Lands of the Future

INTEGRATION AND CONFLICT STUDIES

Published in association with the Max Planck Institute for Social Anthropology, Halle/Saale

Series Editor: Günther Schlee, Arba Minch University, Ethiopia, and Director emeritus at the Max Planck Institute for Social Anthropology

Editorial Board: Brian Donahoe (Max Planck Institute for Social Anthropology), John Eidson (Max Planck Institute for Social Anthropology), Peter Finke (University of Zurich), Jacqueline Knörr (Max Planck Institute for Social Anthropology), Bettina Mann (Max Planck Institute for Social Anthropology), Ursula Rao (Leipzig University), Stephen Reyna (Max Planck Institute for Social Anthropology), Olaf Zenker (Martin Luther University, Halle-Wittenberg)

Assisted by: Viktoria Giehler-Zeng (Max Planck Institute for Social Anthropology)

The objective of the Max Planck Institute for Social Anthropology is to advance anthropological fieldwork and enhance theory building. 'Integration' and 'conflict', the central themes of this series, are major concerns of the contemporary social sciences and of significant interest to the general public. They have also been among the main research areas of the institute since its foundation. Bringing together international experts, *Integration and Conflict Studies* includes both monographs and edited volumes, and offers a forum for studies that contribute to a better understanding of processes of identification and inter-group relations.

Recent volumes:

For a full volume listing, please see the series page on our website: http://www.berghahnbooks.com/series/integration-and-conflict-studies

Lands of the Future

Anthropological Perspectives on Pastoralism, Land Deals and Tropes of Modernity in Eastern Africa

Edited by Echi Christina Gabbert, Fana Gebresenbet,
John G. Galaty and Günther Schlee

berghahn
NEW YORK · OXFORD
www.berghahnbooks.com

First published in 2021 by
Berghahn Books
www.berghahnbooks.com

Library of Congress Cataloging-in-Publication Data
Names: Gabbert, Echi Christina, editor. | Gebresenbet, Fana, editor. | Galaty,
    John G., editor. | Schlee, Günther, editor.
Title: Lands of the future : anthropological perspectives on pastoralism, land deals
    and tropes of modernity in eastern Africa / edited by Echi Christina Gabbert,
    Fana Gebresenbet, John G. Galaty, and Günther Schlee.
Other titles: Integration and conflict studies ; v. 23.
Description: New York : Berghahn Books, 2021. | Series: Integration and conflict
    studies; volume 23 | Includes bibliographical references and index.
Identifiers: LCCN 2020042157 (print) | LCCN 2020042158 (ebook) |
    ISBN 9781789209907 (hardback) | ISBN 9781789209914 (ebook)
Subjects: LCSH: Land use, Rural--Africa, Eastern. | Pastoral systems--Africa,
    Eastern. | Economic development--Africa, Eastern.
Classification: LCC HD978.Z7 L35 2021 (print) | LCC HD978.Z7 (ebook) |
    DDC 333.760963--dc23
LC record available at https://lccn.loc.gov/2020042157
LC ebook record available at https://lccn.loc.gov/2020042158

British Library Cataloguing in Publication Data
A catalogue record for this book is available from the British Library

ISBN 978-1-78920-990-7 hardback
ISBN 978-1-80539-120-3 paperback
ISBN 978-1-80539-378-8 epub
ISBN 978-1-78920-991-4 web pdf

https://doi.org/10.3167/9781789209907

Contents

Part II. Contested Identities and Territories: A History of Expropriation

Part III. Power, Politics and Reactions to State-Building

Part IV. Underdeveloping South Omo

Illustrations

Acknowledgements

This volume is dedicated to our pastoralist and agro-pastoralist friends and families. To them go our deepest thanks and gratitude, not merely for welcoming us in their homes and hosting us in their communities but above all for teaching, challenging and inspiring us in ways that no university in the world could. We hope that this knowledge is faithfully reflected in the work presented here.

We wish to convey our appreciation to the institutions with which we are affiliated and which have supported our work over the years: the Institute for Social and Cultural Anthropology at Göttingen University, the Institute for Peace and Security Studies at Addis Ababa University, the Centre for Society, Technology and Development at McGill University, and the Institutional Canopy of Conservation partnership project, funded by the Social Sciences and Humanities Research Council and the International Development Research Centre of Canada. We are also indebted to our colleagues from around the world, who with their insights, criticism and support have helped in shaping this volume, to Cornelia Schnepel, Viktoria Zeng and Jutta Turner at the Max Planck Institute for Social Anthropology in Halle/Saale, to the anonymous reviewers who contributed valued critical input, and, last but far from least, to our families, who endure our time spent in the field and time tied to our desks with forbearance and grace.

Abbreviations

ACHPR	African Commission on Human and Peoples' Rights
ADLI	Agricultural Development-Led Industrialization
AFC	Awsa Farmers Cooperative
AfDB	African Development Bank
ALARM	Arid Lands and Resource Management Network in Eastern Africa
ALF	Afar Liberation Front
ANLM	Afar National Liberation Movement
ANRS	Afar National Regional State
APF	African Parks Foundation
AU	African Union
AVA	Awash Valley Authority
BEE	Bagamoyo EcoEnergy
CADU	Chilalo Agricultural Development Unit
CHAINS project	Climate-Induced Vulnerability and Pastoralist Livestock Marketing Chains in Southern Ethiopia and Northeastern Kenya
CPRs	Common Pool Resources
CSA	Central Statistical Agency (of Ethiopia)
CSCAR	Consulting for Statistics, Computing & Analytics Research
CSE	Concerned Scholars Ethiopia

DA	Development Agent
DAG	Donor Assistance Group
DFDR	Development-Forced Displacement and Resettlement
DFID	Department for International Development
DRC	Democratic Republic of Congo
EAILAA	Ethiopian Agricultural Investment Land Administration Agency
EDSD	Equitable Development Support Directorate (of Ethiopia)
EEPCO	Ethiopian Electric Power Corporation
EIA	Environmental Impact Assessment
EIB	European Investment Bank
ELF	Eritrean Liberation Front
EPLF	Eritrean People's Liberation Front
EPRDF	Ethiopian Peoples' Revolutionary Democratic Front
ESIA	Environmental and Social Impact Assessment
ESC	Ethiopian Sugar Corporation
ESDC	Ethiopian Sugar Development Corporation
ETB	Ethiopian Birr
EU	European Union
EW	Extension Worker
EWCA	Ethiopian Wildlife Conservation Authority
FAO	Food and Agriculture Organisation of the UN
FCAR	Québec Fonds pour la Formation de Chercheurs et l'Aide à la Recherche
FDI	Foreign Direct Investment
FDRE	Federal Democratic Republic of Ethiopia
FEP	Flora EcoPower
FPIC	Free Prior Informed Consent
GCAO	Government Communication Affairs Office (of Ethiopia)
GDP	Gross Domestic Product
GERD	Grand Ethiopian Renaissance Dam
GFFNW	Glynn Flood Field Notes and Writings
GFJL	Glynn Flood Journal and Letters
GHG	Greenhouse Gases
GTP	Growth and Transformation Plan (of Ethiopia)
HRW	Human Rights Watch
IDRC	International Development Research Centre of Canada

IDP	Internally Displaced People
IFU	Danish Investment Fund for Developing Countries
IGAD	Intergovernmental Authority on Development
ILO	International Labour Organisation
IMPACT	Indigenous Movement for Peace Advancement and Conflict Transformation
INGO	International Non-Governmental Organisation
IPCC	Intergovernmental Panel on Climate Change
IUCN	International Union for Conservation of Nature
IWGIA	International Work Group for Indigenous Affairs
KSDP	Kuraz Sugar Development Project
KSh	Kenyan Shilling
LAPSSET	Lamu Port Southern Sudan-Ethiopia Transport Corridor
LTWP	Lake Turkana Wind Power Project
MAADE	Middle Awash Agricultural Development Enterprise
MetEC	Metals and Engineering Corporation
MIDROC	Mohammed International Development Research and Organization Companies
MoARD	Ministry of Agriculture and Rural Development (of Ethiopia)
MoFED	Ministry of Finance and Economic Development (of Ethiopia)
MoFPDA	Ministry of Federal and Pastoral Development Affairs (of Ethiopia)
MPI	Max Planck Institute for Social Anthropology
MPIDO	Mainyoito Pastoralist Integrated Development Organization
NGO	Non-Governmental Organisation
OBC	Ortelo Business Corporation
OKSDP	Omo Kuraz Sugar Development Project
OLF	Oromo Liberation Front
ONLF	Ogaden National Liberation Front
ONP	Omo National Park
OPDO	Oromo People's Democratic Organization
PASDEP	A Plan for Accelerated and Sustained Development to End Poverty (of Ethiopia)
PASTRES	Pastoralism, Uncertainty and Resilience: Global Lessons from the Margins (research project)

PMAC	Provisional Military Administrative Council (of Ethiopia)
PP	Prosperity Party
REDD	Reducing Emissions from Deforestation and Forest Degradation
RRC	Relief and Rehabilitation Commission (of Ethiopia)
SAGCOT	Southern Agricultural Growth Corridor of Tanzania
SDGs	Sustainable Development Goals
SMNE	Solidarity Movement for a New Ethiopia
SNNPRS	Southern Nations, Nationalities and Peoples' Regional State (of Ethiopia)
SSHRC	Social Sciences and Humanities Research Council of Canada
TPLF	Tigray People's Liberation Front
TPSC	Tendaho Plantation Share Company
TSDP	Tendaho Sugar Development Project
UK	United Kingdom
UN	United Nations
UNDP	United Nations Development Programme
UNDRIP	United Nations Declaration on the Rights of Indigenous Peoples
UNEP	United Nations Environment Programme
UNESCO	United Nations Educational, Scientific and Cultural Organization
UNHCR	United Nations High Commissioner for Refugees
UNOCHA	United Nations Office for the Coordination of Humanitarian Affairs
UNPFII	United Nations Permanent Forum on Indigenous Issues
UN-REDD	United Nations Programme on Reducing Emissions from Deforestation and Forest Degradation
URT	United Republic of Tanzania
USA	United States of America
USAID	United States Agency for International Development
USD	US Dollar
VAT	Value-Added Tax
WADU	Wolaita Agricultural Development Unit
WCMC	World Conservation Monitoring Centre
WSD	Wildlife for Sustainable Development (Ethiopian NGO)

Introduction

Futuremaking with Pastoralists

Echi Christina Gabbert

... the common world is what we enter when we are born and what we leave behind when we die. It transcends our life-span into past and future alike; it was there before we came and will outlast our brief sojourn in it. It is what we have in common not only with those who live with us, but also with those who were here before and with those who will come after us.

—H. Arendt, *The Human Condition*

The future is a hypothesis first. This book is a contribution to futuremaking rooted to the ground, speaking in the here and now, reaching into the depths of history, inspired by the search for visions for the future from a challenging present. Positive futuremaking can be compared to positive peace. Positive peace has a life-enhancing quality that goes beyond freedom from fear of violence and destruction (Davies-Vengoechea 2004; Galtung 2010). It enables people not only to live a good life but also to have the opportunity to lend it greater meaning day by day. Similarly, positive futuremaking aims to create a passage in time that is not defined by an absence, whether of past or present. Rather, it aims to fill past and present with new forms of meaning, moulded in a continuum of time and space. Positive futuremaking acknowledges the importance of how what is decided now influences us and those who come after us. The future comes to be through the alternatives and possibilities offered up by the present (Bell and Mau 1971: 9), captured by the hopes and aspirations expressed in the actions of people with diverse interests but also through their forms of inaction and indifference

(Appadurai 2013). Thus the art of positive futuremaking is shaped by many people – whether as individuals or as spokespersons for civil society, governments or international institutions – with converging understandings of how to live together on a shared planet. While there are various possible futures (Bourne 2006), predictions for coming generations are growing increasingly grim because of the world's exploitation of finite resources, environmental pollution, social and economic inequality, biodiversity loss and climate change. Therefore, futuremaking poses extraordinary challenges to a peaceful global living together. Voices from and for the future are entering in intensified forms into the silence of political indecision and failure to address these urgent global challenges.

In 2002, in southern Ethiopia, the Arbore spokesman, Grazmach Sura, asked the anthropologist Ivo Strecker to film his message for world peace, to be carried not only to other places but also to times to come, explaining that peace lies in the hands of people but that one also has to beg the land and the spirits for peace (Strecker and Pankhurst 2003).[1] In December 2018, the German astronaut Alexander Gerst sent a message from the International Space Station, apologizing to future generations. Humbled by the sight of the fragile beauty of Planet Earth and the harmful human-made changes he observed during his stay in space, he conceded that his generation will have to confess to not having taken care of the future. That same month and year, the 15-year-old Swede Greta Thunberg, who had gained international attention with her continuing Friday school strikes for climate protection, so neglected by her parents' generation, spoke in front of the United Nations Climate Change Conference; and, in 2019, she called out policymakers at the World Economic Forum in Davos for their own inaction and initiated the largest ever global mobilization of youth against climate change. Her story resembles the tale of the child who exposes the emperor who has no clothes, only this time the emperors invited the child to tell them what they already knew about the future, aware that they were doing nothing about it. The Ethiopian artist Girmachew Getnet asks about human unity in his 'circle series' of cardboard paintings, about the interruption of unity in his 'wall series', and about the future of it all in times of destructive consumerism in his '€ waste series'. The pastoralist elder, the astronaut, the schoolgirl and the artist have in common a perception of broader space-time to express the relevance of forms of being and agency in the universe that extends beyond the present. With heightened self-consciousness of the unity of space-time perception, the future speaks to the present for good reason.

Lands of the Future: Pastoralism, Scholarship, Dissonances and Silences

To study carefully an emergent future 'is more difficult than mere political action, and more constructive' (Bell and Mau 1971: xii). The land rush of the twenty-first century – worldwide and, specifically, in the Global South – strongly resembles other historical developments, such as the enclosure of commonly held lands during the course of the agrarian transformation and industrialization in Europe; but it also mirrors the global dissonance between capital and climate, now at a turning point where the finiteness of resources urges humanity to rethink both present and future. The continuous repetition of fast-track industrialization has met much resistance on local and global scales (with that very distinction making less and less sense). Such processes are, however, represented in the media, in public discussions, and in official pronouncements in widely varying ways, thus presenting us with challenges, morally, politically and economically. How can scientists (from the Global North) criticize governments in the Global South? How can governments, some of whose leading members benefit from schemes of investment exploiting distant resources, tell their citizens who are worse off after the investments that all is being done in their own best interest? How can consultants from the World Bank mark out investment zones for a global market without having set foot in the places where they propose to invest? Who establishes the measures that determine the line between destitution and well-being? How can people endure the obvious dissonance between how we understand the future of land and the lands of the future? How does the future of pastoralism fit into all of this?

Pastoralists have always been depicted in divergent terms: poor and vulnerable by some, skilled and self-sufficient by others. This dichotomy is hard to overcome. Our volume is an anthropological contribution to understanding the future of pastoralism and agro-pastoralism in its coexistence with many other forms of livelihood.[2] We show how people and their livestock live not only *off* the land but *with* the land. The volume is a cooperative contribution by people, mainly agro-pastoralists and scientists from the Global South and North, who over the years have come together in many different settings – in pastures, fields, villages and watering places, farms, firms, cities and government offices, universities, conferences and e-correspondence – to augment our joint store of pertinent knowledge about pastoralism in the twenty-first century, by combining practice, knowledge and philosophies rooted in writing and non-writing cultures. Although this volume is focused on Eastern Africa, especially on Ethiopia, the findings are relevant to situations of pastoralists and small-scale farmers around the globe.

This volume is an outcome of the *Lands of the Future* Initiative.[3] When in 2012 a group of researchers came together at Oxford to discuss concerns expressed by our agro-pastoralist counterparts about large-scale land investment schemes occurring across Eastern Africa that were being implemented without the people affected being consulted, it was an Ethiopian colleague who encouraged us to establish the *Lands of the Future* Initiative with a focus widened beyond academic deliberations. He reminded us that we might not be able to say much less publish what we see but that one day it will be important to know what has taken place. His advice, drawn from his painful experiences with the previous Ethiopian regime (the Derg), is another example of how things might, for one reason or another, be quite invisible in the present but attain importance and visibility in the future.[4]

In the wake of the global land rush that followed the financial and food-price crises of 2007 and 2008, *Lands of the Future* was established to bring people from different disciplines together to aim at greater transparency with respect to the dynamics of land deals that were often planned behind closed doors in ministries, international institutions, investment agencies and multinational mining and agro-companies, far from the lands and people most directly affected: nomads, pastoralists, agro-pastoralists and small-scale farmers. Scenarios all over Eastern Africa played out in similar ways. The pragmatic aim of *Lands of the Future* was to distinguish rumour from fact with regard to 'changing land uses' or 'large-scale land acquisitions', to employ the euphemisms of the day. When working on the ground, we discovered that the facts were often grimmer than the rumours, as many land deals materialized as full-fledged land grabs, with violent incidents following the dispossession of agro-pastoralists from the territories they regarded as their home.[5]

The often violent conditions that arose for pastoralists, who were deprived of land and access to pastures and fields in southern Ethiopia, Tanzania, the Sudan and Kenya in order to make room for agro-investments, were more often than not accompanied by stalled research. Researchers and their pastoralist friends, families and counterparts were intimidated and hindered more or less openly, regardless of whether or not they worked specifically on land issues. In this environment of expropriation and exclusion, *Lands of the Future* provided a space where people encouraged each other to pursue genuine observations, research and analyses of realities on the ground; not more, no less.

Since 2013, *Lands of the Future* has kept lines of discourse open and alive in everyday exchange, in workshops and in conferences, always with counterparts from pastoral communities. The initiative continues as a lively international collaboration of pastoralists and non-pastoralists who have lived and studied together for decades.[6] Moreover, *Lands of the Future* shows that 'slow scholarship' has its place in academia. The results presented in this volume are based on long-term research. In contrast to much of the literature rush on the land rush, the findings here are based on listening, observing, learning and oftentimes waiting cautiously before coming to critical conclusions, keeping the safety of all involved in mind.[7] It is telling that our authors did not choose the topic 'land' because it was a 'hot topic' in academia and elsewhere; rather, the land rush had come to the places and people we had already known for decades.

The Trope of the Backward

Peaceful futuremaking needs to be based on understanding of actors and their incentives within their respective settings.[8] Land-use planning to meet the demands of growing populations is, admittedly, urgent; but it cannot be a short-term engagement. On the contrary, for food security[9] and well-being to matter, time is needed to integrate knowledge about the specifics of land, soil and water in the planning. People and the land they regard as their dwelling place cannot be separated without harm because it is not only a place of production but also of belonging (Turton 2011; Lentz 2013), and being forcefully separated from their land is among the most devastating experiences that can occur to people in their lives. As Shauna LaTosky describes in detail in her contribution, the possibility of staying and withholding consent needs to be a viable option for people who live on land earmarked for investment. Also, the option to refrain from planned land deals needs to be a realistic possibility – one resulting from serious evaluation of existing land use practices and of the environmental and social consequences of new land use schemes (Gabbert 2014: 23).[10] Therefore, the art of policymaking should involve the attentive integration of divergent views on and interests in land. Among the agro-pastoral Arbore in southern Ethiopia, it is said that 'land cannot be rushed'. This means that cultivation cycles and livestock movements need to be finely tuned and well attended, and places of ritual importance need to be respected. Especially when it comes to political decisions, elders remind the young to act slowly and with care, *nungu*. 'Make haste slowly, *festina lente*' is what Erasmus von Rotterdam told leaders almost half a millennium ago to help them avoid making the wrong political decisions for their people: 'But one fit of idleness in a prince, one rash decision – just think what storms it sometimes raises and what ruin it can bring with it into the affairs of men!' (Erasmus 2001[1536]: 134).

In the wake of the land rush at the beginning of the twenty-first century, policies that were clearly against pastoralists' interests were implemented at an unprecedented pace and with predetermined rigidity, which repeatedly brought ruin both to the dispossessed and the investors. How was this legitimized? As Günther Schlee describes in his contribution, in the developmental state of Ethiopia, labelling pastoralists as 'backward' became a political 'magic formula' revived in a neoliberal guise and implemented as a licence to dispossess pastoralists from the land they lived with, on and off. The old modernist trope of backwardness legitimized the exclusion of pastoralists in the planning. They were depicted as people for whom decisions had to be made rather than as respected citizens who could contribute to pursuing the common goals of the country. This attitude, well known in the history of development policies (see Hobart 1993), contributed to the violent dimensions of land deals described in this volume. Once people were depicted as inferior, there was no need to approach them respectfully. We often suggested that decision-makers should engage directly with the people whose land they were making decisions about. Instead, meetings often took place in the presence of guards and officials who would often be intimidatory and manipulative of people, as described in the contributions by Wedekind,

LaTosky and Buffavand. Perhaps the outcome of face-to-face communications would have been eye-opening for the planners. Instead, general plans, independent of cultural context, were thought adequate and were implemented. Rather than through talking with people and creating common goals, as stated in the Ethiopian Constitution, policies were designed and put into practice, with the backing of overt force, to achieve the ambitious goals, formulated at the centre, that were most forcefully applied in the lowland peripheries inhabited by agro-pastoralists.[11]

While we do not question the validity and importance of goals such as the right to food, to procure income, to secure health and enjoy quality school services, the decision simply to exploit the lowlands for broader economic goals proved fatal in many respects. We will discuss later how this relates to the greater goal generally announced of securing a better future for all. A common strategy was defined to push for development goals by means of the violent suppression of freedom of opinion. For pastoralists, this approach was accompanied by the stigmatization of their very livelihoods. Once pastoralists were labelled as backward, this eradicated their rights to land use, agency or consent. Stigmatization was extended also to people who defended the rights of pastoralists and the value of pastoralism as a livelihood – for example, researchers who were labelled as 'development spoilers' and 'friends of backwardness and poverty'.[12]

To exclude pastoralists from decision-making was framed as a noble task, to 'relieve' them of their 'backward existence'. In 2018, when listening to a radio report on violent conflicts in Gambella in western Ethiopia, a taxi driver in Addis Ababa had an explanation ready: 'The pastoralists attack the people from the centre because, before the investors came, they did not know how to use the land and now they are jealous because they see agriculture for the first time in their lives' (personal communication, October 2018). This example shows how fictitious divisions are created between those who consider themselves modern, or open to modernity and progress, and those who are denigrated as backward and uninformed. This supported and enforced a conflictual division between people as well as discrimination against agro-pastoralists, not only from a distance but also by migrant labourers on new farms, providing more causes for violence. What would have happened if policy planners had prioritized unity over antagonism? Instead, the paternalistic attitude that has led to the exploitation of the peripheries at least since the beginning of recorded history has persisted into the present, now in a high-modernist framework.[13] As a consequence, the pathway towards the 'integration' of pastoralists' territories was paved with negative connotations and paternalistic notions of how to develop fellow citizens, and unity was defined by the goals and ideals of 'the moderns', not by embracing the rich diversity of the country's citizens. The result was a great divide, as illustrated in Figure 0.1.

'When the word "modern", "modernization", or "modernity" appears', Latour reminds us, 'we are defining, by contrast, an archaic and stable past. Fur-

future	past
center	periphery
modern	backward/traditional/ancient
developed	undeveloped
equilibrium	non-equilibrium
agriculture/industry	pastoralism/nomadism
winners	losers
educated	uneducated
rich/strong	poor/vulnerable

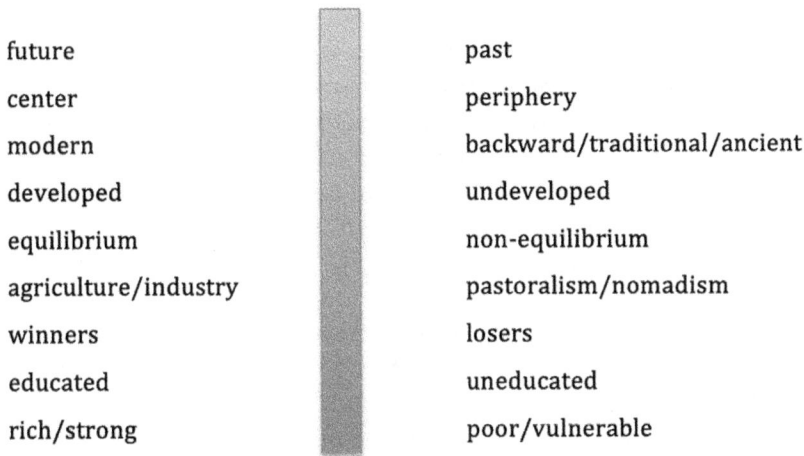

Figure 0.1. The great divide: exclusive futuremaking vs. pastoralists. © Echi Christina Gabbert.

thermore, the word is always being thrown into the middle of a fight, in a quarrel where there are winners and losers, Ancients and Moderns'. This creates a combat zone (Latour 1993: 10). The speech presented by the late Ethiopian Prime Minister Meles Zenawi at the Pastoralist Day in Jinka in 2011, which marks this divide clearly, has been cited often enough.[14] The irony of that speech is further layered with cynicism when one realizes that the very same pastoralists he addressed, and whom he declared to be poor and backward, had been forced to provide substantial amounts of money to help finance the event.[15] The prime minister promised that the pastoralists would benefit from development, and that developers would cooperate with pastoralists in 'their own interest', but these promises were not kept – which may be one decisive reason for the failure of many of these ambitious projects.

The documents setting out the Growth and Transformation Plans of the Ethiopian government provide an interesting illustration of the rhetorical denigration of pastoralists as agents of a common future. In the earlier documents related to the plan – e.g. PASDEP (MoFED 2006) – one finds substantive sections on pastoral livelihoods and expertise, on the importance of mobility, and on cultural and land rights;[16] but, in the Millennium Development Goals report of 2010, pastoralists only appear sporadically, while being depicted as vulnerable and undereducated (MoFED 2010a: 10, 14). In the Growth and Transformation Plan I, those formerly substantive subsections became little more than a few short paragraphs with vague ideas about 'voluntary' resettlement plans, livestock breeding, marketing systems and (mobile) schools (MoFED 2010b). In the Growth and Transformation Plan II, the transformation of 'backward production methods' in the livestock subsector (National Planning Commission

2016: 122) was supposed to lead to an increase in animal production through the further sedentarization of pastoralists, market integration and the provision of veterinary health services, water and fodder. The respective passages in the reports have little to say about existing pastoralist knowledge; for instance, the call for 'voluntary sedentary farming' displays ignorance of time-tested agro-pastoral practices that have flexibly combined animal husbandry with agriculture. Grounded knowledge about agro-pastoralism disappeared in these major government reports that presented the ill-advised land investment phase, in spite of well-founded guidelines from the African Union, such as the 'Policy Framework for Pastoralism in Africa' (AU 2010). As John Markakis points out in his contribution, pastoral land rights, as stated in the Ethiopian Constitution, as well as initial plans for serious studies about pastoralists were, after 1991, 'not mentioned again'.[17] As Schlee has noted, 'many urban Africans, including the political class, do not seem to be aware that the relatively cheap and abundant, as well as "ecologically" produced meat they enjoy does not stem from the "modern" kinds of agriculture they propagate but from pastoralists' (Schlee 2010: 160). One cannot help wondering who was politically responsible for the rhetorical 'evaporation' of pastoralist matters in these plans, the same matters that have been well described by several Ethiopian scholars. Perhaps their work has been seen as too 'realistic' to support the fictitious visions of the future to be discussed in the following sections.[18]

The Trope of Uninhabited Territory

> From a conventional perspective associated with the industrial way of life, the future is the "not yet". It is the realm of potential and possibility, an empty vessel to be filled with dreams and desires, plans and projects. As such, it is stretching out in front of us: vast, unlimited and open-ended. (Adam 2008: 111)

Adam's critical description of the future corresponds to visions of 'empty lands' that called upon global investment to awaken 'sleeping giants' on unused land through 'competitive commercial agriculture for Africa' (World Bank 2009). Indeed, in the 2000s, pastoralists' territories in the Ethiopian peripheries were offered to investors on the Internet through minimally priced leases for supposedly uninhabited, fertile and unused land that were combined with incentive packages for investors such as 'tax holidays' (Lavers 2012). This was a logical consequence of the above-described stigmatization of pastoralists because 'empty spaces are first and foremost empty of *meaning*. . . . (more precisely, unseen)' (Baumann 2000: 103). In a perfectly designed *terra nullius* pattern, land together with its inhabitants was declared empty by planners who then made it available for industrial uses and commodification.[19] The 'backward' existence of pastoralists was regarded as void of agricultural values and economic benefits while disregarding elaborated agro-pastoral practices. This also displayed a lack of understanding of the inseparability of the human, non-human and divine in land (see Buffavand 2016: 477). Patches of land, offered to investors for sell-off prices[20] (Dessalegn 2011, 2014), were in areas that the World Bank had previously identified as 'untapped growth potentialities'. The language used in an initial 2003 concept paper for the World Bank is oftentimes more inflated than factual, using scaling-up rhetoric that perpetuated the global land rush: 'Ethiopia seems to be caught in a poverty trap, plummeted [sic] by dreadful initial conditions, unable to sustain high growth rates' (El Aynaoui 2003: 3). Solutions for this 'very destitute nation with very poor physical and human capital stocks' therefore aim at a 'big push' to 'kick start the economy' (ibid.: 3f). The follow-up report promoted the idea of multipurpose dams and attracting investors (World Bank 2005a). Pastoralism, under the term 'livestock sector/assets', is covered erratically in these documents. Together with a confidential note on the 'Four Ethiopias' (World Bank 2004), in which different regions are evaluated according to their growth potential, these documents were, and continue to be relied upon as, decisive supports for the narrative of the 'undeveloped' (parts of) Ethiopia.

Documents such as these World Bank reports, along with other sets of data produced worldwide for 'action at a distance', particularly for assessing land as a resource, have had an enormous impact on policy, speculation and money flows under the guise of development (Li 2014a). Thus, global market mechanisms and schemes of accumulation, supported by fictions of unused/undeveloped/untapped and, therefore, available land, continue to be applied (a) to dispossess people and (b) to eradicate the meaning that land always has, over and above being, merely, a commodity.[21]

The fictitious joint construction of empty lands and backward citizens has made possible the establishment of the market as the 'sole director of the fate of human beings and their natural environment indeed, even of the amount and use of purchasing power, [that] would result in the demolition of society' (Polanyi 2001 [1944]: 76). In many land-grab scenarios, pastoralists are not even considered as an 'accessory of the economic system' in a Polanyian sense. Rather, together with their livestock, they become extraneous objects within a rigid framework for global social engineering (see Behrends et al. 2014; Bierschenk 2014), conveniently evaporated into insignificance as their displacement and replacement proceeds, as advocated in the development documents mentioned above. As Mbembe (2016: 223) states with reference to black labour power in South Africa: 'Capitalism in its present form might need the territory they inhabit, their natural resources . . . , their forests, or even their wildlife. But it doesn't need them as persons'. In fact, the great majority of workers on the sugar cane farm in southern Ethiopia were labourers from other parts of the country (Kamski 2016), while some pastoralists held only a few petty jobs.[22]

Futuremaking – not with but against pastoralists – is a continuation of the denial of their existence in the tropes of modernity that had established the basis for the taking over of their territory in the first place. The examples in this volume add to numerous works describing similar patterns of land deals all over the world that squeeze smallholders out of their territories (e.g. Tsing 2005; Baviskar 2008; Abbink 2011; Borras and Franco 2012; Cotula 2012; White et al. 2012; Kaag and Zoomers 2014; Li 2014a and 2014b; Edelman, Oya and Borras 2015; Hall et al. 2015). The examples further add to the history of stigmatization, dispossession and forced settlement of pastoralists in state-building schemes – e.g. in Central Asia and Russia (Slezkine 1994; Donahoe 2004; Khazanov and Schlee 2012).[23] Therefore, one aim of this volume is to shed light on the historically repetitive pattern of using land policies for state-building in Eastern Africa in the twenty-first century.

State-Building and Modernity

As we have seen above, to pave the way for the development of land, governments aim to quickly 'melt the solids' (Baumann 2000), such as cultural values, the land as dwelling place, cultural self-esteem and socio-economic relations. State-building[24] in the peripheries, following an established historical pattern, was again implemented through development-forced displacement, resettlement and villagization schemes for pastoralists (see Turton 2015).[25] A World Bank report on Ethiopia describes women and pastoralists as vulnerable citizens and identifies tradition as an obstacle to state-building: 'The analysis furthermore suggests both that traditional institutions remain more important to citizens than the formal organizations that are attempting to bring governance and resources control closer to citizens, and that these efforts are also currently inhibited by informal practices and norms' (World Bank 2005b: 40). To throw pre-modern 'solids' – such as pastoralists with their knowledge and complex understanding of land, community and animal husbandry – into the melting pot is a 'permanent feature of modernity', or rather of those who regard themselves as modern, with the intent to make political and economic challenges and circumstances manageable and the future predictable (Baumann 2000: 3). Through this approach, pastoralists and the land they live on would finally be assimilated into state power and market structures. As Baumann (2000: 8) warns, however, managing a fluid modernity is a greater challenge than those who advocated the melting process anticipated. And as Scott (1998: 318f) warns, relying on generic rules and calculations without regard for local particularities invites failure on the ground.

'With land it is never over' (Li 2014a: 591), and like peacemaking and state-making, futuremaking is a never-ending process. Just as in peacemaking, there are no recipes for futuremaking. Futuremaking can aim for the most positive outcome following painful experiences, but it can also repeat textbook examples of how not to learn from past insights, as David Turton describes in detail in this volume. Accordingly, land policies have often not led to the calculated benefits because the underlying calculations were too unidirectional in space and time.[26] A study commissioned by the Ethiopian government in 2012 found deficient land use applied in areas of large agricultural investments, the exclusion of civil society and a lack of land rights (UNDP 2013), which suggested that much land actually became unused *after* it had been taken away from people. Another report confirmed these conclusions only partially but did assert that large-scale farms provide fewer job opportunities (one job per 20 ha) than small-scale farms (Daniel, Deininger and Harris 2015). Many land investments were reportedly unsuccessful. As a result, the Ethiopian Agricultural Investment Land Administration Agency (EAILAA) began to revoke the licences of unsuccessful investors (Yonas 2016). The question then became: Will such land simply be given to the next best investor, or will the devastating results lead to a thorough rethinking of development policies?

The concentration on the industrial production of export goods such as cotton, sugar cane and flowers, which mainly meet consumer needs in the Global North, helped destroy (agro-)pastoralists' and other small-scale food providers' livelihoods without providing them apparent alternatives and with self-evident disadvantages occurring beyond the direct ones inflicted on displaced community members and on the environment. This also resulted, repeatedly, in the economic failure of entire investment schemes. After the 'subsistence' economy had come to be equated with poverty in order to legitimize modernization, many families, which, previously, had been well integrated into local production and trade networks, experienced a hitherto unknown degree of poverty. There are no statistics pertaining to the collateral damage done to (agro-)pastoralists' economies, which so clearly contradicts the 'win-win' and 'trickle-down' promises that have served to make land deals more palatable. Many investment schemes have produced little if any revenue. And, as Edward G.J. Stevenson and Benedikt Kamski illustrate in their contribution, many displayed significant blind spots in their legitimization narratives before and after the land deals. For the Kuraz Sugar Development Project in southern Ethiopia, the case studies presented in the chapters of this book show that several Sustainable Development Goals (SDGs)[27] were not only not reached but were actually crushed, at least with regard to pastoralists, in the period from 2011 to 2018. Many members of the Mun and Mela communities were, not surprisingly, made more food-insecure by the loss of their land and reduction in biodiversity (SDG 2, 3, 12, 15). They were poorer (SDG 1); they – especially the women – had few job opportunities and were often exploited and underpaid (SDG 5, 8 and 10); they experienced greater social and military conflict; and they were, increasingly, victims of lethal accidents (SDG 16). As of 2019, the overall economic assessment concluded that the project was a failure (SDG 8). 'With at least 3.6 billion US dollars received in loans between 2011 and mid 2016' (Kamski 2016: 568), sugar production is limited because of the shortage of sugar cane, while promised service packages for health services were neglected, as Fana Gebresenbet illustrates in his contribution to this volume (SDG 3, 4, 6, 7, 10). One could add to the list the sole goal that has been seriously targeted: SDG 9, which pertains to industry, innovation and infrastructure. 'Infrastructure' for the farms was established at a rapid pace, without adequate environmental and social impact studies, as David Turton in his contribution shows, while 'innovation' was simply defined through 'industrialization'.[28] The strong resemblance of these scenarios to Marx's (1867) description of the effects of enclosures and dispossession in the eighteenth century has been noted (Makki 2014; White et al. 2012; Fana 2016). The fact that such destructive scenarios are repeated under the helm of the Sustainable Development Goals in the twenty-first century poses profound challenges to world politics (see Makki 2014). It seems that the monumental failure of 'high modernist' and standardized development projects imposed on populations in former colonies or in regions of internal colonialism by both capitalist and socialist regimes extends from the twentieth into the twenty-first century. Yet, there is a difference because 'the expansive modern age has got stuck' (Sachs 2019: xv). The destruction of ecology and livelihoods in the last frontiers across Africa (Abbink 2018), in the tropical forests in Asia (see Tsing 2008; Li 2014b) and Latin America (see Campbell 2015) cannot be extended further, while the spiral of violence against those who are 'squeezed out' of these territories has too often gotten out of control. The time has come to change the causes of these dismal outcomes.

What then, if, instead, the livelihoods of people who use the land without destroying it were regarded as innovative, across a broader space-time frame, and suitable to inform the goals for a 'better future for all', as is envisaged in the UN Sustainable Development Goals?[29] Our contributions show how visions of high modernity continue to sacrifice livelihoods, family farming and animal husbandry, socio-ecological expertise, customary structures and security. Moreover, management and control over the peripheries remains a prominent feature of capital accumulation and state-building, to the detriment of well-managed uses of common land, turning dwelling places into conflict zones and creating battlegrounds for global speculation. The art of living together within the limits of the planet needs to be learnt anew.

The Way to Go: Healing Broken Bonds

'Social reality include[s] a variety of real alternatives or possibilities for the future' (Bell and Mau 1971: xi). Naturally, these alternatives look different to different actors. States and pastoralists have seldom worked together on futuremaking; on the contrary, pastoralism has time and again been replaced by other state preferences, with dispossession and sedentarization as major features utilized to manage and control once mobile populations. This applies to situations of external and internal colonization and predatory expansion, as Asebe Regassa shows in his contribution to this volume. But is it not high time to fully integrate pastoralists into the social body of the state? Mutual futuremaking by states and pastoralists is possible if differences are also regarded as opportunities. To make the best of these opportunities, misconceptions about pastoralists need to be corrected to foster more holistic and realistic discourses about food providers, well-being, sustainability and peaceful futures. This is crucial for a peaceful living together that cannot possibly be built upon or sustained by means of stigmatization and exclusion. What, then, are features of pastoralism that can contribute to peaceful futuremaking?

Economy, Land, Livestock and Crisis Management

As Peter D. Little shows in his contribution, pastoralists' livestock production in the Horn of Africa, even before the advent of modernist growth paradigms, has been anything but peripheral (see also Mahmoud 2013; Catley 2017). The fact that some agro-pastoralists produce agricultural surpluses (see Kurimoto 1996; Gabbert 2018: 300ff) goes largely unnoticed. Moreover, pastoralism is based on flexibility, crisis management, resilience and diversification, developed in response to the challenges posed by difficult geographic and climatic conditions and exclusionary political governance.[30] Pastoralists constantly re-adapt to new challenges under non-equilibrium circumstances. In other words, in changing environments, hardship and abundance are balanced over the long term in communities of humans, animals, plants and spirits with an active bond to the land. In Arbore, the spiritual power of land is also a reminder that it must be used respectfully; to steal and exploit the land will lead to a person's ruin, as the land itself will place a curse upon the thief. Also, the significance of livestock is often barely understood by non-pastoralists. Schlee (1989: 403ff) describes cattle as a means to establish social networks with an insurance factor. Bonte and Galaty (1991: 9) describe cattle as signifiers for 'well-being and abundance, providing fertile objects for metaphorical thought and expression, and representing religious symbols, emblems of divinity and vehicles for sacrifice'. Ginno Ballo from Arbore describes the difference in wealth when comparing cattle to money:

> When I watch my cow, I can see how she is full of life, full of energy, how she breathes, how her colours and patterns are shining in the sun, how she rejoices when I bring her to the watering place and to good pastures. My cow knows my whistle, my voice, my call. Money, you put in your pocket, or you hide it away in a box or in a bank. Our wealth is alive, out there, visible and beautiful. You can respond to it with your heart and with good energy. . . . Cattle open as many ways between people as they have hair on their hide. Every transaction of a cow has to be discussed

thoroughly. Every matter to do with cattle brings together many people and opinions and has to be considered carefully. (Ginno Ballo, personal communication, August 2011)

Being aware of diverse notions of wealth, well-being, land and human and non-human realities corresponds to global efforts to achieve context-specific agrarian justice, food justice and climate justice that considers a plurality of livelihoods (Borras and Franco 2018).[31] Maknun Ashami and Jean Lydall's contribution provides a historical perspective as to how Afar pastoralists in northern Ethiopia, despite endless challenges to their livelihoods coming from plantations and anti-pastoral politics, have chosen ways to continue a livelihood option that has proven to be resilient and well adapted to the ecology of the region over the long term.

Alternative Economies and Sustainability

The reality that multimillion-dollar investments have not resulted in the expected revenues for the national economy, and in the end produced losses instead, is only one reason why such expenditures should have been weighed against the value of pastoralism or other customary economies in the first place. Jonah Wedekind's study of the white elephant agro-investment in Hararghe in eastern Ethiopia is a clear example of agricultural 'development' that produces environmental costs and social externalities that render the projects not only ecologically and socially destructive but economically unsustainable as well, stimulating scenarios of resistance.[32] The warning in Elinor Ostrom's classic study *Governing the Commons* – e.g. 'Privatization of CPRs [common pool resources such as land, water and pastures] need not have the same positive results as privatizing the ownership of an airline' (Ostrom 1990: 22) – could also have helped to produce more realistic calculations about the use of commons before eradicating agro-pastoralism. The repeated failures of land deals show that there is no way around good knowledge about the common use of soil and about living on the land sustainably – that is, with future generations in mind.[33]

The agro-pastoralist Arbore say that 'the land has fathers'. This means that the land hosts its people. It also means that land should be used carefully; not for personal profit but for communal well-being. Common land, therefore, cannot be sold or given away to people who do not use it respectfully over the long term. Lucie Buffavand describes similar patterns for the Mela of southern Ethiopia (Buffavand 2016, 2017). As heterogenous as pastoralist ways are, they have time and again created senses of place that are combined with refined and sustainable agroecological and organic practices, an immense knowledge of biodiversity, of animals, seeds and soils, and a common view of land.

A balanced assessment of the achievements of small-scale farmers and (agro-)pastoralists as food providers shows clearly that their contributions to the responsible use of land and well-being should not be underestimated.[34] As Ostrom notes with respect to villagers, pastoralists often choose common land use for good reasons, and their economic survival depends on the management of limited resources (Ostrom 1990: 61). The wisdom of this corresponds to current searches for alternatives in economic thinking. The critical economist Kate Raworth (2017: 156) states: 'Today's economy is divisive and degenerative by default. Tomorrow's economy must be distributive and regenerative by design.' In a similar vein, Järvensivu et al. (2018: 2), in their latest background report on economic transformation for the Global Sustainable Development Report, stress that today's economies, which were developed during an era of material abundance, need alternative 'economic-theoretical thinking that can assist governments in channelling economies toward activity that causes a radically lighter burden on natural ecosystems and simultaneously ensures more equal opportunities for good human life'. This position does not support the idea that pastoralists should be coerced into market-based arrangements or that their knowledge should be misused for the building of new economies (see Trouillot 2003: 138f; Borras et al. 2018: 1232; Borras and Franco 2018). On the contrary, it suggests the fundamental rethinking of economic paradigms and of values that create well-being beyond the global marketplace, taking into account the profound variation in definitions of what constitutes a good life. To become a watchman on an industrial plantation might be an option for some people in one setting, but it might be a nightmare for a herder who cherishes autonomy and food sovereignty in another. What Walsh contends about the application of the concept of *buen vivir*[35] in South America is also valid here: it is necessary to stay open to interepistemic transformations that allow for different 'philosophies, cosmovisions and collective relational modes of life' (Walsh 2010: 20). In fact, pastoralists' views of land, their highly adaptive land-use practices and their organization of the commons may contribute substantively to the development of alternatives, within the field of economics, to mainstream models positing the inevitability or desirability of rapid and unsustainable growth. This is especially relevant in the search for climate-friendly solutions for food production. In combination with Latour's (1993, 2013) claim that 'the moderns have never been modern', this creates a basis for the acceptance of parallel modes of existence beyond the modern/ not modern divide – an acceptance that makes mutually informed futuremaking possible.

Innovation, Change and Democratic Egalitarian Principles

Pastoralists, as shown throughout this volume, are not confining themselves to remote areas in order to escape the present. They are constantly reacting to ecological, climatic and political changes and fluctuations. This environmental knowledge is 'contained, created, and realized, or "constructed" in dynamic processes of social interaction' (Schareika 2014) and of course managed through mobility. Nor can pastoralists be dismissed as denizens of an archaic era or as reactionaries; rather they are constantly recombining knowledge, realities and possibilities in a way that is expressed clearly in this quotation from an Arbore elder on school education: 'What we want are good schools that integrate the knowledge and respect that even the smallest Arbore children have, so they can proudly and in good health combine it with things we cannot teach them' (personal communication, December 2007). This statement also makes another important point. Not all is well in pastoralist communities, and there is much that can be improved; for example, in quality services for health and schooling. Unfortunately, pastoralists are often depicted as traditionalists who are not interested in change. While one should not romanticize pastoralism nor support an idealized stereotype of pastoralists, one should recognize that the choice for autonomy (e.g. rejection of school models that lack respect and understanding for pastoralism) is not to be confused with traditionalism (see also Girke 2018). There is often an emancipatory quality in statements made by pastoralists, which express their views of a good life, grounded in egalitarian principles, and of people's desire for 'equal access to the powers needed to make choices over their own lives and to participate in collective choices that affect them' (Wright 2010: 18). This comes close to the pastoralists' view of a social order, where community and lineage values still are key, and in which social, ecological, economic and political choices cannot be made by individuals alone.

Many pastoralists who pursue other professions continue to invest in their family herds. Mobile technology is used to tend to the herds, to find lost animals or to manage conflicts and peace negotiations. A balance is sought among various life choices: choosing the best pastures, fields, waterplaces and dwelling places; making decisions about dual education (in pastoralists practice and in schools, colleges and universities); and diversifying subsistence practices and engagement in trade (see also Schareika 2018). In many pastoralist communities, living with and on the land requires consideration of the human and the non-human, of new and old practices and techniques, of the living, the deceased and the ones who are not yet born. Choices, changes, cooperation and conflicts are weighed and intensely discussed as matters concerning families, lineages, clans, and larger groups and alliances of groups who live in the wider cultural neighbourhood (Gabbert and Thubauville 2010). Often, age- and generation-sets provide platforms for orderly communication within and between generations, including in matters concerning land. In the eyes of state administrators, the self-governing and egalitarian features of pastoralist social order have been seen as a hindrance to modernization; but, instead, exactly these features might be taken to indicate that pastoralists with their own ideas, organizations, and opinions are part of 'the multitude of those who have felt, well ahead of the others, the extent to which it was necessary to flee posthaste from the injunction to modernize' (Latour 2018: 42). This does not mean that the pastoralists are pre-modern or anti-modern but that they may help us to learn how to avoid those distorted forms of modernization that are destructive and unsustainable. When our present dilemmas indicate to us that we should not buy into dichotomies of modernization and backwardness, then the cooperation of people with divergent views of life can begin. This requires the abandonment of bulldozer policies in favour of greater political and agrarian justice and of democratic principles enabling us to create 'a community of life' (Mbembe 2011: 1). Pastoralists, agro-pastoralists and farmers, whose socio-ecological principles are both grounded and diverse, can contribute to peaceful futuremaking and, beyond that, may have other, unanticipated roles to play.

States, Land Rights, Human Rights and Peace Formation with Pastoralists

At the World Economic Forum in Davos in 2019, Ethiopia's Prime Minister Abiy Ahmed recited this Ethiopian saying: 'If you want to go fast, go alone; if you want to go far, go together,' which prompts the question: Who is included in this 'togetherness'? Who belongs together with whom and why (Schlee 2009)? One would like to imagine that togetherness and unity are not achieved solely by moving in the direction prescribed by 'master plans' of governments and investors, but instead by addressing all and listening to many so as to make peaceful synergies thinkable. Too often, states and investors form alliances to the detriment of pastoralists and smallholders. If the answer to the question 'who belongs together with whom and why?' is that pastoralists and states (also) belong together, then the question of 'how they belong together' needs to be explored seriously. Many pastoralists are waiting for constructive approaches from their governments that allow them to come to terms with a painful past and present and enter into a future that provides space for peaceful living together without forced homogenization.[36] Continued discrimination against marginalized groups, such as pastoralists, agro-pastoralists and hunter-gatherers, cannot possibly lead to a peaceful living together. The case studies in this volume show that policies regarding pastoralist territories foster conflict if they are solely based on external imposition rather than on consultation and cooperation. Richmond (2013a, 2013b) describes this as the very pattern that has resulted in the failure of state-building and peace-building. Yet he also asserts that peace formation, if built on local capacities, can result in a state that is 'more fully representative of all identity groups in society' (Richmond 2013a: 282).

It should not be necessary to advocate pastoralism, but it is necessary to remind ourselves of the significance of drylands and lowlands, which are not empty but full of life. Within a broader temporal and spatial perspective, one broader in scope than this book, pastoralists do not need to be rehabilitated when it comes to land use. Their expertise simply should be recognized. Just as books that are seminal contributions to the understanding of particular topics should be consulted, if one wants to be well-informed, so knowledge of (agro-)pastoralists should be part of the syllabus for developing an understanding of land use. In weighing pastoralists' ways of living with and off the land against forms of capital investment and 'development', it is not too late to learn important lessons that can help multiple actors achieve a future based on the reconciliation of interests that are now in conflict.

In their contribution to this volume, Elifuraha I. Laltaika and Kelly M. Askew remind us of the significance of the UN Declaration of the Rights of Indigenous Peoples, which has, however, been received with obvious scepticism on the African continent. Such scepticism might be overcome if the concept of indigeneity were broadened to include people 'whose social and economic sustenance depends upon the management of a territory, according to their collective customs' (Milanez and Wedekind 2016: 6). Understood in this way, an emphasis on indigenous rights could be combined with the ratification of the ILO (International Labour Organization) Convention 169 on Indigenous and Tribal Rights, which acknowledges people's national right to self-determination. Another approach that corresponds well to respecting (agro-)pastoralist ways of life is 'food sovereignty', which is the 'right of peoples to healthy and culturally appropriate food produced through ecologically sound and sustainable methods, and their right to define their own food and agriculture systems' (Declaration of Nyéléni 2007). Last but not least among the ways of contributing to positive futuremaking in southern Ethiopia and neighbouring regions is the proper translation of pastoralist land use practices into policies and the *de facto* use of commons as entailing communal land rights, as has been specified by the Voluntary Guidelines on the Responsible Governance of Tenure (FAO 2012) and other sources (e.g. Mohammud 2007; Imeru 2010; Amanor 2012: 45; Abebe and Solomon 2013; Strecker 2014; Yonas 2016). So far, these approaches have been largely neglected when analyzing the dispossession of (agro-)pastoralists in the interest of capital accumulation by outside investors and local elites. In and of themselves, they cannot provide blueprint solutions, but their contextual integration in policymaking could provide cornerstones for a revision of harmful land deals.

Conclusion

> If the future is developed peacefully and respectfully, everyone can learn and listen and change and open their minds. But if we are treated as inferiors, where is understanding, where is respect, where is the peace of mind that opens minds and hearts? (Pastoralist, Arbore, Southern Ethiopia, name withheld, 2016)

The future is a hypothesis first. The statement above is drawn from one of many conversations with my friends about their possible future as pastoralists in Ethiopia. The longing for peaceful and respectful living together is paramount in these conversations. It shows that people would like to identify with their state but cannot. The call for insight, genuine communication and respect by the government with and for its people mirrors the bitterness and discontent about suppressive policies, silencing and violence that cannot possibly lead to a positive identification with the state. Excluding pastoralists from futuremaking in the name of development and modernity has created what in chemistry is known as toxic synergy.[37] Development patterns that seemed to make sense in one institutional framework (Sustainable Development Goals) have been matched with market mechanisms that seemed to make sense in another institutional framework (economic growth and investment). By ignoring possible synergies and convergence with pastoral livelihoods, this match has created toxic environments of global social engineering and state-building that are marked by expropriation, conflict and cultural, environmental and economic losses, which, in their harmful effects, are much greater than the sum of their parts.

In his contribution to the volume, John G. Galaty describes how concepts of modernity have become a weapon of class struggle all over the Horn of Africa. Such concepts, and the exercise of power that they serve to legitimize, affect the conditions of rural land holding in much of the world while hindering the mutual exchange of opinions, existing knowledge and visions for the future. The paternalistic assumption that everyone wants what the planners think they want is based on a fundamental underestimation of people's agency and cultural self-esteem. Such assumptions construct a local, national and global divide between enforced modernity and artificially constructed backwardness, propagating images of pastoralists as poor and vulnerable, without asking whether such images correspond to pastoralists' self-understanding or calculating the costs of removing pastoralists from the matrix of futuremaking.

Positive futuremaking is an expressive and creative way of dealing with the past, especially if current understandings of the past, present and future call for improvement. As previously stated, to respect and support visions of development as a means to improve people's lives is a basis for constructive discussion. Likewise, to respect and understand people's views of land, especially the views of people who are most familiar with their land, is not an optional act of benevolence but an essential part of the opportunity to create the best possible solutions to pressing challenges to food provisioning worldwide. The responsibility for food security has increasingly been concentrated in the hands of people who have very little knowledge about land beyond its value as a commodity. Their understanding of 'food security' may, however, be illusory: 'If you take away land from others, it might appear sweet to you first; later you will awake and realize it has ruined you. Even with millions in your bank account, one day you will live to see: money from stolen land has a curse on it' (Arbore man, 25 February 2019, name withheld).

'The future needs heritage,' says the philosopher Marquard (2003). He calls for sustaining the tension between rapid innovation and a moderate or slow approach to seeking necessary improvements; but these formulations still associate speed with modernity and slowness with tradition, thus reinforcing a divide that has contributed to the disintegration of the ties that link people, land and politics. It is a divide that has made economics the science of the future and, thus, the launching pad for policymaking while diminishing the cultural actor as 'a person of and from the past' (Appadurai 2013: 180). Instead of reinforcing oppositions between the future and heritage or modernity and tradition, anthropologists have time and again called for syntheses of economic, sociocultural and practical perspectives beyond the 'alluring spectacle of modernity' and development (Fratkin 2014: 109).[38] For these repeated calls to resonate more clearly, it might be helpful to take a step away from the time-bound illusion of the modernity paradigm – that is, the fads and fashions of immediate situations – and to enter the timeless domain of value (Bell and Mau 1971: xi), in the hope of discovering what the pastoralist elder, the astronaut, the schoolgirl and the artist have envisioned: what is and will be relevant in a broader, more inclusive space-time concept for life on earth.

'Modernity starts when space and time are separated from living practice' (Baumann 2000: 8). In thinking about land, water and living together in the twenty-first century, the divisions between theory and practice, modern and backward, states and pastoralists, have stood in the way for too long. Modernity also started when it was defined in opposition to all that is not regarded as modern. In the twenty-first century, such understandings of modernity increasingly resemble features of a past that used to be regarded as modern but is no longer seen as such. Positive futuremaking starts when space, time and land with its inhabitants are brought together to be thought together, when diverse forms of life on, with and off the land can be accepted as valid elements of futuremaking; when unnecessary distinctions among livelihoods and forms of existence are overcome; and when all members of society are trusted to cooperate to 'build peace and states' (Richmond 2013a: 282). Furthermore, when the social, ecological and economic factors are not construed as antagonistic but as integral parts of futuremaking, then knowledge about the land as soil and ground fosters knowledge about the world (see Latour 2018: 92). As an outcome, tradition would be relieved of the stigma of backwardness and instead be recognized as a synergetic element of a common future in which 'dualistic categories' are seen as 'relational, dynamic and essential for each other's existence' (Sullivan and Homewood 2018: 120). Sometimes, this is expressed in playful ways, as is the case with an Ethiopian coffee producer whose slogan is 'Where the tradition is progress'; is made accessible in inspiring academic collaborations such as in the volume *The River: Peoples and Histories of the Omo-Turkana Area* (Clack and Brittain 2018); or becomes visible in artistic ways, as in the paintings of Girmachew Getnet, which leave spaces for differences without breaking the circles that hold everything together.

This volume, although based on long-term anthropological engagement and research, is not an anthropology of the future of pastoralism. 'At the time of the

Anthropocene, anthropology is not a specialized discipline' (Latour 2017: 48); rather, it is one possibility to rethink the current local and global state of affairs. The future is a common destiny of people with many different views on life. And no single view can claim ownership over knowledge of what the future is or will be. In futuremaking, humans have only one part to play, without being able to control the future or the role non-human components will play in it. From a global perspective, modern contributions to the well-being of the world in the Global North are as remarkable as they are limited but up to now have not been characterized by equity but by selective enrichment through exploitation. As the greatest contributors to global warming, many 'developed' countries considered themselves modern for the longest time until discovering that their approaches were outmoded and even untimely when they were faced by a pressing need to finally develop sustainable ways of living within planetary limits. To ask countries from the Global South to slow down efforts to feed their populations and create income possibilities would be cynical, and this is not our intention. Access to healthcare, integrated education and the right to food should not be negotiable. They form a crucial basis for a peaceful living together. But have the scenarios described truly been designed with the intention to provide such access? The case studies in the volume answer this question rather forcefully: most land deals provided platforms for harmful and exploitative developments in global food production, creating toxic global synergies characterized by structural violence rather than new forms of peaceful synergy. A deep rethinking of agricultural knowledge, supported, for example, by agroecology and food sovereignty, is a far cry from the present reality. The global state of affairs, the climate crisis and the uncertainty about the future voices demands for desirable, viable, achievable and sustainable ways that 'are well thought out and understood' (Wright 2010: 23), drawing from all sources available.

Peaceful futuremaking needs many opinions, much expertise, and the ability to turn present dissonances into transformative moments. This is hard work. No discipline alone will identify answers that in themselves are sufficient. No peace-building mechanism can itself serve as a sole recipe. No land use practice alone will feed the world. To create enabling environments for a blend of organic farming, (agro-)pastoralism and other innovative farming systems is the challenge for policymakers dedicated to supporting liveable and peaceful futures in a global neighbourhood (see Reganold and Wachter 2016; Gabbert 2018). (Agro-)pastoralists have much to contribute to this endeavour.

To respect and fully integrate pastoralists' knowledge would first require the immediate correction of unjust land deals. Reparations for losses in land, food and well-being that still go unacknowledged are necessary to re-establish trust and stability in the affected regions. Pastoralist territories should not be declared empty, unused and available. Failed land deals cannot be corrected by simply bringing in new investors. Rather, pastoralists' rights to land, if clearly recognized by law, could prevent a replacement of common resources by monop-olization and privatization and foster fluid tenure solutions (see Galaty 2016). The narrative of the backward pastoralist can be corrected in informed ways, not to be confused with romantic pictures that perpetuate the image of the ex-otic other in equally questionable ways. To address this, pastoralists, scholars, the media, government authorities and donors together can play constructive roles. An important step towards this was made in the speech of the Deputy Prime Minister of Ethiopia, Demeke Mekonnen, on the Ethiopian Pastoralist Day in Jinka in January 2019, acknowledging the immense contribution of pastoralists as a 'national treasure', revoking the backward label and criticizing ill-advised development projects.

Although we criticize 'development' that is harmful to pastoralists, our aim in this book is not to advocate pastoralism or rehabilitate pastoralist knowledge. Rather, by conveying a realistic view of pastoralism and agro-pastoralism as equally valid modes of existence, representing one of the many ways in which certain kinds of land may be used effectively, we want to show that the alienation of pastoralists from productive lands is unwarranted, unproductive and inadvis-able. Again, this is not based on romantic notions of traditional land use practices but on time-tested evidence that pastoralism, like nomadism, is 'a rather sophis-ticated, economically successful and sustainable way of life' in certain areas of the world (Scholz and Schlee 2015: 838). Nomads and pastoralists who know how to use drylands in highly adaptive, flexible and organized ways are the major experts to be consulted together with other small-scale food providers at 'the helm of shaping food policies' (Gabbert 2018; Schiavoni et al. 2018: 1360).

The winds of change in Ethiopia and elsewhere give hope, as terms such as 'backward' and 'primitive' are becoming less frequent in official speeches. Yet, a change of tone alone is not sufficient, because, as Dessalegn Rahmato (2014: 239) states, we 'must focus not merely on issues of inadequate governance and lack of management capacity, but rather on fundamental issues of policy choice and principle'. In other words, an economically successful land grab is still a land grab; and, as such, it is a source of conflict to be avoided in favour of peaceful solutions. Instead of perpetuating injustice in the name of 'development', an important sentence in the Ethiopian Constitution – that the right to land owner-ship 'is vested in the State *and in the peoples of Ethiopia*' – could be realized fully, not in top-down state-building but in mutual state-making.

In this sense, this volume does not provide comfortable truths. On the contrary, while genuinely acknowledging the urgency of the obligation of gov-ernments to provide good living conditions for their citizens, it exposes, in an-thropological detail, the painful, harmful and deeply dissonant developments that first brought people together in the *Lands of the Future* Initiative. The com-poser Arnold Schönberg explained that dissonance, as unsettling as it can be, is not merely ugly but also a driver of movement (Bohemia 1912). This is a volume full of dissonances. It will not curry favour with self-proclaimed modernizers. It takes a stand against power inequalities, harmful development, short-sighted growth paradigms and forms of repression on a global scale.

To diagnose and criticize processes that cause harm is a fundamental goal of emancipatory social science (Wright 2010: 11). Still, our criticism is only a distant echo of the deep discord and chaos that lies at the heart of our descriptions: the experiences of friends and counterparts who have lost their land and the grounds on which to choose the lives they want to live – a way of life dissonant from the plans made for them in national and global institutions and business centres. It is time to learn to listen to this dissonance in order to create a respectful space for transformation. Moments that call for transformation can neither be pushed aside in haste nor resolved through slight changes of tone or through whitewashing injustices. To create more pacific spaces in the future will require much energy, synergy, cooperation and the recognition of grievances. Only in these ways will it be possible to develop workable solutions that are based on 'encounters across difference' (Tsing 2005), in order to develop shared goals, including those that have been ignored or intentionally displaced for no good reason.

When seeking resolution in moments of pessimism, when places are dissolving and the present seems vulnerable, the philosopher Mbembe (2015) says: 'A proper critique requires us to first dwell in the chaos of the night in order precisely to better break through into the dazzling light of the day.' If our volume, through sound critique, can broadcast the dissonance produced by the misrepresentation of (agro-)pastoralists in the past and present – and if decision-makers and their advisors can endure the discomfort with which they react to this dissonance – then, together, we might succeed in taking the first steps towards making a new start, one based on deep rethinking, peaceful synergy, deep reform and informed practice, towards transformation, cooperation and respect. Hopefully, this volume can be one contribution among many to positive futuremaking, to entry into the light of day, whether by amplifying invisible silences, by accepting emancipated dissonances, or by resonating with one another in our common world.

The Case Studies

John G. Galaty, in 'Modern Mobility in East Africa: Pastoral Responses to Rangeland Fragmentation, Enclosure and Settlement', highlights the relationship of pastoralists and states with modernity after neoliberal trends have devalued local land uses in favour of its commercialized exploitation. As pastoral land is traversed and not 'held', the demand that pastoralists settle is linked to the call to modernize. Galaty focuses on new forms of mobility that have arisen as responses to, and reformulations of, the challenges created by social change, sedentarization and displacement: first, the growth of small towns in arid lands, and second, novel techniques of claiming and moving into lands hitherto unavailable because of enclosure, land fragmentation and settlement. Various examples from Ethiopia and Kenya show that modernity, rather than being seen simply as a counterpoint to traditionalism, is conceived as a strategic stance towards innovation, where current conditions are refashioned as opportunities and continuing mobility represents modern responses to fragmented and bounded landscapes in an increasingly complex and globalized world.

Günther Schlee, in 'Unequal Citizenship and One-Sided Communication: Anthropological Perspectives on Collective Identification in the Context of Large-Scale Land Transfers in Ethiopia', scrutinizes notions of equality and realities of inequality in Ethiopian politics. Looking at Ethiopian ethnic federalism, Schlee describes the conundrum of shifting discourses about the equality of individuals and groups in relation to concepts of citizenship. While rights to territories move along ethnic, administrative, linguistic and historical lines and can be negotiated, there is one magic formula: if a group is classified as backward, then ethnicity is not associated with any entitlement to resources and does not have a voice in politics. This can be seen as a new class division that runs throughout the country. The lack of communication with 'backward' people has been bolstered by criminalization and silencing. Like a radio that can be switched off, this ignorance of citizens affects the core of ethnic federalism: cultural pluralism. To abolish the label 'backward' and to respect the land rights, knowledge and potential of pastoralists is an absolute requirement for the establishment of citizenship, in which everybody has a say in determining their own fate and that of the nation. This is essential for the cohesion of the country.

Peter D. Little, in 'Global Trade, Local Realities: Why African States Undervalue Pastoralism', rectifies state-skewed representations of economic realities by pointing to the immense contributions that pastoralists have been making to national economies in the Horn of Africa. He scrutinizes the hypocrisy in policymaking that fails 'to recognize that growth in exports of livestock and livestock products are dependent on existing forms of pastoralism'. Little shows how high-modernity utopias that regard their antagonists as 'unmodern' also create critical blind spots in their economic visions. These blind spots lead them to attempt to replace pastoralism with unsuccessful development schemes, such as implementing massive water development and farming schemes in Borana, prioritizing commercial ranching schemes over common land use, and criminalizing cross-border trade, thus constraining mobility and increasing inequality.

Elifuraha I. Laltaika and Kelly M. Askew, in 'Modes of Dispossession of Indigenous Lands and Territories in Africa', discuss indigenous rights on the African continent. Although all African states are united in their insistence that the concept of indigeneity does not apply to them, based on the claim all Africans are equally indigenous, the authors describe how identification as indigenous became increasingly significant in environments of violent discrimination against marginalized groups such as pastoralists, agro-pastoralists and hunter-gatherers.

With violence increasing alongside the appropriation of land, water and other resources in the course of the global land rush, they describe and analyse six modes of land loss and dispossession, with cases drawn from across the continent – agribusiness, conservation, extractive industries, infrastructure projects, competition with cultivators and internally displaced persons – to emphasize the global responsibility to create a respectful path of development.

John Markakis, in 'Land and the State in Ethiopia', embeds recent policies for pastoralists in the history of the Ethiopian arid lowland peripheries. He scrutinizes the continuing lack of synergy between the local economy and the plantation economy within different political frameworks. After offering vast amounts of available land in the peripheries in the twenty-first century, Ethiopia became a major participant in the 'second scramble for Africa', with the 'feeding frenzy' involving state, private and foreign capital in outsized amounts. Resettlement and villagization processes were often supported by the local intelligentsia that had been groomed into an auxiliary elite, which was recruited into the EPRDF-affiliated local political party and local administration. The technocratic interpretation of future economic gains that clash with often disastrous outcomes for people in the periphery and the environment is accompanied by accounts of failed investments squeezed between the political power of the state and the increasing discontent of lowlanders.

Maknun Ashami and Jean Lydall, in 'Persistent Expropriation of Pastoral Lands: The Afar Case', draw from rich historical material to review the commercial agro-industry projects and development policies for Afar of different governments as well as reactions from Afar elites and pastoralists. Including hitherto unknown material from the late Glynn Flood, they describe the similarities between the set of assumptions that puts regions and peoples under feudal obligation, the revolutionary ideology that establishes all land may be held by, and at the disposal of, the state, and finally a neoliberal philosophy that grants the state the right to allocate land for capitalist development to the detriment of a pastoral livelihood. They conclude by noting that in spite of losing crucial flood-fed grazing areas, the great majority of Afar still survive, for better or worse, as pastoralists and agro-pastoralists.

Jonah Wedekind, in 'Anatomy of a White Elephant: Investment Failure and Land Conflicts on Ethiopia's Oromia–Somali Frontier', provides an example of state formation at high cost embedded in global market schemes for agro investment. Here the transformation of agro-pastoralist livelihoods not only failed economically in the short term but also backfired politically over the long term. The case can be regarded as a forerunner of the social, economic and ecological harm created by similar projects in Ethiopia. Attracted by cheap land lease, water and labour and promises of the global boom in biofuels, land was appropriated by officials and investors through extreme measures when co-opting customary figures and establishing tightly controlled agricultural schemes to produce castor oil.

Complex entanglements led to a lack of cooperation and to resistance by farmers and agro-pastoralists and finally to the repeated bankruptcy of the project for Israeli and German investors, leaving behind deteriorated relationships between local communities and the federal and regional state long after the investors left the country.

Asebe Regassa, in 'From Cattle Herding to Charcoal Burning: Land Expropriation, State Consolidation and Livelihood Changes in Abaya Valley, Southern Ethiopia', argues that the current land regimes represent a continuation of past Ethiopian strategies of state expansion and resource exploitation as paths to the consolidation of state power. Large-scale agribusiness projects are mechanisms of exclusion, separating local people from their customary resource bases in processes of exclusion and expropriation to reconfigure property regimes pertaining to the ownership, utilization and control of natural resources. Using the example of a combined sugar cane cultivation and dam-building scheme, Asebe presents the voices of the Guji Oromo pastoralists. After having been dispossessed of their habitat and large portions of their herds, the Guji reacted by establishing private enclosures for charcoal burning, given the dwindling space for a pastoralist way of life.

Fana Gebresenbet, in 'Villagization in Ethiopia's Lowlands: Development vs. Facilitating Control and Dispossession', unveils the political objectives of villagization programmes for pastoralists in Ethiopia's lowlands within an historical context by asking, 'What was villagization really about?' Focusing on the clash of values between the 'developers and the developing', he shows that the realities of so-called development projects in the lowlands can be understood as a process of state-making by de-skilling pastoralists through central development paradigms. Villagization contributed to making society legible, governable and controllable. Whereas the need to address food security, health and improved schooling is accepted, the broken promises of integrated social services show that development rhetoric served to veil political and economical goals, with local communities losing out. Although Fana contends that 'equitable development is not on the horizon', he also argues that differences in worldview are surmountable when the capacity to aspire to a common future is reclaimed.

David Turton, in '"Breaking Every Rule in the Book": The Story of River Basin Development in Ethiopia's Omo Valley', guides us into the policies behind the Gibe III dam, part of the largest planned irrigation complex in Ethiopia constructed along the River Omo in southern Ethiopia, and the establishment of the plantation for the Ethiopian Sugar Corporation. After a description of the integrated and viable agro-pastoral economy that he has studied for decades, Turton describes the inadequate social and environmental impact assessments of the combined megaprojects that basically ignored the populations who lived along the river. The flaws in planning were followed by the disastrous effects of development-forced displacement and resettlement based on fictitious descriptions of people's livelihoods. By asking 'how did it come to this?', Turton embeds the current developments in historical state-building processes 'fundamentally authoritarian, repressive and racist' and observes that genuine consultation, warning and advice were not given the space to avoid disaster.

Lucie Buffavand, in 'State-Building in the Ethiopian South-Western Low-lands: Experiencing the Brunt of State Power in Mela', complements Turton's chapter with a description of the effects on the Mela (Bodi) of the Gibe III dam and the irrigation schemes of the sugar cane plantation along the Omo River. Buffavand examines state-building mechanisms 'by which the Ethiopian state has attempted to secure the compliance of people whose land it takes'. With a focus on the actions of military personnel together with farm management and government workers, she provides ethnographic detail about land appropriation marked by violence, force and threats within the framework of historically estab-lished centre-periphery relations, with the deployment of heavily armed troops that targeted young Mela men in an exaggerated display of military might. So-called consultancy meetings were held in an atmosphere of fear and suspicion to implement villagization schemes under immense pressure. Deprived of land and time-tested coping mechanisms, the Mela pay the price for the new devel-opment – hunger. Whether the shifts towards less coercive modes of governance will reach the lowlands remains an open question.

Shauna LaTosky, in 'Customary Land Use and Local Consent Practices in Mun (Mursi): A New Call for Meaningful FPIC Standards in Southern Ethi-opia', adds another dimension to the industrialization efforts around the sugar cane projects in southern Ethiopia. She shows how development and villagization schemes still struggle to honour and uphold culturally appropriate free, prior and informed consent (FPIC) guidelines with agro-pastoralists. By unveiling how the Mun gave their 'full consent' under an extreme, hostile climate of intimidation and discrimination after investments had already begun, it is clear people's fun-damental right to FPIC, including the right to withhold consent, has not yet been realized. She shows, in a rich cultural translation, not only what 'consent' means but how understandings about territory need to be reached before any meaningful agreement about land use can take place. To restore dignity, decrease conflict and include pastoralists' ideas of development, LaTosky calls for all actors to come together to seriously work on future land use plans.

Edward G.J. Stevenson and Benedikt Kamski, in 'Ethiopia's "Blue Oil"? Hydropower, Irrigation and Development in the Omo-Turkana Basin', look at water, 'the hydrological equivalent' to land, as an asset in the global market, com-plementing the contributions of Turton, Buffavand and LaTosky in the Omo region. By scrutinizing the divided perceptions with respect to megaprojects – high potential or human disaster – they show that the (rhetorical) 'framing' of the issue often decides the outcome of its evaluation and implementation. While, for example, the Italian contractor frames its activities as positive development, counter-narratives tell of human rights abuses, impoverishment, failure of investment schemes, conflict potential across national boundaries and the silencing of critical voices. The authors do not seek to pick a 'winning horse' in the race but instead to expose the hypocrisy of partial truths, especially on the side of the planners; to emphasize the necessity to cast light on shadowy reasoning and foreground the impacts on people and ecosystems on both sides of the international border; and in conclusion to stress that water cannot be likened to oil.

Echi Christina Gabbert is an anthropologist and a lecturer at the Institute for Social and Cultural Anthropology at Göttingen University, Germany. Her research foci are agro-pastoralism, music and oral history, political ecology and peace and conflict studies. Her long-term fieldwork in Ethiopia resulted in the award-winning PhD thesis 'Deciding Peace'. She extended the 'Cultural Neighbourhood Approach' to 'Global Neighbourhood' scenarios, where global investment schemes meet smallholder's livelihoods, and is coordinating the *Lands of the Future* Initiative, an interdisciplinary project about pastoral livelihoods in the twenty-first century.

Notes

1. The Arbore (also Hor) are agro-pastoralists in southern Ethiopia. The late Grazmach Sura was a spokesman for peace during interethnic conflicts in southern Ethiopia. The peacemaking efforts of the Arbore are described in 'Deciding Peace' (Gabbert 2012).
2. As many pastoralist communities also practise agriculture; in this volume we use the terms pastoralism and agro-pastoralism/(agro-)pastoralism.
3. The name *Lands of the Future* was borrowed from an article by John G. Galaty (2013: 153) in which he argues that states should 'demonstrate more confidence in their people's ingenuity . . . rather than looking elsewhere for eager hands of investors in which to place the lands of the future and the future of the land'.
4. The *Lands of the Future* Initiative has been supported and financed by the Max Planck Institute for Social Anthropology, Department 'Integration and Conflict', in Halle (Saale), Germany.
5. At the beginning of our research, we used the neutral term 'changing land use' until there was sufficient evidence to specify the use of terms such as 'land grab' (on the terminology of land deals in research, see Hall 2013).
6. The *Lands of the Future* position paper, co-authored by thirteen anthropologists (Abbink et al. 2014), gained wide attention, including from the development agencies of donor countries. For a list of workshops and panels at international conferences of the initiative, see https://www.eth.mpg.de/lof.
7. Edelman (2013) warns about the lack of understanding of land tenure, size and scale in the global land rush literature (see also Kaag and Zoomers 2014; Edelman, Oya and Borras 2015).
8. In the 'global neighbourhood approach', diverse views on land use are described with a focus on understanding all actors in given investment schemes (Gabbert 2014, 2018).

9. The term 'food security' here is used in the context of a global food policy framework, whereas in the context of small-scale food providers the term 'right to food' is preferred (see also Schiavoni et al. 2018).

10. Sustainable procurement processes are intended to help in serious-minded calculations regarding future social, economic and ecological factors and external costs ('externalities' in economic jargon) before operations are underway.

11. For descriptions of frontier dynamics in pastoralist territories, see Schlee and Watson (2009), Markakis (2011), Schlee (2011), Behnke and Kerven (2013), Dereje (2013), Girke (2013), Meckelburg (2014), Turton (2015), Wagstaff (2015), Fana (2016), Hennings (2016), Mosley and Watson (2016), Nalepa, Short Gianotti and Bauer (2017), Asebe, Yetebarek and Korf (2018).

12. As voiced in the speech of the late Prime Minister of Ethiopia Meles Zenawi on the Pastoralist Day in Jinka in 2011 (Meles 2011). Civil servants in southern Ethiopia were reportedly warned in official meetings about anthropologists who were 'enemies of development'.

13. Sources on the history of state expansion and forced displacement in Ethiopia, and on the South as a zone for enslavement, hunting and feudal control, are, among others, Pankhurst (1997), Donham and James (2002), Strecker (2006), Pankhurst and Piguet (2009), Lydall (2010), Gabbert (2012: 44ff).

14. 'I promise you that, even though this area is known as backward in terms of civilization, it will become an example of rapid development' (Meles 2011).

15. Several individuals who did not agree to the payment for the visit were consequently imprisoned for a few days.

16. For example: 'Institutionally, the major policy steps implemented so far by the Federal Government include securing the constitutional right of pastoralists not to be displaced from their own land' (MoFED 2006: 192).

17. Article 40.5 of the Ethiopian Constitution: 'Ethiopian pastoralists have the right to free land for grazing and cultivation as well as the right not to be displaced from their own lands. The implementation shall be specified by law'.

18. See Galaty's note on rational choices and self-interested judgements in policies for pastoralists (Galaty 2011).

19. In the recent land rush in Eastern Africa, *terra nullius* was not applied in its legal sense, as known, for example, from British colonial rule, when 'uninhabited' land could be appropriated by law. Nevertheless, *terra nullius* rhetoric that justified appropriation when land was not used according to the expectations of colonial rulers was clearly applied to pursue and legitimize land deals (see also Geisler 2012; Makki 2014).

20. Dessalegn (2011: 18) reports lease rates per hectare per year in 2009 of between 1.20 and 12 US dollars.

21. It remains to be seen how more differentiated approaches – e.g. in the latest report of the World Bank Group and the UK's Department for International Development (2019) – will be merged with the Pastoral Development Policies Strategy of the Ethiopian Government.

22. From the envisaged 700,000 new jobs created by the sugar industry in the Omo Valley, only 30,000 materialized (Kamski 2016). The numbers from various sources differ dramatically. LaTosky reports that from the pastoral community only thirty-four Mun have been employed. Buffavand reports significant differences in the payment of locals versus migrant workers, with cases of local workers receiving lower wages and of women who were actually deprived of their payment (personal communication October 2018).

23. 'The "virgin lands campaign" in the Kazakhstan steppes in the 1950s and the introduction of a cotton monoculture in Uzbekistan are just two examples of culturally and ecologically devastating Soviet initiatives . . .' (Donahoe 2004: 2017f).

24. While acknowledging that the 'state is always in the making' (Lund 2016: 1200), the term 'state-building' here is used according to the following understanding: 'It is normally aimed at producing the basic framework of a neoliberal state in a procedural and technocratic sense, and is less interested in human rights norms or civil society' (Richmond 2013b: 383).

25. For a historical perspective on development policies for pastoralists, see Schareika (2018) and Sandford (1983).

26. Benefits are difficult to evaluate because (a) quantative reports on the performance of agricultural investment often contradict each other, and (b) evaluation of costs alone does not include the meaning of land and well-being beyond economic calculations. On the unreliability of data regarding land deals, see Cotula et al. (2014).

27. Sustainable Development Goals set by the United Nations Assembly in 2015 to 'achieve a better and sustainable future for all': 1: No Poverty, 2: Zero Hunger, 3: Good Health and Well-being, 4: Quality Education, 5: Gender Equality, 6: Clean Water and Sanitation, 7: Affordable and Clean Energy, 8: Decent Work and Economic Growth, 9: Industry, Innovation and Infrastructure, 10: Reduced Inequality, 11: Sustainable Cities and Communities, 12: Responsible Consumption and Production; 13: Climate Action, 14: Life below Water, 15: Life on Land, 16: Peace and Justice Strong Institutions, 17: Partnerships to Achieve the Goal (https://www.un.org/sustainabledevelopment/sustainable-development-goals/).

28. Similar findings have been made for Beni Shangul Gumuz and Gambella, concluding that large-scale agricultural projects 'fail in all aspects' (Atkeyelsh 2019:127ff).

29. The *Guardians of Productive Landscapes* Project, which evolved from the *Lands of the Future* Initiative, is looking at well-functioning, sustainable, organic and highly productive land use practices that make up the backbone of food production (Schlee et al. 2017: 17ff).

30. See Scoones (1994, 2004), Lane (1998), Little et al. (2001), Galaty (2005), Schlee and Shongolo (2012), Catley et al. (2013), Schlee (2013), Abbink et al. (2014), Krätli (2015), Zinsstag et al. (2016), Gabbert (2018).

31. The international PASTRES (Pastoralism, Uncertainty and Resilience: Global Lessons from the Margins) project is building on pastoralists' expertise to apply it to global challenges, such as financial systems, critical infrastructure management, disease outbreak response, migration policy, climate change, and conflict and security governance.

32. Studies show the hidden costs for seemingly 'successful' food production (see Fitzpatrick et al. 2017 for the UK).

33. A groundbreaking contribution to the meanings of sustainability in the twenty-first century is *The Anthropology of Sustainability* (Brightman and Lewis 2017).

34. In 2013, a comprehensive UN report emphasized the need for a long-term paradigm shift from industrial monoculture to polyculture and small-scale agriculture in order to secure world food security (UN 2013). The technological and political dimensions of agroecology and food sovereignty provide viable insights into alternatives to unsustainable industrial agricultural practices and policies (Rosset and Altieri 2017; Pimbert 2018).

35. The concept of *buen vivir*, roughly translatable as 'the good life', has been incorporated into the constitutions of Ecuador and Bolivia, where it articulates alternatives from below to 'development' based on Western models. In this understanding, *buen vivir* is only possible within a community (Gudynas 2011).

36. In the volume *To Live with Others*, such principles of diversity have been described for the cultural neighbourhood of southern Ethiopia (Gabbert and Thubauville 2010).
37. Chemical substances – e.g. pesticides – that might not lead to harm in separate exposures can lead to toxic chemical reactions when mixed (see Lydy et al. 2004).
38. See also Elwert and Bierschenk (1988), Olivier de Sardan (2001), Schlee (2008: 21), Rottenburg (2009).

References

Abbink, J. 2011. '"Land to Foreigners": Economic, Legal, and Socio-cultural Aspects of New Land Acquisition Schemes in Ethiopia', *Journal of Contemporary African Studies* 29(4): 513–35.

Abbink, J. (ed.). 2018. *The Environmental Crunch in Africa: Growth Narrative vs. Local Realities*. Cham: Palgrave Macmillan.

Abbink, J. et al. 2014. 'Lands of the Future: Transforming Pastoral Lands and Livelihoods in Eastern Africa', *Max Planck Institute for Social Anthropology Working Papers* No. 154. Retrieved 8 December 2016 from https://www.eth.mpg.de/pubs/wps/pdf/mpi-eth-working-paper-0154.

Abebe Mulatu, and Solomon Bekure. 2013. 'The Need to Strengthen Land Laws in Ethiopia to Protect Pastoral Rights', in A. Catley, J. Lind and I. Scoones (eds), *Pastoralism and Development in Africa: Dynamic Change at the Margins*. London and New York: Routledge, pp. 57–70.

Adam, B. 2008. 'Future Matters: Futures Known, Created and Minded', *Special Issue: Twenty-First Century Society* 3(2): 111–16.

Amanor, K.S. 2012. 'Land Governance in Africa: How Historical Context Has Shaped Key Contemporary Issues Relating to Policy on Land', *Framing the Debate Series*, no. 1. Rome: ILC.

Appadurai, A. 2013. *The Future as Cultural Fact: Essays on the Global Condition*. London: Verso.

Arendt, H. [1958] 1998. *The Human Condition*. Chicago and London: University of Chicago Press.

Asebe Regassa, Yetebarek Hizekiel and Benedikt Korf. 2018. 'Civilizing the Pastoral Frontier: Land Grabbing, Dispossession and Coercive Agrarian Development in Ethiopia', *Journal of Peasant Studies*.

Atkeyelsh G.M. Persson. 2019. *Foreign Direct Investment in Large-Scale Agriculture in Africa: Economic, Social and Environmental Sustainability in Ethiopia*. Abingdon and New York: Routledge.

AU (African Union). 2010. *Pastoral Policy Framework in Africa: Securing, Protecting and Improving the Lives, Livelihoods and Rights of Pastoralist Communities*. Addis Ababa: AU.

Baumann, Z. 2000. *Liquid Modernity*. Malden, MA: Polity Press.

Baviskar, A. (ed.). 2008. *Contested Grounds: Essays on Nature, Culture and Power*. Oxford and New York: Oxford University Press.

Behnke, R., and C. Kerven. 2013. 'Counting the Costs: Replacing Pastoralism with Irrigated Agriculture in the Awash Valley', in A. Catley, J. Lind and I. Scoones (eds), *Pastoralism and Development in Africa: Dynamic Change at the Margins*. Abingdon and New York: Routledge, pp. 57–70.

Behrends, A., S.-J. Park and R. Rottenburg. 2014. *Travelling Models in African Conflict Resolution: Translating Technologies of Social Ordering*. Leiden: Brill.

Bell, W., and J.A. Mau. 1971. *The Sociology of the Future: Theory, Cases and Annotated Bibliography*. New York: Russell Sage Foundation.

Bierschenk, T. 2014. 'From the Anthropology of Development to the Anthropology of Global Engineering', *Zeitschrift für Ethnologie* 139(1): 73–98.

Bohemia. 1912. 'Bei Arnold Schönberg: Eine Unterredung vor Zugsabgang', *Bohemia* Morgenausgabe 2. März. 1912. Retrieved 2 February 2019 from https://www.schoenberg.at/index.php/de/bei-arnold-schoenberg-eine-unterredung-vor-zugsabgang.

Bonte, P., and J.G. Galaty. 1991. 'Introduction', in J.G. Galaty and P. Bonte (eds), *Herders, Warriors, and Traders: Pastoralism in Africa.* Boulder, CO: Westview Press, pp. 3–30.

Borras Jr, S.M., and J.C. Franco. 2012. 'Global Land Grabbing and Trajectories of Agrarian Change: A Preliminary Analysis', *Journal of Agrarian Change* 12(1): 34–59.

———. 2018. 'The Challenge of Locating Land-Based Climate Change Mitigation and Adaptation Politics within a Social Justice Perspective: Towards an Idea of Agrarian Climate Justice', *Third World Quarterly* 39(7): 1308–25.

Borras Jr. S.M. et al. 2018. 'Converging Social Justice Issues and Movements: Implications for Political Actions and Research', *Third World Quarterly* 39(7): 1227–46.

Bourne, C. 2006. *A Future for Presentism.* Oxford: Oxford University Press.

Brightman, M., and J. Lewis (eds). 2017. *The Anthropology of Sustainability.* New York: Palgrave Macmillan.

Buffavand, L. 2016. '"The Land Does Not Like Them": Contesting Dispossession in Cosmological Terms in Mela, South-West Ethiopia', *Journal of Eastern African Studies* 10(3): 476–93.

———. 2017. 'Vanishing Stones and the Hovering Giraffe: Identity, Land and the Divine in Mela, Southwest Ethiopia', Ph.D. dissertation. Halle (Saale): Martin Luther University Halle-Wittenberg, Institute for Social Anthropology.

Campbell, J.M. 2015. *Conjuring Property: Speculation and Environmental Futures in the Brazilian Amazon.* Seattle and London: University of Washington Press.

Catley, A. 2017. *Pathways to Resilience in Pastoralist Areas: A Synthesis of Research in the Horn of Africa.* Boston: Feinstein International Center, Tufts University.

Catley, A., J. Lind and I. Scoones (eds). 2013. *Pastoralism and Development in Africa: Dynamic Change at the Margins.* London and New York: Routledge.

Clack, T., and M. Brittain (eds). 2018. *The River: Peoples and Histories of the Omo-Turkana Area.* Oxford: Archaeopress.

Cotula, L. 2012. 'The International Political Economy of the Global Land Rush: A Critical Appraisal of Trends, Scale, Geography and Drivers', *Journal of Peasant Studies* 39(3–4): 649–80.

Cotula, L. et al. 2014. 'Testing Claims about Large Land Deals in Africa: Findings from a Multi-country Study', *Journal of Development Studies* 50(7): 903–25.

Daniel Ayalew Ali, K. Deininger and A. Harris. 2015. 'Using National Statistics to Increase Transparency of Large Land Acquisition: Evidence from Ethiopia', *Policy Research Working Paper Series* 7342. Washington DC: World Bank.

Davies-Vengoechea, X. 2004. 'A Positive Concept of Peace', in G. Kemp and D.P. Fry (eds), *Keeping the Peace: Conflict Resolution and Peaceful Societies around the World.* New York and London: Routledge, pp. 11–18.

Declaration of Nyéléni. 2007. Retrieved 16 February 2019 from https://nyeleni.org/IMG/pdf/DeclNyeleni-en.pdf.

Dereje Feyissa. 2013. '"Centering the Periphery"? The Federal Experience at the Margins of the Ethiopian State', *Ethiopian Journal of Federal Studies* 1(1): 155–92.

Dessalegn Rahmato. 2011. 'Land to Investors: Large-Scale Land Transfers in Ethiopia', discussion paper. Addis Ababa: Forum for Social Studies.

————. 2014. 'Large-Scale Land Investments Revisited', in Dessalegn Rahmato, Meheret Ayenew, Asnake Kefale and B. Habermann (eds), *Reflections on Development in Ethiopia: New Trends, Sustainability and Challenges*. Addis Ababa: Forum for Social Studies, Friedrich Ebert Stiftung, pp. 219–45.

Donahoe, B.R. 2004. 'A Line in the Sayans: History and Divergent Perceptions of Property Among the Tozhu and Tofa of South Siberia', Ph.D. dissertation. Indiana University, Department of Anthropology.

Donham, D., and W. James (eds). 2002. *The Southern Marches of Imperial Ethiopia*. Oxford: James Currey.

Edelman, M. 2013. 'Messy Hectares: Questions about the Epistemology of Land Grabbing Data', *Journal of Peasant Studies* 40(3): 485–501.

Edelman, M., C. Oya, and S. Borras, Jr. (eds). 2015. *Global Land Grabs: History, Theory and Method*. London and New York: Routledge.

El Aynaoui, K. 2003. *Ethiopia – Country Economic Memorandum – Concept Paper*.

Elwert, G., and T. Bierschenk. 1988. 'Development Aid as an Intervention in Dynamic Systems: An Introduction', *Sociologia Ruralis* 28(2/3): 99–112.

Erasmus, D. 2001 [1536]. *The Adages of Erasmus. Selected by William Barker*. Toronto: University of Toronto Press.

FAO. 2012. *Voluntary Guidelines on the Responsible Governance of Tenure of Land, Fisheries and Forests in the Context of National Food Security*. Rome: Food and Agriculture Organization of the United Nations.

Fana Gebresenbet. 2016. 'Land Acquisitions, the Politics of Dispossession, and State-Re-Making in Gambella, Western Ethiopia', *Africa Spectrum* 51(1): 5–28.

Fitzpatrick, I. et al. 2017. *The Hidden Costs of UK Food*. Bristol: Sustainable Food Trust.

Fratkin, E. 2014. 'Ethiopia's Pastoralist Policies: Development, Displacement, and Resettlement', *Nomadic Peoples* 18(1): 94–114.

Gabbert, C. 2012. 'Deciding Peace: Knowledge about War and Peace among the Arbore of Southern Ethiopia', Ph.D. dissertation. Halle (Saale): Martin Luther University Halle-Wittenberg, Institute for Social Anthropology.

Gabbert, E.C. 2014. 'The Global Neighbourhood Concept: A Chance for Cooperative Development or *Festina Lente*', in M.G. Berhe (ed.), *A Delicate Balance: Land Use, Minority Rights and Social Stability in the Horn of Africa*. Addis Ababa: Institute for Peace and Security Studies, Addis Ababa University, pp. 14–37.

————. 2018. 'Future in Culture: Globalizing Environments in the Lowlands of Southern Ethiopia', in J. Abbink (ed.), *The Environmental Crunch in Africa: Growth Narrative vs. Local Realities*. Cham: Palgrave Macmillan, pp. 287–317.

Gabbert, E.C., and S. Thubauville (eds). 2010. *To Live with Others: Essays on Cultural Neighborhood in Southern Ethiopia*. Cologne: Köppe.

Galaty, J.G. 2005. 'States of Violence: Ethnicity, Politics and Pastoral Conflict in East Africa', *Geography Research Forum* 25:105–27.

————. 2011. '(Non) Rational Choice', paper presented at the Workshop organized on the Occasion of the 60th Birthday of Günther Schlee, Roundtable on Rational Choice and Challenges, 10–12 July 2011. Max Planck Institute for Social Anthropology, Halle (Saale).

————. 2013. 'Land Grabbing in the Eastern African Rangelands', in A. Catley, J. Lind and I. Scoones (eds), *Pastoralism and Development in Africa: Dynamic Change at the Margins*. Abingdon and New York: Routledge, pp. 143–53.

————. 2016. 'Reasserting the Commons: Pastoral Contestations of Private and State Lands in East Africa', *International Journal of the Commons* 10(2): 709–27.

Galtung, J. 2010. 'Peace, Negative and Positive', in N.J. Young (ed.), *The Oxford International Encyclopedia of PEACE, Vol. 3*. Oxford: Oxford University Press, pp. 352–56.

Geisler, C. 2012. 'New Terra Nullius Narratives and the Gentrification of Africa's "Empty Lands"', *Journal of World-Systems Research* 18(1): 15–29.

Girke, F. 2013. 'Homeland, Boundary, Resource: The Collision of Place-Making Projects on the Lower Omo River, Ethiopia', *Max Planck Institute for Social Anthropology Working Papers* No. 148. Retrieved 6 July 2014 from https://www.eth.mpg.de/pubs/wps/pdf/mpi-eth-working-paper-0148.

———. 2018. *The Wheel of Autonomy: Rhetoric and Ethnicity in the Omo Valley*. New York and Oxford: Berghahn.

Gudynas, E. 2011. 'Buen Vivir: Today's Tomorrow', *Development* 54(4): 441–47.

Hall, D. 2013. 'Primitive Accumulation, Accumulation by Dispossession and the Global Land Grab', *Third World Quarterly* 34(9): 1582–604.

Hall, R., I. Scoones and D. Tsikaka (eds). 2015. *Africa's Land Rush: Rural Livelihoods and Agrarian Change*. Woodbridge: James Currey.

Hennings, A. 2016. 'Das Konfliktpotenzial exklusiver Landgrabbing-Praktiken: Eine Herausforderung für den regionalen Frieden', *ZeFKo - Zeitschrift für Friedens- und Konfliktforschung* 5(2): 221–248.

Hobart, M. 1993. 'Introduction: The Growth of Ignorance', in M. Hobart (ed.), *An Anthropological Critique of Development: The Growth of Ignorance*. London and New York: Routledge, pp. 1–30.

Imeru Tamrat. 2010. 'Governance of Large Scale Agricultural Investments in Africa: The Case of Ethiopia', paper presented at the World Bank Conference on Land Policy and Administration.

Järvensivu, P. et al. 2018. 'Governance of Economic Transition: Global Sustainable Development Report 2019', drafted by the Group of Independent Scientists. Invited background document on economic transformation, to chapter: Transformation: The Economy. Retrieved 6 April 2019 from https://bios.fi/bios-governance_of_economic_transition.pdf.

Kaag, M., and A. Zoomers (eds). 2014. *The Global Land Grab: Beyond the Hype*. London: Zed Books.

Kamski, B. 2016. 'The Kuraz Sugar Development Project (KSDP) in Ethiopia: Between "Sweet Visions" and Mounting Challenges', *Journal of Eastern African Studies* 10(3): 568–80.

Khazanov, A.M., and G. Schlee. 2012. 'Introduction', in A.M. Khazanov and G. Schlee (eds), *Who Owns the Stock? Collective and Multiple Property Rights in Animals*. New York and Oxford: Berghahn, pp. 1–23.

Krätli, S. 2015. *Valuing Variability: New Perspectives on Climate Resilient Dryland Development*. London: International Institute for Environment and Development.

Kurimoto, E. 1996. 'People of the River: Subsistence Economy of the Anywaa (Anyak) of Western Ethiopia', in S. Sato and E. Kurimoto (eds), *Essays in Northeast African Studies*. Osaka: National Museum of Ethnology, pp. 29–57.

Lane, C.R. (ed.). 1998. *Custodians of the Commons: Pastoral Land Tenure in East and West Africa*. Abingdon and New York: Earthscan/Routledge.

Latour, B. 1993. *We Have Never Been Modern*. Cambridge, MA: Harvard University Press.

———. 2013. *An Inquiry into Modes of Existence: An Anthropology of the Moderns*. Cambridge, MA: Harvard University Press.

———. 2017. 'Anthropology at the Time of the Anthropocene: A Personal View of What Is to Be Studied', in M. Brightman and J. Lewis (eds), *The Anthropology of Sustainability*. New York: Palgrave Macmillan, pp. 35–49.

———. 2018. *Down to Earth: Politics in the New Climatic Regime*. Cambridge and Medford: Polity.

Lavers, T. 2012. 'Patterns of Agrarian Transformation in Ethiopia: State-Mediated Commercialization and the "Land Grab"', *Journal of Peasant Studies* 39(3–4): 795–822.

Lentz, C. 2013. *Land, Mobility, and Belonging in West Africa*. Bloomington: Indiana University Press.

Li, T.M. 2014a. 'What Is Land? Assembling a Resource for Global Investment', *Transactions of the Institute of British Geographers* 39(4): 589–602.

———. 2014b. *Land's End: Capitalist Relations on an Indigenous Frontier*. Duke University Press.

Little, P.D. et al. 2001. 'Avoiding Disaster: Diversification and Risk Management among East African Herders', *Development and Change* 32(3): 401–33.

Lund, C. 2016. 'Rule and Rupture: State Formation through the Production of Property and Citizenship', *Development and Change* 47(6): 1199–228.

Lydall, J. 2010. 'The Paternalistic Neighbor: A Tale of the Demise of Cherished Traditions', in E.C. Gabbert and S. Thubauville (eds), *To Live with Others: Essays on Cultural Neighborhood in Southern Ethiopia*. Cologne: Köppe, pp. 314–34.

Lydy, M. et al. 2004. 'Challenges in Regulating Pesticide Mixtures', *Ecology and Society* 9(6): 1. Retrieved 8 July 2019 from http://www.ecologyandsociety.org/vol9/iss6/art1/.

Mahmoud, H.A. 2013. 'Pastoral Innovative Responses to New Camel Export Market Opportunities on the Kenya/Ethiopia Borderlands', in A. Catley, J. Lind and I. Scoones (eds), *Pastoralism and Development in Africa: Dynamic Change at the Margins*. Abingdon and New York: Routledge, pp. 98–107.

Makki, F. 2014. 'Development by Dispossession: *Terra Nullius* and the Social Ecology of New Enclosures in Ethiopia', *Rural Sociology* 79(1): 79–103.

Markakis, J. 2011. *Ethiopia: The Last Two Frontiers*. Woodbridge and Rochester: James Currey.

Marquard, O. 2003. *Zukunft braucht Herkunft: Philosophische Essays*. Stuttgart: Reclam.

Marx, K. 1966 [1867]. *Das Kapital: Kritik der Politischen Ökonomie*. Erster Band. Berlin: Dietz Verlag.

Mbembe, A. 2011. 'Democracy as a Community of Life', *Johannesburg Salon* (4):1–10.

———. 2015. 'The Value of Africa's Aesthetics'. Retrieved 3 February 2019 from https://www.doppiozero.com/materiali/why-africa/value-africa-s-aesthetics.

———. 2016. 'Africa in Theory', in B. Goldstone and J. Obarrio (eds), *African Futures: Essays on Crisis, Emergence and Possibility*. Chicago and London: University of Chicago Press, pp. 211–30.

Meckelburg, A. 2014. 'Large Scale Land Investment in Gambella, Western Ethiopia: The Politics and Policies of Land', in M.G. Berhe (ed.), *A Delicate Balance: Land Use, Minority Rights and Social Stability in the Horn of Africa*. Addis Ababa: Institute for Peace and Security Studies, Addis Ababa University, pp. 144–65.

Meles Zenawi. 2011. 'Speech during the 13th Annual Pastoralist Day Celebrations, Jinka, South Omo', 25 January. Retrieved 4 December 2018 from http://www.mursi.org/pdf/Meles%20Jinka%20speech.pdf.

Milanez, F., and J. Wedekind. 2016. 'Beyond Principles and Declarations: Taking Indigenous Rights Seriously', *Findings and Recommendations from the ENTITLE FP7 Research Project*. Retrieved 26 February 2019 from www.politicalecology.eu/documents/courses/85-pb-milanez-et-al/file.

MoFED (Ministry of Finance and Economic Development). 2006. *Ethiopia: Building on Progress – A Plan for Accelerated and Sustained Development to End Poverty (PASDEP), (2005/06–2009/10), Vol. 1: Main Text*. Addis Ababa.

———. 2010a. *Ethiopia: 2010 MDGs Report: Trends and Prospects for Meeting MDGs by 2015*.

———. 2010b. *Federal Republic of Ethiopia: Growth and Transformation Plan, 2010/11–2014/15. Vol. I. Main Text*. Addis Ababa.

Mohammud Abdulahi. 2007. 'The Legal Status of the Communal Land Holding System in Ethiopia: The Case of Pastoral Communities', *International Journal on Minority and Group Rights* 14: 85–125.

Mosley, J., and E.E. Watson. 2016. 'Frontier Transformations: Development Visions, Spaces and Processes in Northern Kenya and Southern Ethiopia', *Journal of Eastern African Studies* 10(3): 452–75.

Nalepa. R.A., A.G. Short Gianotti and D.M. Bauer. 2017. 'Marginal Land and the Global Land Rush: A Spatial Exploration of Contested Lands and State-Directed Development in Contemporary Ethiopia', *Geoforum* 82: 237–51.

National Planning Commission. 2016. *Federal Democratic Republic of Ethiopia: Growth and Transformation Plan II (GTP II) (2015/16–2019/20), Vol. I: Main Text*. Addis Ababa: National Planning Commission.

Olivier de Sardan, J.-P. 2001. 'Les trois approches en anthropologie du développement', *Revue Tiers Monde* 42(168): 729–54.

Ostrom, E. 1990. *Governing the Commons: The Evolution of Institutions for Collective Action*. Cambridge: Cambridge University Press.

Pankhurst, A., and F. Piguet (eds). 2009. *Moving People in Ethiopia: Development, Displacement and the State*. Oxford: James Currey.

Pankhurst, R. 1997. *The Ethiopian Borderlands: Essays in Regional History, from Ancient Times to the End of the Eighteenth Century*. Lawrenceville, NJ: Red Sea Press.

Pimbert, M.P. (ed.). 2018. *Food Sovereignty, Agroecology and Biocultural Diversity: Constructing and Contesting Knowledge*. London and New York: Routledge.

Polanyi, K. 2001 [1944]. *The Great Transformation: The Political and Economic Origins of Our Time*. Boston: Beacon Press.

Raworth, K. 2017. *Doughnut Economics: Seven Ways to Think Like a 21st-Century Economist*. London: Random House.

Reganold, J.P., and J.M. Wachter. 2016. 'Organic Agriculture in the Twenty-First Century', *Nature Plants* 2: 1–8.

Richmond, O. 2013a. 'Peace Formation and Local Infrastructures for Peace', *Alternatives* 38(4): 271–87.

———. 2013b. 'Failed Statebuilding versus Peace Formation', *Cooperation and Conflict* 48(3): 378–400.

Rosset, P.M., and M. Altieri. 2017. *Agroecology: Science and Politics*. Black Point, Nova Scotia: Fernwood.

Rottenburg, R. 2009. *Far-Fetched Facts: A Parable of Development Aid*. Cambridge, MA: MIT Press.

Sachs, W. 2019. 'Foreword: The Development Dictionary Revisited', in A. Kothari, A. Salleh, A. Escobar, F. Demaria and A. Acosta (eds), *Pluriverse: A Post Development Dictionary*. Shahpur Jat, New Delhi: Tulika Books, xi–xvi.

Sandford, S. 1983. *Management of Pastoral Development in the Third World*. Chichester: John Wiley & Sons.

Schareika, N. 2014. 'The Social Nature of Environmental Knowledge among the Nomadic Woɗaaɓe of Niger', *Ecology and Society* 19(4).

———. 2018. 'Nomads/Pastoralists and Development', in H. Callan (ed.), *The International Encyclopedia of Anthropology*, Vol. 9. Oxford: John Wiley, pp 1–11.

Schiavoni, C. et al. 2018. 'Analysing Agricultural Investment from the Realities of Small-Scale Food Providers: Grounding the Debates', *Third World Quarterly* 39(7): 1348–66.

Schlee, G. 1989. 'The Orientation of Progress: Conflicting Aims and Strategies of Pastoral Nomads and Development Agents in East Africa – A Problem Survey', in E. Linnebuhr (ed.), *Transition and Continuity of Identity in East Africa and Beyond – In Memoriam David Miller*. Bayreuth African Studies Series. Bayreuth: E. Breitinger, pp. 397–450.

———. 2008. *How Enemies Are Made: Towards a Theory of Ethnic and Religious Conflicts*. New York and Oxford: Berghahn.

———. 2009. 'Introduction', in G. Schlee and E.E. Watson (eds), *Changing Identifications and Alliances in North East Africa: Ethiopia and Kenya, Vol. 2*. New York and Oxford: Berghahn, pp. 1–13.

———. 2010. 'A Comment on the "Policy Framework for Pastoralism in Africa", adopted by the African Union in January 2011', *Nomadic Peoples* 14(2): 158–63.

———. 2011. 'Territorializing Ethnicity: The Imposition of a Model of Statehood on Pastoralists in Northern Kenya and Southern Ethiopia', *Journal of Ethnic and Racial Studies* 36(5): 857–74.

———. 2013. 'Why States Still Destroy Pastoralism and How They Can Learn That in Their Own Interest They Should Not', *Nomadic Peoples* 17(2): 6–19.

Schlee, G., and Abdullahi Shongolo. 2012. *Pastoralism and Politics in Northern Kenya and Southern Ethiopia*. Woodbridge: James Currey.

Schlee, G., and E.E. Watson (eds). 2009. *Changing Identifications and Alliances in North-East Africa, Vols. I and II*. Oxford and New York: Berghahn.

Schlee, G. et al. 2017. 'Guardians of Productive Landscapes', *Max Planck Institute for Social Anthropology, Report 2014–2016*. Department 'Integration and Conflict', pp. 17–19.

Scholz, F., and G. Schlee. 2015. 'Nomads and Nomadism in History', in J.D. Wright (ed.), *International Encyclopedia of the Social and Behavioral Sciences* 2. Amsterdam: Elsevier, pp. 838–43.

Scoones, I. (ed.). 1994. *Living with Uncertainty: Directions in Pastoral Development in Africa*. London: Intermediate Technology Publications.

———. 2004. 'Climate Change and the Challenge of Non-Equilibrium Thinking', *IDS Bulletin* 35(3): 114–19.

Scott, J. 1998. *Seeing Like a State: How Certain Schemes to Improve Human Conditions Have Failed*. New Haven, CT: Yale University Press.

Slezkine, Y. 1994. *Arctic Mirrors: Russia and the Small Peoples of the North*. Ithaca: Cornell University Press.

Strecker, I. 2006. 'A History of Pride and Confrontation in South Omo', in I. Strecker and J. Lydall (eds), *The Perils of Face: Essays on Cultural Contact, Respect and Self- Esteem in Southern Ethiopia*. Berlin: Lit, pp. 151–84.

———. 2014. 'Implications of the International Investors Code of Conduct: The Case of the South Ethiopian Rift Valleys', in M.G. Berhe (ed.), *A Delicate Balance: Land Use, Minority Rights and Social Stability in the Horn of Africa*. Addis Ababa: Institute for Peace and Security Studies, Addis Ababa University, pp. 38–63.

Strecker, I., and A. Pankhurst. 2003. *Bury the Spear! Cursing War and Blessing Peace at Arbore, Southern Ethiopia*. Digital video, colour, 76 minutes. Göttingen: IWF.

Sullivan, S., and K. Homewood. 2018. 'On Non-Equilibrium and Nomadism: Knowledge, Diversity and Global Modernity in Drylands', in M. Pimbert (ed.), *Food Sovereignty, Agroecology and Biocultural Diversity: Constructing and Contesting Knowledge*. London and New York: Routledge, pp.115–68.

Turton, D. 2011. 'Wilderness, Wasteland or Home? Three Ways of Imagining the Lower Omo Valley', *Journal of Eastern African Studies* 5(1): 158–76.

———. 2015. 'Hydropower and Irrigation Development in the Omo Valley: Development for Whom?', paper presented at the 19th International Conference on Ethiopian Studies, 'Ethiopia: Diversity and Interconnections through Space and Time', Warsaw, 24–28 August 2015.

Trouillot, M.R. 2003. *Global Transformations: Anthropology and the Modern World*. New York: Palgrave Macmillan.

Tsing, A.L. 2005. *Friction: An Ethnography of Global Connection*. Princeton, NJ, and Oxford: Princeton University Press.

———. 2008. 'Natural Resources and Capitalist Frontiers', in A. Baviskar (ed.), *Contested Grounds: Essays on Nature, Culture and Power*. Oxford and New York: Oxford University Press, pp. 137–57.

UN. 2013. *Wake Up before It Is Too Late: Make Agriculture Truly Sustainable Now for Food Security in a Changing Climate*. UNCTAD. Trade and Environment Review Series. New York and Geneva: United Nations.

UNDP. 2013. *An Assessment of Operation and Performance of Commercial Farmers in Ethiopia: Summary of Commissioned Studies*. UNDP Ethiopia.

Wagstaff, Q.A. 2015. 'Note 13: Development, Cultural Hegemonism and Conflict Generation in Southwest Ethiopia: Agro-Pastoralists in Trouble', *Observatoire des enjeux politiques et sécuritaires dans la Corne de l'Afrique*. Bordeaux: Sciences Po, Les Afriques dans le Monde (LAM).

Walsh, C. 2010. 'Development as *Buen Vivir*: Institutional Arrangements and (De)Colonial Entanglements', *Development* 53(1): 15–21.

White, B. et al. 2012. 'The New Enclosures: Critical Perspectives on Corporate Land Deals', *Journal of Peasant Studies* 39(3–4): 619–47.

World Bank. 2004. *Ethiopia: Country Economic Memorandum. Four Ethiopias: A Regional Characterization*. Assessing Ethiopia's Growth Potential and Development Obstacles. Background Report. Washington, DC: World Bank.

———. 2005a. *Ethiopia: A Strategy to Balance and Stimulate Growth: A Country Economic Memorandum*. Washington, DC: World Bank.

———. 2005b. *Ethiopia: Well Being and Poverty in Ethiopia: The Road of Agriculture and Agency*. Country Department for Ethiopia. Washington. DC: World Bank.

———. 2009. *Awakening Africa's Sleeping Giant: Prospects for Commercial Agriculture in the Guinea Savannah Zone and Beyond*. Washington, DC: World Bank.

World Bank Group and the UK's Department for International Development. 2019. *Poverty and Vulnerability in the Ethiopian Lowlands: Building a More Resilient Future*. Washington, DC: World Bank.

Wright, E.O. 2010. *Envisioning Real Utopias*. London and New York: Verso.

Yonas Birmeta Adinew. 2016. 'Land Rights and Agricultural Investments in Ethiopia', Ph.D. dissertation. Halle (Saale): Martin Luther University Halle-Wittenberg.

Zinsstag, J. et al. 2016. 'The Future of Pastoralism/L'avenir du pastoralisme/El futuro del pastoreo', *Scientific and Technical Revue* 35(2).

Part I

Setting the Context

Modernity and Citizenship in Pastoral Areas

Chapter 1

Modern Mobility in East Africa

Pastoral Responses to Rangeland Fragmentation, Enclosure and Settlement

John G. Galaty

Introduction

Pastoralists have not had an easy relationship with modernity. By 'modernity', I refer less to the technological, economic and political state of affairs launched by the Enlightenment and brought to flower during the last century than with the accusation, first by colonialism and then by a self-satisfied urban elite, that modernity is something essential that rural communities are seen to lack. The circulation of stereotypic images and attributions of blame ramify beyond the world of words when they begin to influence policy and practical action. Such is the case with African pastoralists, who, characterized as resisting modernity, have become subject to forced changes that often leave them even farther behind, or, having been characterized as perpetrators of degradation, desertification, poaching and other crimes against the rangeland environment, have too often seen their well-adapted strategies of land use undermined or their lands taken away (Galaty 2002b). The concept of modernity has in this way become a weapon of class struggle, not just between development aid givers and recipient communities but between urban and rural, rural elites and commoners, and between pastoralists, peasants and aspiring rural landholders and those wishing to retain land against individuals and companies wishing to appropriate it or to divert it to alternative uses, whether for plantations, industries, tourism, conservation or speculation (Ellis 2012). More broadly, current processes of large-scale acquisition of land, as part of a neoliberalized trend to devalue local land use in favour of its commercialized exploitation, is now altering the conditions of rural land holding in much of the developing world (Galaty 2013b). The undermining of peasant and pastoral land holding is both legal and ideological, underpinned by unfounded accusations that they resist 'modern' attitudes, interests and land use strategies. But it is not that poorer rural dwellers do not like modernity; generally, their opinion is that they do not get enough of it!

What may be called the Modernity-Wars have been waged in rural Africa over education, the cultures of fashion and music, market participation, democratic representation, producing for markets or subsistence and, most crucially here, territoriality and land tenure. The fact that pastoral lands are not just 'held' (from *tenir*, fr., giving rise to 'tenure') but 'traversed' makes pastoral systems of territoriality exceptional in a world dominated by the ideology and practice of sedentarism (Malkki 1997). Linked to the call for pastoralists to modernize is the associated demand that they settle (Ikeya 2017). Clearly, sedentarization does facilitate access to schools, health clinics, trading centres selling food and household commodities, medical and veterinarian drugs, livestock markets, and offices of the growing number of organizations of civil society dedicated to mobile peoples (Fratkin and Roth 2005). But these services and connections are sufficiently appreciated by pastoralists that patterns of mobility are already skewed towards making town-based services accessible to people who continue to move, while sometimes – but all too infrequently – services in education and health and trade are actually delivered in a mobile fashion, as pastoral students, patients and customers are actually followed around by service providers.

The contrast between traditionalism and modernity seems tired and outmoded, especially when icons of the 'traditional' have become part of a hyper-commercialized world and cosmopolitan secretions pervade senses of self in every dusty corner of the globe (see Comaroff and Comaroff 2009). Traditionalism itself has become a modernist stance, conveying nostalgia for some, refusal or even resistance for others, and representing performances, whether in celebration or parody, never without irony; portrayals of tradition proclaim 'this-is-who-I-really-am' while slipping a subliminal wink to the never-absent audience that whispers a satiric subtext: 'this-is-the-I-that-I'm-performing, not-that-one-that-I-now-am'. Nonetheless, rural livelihood practices – of peasants, foragers, fishers, pastoralists – are not pursued in order to uphold 'traditionalism' but as pragmatic exercises drawing from a ready repertoire of skills to produce value in politically and culturally complex settings, structured horizontally by relations with a variety of other local actors and vertically with agencies of power that bring global paradigms of ideas, values, market demands, and expectations of governance to bear on localities.

Consider one noteworthy trend in pastoral territoriality seen across the African continent that illustrates the convergence of local political dynamics and a global paradigm: the inexorable demarcation and enclosure of rangelands, where pastoral families are increasingly being settled or from which they are being displaced. Faced with encouragement and pressure to settle, a process long seen as a step towards modernization, pastoralists have demonstrated initiative and ingenuity in devising responses that mitigate the worst effects of sedentarization while securing their livelihoods. Are they being overcome by the inexorable processes of land grabbing through which millions of hectares of land are being appropriated by urban elites, national officials, or international companies pursuing mining, commercial agriculture or conservation and tourism? While large-scale land appropriation is a global phenomenon, embracing lands said to be 'available' or 'unused' in Latin America and Southeast Asia, it is especially in Africa where states have failed to resist or have actively abetted the movement of lands from use by peasants and pastoralists into the hands of investors (Galaty 2013a).

'Enclosure' of lands evokes the processes experienced in Scotland and Ireland from the mid-seventeenth to the mid-nineteenth centuries. Here, shifts in tenure privileged elites, who were subsequently seen as sole proprietors of lands where cottars and other tenants had previously held rights of occupancy and farming or had enjoyed use of common lands (Devine 2018). The consolidation of cottars' fields and villages into extensive grazing lands, to feed a growing market for livestock produce, led to the subsequent dispossession of many in 'the clearances'. This case contrasts with enclosures underway in Africa, where extensive commonly held pastures are being privatized and subdivided into small holdings, sometimes for cultivation; the dispossession process may occur if lands are appropriated for allocation to companies or investors, or through the market as smallholders sell their parcels.

Lands susceptible to appropriation are rich in some key resource, which, although often central to the livelihoods of rural landholders, represents a fertile source of investment for outsiders who dream of large-scale agricultural plantations, mining or tourism in wildlife-rich forests and savannahs. So it is, in a neoliberal age, that states and their leaders envision their own well-being, and that of their often poor countries, as dependent not on the development of their own landholders but on investments from abroad. Consider what Pearce (2012) calls the 'land wars' that are occurring in the lowlands of western Ethiopia, throughout the Omo River basin, and in the Awash Valley, where pastoralists have been displaced in favour of sugar cane, dams and irrigation, and wildlife refuges (Catley et al. 2013). River valleys that are critical for neighbouring herders and cultivators alike are attractive for commercial farming enterprises, in Somalia, Kenya, and the Sudan. But appropriation of the wetlands in the drylands, so critical for dry season grazers, and forests in the drylands, so important for wildlife and livestock alike, is how pastoral communities are caught in the vice between outside investors and their enterprises and endogenous forces of enclosure and settlement, which will be subsequently described. The view here is from below, of local processes that in fact are global in nature, with localities being where global influences and investments arrive to influence the 'struggles over autonomy' that implicate property and territory throughout the world (Coleman 2011).

Encountering, resisting and embracing forces of social change, pastoral communities respond in apparently contradictory ways to focal problems that are very local but bear global signatures: asserting rights to critical resources in the face of heightened competition, sometimes from commercial enterprises of national or international origins; some affirming and some selling ancestral territories; ignoring local politics while demanding a voice in them; proclaiming environmentalist values while resisting conservationist claims and interests; demanding schools but resisting education, wary of its economic and cultural implications; calling for individual human rights within a framework of collective rights; pressing for indigenous status while seeking the protection of national citizenship; decrying the violence that they meet while responding with counter-violence; and so on. Increasingly, rural communities that use land extensively through continuing mobility devise political strategies and carry out decision-making informed by transnational personal and electronic linkages.

This chapter focuses on new forms of mobility that have arisen as responses to and reformulations of the challenges of social change, some of which were just enumerated. Rather than modernity being seen just as a counterpoint to traditionalism, or – as suggested above – only a set of accusations aimed at disarming marginalized populations, it is conceived here as a strategic stance towards innovation, where current conditions are refashioned as opportunities. In particular, how do pastoralists respond to growing constraints on herd and household mobility long represented by emblematic methods to deal with the social and ecological constraints of drylands – is it by finding new avenues and mechanisms for pursuing 'Modern Mobility'? The chapter examines types of Modern Mobility that reflect two major transformations altering the profile of rural life: first, the growth of small towns in arid lands, which tend to exercise a sort of social magnetism by bending settlements and movement patterns towards the attractions and services of settled life; second, novel techniques of claiming and moving into lands hitherto unavailable because of enclosure, land fragmentation and settlement, thus evading and resisting contemporary constraints. I have elsewhere addressed a third means of facilitating modern mobility, through cultivating new strategies of communication, including using mobile phone technologies that both reduce the need to move and make its practice easier! How is relative sedentarization reconciled with continuing herd movement, and how are new forms of mobility used to circumvent the constraints of sedentary forms of life and governance? In addition, what are the implications of new information technologies and global institutional relations for the political and economic strategies pursued by 'wired nomads'?

Territoriality and Mobility in the Context of Roads and Small Towns

Systems of territoriality among African pastoralists have long hinged on two sorts of mobility: firstly, continuous, short-term movement of herds between critical resources; secondly, punctual, longer distance, often seasonal transhumance to access pastures arising from cycles of rainfall (Galaty 2013a). For many herders, the first form of mobility represents a spatial articulation of a herd with pastures, water and a protective homestead base; the second form of mobility involves the transfer elsewhere of the entire configuration as the herder seeks an improved setting (McCabe 1994). In the longer-term politics of mobility, a herder seeks a locale where resources are sufficient – in relation to the competition – and as a community defends or expands its control of space, while in the shorter-term politics of mobility, herders seek to successfully insert their herds into a neighbourhood process of allocating and conserving local supplies of grass, water and minerals (Homewood 2008).

But under contemporary conditions, this geometric articulation of herd with herbage, water and home is no longer sufficient to account for patterns of pastoral mobility. Rather, we must factor in diverse influences that attract or deter pastoralists: the presence of trading centres, churches, clinics, missions, schools, boreholes and roads, and the availability of farmland, famine relief and markets. True, where pastoral domains lie depends on historical land use patterns, regional recognition of rights that accrue to certain groups and communities, and the creation of borders by the modern colonial and postcolonial state. But the irrepressible nature of pastoral mobility and the continuous need to sustain herds still often lead herders to press into new grounds, ignoring formal limits and reshaping pastoral terrain. It is within this evolving territoriality that intersecting lined patterns of roads and tracks, punctuated by nodal points of trading centres, towns and water sources, have been inscribed across the rangeland map (Galaty 2013b).

Scott (1998) has described how it is in the nature of the state to make otherwise inscrutable societies 'legible' through fixing communities in place, establishing borders and boundaries and committing acts of knowledge such as census taking, land registration and map making. For sedentary communities, the checkerboard of fields, streams and forests indicates how cultivation has inscribed itself upon farmland, providing the state with contours amenable to formalization, not least in the form of land titles. But mobile rangeland communities in an unfenced condition have no natural blocs equivalent to fields ploughed or hoed, or hedgerows and fences dividing crops and plots. Rather, the pastoral landscape is shaped less by the circumferences etched by fences than by a very loose lattice of lines and points identifying paths of mobility and temporary destinations, signifying the paths of livestock to and from resources and home, and the larger routes and centres of commerce and organized transport. But it is in such centres and along such roads that the localized institutions of modernity are arrayed, to which herding families are drawn and around which social life increasingly turns. Few herders with herds actually walk along the roads made by states (though they are avid users via buses, trucks and taxis), but they follow paths and tracks that emanate star-like from locales of compelling interest, thus connecting their homesteads and families to sites of modernity.

If one scrutinizes contemporary maps, or scans Google Earth up close, what is most striking is how few lines emblematic of motor transport transect the arid lands compared to the dense criss-crossing matrix inscribed in regions of fertile cultivation, not to mention the dense board-like delimitations of urban life. Their scarcity lends dryland roads even greater importance as links not just between major cities but between multitudinous trading centres, which spring up along its byways like grass watered by the run-off of rain from a road. Many examples could be cited. A long, dusty road – a long piece of unfinished business along the Cape to Cairo route – has run from just north of Mount Kenya at Isiolo northwards to Ethiopia since the colonial period.[1] This Marsabit Road, which was being paved from Isiolo to Marsabit in 2010 and 2011 and has now been completed, traverses numerous pastoral territories in northern Kenya: Somalis living in and near Isiolo, Borana who occupy territories on either side of the Ewuaso Ng'iro and northward along the east, communities of Turkana and mixed Turkana/Samburu called *Ilgira*, Samburu proper, Rendille camel-herders, the mixed Samburu-Rendille community called *Ariaal*, the ethnically complex Marsabit Mountain, with town or peri-urban Rendille, Ariaal, Borana, Gabra, and Burji and a mix of Meru from Kenya and Konso from Ethiopia, and more pastoralists northward to the Ethiopian border, namely Gabra with camels, Borana with cattle, and Sakuye, Garre and Ajuran with both (Schlee and Shongolo 2012).[2] The long road runs through a multitude of towns and trading centres, small and large; or, to be more correct, the original construction of the track north in the colonial period resulted in a series of small licensed trading centres being built up at key junctions, where we now find increasing concentrations of population in small towns.

In 2010 and 2011, the slow approach of the paved road from the south had altered social and economic expectations – and land values – in the small towns to the north. The paved road progressively advanced from Isiolo to Archer's Post, Lerrata, Serrolipi, Merille and Laisamis, before crossing the low-lying Kaisut Desert to Logologo, and rising up to Mount Marsabit. By the end of 2010, the tarmac – which has since been completed – had almost reached the town of Merille. But in Merille, 'development' anticipated the arrival of the improved road, as the town was already being subdivided into commercial 'plots' allocated by the Chief and the local Councillor to long-term residents. Some town plots came in lots of 50 x 100 feet; others 30 x 80 feet; still others 50 x 50 feet, depending on the location and intended utilization. Plot holders paid fees of Kenyan shilling (KShs) 300 per year for the land but may pay KShs 2,000 to 4,000 per year for a shop (a rough approximation of value at that time saw 80 KShs about equal to a US dollar). Ideally, the allocation of a plot is followed by the development of a business. But many who acquire a plot through allocation actually intend only to sell it, since their own interests may still lie in the pastoral sector. So, although neither seller nor buyer has exclusive rights to the land, or the legitimate power to buy or sell it, a very lively informal land market has arisen, perhaps encouraged by the failure of the Government of Kenya to bring order to 'The Land Question' that boils throughout the country. During the year when the paved road slowly crept from Isiolo towards Merille, 99 plots were sold to 37 individuals. Roads became vectors of social and economic change.

In a strict sense, the sellers do not really legally 'own' the land but through connivance with the Chief or Councillor are 'allocated' the land in the presence of elders, which lends sufficient local legitimacy to allow them to use or sell it. Most buyers wish to develop the land commercially, by building shops or businesses; this accounts for 93 out of 99 plots. Six other plots will be used residentially. Two-thirds of buyers are from the predominant groups from the region, the Rendille (8) and the Ariaal (16), with the remaining third being distributed among other groups from the regions to the north, Burji (4), Somali (5) and Boran (1), or from the greater Mount Kenya region to the south, like Meru (2) and Kamba (1). Payments received were significant in relation to the regional economy, though modest in global context; 99 plots, at an average of about KShs 10,300 (slightly under US$130 each), were exchanged for slightly over KShs 1m (or almost $13,000), or about KShs 27,500 per person (c. US$344).

So, pastoralists from the region are cashing in their local land rights for financial returns roughly equivalent to the sale of about one head of cattle, to the benefit of more commercially minded individuals from their own or nearby groups able to invest modest amounts in urban land. What the sellers retain are social ties to town within a moral economy that dictates that transactions are never completely finalized, so buyers always still owe sellers something, and sellers always retain what I have elsewhere called 'residual rights' over whatever they have given away or sold (Galaty 2005). So, paradoxically, as first-generation pastoral rights-holders are displaced of their urban territories by prospective town-dwellers who have money and value land, the former may in reality be anchoring their long-term claims in towns, not to plots but to people.

This new 'rural urbanism' represents a phenomenon of enormous sociological and economic importance, defining sites of economic diversification, interethnic conviviality, and cultural *métissage* (Amselle 1998). Rangelands largely thrive, despite dramatic increases in population in arid and semi-arid regions of Africa, because people gravitate to small towns and centres, pursuing activities outside of herding. But towns and trading centres along the long Marsabit road also serve as magnets for pastoralists, whose homesteads increasingly lie in the urban periphery in a series of increasingly distant concentric circles, or who periodically visit to purchase vital goods and to sell livestock or other products and make routine use of the medical, educational, religious and commercial services provided there. Small towns have become valuable to those who settle and invest in them but also to those more mobile people who move through towns, gravitate towards them, and exercise transactional rights over them by creating reciprocal links with enterprises, traders and service providers alike.

This informal and pervasive tendency for pastoralists to curtail their cycles of movement in order to access towns and institutions identified with the modern is a gesture towards 'relative sedentarization', whether or not a family definitively settles in town (Galaty 2005). In the desertic area that surrounds Marsabit Mountain and its urban concentration, the movement cycles of pastoralists have been profoundly influenced by another manifestation of modernity: the diffusion of automatic weapons that has occurred over the last 20 years (Schlee 1989; Schlee and Shongolo 2012). I have described elsewhere the stages by which first the Dassanech then the Gabra and Borana, and finally the Rendille and Samburu, have acquired arms (Galaty 2002a). When Gabra first attacked Rendille near Kargi in the early 1990s, Rendille responded by retreating to towns like Kor to the south, where large encampments were concentrated. Thus, because of reverberations of drought and violence, many adopted a form of sedentarization in sites that grew because of the security of numbers, the availability of social services, and the provision of emergency food aid (Galaty 2016).

I have used northern Kenya as an illustration of a pervasive trend in Africa towards pastoral inertia, slowing centrifugal grazing movements in response to the attractions of small urban centres, which create greater concentrations of population as communities withdraw from sites of insecurity (Schlee and Shongolo 2012). Towns, however, are locally significant for cultural as well as political and economic reasons: they are seen as sites of modernity, where news, fashion and excitement can be experienced, opening a locality to a wider regional and national society and providing a symbolic connection to global culture. However, regional prosperity and the economic resilience of towns in arid and semi-arid lands rest on livelihoods based on domestic animals and a livestock industry linked to markets, and these rely on mobile strategies of land use. Without a vibrant rural economy, towns would not thrive no matter how much their magnetic properties influence livestock and human flows (McPeak and Little 2006).

Keep on Moving: Mobility in the Face of Enclosure

In the African drylands, transhumance and punctuated movement strategies are aimed at accessing sparse and unpredictable pasture resources (Scoones 1995). But along with grass and water, an inventory of critical resources must now include social services and commercial opportunities, as well as regional sociability. The exigencies of continuing pastoral mobility sometimes contradict the process of settlement, whether carried out through informal processes, such as experienced in northern Kenya (Fratkin and Roth 2005), or through planned change and land reform, such as experienced in southern Kenya (Rutten 1992; Mwangi

2007). It is important to point out that the ecological and political need for live-stock herders to move has not disappeared with enclosure or with settlement! But there are apparently contradictory processes in modern mobility that see both a slowing and a narrowing of cycles of displacement and a defensive re-energizing of movement under new conditions.

For instance, two remarkable processes of pastoral expansion in Africa con-tinue. Fulfulde speakers have spread from Senegal and Mauritania on the Atlantic Coast across the West African Sahel through northern Nigeria, Niger, Cameroon and Central African Republic, eastward into the Sudan and now into western Ethiopia (Dereje and Schlee 2009). Maa speakers, originally from the central and southern Sudan, now stretch from northern Kenya, where Ariaal live on Marsabit Mountain and surrounding lowlands, to the Samburu, Laikipiak and Chamus of north-central Kenya, to the Maasai who occupy southern Kenya to central Tanzania (including the Arusha of Mount Meru), with the Parakuyo of eastern and south-central Tanzania still moving southward, stimulated by displacements and conflicts over land, to southern Tanzania and northern Zambia (Galaty 1993). These processes involve perpetual short-term movement to access pasture, which cumulates in progressive and incremental spreading, as well as abrupt leap-frog movements to access sites of favourable pasture. So not only incessant herd-ing movements but also long-term pastoral expansion continues (Homewood 2008). As a result of displacement from home territories due to the creation of commercial ranches, wildlife reserves, and mining concessions, Tanzanian pasto-ralists – among them Maasai, Parakuyo and Barabaig – have migrated to Bagam-oyo District near the coast and to the Usangu Plains in southern Tanzania (Galaty 1989). Thus, paradoxically, land reform and formalization of tenure rights in one region – aimed at sedentarization – often exert pressure that stimulates pastoral expansion into another (Ikeya 2017).

The experience of the Kenyan Maasai and Samburu thus illustrates how the experience of sedentarization through land reform does not preclude continuing pastoral mobility; indeed in some cases it may accelerate it. 'Enclosure' involved the gradual colonial process of demarcating lands identified with particular groups or particular activities, such as pastoralism, by creating boundaries around territorial units (from national, provincial, district to local levels) that were sub-sequently inscribed around smaller pastoral domains. Maasai went through five stages of progressive demarcation and enclosure: the division of the entire group between 1886 and 1906 when the international boundary between Kenya and Tanzania was established; the creation of a single, integrated Masai Reserve in Kenya following the Masai Treaty of 1911 (Hughes 2006); the subsequent divi-sion of the Reserve into districts and the demarcation of sectional boundaries in the late colonial period; the postcolonial creation of Group Ranches from around 1970; and finally a strong and ongoing trend towards the subdivision of Group Ranches into individualized ranch holdings from the mid-1980s.[3] This historical delimitation of pastoral lands in progressively smaller and more sharply bounded fragments has rendered Maasai territories less opaque and more 'legible' to the state (Scott 1998) but has also had other outcomes. The resulting land parcels, now under individual titles, are much less viable for livestock production than was the case with ecologically larger and more integrated areas and are more practical as units of commercial exchange, most importantly for sale. And when subject to active border controls and even fencing, individual land parcels inhibit the sort of opportunistic grazing that has been a reliable strategy in pastoral land use.

Towards the end of the first decade following Independence in 1963, Maasai districts were divided into Group Ranches under private title, side by side with a limited number of individual private ranches allocated to the aspiring and educated elite (Galaty 1994). Individual ranchers tended to continue using group holdings as their reserve grazing, while influential members of Group Ranches were able to extract land parcels from group holdings to form their own individual ranches. Some individual ranchers began to sell portions of land, often returning to the group to ask for more. As a result, in many Group Ranches a sense of land panic set in that underpinned a growing consensus that comprehensive subdivision of group holdings was needed, partly to achieve the purported benefits of private land but mainly to allow ordinary pastoralists to secure some assets at a time commonly held land was being rapidly dissipated. At present, the corruption that has surrounded subdivision and the allocation of shares in group holdings to members has resulted in some Group Ranches halting subdivision procedures and starting over, thus reversing some unfair and inequitable allocations of land (Riamit 2014). In other areas, dramatically unequal allocations have been upheld, leading to the utter dispossession of some. That enclosure, which has in many areas already occurred, has led some pastoralists who inhabit undivided areas managed under group title to establish more permanent homesteads in order to stake claims for anticipated subdivision in the future (Galaty and Munei 1999).

With the closing of borders around ranching areas, the proliferation of fences across a hitherto undivided range and the establishment of permanent or semi-permanent homes, effective enclosure has occurred (Galvin et al. 2008). The goal and ethic of modernity was instrumental in justifying policies of demarcation and enclosure; pastoralists who otherwise have resisted the challenges and opportunities of the modern neoliberal world would experience positive outcomes if the critical land factor were transformed through privatization. Indeed, the notion that pastoralists were pre-modern in economy and anti-modern in environmental practice informed the quite radical venture of privatizing pastoral lands that has given rise to the subsequent fragmentation of viable rangeland into non-economic and unsustainable ecological units (ibid.). Experience has countered the myth that formalized land title establishes greater 'security' of occupation, accompanied by the benefits of modernity. It has become clear that the major function of privatization has been the transfer of land away from resident pastoralists, with land reforms tied to programmes of range development in fact achieving dramatically evaporating security of land holding. Under conditions of enclosure, many pastoralists have become marginalized and landless, a process only accelerated by the growing amounts of land taken for commercial ranching, large-scale commercial wheat farming, wildlife reserves, tourism, and mineral extraction. But many others have responded to the formal demarcation of land through devising ingenious methods for moving domestic animals within and across boundaries to access the pastures they need, despite the practical problems posed by land fragmentation (Homewood, Kristjanson and Trench 2009).

Looking to the past, lands in Kenya's central Rift Valley have been largely inaccessible to Maasai pastoralists since they were ceded to the colonial state to allocate for White settlement in 1904/5 (Sorrenson 1968; Hughes 2006). With decolonization almost 60 years later, some settler ranches were allocated to members of the political elite and others for smallholder resettlement of landless Kikuyu, themselves displaced earlier (1910s to 1930s) by the creation of highland settler farms and later (1950s) by land reform in Central province aimed at the dispossession of residents associated with the Mau Mau insurgency (Berman 1990; Elkins 2005). Little of this previously Maasai-held land has been directly returned to them, though much of it now circulates through land markets or is 'grabbed' through political machinations. But underlying claims based on Maasai historical rights have not been forgotten. In rhetorical terms, Maasai claim residual non-extinguished rights over all lands that were taken from them as a result of the 1904 and 1911 Maasai Treaties, no matter how remote their chances are of ever reoccupying those lands. Demonstrating this sense of grievance, a petition was prepared in 2009 for presentation to the Attorney General of Kenya, calling on restoration of Maasai lands in the context of the drafting of the new Kenyan Constitution. Noting that in 1905 the Maasai became Kenya's 'first IDP's' (Internally Displaced People), the petition claims that the Petitioners are 'aggrieved by the manner in which the Maasai people have progressively been deprived and dispossessed of their lands, land rights and land-based resources' (ibid.: 4). Indeed, between 2010 and 2011, Maasai violently protested when former settler lands on Mau Narok that had been acquired by the Kenyan government were due to be distributed to non-Maasai IDPs who had been caught up in and dislodged from sites they had settled elsewhere by the post-electoral violence of early 2008 (Galaty 2008). These grievances were reawakened a decade later, in 2018, when the Kenyan Cabinet Secretary for Environment and Forestry promised to 'undertake efforts to rehabilitate the Enoosupukia forest' on the Mau Escarpment, ordering that 'The remaining illegal settlers must move out immediately', in order to protect all forest ecosystems in the country (Ministry of Environment and Forestry website, 2 October 2018). The principle underlying these protests is that if anyone is granted the right to occupy forestlands that had been taken from the Maasai, they should be Maasai.

While Maasai lost legal title to this vast territory in 1905, they have since used diverse strategies of modern mobility to regain access. If modern mobility includes using contemporary law to move into and formally claim residual land rights held over from the past, it may also include accessing land on which no formal rights can be asserted apart from the urgency of need. Amusing to many, it has been often repeated that Maasai claim all grass as their right as pastoralists; in fact, the serious philosophical point being made, that in desperation the right to life trumps the exclusivity of property, has informed pastoral pleas and demands for access to pasture in times of environmental stress. In a legal environment where 'adverse possession' can trump freehold title, pastoral claims to the intrinsic right to move to where there is sustenance for livestock can be galvanizing for property owners who have acquired previous pastoral lands but are not in effective occupation of their lands. Yet many aspects of Kenyan property law were designed precisely to undermine customary land claims in favour of those who wish to acquire lands, on which to settle or with which to speculate, through government allocation or the market; indeed, 'property' itself is a concept less about unmediated rights to land one already holds than claims to land one does not hold. Such claims to residual customary rights through 'adverse possession' are strategies of modern mobility, used to facilitate gaining access to lands once held and now being reclaimed.

A central aim of launching programmes of enclosing pastoral lands through programmes of demarcation, subdivision and titling was to encourage pastoral settlement in order to anchor herders within fixed and often fenced territories, thus inhibiting human and livestock mobility. The functions of enclosure were, broadly, to create 'modern' citizens by anchoring them in place, by making them 'legible' to the state (Scott 1998), to bring them under more rigorous systems of governance, to modernize the agrarian economy by establishing the linkage between livestock husbandry, fixed parcels of land, extension services and markets, and to diminish land degradation associated with herd movement and pastoralism. Whatever the political wisdom of 'capturing' pastoralists through sedentarization, the effects of land enclosure on husbandry and conservation have clearly been the opposite of what was intended, as the actual practices of dryland husbandry require livestock to systematically shift between available pastures, with mobility being an essential element both of economic efficiency and sustainability of land use (Scoones 1995; Platteau 2000; Schlee and Shongolo 2012). In arid and semi-arid lands, rainfall is sufficiently sparse, unpredictable and varied in its temporal and spatial distribution that fixity is a recipe for disaster. Where land holding is increasingly fragmented through practices of subdivision, diversified land use and fencing but where livestock mobility remains essential because of climatic and grazing exigencies, modern mobility must be informed by increasing ingenuity (Galvin et al. 2008).

Following subdivision of group ranches, two strategies have emerged to confront the contradiction between mobility and enclosure: in the first, pastoralists cluster their homes on the land of one land holder, leaving the land of others available for sequenced grazing; in the second, pairs of herders establish an arrangement whereby they are able to move their animals back and forth between their respective pasture areas as weather and grass availability dictates. In times of drought, such as have occurred in southern Kenya several times in the last 20 years, including the periods of 2008–09 and 2015–16, numerous opportunistic strategies of herd movement were used. Public lands were exploited for the unused grasses that they harbour, as pastoral herds were moved along the byways of highways and roads, into parks and protected forests, and into open lands in urban areas between housing developments. In Karen and Lang'ata, now suburbs of the capital city, Nairobi, fields of grass that lie between residential developments were occupied by herders who built temporary homes and livestock enclosures as they grazed pastures otherwise unused. In the latter years of the Moi administration, pastoralists requested access to the lawns and glades of State House, and permission was granted! Herders approached large farm owners, whose land included unused pastures, and purchased access to grazing for fixed sums per head per month. In one case in our sample of subjects concerning drought mobility, I was told that a herder sought access to a white-owned farm in Central Province via a relative of his wife, who served as a farm watchman; surreptitiously, the herds were brought from outside where they rested during the day to graze quietly at night, withdrawing before sunrise. To sustain domestic stock as they move, or to make staying home feasible, many pastoralists with higher cash incomes or revenues from livestock sales invest in veterinary drugs and supplementary feed in the form of increasingly costly hay made available through highland/lowland trade.

Some of the farms of the central Rift Valley, which were never very productive for farming, have been left fallow, making them accessible to enterprising herders who have settled in those areas. A few individuals have joined land-buying companies to ensure access to lands that their ancestors once possessed by right. In areas of Nakuru District, adjacent to Lake Naivasha, lands once owned by Lord Delamere, the foremost leader of the colonial settlers, have been reallocated for resettlement, some for herders. In one area, a Maasai community has now settled for a sufficient time that they have put forward legal claim based on long-term occupancy, which has been granted. National Parks are sites of 'fortress conservation', where wildlife occupies areas from which all local residents have been evicted. But near the Masai Mara National Reserve in Narok, pastoralists live in adjacent ranches from which they and their livestock attempt – and often succeed – to enter the park for quiet grazing at night, especially during times of environmental stress. In late 2008, herders from our sample of households from more distant areas in Narok District moved their livestock into the Mara vicinity, both to access areas where pastures were more abundant than was the case further north and to participate in the sort of quiet invasion of the park that depends on neighbourly relations with pastoralists and park officials alike.

Most interesting from the perspective of boundary theory is that many pastoralists from southern Kenya moved their herds directly into northern Tanzania, where more rainfall had fallen and which had retained more abundant pastures than had Kenya. From the Rift Valley regions of Keekonyokie near Oltepesi and Lodokilani south of Magadi, Maasai herders moved into the area of Enkare Sero and Oldoinyo Lenkai, south of Lake Natron; others from Loitokitok and Matapato, near Namanga, moved into the Simanjiro plains in Kiteto District, east and south of Tarangire National Park, a home of Kisongo Maasai. While the Tanzanian authorities objected to the presence of Kenyan herders, the Maasai of the region were surprisingly accommodating, recognizing in practice what had been often asserted in rhetoric that all Maasai have a cultural right to graze on one another's lands in perilous times. But even they recognize that while their lands are still relatively undivided, except into village holdings (and despite further ingression of tour and hunting operators and commercial farmers), the Kenyans are increasingly not in a position to reciprocate given the privatization and fragmentation of their lands. In 2018, the Tanzanian Government began to harden the border by confiscating and even shooting livestock brought in by Kenyan pastoralists, and the generosity offered by their Tanzanian counterparts was more constrained.

Conclusion

In a presentation I made to the conference on The Future of Pastoralism in Africa, in 2011, on changes pastoralists have experienced over the last 30 years, I pointed to the following: dramatic population growth, fragmentation of rangelands due to land privatization and changing land use, livelihood diversification, the growth of small towns, and increasing participation in global institutions, most especially in education, health, trade and religion. The Modernity-Wars mentioned at the beginning of this chapter are played out on the stage provided by these sources of friction, which together define pastoralism today: more people making use of decreasing parcels of land to pursue a combination of pastoralism, agriculture and diverse income- generating activities, within or in close proximity to small and larger town life, informed by formal education and health services and the spread of Islam or Christianity.

In this chapter, I have investigated how two of these factors, growth of small towns and increasing demarcation and fragmentation of land, have both constrained and given rise to innovations in Modern Mobility: patterns of pastoral movement that both react to and positively exploit conditions of change. Although development planners have long hoped that sedentarization coupled with static animal husbandry and the cessation of herd and household movement would bring about pastoral modernization, pastoralists themselves have responded to the pressures of change by coupling land fragmentation and sedentarization with continued mobility. They have done so because their knowledge and skills in husbandry and managing range resources have told them that the health of grazing resources and pastoral productivity depend on the foundational element of pastoral systems: moving livestock to grasses (that in drylands are sparse, sporadic and widely distributed) rather than grasses to livestock (which is expensive, time-consuming and labour intensive), thus efficiently nourishing animals while avoiding range degradation (Reid 2012). The contradiction that contemporary pastoralism faces is how to reconcile continuing mobility with the constraints mentioned above that militate in favour of settled lives – that is, of growing human populations, land fragmentation, livelihood diversification, urban growth and participation in global institutions. Modern Mobility involves eluding fences and boundaries, exploiting legal stratagems to gain access or title to new lands, forming coalitions among themselves, striking agreements and contracts with land owners, accepting commercialized relations to access pastures or provide feed supplements, seeking out pockets of grazing that modern institutions have little use for, and using modern communication technologies to gain information about where grazing can be found, to negotiate with land owners, and to decrease the risk of moving ahead of time by identifying the most secure routes or points of arrival. Modern Mobility, of course, continues to rely on time-tried strategies of herd movement combined with persuasion and force, building temporary houses and enclosures while in transit, evoking cultural, clan and age-set ties while seeking hospitality, moving within political sections and between sections that recognize long-term solidarity, dividing household labour efficiently to allow for herds to be separated out and rapidly moved, negotiating access to water during moves, and weighing the risks and benefits of moving versus staying.

Under conditions of modernity, pastoralists have been subjected to progressive enclosure and sedentarization, partly on the grounds that these changes would serve to 'modernize' pastoralists, whatever that might mean for livestock keepers, who accommodate herding to the opportunities offered by contemporary society – markets, towns, schools or clinics. But in fact, sedentarization has not always proven fruitful for rural dwellers dependent on animals, because of the importance of maintaining systematic mobility in order to best extract necessary resources from a dry and arduous terrain. Despite the enclosure of land and complex processes of sedentarization, described here, pastoralists have for very good reasons continued to practise herd and household movements. But the forms mobility takes are modern; that is to say, they emerge from contemporary political conditions and represent dynamic responses to the exigencies of utilizing range resources to raise animals that link herding communities to wider markets. Thus not only settlement, with the establishment of fixed ranching domains, but continuing mobility represent modern responses to fragmented and bounded landscapes in an increasingly complex and globalized world.

John G. Galaty is a Professor of Anthropology at McGill University in Montreal, Canada. Focused on eastern Africa, his research has covered pastoralism and social change, rangeland development, land tenure transitions, borderland conflict, the culture of political process, including identity, ritual and age-organization, and currently a partnership project on community conservation.

Notes

Research pursuits over time were supported by the Social Sciences and Humanities Research Council of Canada (SSHRC), the Québec Fonds pour la Formation de Chercheurs et l'Aide à la Recherche (FCAR), and the International Development Research Centre (IDRC), for the Arid Lands and Resource Management (ALARM) project, through affiliation with the Ethnography Unit of the Kenya National Museum, the Pastoral Property and Poverty Project, in collaboration with the Mainyoito Pastoralist Integrated Development Organization (MPIDO) and its network of Community-based Organizations, and the Institutional Canopy of Conservation partnership project, through affiliation with the African Conservation Centre and other participating organizations. I acknowledge the assistance of Joseph Ole Simel, Amos Ole Kaitei, Justus Lesiamon and Daniel Lemoille in Kenya, and Julia Bailey, Stephen Moiko and Anne-Elise Keen at McGill and the institutional support of the Max Planck Institute for Social Anthropology in Halle/Salle and the Centre for Society, Technology and Development at McGill University.

 1. The overthrow of Haile Selassie by the Marxist Derg made the Kenyan government cautious about completing the road into Ethiopia, as they envisioned the new road potentially accommodating an influx of tanks to spread the Ethiopian revolution. As a result, the road remained unpaved for 40 more years until now.
 2. A partial list of the rich ethnographic record here would include Schlee (1989) for an overview, Fratkin (1991) for the Ariaal, Hjort (1981) on the Ilgira, Dahl (1979) on the Waso Borana, McPeak and Little (2006) and Fratkin and Roth (2005) for northern Kenya, Little (2003) on the Somali, and so forth.
 3. The Masai Reserve was first divided into Kajiado and Narok Districts, which in light of the 2010 Constitution have become Counties under systems of devolved governance.

References

Amselle, J.-L. 1998. *Mestizo Logics: Anthropology of Identity in Africa and Elsewhere*. Stanford: Stanford University Press.

Berman, B. 1990. *Control and Crisis in Colonial Kenya: The Dialectic of Domination*. London: James Currey.

Catley, A., J. Lind and I. Scoones (eds). 2013. *Pastoralism and Development in Africa: Dynamic Change at the Margins*. London: Earthscan from Routledge.

Coleman, W. (ed.). 2011. *Property, Territory, Globalization: Struggles over Autonomy*. Vancouver: UBC Press.

Comaroff, J., and J. Comaroff. 2009. *Ethnicity Inc*. Chicago: University of Chicago Press.

Dahl, G. 1979. *Suffering Grass: Subsistence & Society of Waso Borana*. Stockholm: Stockholm University Press.

Dereje Feyissa, and G. Schlee. 2009. 'Mbororo (Fulbe) Migrations from Sudan into Ethiopia', in G. Schlee and E. Watson (eds), *Changing Identifications and Alliances in North-East Africa: Vol. 3: Sudan, Uganda and the Ethiopia-Sudan Borderlands*. New York and Oxford: Berghahn, pp. 157–78.

Devine, T. M. 2018. *The Scottish Clearances: A History of the Dispossessed*. London: Penguin Random House.

Elkins, C. 2005. *Imperial Reckoning: The Untold Story of Britain's Gulag in Kenya*. New York: Henry Holt and Co.

Ellis, S. 2012. *Season of Rains: Africa in the World*. Chicago: The University of Chicago Press.

Fratkin, E. 1991. *Surviving Drought and Development: Ariaal Pastoralists of Northern Kenya*. Boulder: Westview Press.

Fratkin, E., and E. Roth (eds). 2005. *As Pastoralists Settle: Social, Health, and Economic Consequences of Pastoral Sedentarization in Marsabit District, Kenya*. New York and London: Kluwer Academic Publishers.

Galaty, J. 1989. 'Pastoral and Agro-Pastoral Migration in Tanzania: Factors of Economy, Ecology and Demography in Cultural Perspective', in J. Bowen and J. Bennett (eds), *Power and Autonomy: Anthropological Studies and Critiques of Development*. Washington, DC: University Press of America, pp. 163–83.

———. 1993. 'Maasai Expansion and the New East African Pastoralism', in T. Spear and R. Waller (eds), *Being Maasai: Ethnicity and Identity in East Africa*. London: James Curry, pp. 61–86.

———. 1994. 'Rangeland Tenure and African Pastoralism', in E. Fratkin, K. Galvin and E. Roth (eds), *African Pastoralist Systems: An Integrated Approach*. Boulder and London: Lynne Rienner, pp. 185–204.

———. 2002a. 'Une vue sur des conflits pastoraux au Kenya', *Anthropologie et Sociétés, Politiques, jeux, d'espace* 26(1): 107–26.

———. 2002b. 'How Visual Figures Speak: Narrative Inventions of "The Pastoralist" in East Africa', *Visual Anthropology*, Spec. Issue 'Persistent Popular Images of Pastoralists', R. Gordon and C. Kratz (eds) 15(3–4): 299–319.

———. 2005. 'Time, Terror and Pastoral Inertia: Sedentarization and Conflict in Northern Kenya', in E. Fratkin and E. Roth (eds), *As Nomads Settle: Social, Health, and Ecological Consequences of Pastoral Sedentarization in Northern Kenya*. Boston, MA: Kluwer Academic, pp. 53–68.

———. 2008. 'Violence and Its Mediations: Civil Society, Community Conflict and the State in East Africa', in A. Bellagamba and G. Klute (eds), *Beside the State: Emergent Powers in Contemporary Africa*. Cologne: Rüdiger Köppe, pp. 23–54.

———. 2013a. 'The Indigenization of Pastoral Modernity: Territoriality, Mobility, and Poverty in Dryland Africa', in M. Bollig, M. Schnegg and H.-P. Wotzka (eds), *Pastoralism in Africa: Past, Present and Future*. New York and Oxford: Berghahn, pp. 473–510.

———. 2013b. 'Land Grabbing in the Eastern African Rangelands', in A. Catley, J. Lind and I. Scoones (eds), *Pastoralism and Development in Africa: Dynamic Change at the Margins*. London and New York: Earthscan from Routledge, pp. 143–53.

———. 2016. 'Boundary-Making and Pastoral Conflict along the Kenyan-Ethiopian Borderlands', *African Studies Review* 59(1): 97–122.

Galaty, J., and K. Ole Munei. 1999. 'Land, Law, and Dispossession', *Cultural Survival Quarterly: Uprooted: Dispossession in Africa* (J. Galaty, guest editor) 22(4): 68–71.

Galvin, K. et al. 2008. *Fragmentation in Semi-Arid and Arid Landscapes: Consequences for Human and Natural Systems*. New York: Springer.

Hjort, A. 1981. 'Ethnic Transformation, Dependency and Change: The Ilgira Samburu of Northern Kenya', in J. Galaty and P. Salzman (eds), *Change and Development in Nomadic and Pastoral Societies, Journal of Asian and African Studies* 16(1–2). Leiden: Brill, pp. 50–67.

Homewood, K. 2008. *Ecology of African Pastoralist Societies*. Oxford: James Currey.

Homewood, K., P. Kristjanson and P.C. Trench (eds). 2009. *Staying Maasai: Livelihoods, Conservation and Development in East African Rangelands*. New York: Springer.

Hughes, L. 2006. *Moving the Maasai: A Colonial Misadventure*. Houndsmills and New York: Palgrave McMillan.

Ikeya, K. (ed.). 2017. *Sedentarization among Nomadic Peoples in Asia and Africa*. Osaka: National Museum of Ethnology, Senri Ethnological Studies 95.

Little, P. 2003. *Somalia: Economy without State*. Oxford: James Currey.

Malkki, L.1997. 'Speechless Emissaries: Refugees, Humanitarianism, and Dehistoricization', in K. Olwig and K. Hastrup (eds), *Siting Culture: The Shifting Anthropological Object*. New York: Routledge, pp. 223–54.

McCabe, J.T. 1994. 'Mobility and Land Use Among African Pastoralists: Old Conceptual Problems and New Interpretations', in E. Fratkin, K. Galvin, and E. Roth (eds), *African Pastoralist Systems*. Boulder: Lynne Rienner, pp. 69–89.

McPeak, J., and P. Little. 2006. *Pastoral Livestock Marketing in Eastern Africa: Research and Policy Challenges*. Bourton on Dunsmore: Intermediate Technology Publications.

Mwangi, E. 2007. *Socioeconomic Change and Land Use in Africa: The Transformation of Property Rights in Maasailand*. New York: Palgrave MacMillan.

Pearce, F. 2012. *The Land Grabbers: The New Fight over Who Owns the Earth*. Boston: Beacon Press.

Platteau, J-P. 2000. 'Does Africa Need Land Reform?', in C. Toulmin and J. Quan (eds), *Evolving Land Rights, Policy and Tenure in Africa*. London: Institute of Environment and Development, pp. 51–74.

Reid, R. 2012. *Savannas of Our Birth: People, Wildlife, and Change in East Africa*. Berkeley: University of California Press.

Riamit, S.K. 2014. 'Dissolving the Pastoral Commons, Enhancing Enclosures: Commercialization, Corruption and Colonial Continuities amongst the Maasai Pastoralists of Southern Kenya', MA Thesis. Department of Anthropology, McGill University.

Rutten, M. 1992. *Selling Wealth to Buy Poverty: The Process of the Individualization of Land Ownership among the Maasai Pastoralists of Kajiado District, Kenya, 1890–1990*. Saarbrücken: Verlag für Entwicklungspolitik.

Schlee, G. 1989. *Identities on the Move: Clanship and Pastoralism in Northern Kenya*. Manchester: Manchester University Press.

Schlee, G., and A. Shongolo. 2012. *Pastoralism and Politics in Northern Kenya & Southern Ethiopia*. Woodbridge: James Currey.

Scoones, I. 1995. 'New Directions in Pastoral Development in Africa', in I. Scoones (ed.), *Living with Uncertainty: New Directions in Pastoral Development in Africa*. London: Intermediate Technology Publications, pp. 1–36.

Scott, J.C. 1998. *Seeing Like a State: How Certain Schemes to Improve the Human Condition Have Failed*. New Haven: Yale University Press.

Sorrenson, M.P.K. 1968. *Origins of European Settlement in Kenya*. Nairobi: Oxford University Press.

Chapter 2

Unequal Citizenship and One-Sided Communication

Anthropological Perspectives on Collective Identification in the Context of Large-Scale Land Transfers in Ethiopia

Günther Schlee

Modern ideas of citizenship imply equality. They are of fairly recent origin. The three-class franchise that gave different weight to the votes of different categories of people according to property and status was abolished in certain parts of Germany only in the early twentieth century, and women's suffrage was introduced in many parts of the world even later. Racial equality and non-discrimination against sexual minorities are still hotly debated political issues even in the so-called developed world and remain matters of changing legislation. The principle that all citizens of a country have the same citizenship rights is called the universalist notion[1] of citizenship,[2] not to be confused with global citizenship or cosmopolitanism, which refers to forms of political agency and notions of responsibility in a wider framework.[3] For some Westerners, to agree with this universalist notion is an indicator of civilization, and they impatiently urge Africans to share and implement it. This makes one wonder whether they would regard their own parents and grandparents as uncivilized, since even in Western countries this standard has been met only recently and imperfectly. Still, at the normative level, universalist citizenship has been universally (in the sense of globally) accepted.[4] This makes any attempt to grant special rights to defined categories of people in a special area within a nation-state subject to demands for justification. How can special rights be reconciled with the demands of equality and universal, uniform citizenship? After all, the more rights that are invested in you as a member of an ethnic group in a given part of your country, the fewer rights you have in other parts of your country, where others hold these special rights. And the more rights you claim as a citizen of the wider unit, the more rights you will have to concede to others within your ethnic territory who are not your co-ethnics, in accordance with universal citizenship. That is a kind of zero-sum game: claiming special rights in one territory means losing them elsewhere, where others would follow suit and claim these rights for themselves. You have to strike a balance between ethnic entitlements and universal citizenship. Ethnic movements should consider well how far to go. If they are too successful, they become self-defeating: the rights they lose elsewhere might be more valuable than the rights they gain in their own territory. Thus the groups they stand for might lose more than they gain, especially if their ethnic territory is relatively small. Loss of rights elsewhere would not matter if everyone stayed in their own territory, but that seems to be an ethnonationalist phantasy, hard to combine not only with the notion of free-dom but also with the reality of migration.

Ethiopia: Its Constituent Units, Their Shapes and Functions

In Ethiopia, a country that has introduced a form of federalism comprising re-gional states based on ethnicity or a plurality of ethnicities since 1991, the ques-tion of how these special rights can be reconciled with the demands of equality and universal, uniform citizenship has been asked often and in many variations, and the answers are many. They include that demands of equality at the individ-ual level do not address problems of inequality between groups. Groups might deserve special consideration to address past imbalances and injustices.[5] One may also argue that ethnic federalism and other forms of organized pluralism are mainly concerned with cultural and linguistic rights and that all Ethiopians, for example, have the right to live and work and vote in any part of the country, although the proponents of this argument would have to concede that things do not always work out this way in practice. A third answer would be that a consti-tution can be written in such a way as to give equal voice to all component re-gional states, including both those named after an ethnic majority and the more composite ones, so as to grant equality at a collective level with the implication that citizenship at the federal level is only partly direct and in addition has an indirect component. One is a member of a federation by virtue of being a mem-ber of an ethnic group or having citizenship in a regional state and through these institutions. One is Ethiopian by virtue of being Gurage or Hadiya or Amhara or whatever, and in that context one ethnic identity is as good as another. So the discourse can shift from the equality of individuals to the equality of groups.

Not only does the vocabulary by which right-bearing units are described (na-tions, nationalities and peoples) go back to Stalin and follow the Soviet model. Also the resulting maps look similar. Boundaries have many corners and bulges aimed at including one village that speaks language A on the generally B-speaking side and one village speaking language B on the A-speaking side. Along the bor-der between Uzbekistan and Tajikistan, you have long narrow protrusions, like peninsulas surrounded by the other state, and you have exclaves and enclaves. The border faithfully follows the linguistic map so that a village with an Uzbek-speaking majority would belong to Uzbekistan and a Tajik-speaking village to Tajikistan. These borders were never meant to be closed, as they were interior boundaries within a larger unit, the Soviet Union. But when I travelled in the area in 2006, at a time when the Soviet Union was already a thing of the past, the border between Uzbekistan and Tajikistan was closed. We needed a special permit to cross from Uzbekistan to Khojand in a northern protrusion of Tajikistan, and from there we took an aeroplane to reach the main part of the country and the capital city, Dushanbe, behind a mountain range 5,000 metres high. Geographical proximity was ignored, as towns were cut off from their hinterland and the existing road infrastructure interrupted by road blocks. People had to learn that existing neighbourhoods and business links no longer mattered and that they belonged with those others behind the mountains who speak the same language.

In Ethiopia, each regional state has the constitutional right to separation, and there is a fixed procedure for it, which makes Ethiopia unique in the world, but the procedure requires a consensual solution, so that a one-sided demand for separation is not sufficient (and that is what one thinks of when one hears 'right of separation'). So the 'right of separation' in Ethiopia is a bit like according the right of divorce to a woman *if* her husband grants it. Nor is separation a practical possibility. The states are not designed for separation. If you want to go from Yem, a special *woreda* (administrative district) of the Southern Nations, Nationalities and Peoples' Regional State (SNNPRS), to Awassa, the capital of that state, you have to travel via Addis Ababa, twice crossing a part of Oromia (Popp 2001: 371). Likewise, people in Beni Shangul-Gumuz, living to the north and to the south of the Blue Nile, might as well meet in Addis Ababa, since it is not possible to reach one part of the state from the other. Replace the river gorge with a mountain range and you almost feel like you are in Tajikistan. If Oromia actually separated from the federation, all these people would need a visa to go to Addis Ababa or to visit another regional state on the other side of Oromia. The contested status of Addis Ababa itself would generate more problems. Does it belong to Oromia in spite of its function as a federal capital? Would it go if Oromia goes? Or would it become an Ethiopian exclave – that is, an enclave within Oromia? So I would not advise anyone to put the constitutional right of separation to the test. You might face a lot of opposition, constitutional and unconstitutional. Dissolution is one of the elements of the Soviet model that Ethiopians should not emulate.

Like the Soviet model, the delineation of boundaries in Ethiopia has followed the linguistic principle. Minimal dialect differences were used to claim special rights, down to the *woreda* level. Ethnic groups reacted to the incentives given and multiplied. But also very distant linguistic relationships were used for identity discourses.

In 1991, a Boran friend from Moyale, Kenya, Abdullahi Shongolo, and I walked across the boundary into Moiale, Ethiopia. There was no state on the Ethiopian side, and we left our passports with the Kenyan border post to be collected on our way back. But there was a new government in Addis Ababa, and it was in the air that one day it would extend its power through the whole country and that the new units of administration would follow ethnic lines. We walked straight into the OLF (Oromo Liberation Front) office and found a group of men standing around a table, bent over a map of Ethiopia. They were designing Oromia. What should be done with the Burji? We were speaking Boran. The new official Oromo language, which is heavily influenced by the Wollega dialect, had not developed by then. The men explained to us, '*Worri sun Oromoonit ammo* Cushites'. 'These people are not Oromo but Cushites', and 'Cushites' was the one word that came across in English. The Burji are Cushites like the Oromo, and being Cushites should be good enough for inclusion into Oromia. History took a different course and the Cushitic-speaking western neighbours of the Oromo, like the Burji, Konso, Sidama and Gedeo, later ended up in the Southern Nations, Nationalities and Peoples' Regional State (SNNPRS). But what I find remarkable is that classifications by European and American scholars of the nineteenth and twentieth centuries, which had never played a role in Ethiopian identity discourses, had found their way into political language (Schlee 1994: 977; Schlee 2008: 47).

Expectations about the new regional order went far beyond linguistic rights. Boran traders rejoiced at the prospect of having a regional state just for Oromo like themselves. This would enable them to expel their Gurage competitors. To the best of my knowledge, this never actually happened, but the recent history of the area is replete with other atrocities of this kind.

These days, the huge refugee[6] camps of Gedeo expelled by Guji from their villages make headlines. Taddesse Berisso dates violent clashes between Guji and Gedeo to a major war in 1998. Traditionally, the Guji, who are Oromo speakers, had hostile relationships with all their neighbours, in particular with those of their neighbours who are also Oromo, namely the Arsi and Boran. These other Oromo were recognized as speaking the same language, stemming from the same ancestor and being equals in cultural terms, such as embracing the values associated with the *Gadaa* systems and warlike virtues. That is why killing them carried a much higher prestige than killing non-Oromo. So much for linguistic and cultural similarity and its effect on interethnic relations. The only two groups with whom the Guji mostly lived in peace are two non-Oromo groups that now belong to the SNNPRS: the Sidama and Gedeo. The relationships with Gedeo were economically and ritually interdependent, and the settlement patterns were interspersed. There was no way to draw a boundary that would include all Gedeo villages and hamlets on one side and all Guji on the other. Linguistic classification and territoriality along linguistic lines did not take long to develop into resource conflict. Local administration and schools changed to the Gedeo language on one side and to Oromo on the other. Speakers of the respective other language felt excluded from the public service and neglected by it.

The next thing was the land question. Could people on the wrong side of the boundary till land there or should they go to 'their own' side? Ethnic federalism was thought to be a solution to the 'nationality question'. So why has the problem not been solved over the past two decades with the instruments of ethnic federalism? The answer is that territorial ethnicity here could not be the solution, because it was the cause of the conflict. Political activists had taught the Arsi and Guji and also the Boran that they were Oromo. I can testify from the 1970s and 1980s that at least the Boran of northern Kenya were not aware that they were included in that category. When asked who the Oromo were, the answer was that the Oromo are a people to the north who speak a language that is similar to Boran but a bit strange and that one can sometimes hear them on Ethiopian radio. Within Oromo, the Arsi, Boran and Guji belong to the same dialect group and were aware of their similarities, but that did not, as we have seen, translate into peaceful relationships, not to mention Oromo nationalism. But now there was this new identity, and a territorial boundary needed to be drawn around it. According to Asnake Kefale (2013: 53), boundary-making was the cause of the conflict between Guji and Gedeo, who before had both belonged to Sidamo Province. No amount of boundary corrections with more little bends and bulges can rectify the situation, because boundary-making itself is the problem. In the 2009 *Changing Identifications and Alliances in North-East Africa*, the chapter by Taddesse highlights the shifting alliances of the Guji-Oromo and their neighbours, and in the case of the Guji the change of alliances could not have been more radical. They sided with their Oromo arch-enemies against their former non-Oromo neighbours and in-laws, comprising the Gedeo.

On the other, eastern side of Oromia, there are long-standing conflicts, not solved by many local referendums, along the contested boundary between Oromia and the Somali region. One of the problems is the imposition of a binary classification. Groups who are neither Oromo nor Somali (but claimed by both) and might have clan ties to one side and linguistic proximity to the other, or vice versa, had to please make up their minds as to which side they belonged, and tactical and strategical considerations might have played a role in the choices they made. Pasture and water rights had never been exclusive. Pastoralists migrating with their herds in times of peace might be given water only once by the owners of a well and then be told to leave, but there were no lines in the ground separating one group from the other. The drawing of such lines led to violence and expulsions (Fekadu 2009; Dejene Gemechu 2012; Schlee with Shongolo 2012a and Schlee and Shongolo 2012b).

So the issue of what ethnic rights an ethnic territory actually comprises is still violently contested in many parts of Ethiopia and, conversely, which rights you have as an Ethiopian in any part of Ethiopia (as a citizen of a 'nation'-state). Rights on paper might be worth little in places where you do not dare to go, and the issue of citizenship, entitlement and political empowerment is far from being solved in practice. After twenty-seven years of ethnic federalism, not only is it still contested as to which rights or practical opportunities to access resources are associated with one's ethnic identity, but even the more basic question of who has the authority to define one's ethnic identity has not been solved. To exemplify the problem, Assefa Fiseha (2018: 337) asks whether it is enough to speak the Afar language or whether you have to be of Afar descent to become the president of that regional state. The global trend is to regard ethnicity as a matter of self-declaration. But to simply declare yourself as Afar might not be good enough if you want to be elected or hired by others. Branches of the public service in these long years of ethnic politics have become ethnicized, just like other spheres of life, like religion (ethnic churches with vernacular services splitting into smaller churches to cultivate differences of dialect), music, commercial banks,[7] transport companies, education and many other fields where ethnic identity is not just of symbolic value but is tied to material resources. Dominant ethnic networks forge alliances or compete for power at the national level; less powerful ones defend access to resources at the regional or local level. In many different and complicated ways, ethnic identities or the claims to represent them are used as entitlements.

Land and To Whom It Belongs

The key material resource, land, is hotly contested. In the literature that discusses the recent crisis, which led to a change of government in 2018, the major problem is not due to the federal government increasingly infringing on the land rights of constituent states or nationalities in recent years. The problem seems to be much older. The authors of the constitution in 1994 had already chosen an ambiguous wording: Article 40(3) specifies: 'The right to ownership of rural and urban land, as well as of all natural resources, is exclusively vested in the State and in the peoples of Ethiopia. Land is a common property of the Nations, Nationalities and Peoples of Ethiopia and shall not be subject to sale or to other means of exchange.' If all Nations, Nationalities and Peoples of Ethiopia own the land in common, through which institution do they administer it? Isn't the federal government the only institution they all have in common? Does this article not say the opposite of what it appears to say, namely that the land does not belong to the single Nations, Nationalities and Peoples but to the federal government? This ambiguity reminds us somewhat of the right of separation, which is first granted and then specified in a way that denies it, because the House of Federation has to agree and unilateral separation is not possible. The constitution, cited as it is in the context of ethnic federalism, also lays the foundations for the negation of ethnic federalism, through a top-down centralist developmental autocracy, if a strong leader comes along. No wonder conflicting policies, endless debates and high levels of violence have resulted from these ambiguities.

In other words, every Ethiopian has the right to a piece of land where he can speak his own language but not necessarily to a piece of land where he or she can grow what she wants the way she wants. To whom the land is granted and along which lines it is to be tilled and developed is decided by the federal government.

Many of the smaller groups in South Omo (an example would be the Bodi discussed by Stevenson and Buffavand 2018; Buffavand, this volume) seem to have little power to translate their 'sovereignty' (which the constitution grants them because they are 'a people') into tangible benefits. In spite of the cultural relativism that pervades official rhetoric, they are classified as backward, their forms of land use are not respected and (counterfactually) not attributed economic value, and large tranches of their land are given to foreign investors (Abbink et al. 2014). The Nilotic groups of Gambella in the far west of Ethiopia do not seem to fare better (Fana Gebresenbet, this volume). So, despite the constitution giving rights to 'peoples' as such, some peoples seem to have more say than other peoples. Therefore we have to examine case by case what belonging to a given 'people' is worth.

The Exchange Value of Ethnicity

The main test for determining the value of something is to exchange it for something else. Esau sold his birthright to Jacob for a dish of lentils, so we know that being a first-born son is at least worth a dish of lentils, or so it was in that Biblical context. Try to sell your birthright as a first-born or whatever to your sibling, friend or neighbour and in many modern contexts you might find that it does not even buy you a dish of lentils. Obviously, how symbolic values translate into material values is a matter to be studied, case by case. We have to study what people get for dropping claims or giving up rights.

One such natural experiment has taken place in the northern parts of the Borana zone of Oromia, where we find many Guji. As explained above, the Guji and Boran share the wider Oromo identity, so they are Oromo sub-ethnicities.[8] At least since 1991 their educated elites have spread the knowledge among them that they are Oromo, and since then they have fought alongside each other in a border issue with the Gedeo, as Taddesse Berisso (2009) has shown.

Traditionally, they had been preferred or respected enemies. For a Boran, it brought prestige to kill a Guji, and vice versa. In 1999, a separate Guji zone was established, but it did not include the Guji-inhabited areas in the northwest of the Boran zone. So in 2006, as Dejene Gemechu, to whom I owe this story, describes in his doctoral thesis (Dejene 2012), there was a demand for a second Guji zone with Bule Hora (formerly known by its Amharic name Hagere Mariam) as its capital. That this demand was not based on the desire for Guji unity is obvious because that desire would have been better expressed by joining the existing Guji zone. To want a second zone obviously had to do with urban development and new jobs.

From the pastoralists' point of view, it was further obvious that the creation of such a zone would enable the Guji to push the Boran and Gabra and their herds southwards, thus vacating pastures in favour of the herds of the Guji. This is quite against the traditional southern Oromo grazing management system (Schlee and Shongolo 2012b). That system was based on mutual hospitality and some regulation by allocation of water from the wells in the dry season (*herega*), not by territorial boundaries. But by 2006, it seemed clear that pastures in a 'Guji' zone would be exclusively used by Guji. Such fragmentation of pasture-land is incompatible with risk management in semi-arid areas and harmful to the overall productivity of pastoralism, but that is the price people seemed to be ready to pay for their sub-ethnic territoriality. I am not aware of any formal legislation giving the rights to pasture in the Guji zone only to Guji. This seems to illustrate that the question raised above, 'what ethnic rights an ethnic territory actually comprises', does not have any hard and fast answers but is something that develops informally through local power relations, latent threats and getting used to actual practices.

The plans for a second Guji zone failed, for the time being, but they were not given up without compensation. Bule Hora got a university, one of the few uni-versities in a district capital in Ethiopia. (Ethiopian universities tend to be found in zonal or state capitals and, of course, in the federal capital.) The university was founded in 2008. So ethnicity sometimes does have a material value. One may get a university for giving up an ethnic-based claim. Much later, in 2016, after Dejene Gemechu had finished his research and therefore because of circum-stances not known to me, a second Guji zone (the present West Guji Zone) was established. In the end, Esau had the dish of lentils and kept his birthright all the same.

We shall discuss below cases in which ethnic ascriptions, combined with the label 'backward' and referring to smaller groups, entail no rights at all when it comes to material resources. As for the above case, which took place before an Oromo became prime minister in April 2018, Oromo subgroups show that they had gained – at least against other Oromo – a much stronger bargaining position. True, the Oromo also like to depict themselves as victims of Amhara imperialism, and Asebe (this volume) describes an Oromo group who are victims of miscon-ceived development, but there is no way to deny that Oromo elites have in many cases proven more educated, better connected and more powerful when it comes to asserting ethnic rights or trading these ethnic rights for something else, as in the Bule Hora case. Oromo have always been found on both sides of the dividing line between rulers and ruled.

Backwardness

The Ethiopian constitution celebrates ethnic diversity and encourages peoples to stress their particularities, giving special rights to smaller and smaller administrative units to the delight of the elites, who find employment there, and to the chagrin of the taxpayer, who has to pay for it all. There is, however, one magic formula that enables governments to ignore ethnic rights completely: 'backwardness'. 'Backwardness' is the opposite of 'high modernity', which comes in 'modernity packages' (see Fana Gebresenbet, Asebe Regassa and Turton, this volume; Gabbert 2018). If your group is classified as backward, then your ethnicity is not associated with any entitlement to resources and does not have a voice in politics. So this distinction might mark a new class division that runs across the entire country. Ethiopia is divided into those who know the direction of progress and therefore know where the directions 'forward' and 'backward' point and those who are said not to know. 'Forward' and 'backward' depend, of course, on where you are heading. In Marsabit, Kenya, I have come across a tale about an old Somali man, the shop owner Ducale, who once, on a public holiday, participated in a running competition. He joined the others at the starting line. Ready, steady, go! Ducale ran in the opposite direction and everyone laughed at him. He responded by saying that in his direction he was first. So forward and backward, progress and backwardness, are defined in relation to one's aim. The people engaged in the developmental democracy discourse do not hesitate to state their aims, although the effects of their interventions do not always lead in the direction of those stated aims. In this they differ from Ducale, who indeed runs in the direction he has defined as his. Therefore, their targets cannot be inferred from where they are actually moving but must be gleaned from their discourses. If they say, 'Our aim is to achieve development targets a, b and c', we have to believe them. Or maybe not, if we suspect a hidden agenda. Often development measures simply fail because of incompetence or corruption, while sometimes subjects seem to pursue other aims than the stated ones (Fana Gebresenbet, Stevenson and Kamski, this volume).

In which ways and to what degree project failures are due to incompetence and lack of understanding of local givens and to what extent due to the pursuit of unstated aims is a matter of interpretation. We often find a mix of many components, and the different actors involved might share neither the same aims nor the same perceptions of what is going on. An example for this is provided by Wedekind (this volume). There are elements of ignorance: in his example of a castor oil production scheme on the border of two regional states, Oromia and the Somali Regional State of Ethiopia, the arguments in favour of growing castor for oil production were based on faulty calculations – that is, the assumption that the local farmers produced only subsistence goods was wrong, the value of their cash crops (*khat*, groundnut and vegetables for the market) was not part of the equation, and the fact that the value of food crops would probably rise when large surfaces were converted to non-food crops was not taken into account. That existing forms of land ownership were ignored goes almost without saying when one looks at the broader picture. Then on the side of the government, unacknowledged aims might have played a role in favouring a project that was highly unlikely to achieve its economic aims. One such tacit aim may have been to defuse land competition along a contested boundary between Oromo and Somali users by giving land to a foreign company, another to achieve 'a proxy ban' on *khat* production. As political intentions were no replacement for economic success, the level of failure, when measured against all aims, stated and unstated, was extraordinary.

The power to define aims – that is, to define in which direction to move forward – implies the power to denounce others as backward. In the first parts of the chapter, we discussed the costs and benefits or claiming particular or universal citizenship rights. We then discussed what ethnic claims or giving them up might be worth in material terms. With the 'backward' peoples, we now come to a category of people who do not have to face these questions, because they are not asked. 'Developed' people decide in Ethiopia about 'backward' people. We might say that in practice the latter are not citizens but wards, and wards of not very sympathetic guardians.

'Backward' people are not consulted. They are taught. Where teaching fails, they are forced. In his booklet *Land to Investors: Large-Scale Land Transfers in Ethiopia*, Dessalegn Rahmato (2011: 37) concludes that 'the state has used its hegemonic authority over the land to dispossess smallholders and their communities without consultation or consent'. On the other hand, according to researchers from MPI, there seems to have been a lot of communication between different levels of government and the government and the population, including the segments of population affected by land transfers. Dessalegn Rahmato cannot have ignored all this communication. This raises the question of what went wrong with this communication so that Dessalegn Rahmato could not accept it as consultation. The answer may be that, in agreement with their common usage in English, for Dessalegn Rahmato the concept 'consultation' implies listening and 'consent' needs to be voluntary (see also LaTosky, this volume, on 'free, prior and informed consent').

There are stages in the procedure of land transfer to investors in which one would communicate with the affected people. As Dessalegn Rahmato (2011: 14) explains, 'once the land to be handed over is determined, the investor is asked to prepare an environmental impact report which is reviewed by MoARD.' MoARD stands for Ministry of Agriculture and Rural Development. I assume the environmental impact study, which deals with effects of a project on the ecosystem, has to include humans. In spite of the rhetoric that 'unused land' is given to investors, the land in question invariably is inhabited by humans and the other mammals with whom humans live in symbiosis, like cattle, camel, sheep, goats and horses, as well as the plants further down the food chain, to put the matter in ecological terms. As the impact reports are provided by the investors, one may expect that the experts employed for writing these reports are paid by the investors and therefore are biased in their favour. This may well be the case. But does it have to be the case?

I have never been asked to provide such a report, but one of my former doctoral students has. After he had finished the job, I asked him whether he did not have to struggle with moral dilemmas. The answer was no. The researcher was perfectly free to write the truth about what he had found out. In the area earmarked for 'development' there were many pastoralists who would be deprived of their pastures, an even larger population of smallholder agriculturalists and agro-pastoralists who would lose their land, and also hunter-gatherers, including beekeepers, who would lose their livelihood by reduction of the forest cover. He could and did write all that. The researcher explained to me that the important point was that the impact report had been done, not what it contained. It had to be there, on the shelf, so that in further proceedings the impact report could be checked off as done. The academics involved in writing such reports were thus completely free to be as critical as they felt they needed to be, without any harm being done to the planned investment. It is the other side of the equation mentioned by Dessalegn Rahmato that we need to look at: the reviewing ('the investor is asked to prepare an environmental impact report which is reviewed by MoARD'). If the reviewing consists of merely the formalities – that is, confirming that a report of the required length exists, no matter the content – it provides a perfect filter against undesired content: you can safely ignore it.

One kind of undesired evidence that is rarely adduced and never properly discussed is the shadow costs or opportunity costs of development measures. What is the value of an economy that must make space for the new 'developed' form of economy to be introduced? For this, the knowledge of local producers should be taken into account more seriously. By local producers, I mean peasants, pastoralists and craftsmen – whoever makes a living in the contested areas, irrespective of standards of ethnic purity or whether they are ethnically mixed. I am not speaking of 'the culture' of this or that group.

The longest-running large-scale irrigation-based development scheme in Ethiopia is the one in the Awash Valley. It dates back to the times of Haile Selassie. Concerning this scheme, Behnke and Kerven (2013) have come to the conclusion that in the interest of the overall economy it would have made more sense to leave the nomadic livestock production of the Afar in place. But the interests of decision-makers, of course, do not need to be in the service of the overall economy or well-being (Schlee 2013). There is a vast literature to substantiate this point. The most recent addition to it is an edition of the field notes of Glynn

Flood, an anthropologist who was killed in this context among his Afar friends in 1975 (Ashami, Flood and Lydall 2018).

Lack of concern over existing economies also leads to an emphasis on alternatives to what is there rather than combining with what is there. Along the Lower Omo, immense areas of open range where the cattle of local groups once grazed are converted into irrigation schemes for sugar cane. The sugar cane tops – that is, the end of the stalk above the last well-formed node with the top three or so leaves, which are chopped off when the plant is harvested – would be valuable cattle feed. These tops alone could feed 1 LU (livestock unit, a cow) per hectare per year (Naseeven n.d.).[9] One hectare is about what one would have to calculate for one cow in Europe, under optimal climatic conditions. Under conditions of natural pasture in unirrigated semi-arid areas, one would need a much larger surface. And the sugar cane tops are just waste, often not even regarded as a by-product. Through negotiations over the by-products of sugar and biofuel production, one could have struck deals with local pastoralists instead of violently expelling them and destroying their livelihoods.

So the question is not whether irrigated agriculture is more efficient than natural pastures in arid areas. It would require a lot of mismanagement to produce less with a lot of water than without it. The question is to whom products and by-products should belong. What is the share for the local cows that have been deprived of their natural pastures?

In a drastic way, the effects of lack of communication can be shown in a case of well-intended intervention. Kaleb Kassa (2018) reports that in 2014, a year in which the reservoir of the hydroelectric Gibe III dam was filling up and the yearly floods of the Lower Omo did not take place, an artificial flood was produced by releasing a tidal wave of water in order to irrigate the lands of the riverine farmers who practise flood recession agriculture. In principle, a good idea. But the plan was not announced in advance to many who needed to know, and at the time of the flood, the Dassanech had already sown their fields, and the new crop was sprouting. The flood washed it away. There seems not to have been any routine communication with these 'backward' people and no shared common sense.

Communication

From all this, we can conclude that there is something wrong with the communication between government and people, and more specifically the section of the people that is not treated as citizens but as 'backwards'. At least in one direction something goes wrong. We do not need to worry about the government's outlets of communication. The government has enough control of the media to make itself heard; it can call meetings; it can even pass its orders down a chain of command. So we do not need to worry about top-down communication. It is bottom-up communication that does not seem to work. To take a closer look, we can use a simple, conventional communication model.

sender —> channel —> receiver

A sender sends a message through a channel to a receiver.

Think of a public meeting in which state officials explain the benefits of development to a gathering of local peasants who will be affected by it, or 'benefit' from it, as the wording would more likely be. Since we are interested in bottom-up communication, it is the responses by members of the public that are of interest to us. So, in our model, we define the local peasants as the senders. There have been protests, even violent protests, but what has often been observed in these meetings is that the peasants remain silent. It has been made abundantly clear to them by their own 'elites' and by local administrators that to be 'anti-development' is to be anti-government, and to be anti-government is forbidden (a strange idea in a self-styled democracy). In other words, there is criminalization of dissent, and dissenting voices are silenced, like a radio that you have switched off. So, one way of blocking the message is to switch off the sender.

To stay with the metaphor of the radio: if you do not like the music, there is an alternative to switching off the radio. You can change to another radio station; you can choose another sender. That has also been done in public consultations about development programmes. Let us examine how.

The most elaborate example about the selectivity involved in choosing who is allowed to deliver his message can be found in the recent thesis by Kaleb Kassa. He writes about government-sponsored peace meetings among the Dassanech and their neighbours on the boundary with Kenya. These meetings concern land use disputes between pastoralist groups, not between pastoralists and investors. One may raise the question of whether the procedures involving meetings about direct investment are much different. The following is a slightly shortened and lightly edited version of Kaleb's account:

> There are always debates regarding the identities of personalities involved and criteria employed to include and exclude pastoralists in state-initiated and organized peace meetings. The question 'who are these people?' needs to be answered. When peace gatherings are planned, the state authorities at *woreda* level often send a car to collect selected members of the *kebele* peace committee,[10] most often administrators and 'a community spokesperson'. In a more comprehensive peace event where a relatively large number of participants is expected, a *kebele* vice administrator, executive secretary, a woman representative and more recently 'youth' delegates are added to the list of attendees mentioned above. From a local state's point of view, these groups of people are labelled 'positive thinkers'

for the fact that, at least in principle, they endorse the ideas of government officials and their interests. These groups of people constitute what are called 'model' pastoralists, who are willing to make peace with neighbouring groups, teach fellow herdsmen to obey the officials and take care of the service centres in the rural area. These 'model pastoralists' in their eyes are, however, seen by the majority of pastoralists simply as 'collaborators' who serve the state in return for personal benefits. Their main discontent is that the government officials select these people on the basis of their affiliation to agents and structures of the state.[11]

When there are peace gatherings (workshops, conferences and trainings) to be held, the *woreda* authorities communicate with *kebele* administrators, who follow the same 'principle of suitability' to recruit participants to accompany them from their *kebele* administration at times when large numbers of participants are required. Along horizontal or vertical chains of relations, the peace process operates through multilevel networks of reciprocity in order to legitimize its actions. *Kebele*-level 'collaborators' and their clients strive to maintain their positions, showing loyalty to each other and to the district-level government authorities. Any attempt to add new people to the existing networks ignites a heated debate and resistance.

In his thesis about a border region between Beni Shangul and Oromia, where land is contested between the two ethnic groups and investors from elsewhere, Ameyu Godesso (2017) writes:

As to the makeup of the joint peace committees, a division can be made in terms of how members are selected: that is, ownership versus client interest. If peace committees are established by asking the community to assign 'prominent elders' and take a proactive role in peacebuilding, members of the committees or [all of them] as a unit tend to be viewed more or less as *jaarsa-biyyaa* [which is Afaan Oromo and means elders of the people] and are expected to abide by *dhugaa lafaa*, literally 'the truth of the land'. However, if peace committees are assembled by members recruited by governmental bodies and whose role in peacebuilding is thereby compromised, the committees are perceived as agents with an affiliation to E[P]RDF party politics and are branded as mere party mouthpieces.

There is also suspicion that their main motivation for taking part in meetings is to collect their per diems.

This makes clear that in some cases the government relies on the option of picking local representatives of their choice. Or to revisit the radio metaphor: they can choose the radio station to which they want to listen.

Between sender and receiver is the channel. Up the chain you report only what your superior wants to hear. Messengers appear to be afraid to be blamed for the content of their messages and only report what they think will please higher levels of government.

As for the last part of our tripartite model, selectively ignoring information that is detrimental to one's aims is something the receiver can practice. One such example is the above-discussed impact assessment report that was simply shelved. Top-down communication and expropriation by force lead to violent reactions, social disruption and alcohol abuse, which then encourages the qualification of the victims of land alienation as 'backward' people (Stevenson and Buffavand 2018).

Some Conclusions

Being deemed 'backward' not only deprives part of the Ethiopian citizenry of their land rights. It also affects the core of ethnic federalism: cultural pluralism. You are denied the right to perform cultural practices if you are classified as 'backward' and your practices as 'harmful', like inserting lip plugs or scarification (LaTosky 2015). So 'backwardness' is the one button you have to press if you want to reverse the whole project of ethnic federalism and reset it back to zero, as far as *they* are concerned; you might still claim group rights if you manage to define yourself as advanced or whatever the opposite of 'backward' may be. There is a line running through Ethiopia between those who can classify others as backward and those who lack the means to reject this label.

This dividing line follows ethnic distinctions to some extent but not neatly. We already mentioned that the Oromo straddle it. They comprise local and genealogical groups, some of whom, when the Ethiopian empire under Menelik expanded, belonged to the conquerors and others of whom belonged to the conquered. Also the 'Semites', often attributed the status of comprising the Semitic core of the empire, cannot invariably be found at the higher echelons of the ethnic hierarchy. The Gurage are among the conquered. Even among the Amhara and Tigre, who during different time periods have been regarded as rulers, the majority have always been ordinary peasants. But, then, the northern peasantry has always been a power base of whoever ruled Ethiopia in the imperial times and ever since, so their land rights, customs and laws could not be so easily ignored as those of small-scale farmers and pastoralists elsewhere.

So who are the typical 'backward' people in Ethiopia? They are likely to belong to one of the smaller linguistic communities, speaking Nilotic, Omotic or Cushitic languages, and they tend to live in the lowlands. Pastoralists are often labelled as 'backward'. Some reasons for this can be found in popularized academic theories about the evolution of food production, which claim that pastoralism preceded agriculture and is an archaic way of life. These theories have long been refuted (Schlee with Shongolo 2012a), but they still persist in popular perception, including that of planners and politicians. Since they are mobile and use pastures intermittently, they risk having their land declared 'vacant' and their resources designated as inefficiently used, although they produce most of the meat consumed by urbanites.

To abolish the label 'backward', to fairly and realistically assess the value of the local economies said to be 'backward' and to respect the land rights, the knowledge and the potential of the people practising these economies is an absolute requirement for the introduction of a uniform citizenship, in practice not just in law – a uniform citizenship in which everyone has a say in determining their own fates and that of the nation. And that is essential for the cohesion of the country. The conflicts in Ethiopia which at present (July 2020) receive most attention are those among present and former dominant ethnic and sub-ethnic groups: Amhara and Tigray who feel sidelined since an Oromo Prime Minister came to power in April 2018, and, worst of all, different groups of Oromo. If the country manages to preserve its territorial shape, if the inter-elite conflicts reach some conclusion and Ethiopia continues to exist, it will be high time to address another pressing problem, and that is not which type of highlanders rule, but how the country manages to integrate its lowland periphery and to offer people there a fair deal not as 'backwards' but as citizens.

Günther Schlee is Professor of Social Anthropology at the Arba Minch University, Ethiopia. He is Director emeritus at the Max Planck Institute for Social Anthropology in Halle, Germany, co-founded by him in 1999. Prior to this appointment, he was Professor of Social Anthropology at the University of Bielefeld. He conducted fieldwork in Kenya, Ethiopia and Sudan and was a guest lecturer in Padang (Sumatra) and at the École des Hautes Etudes en Science Sociales in Paris.

Notes

1. By analogy with 'universal suffrage'.
2. 'The universalist or unitary model defines citizenship primarily as a legal status through which an identical set of civil, political and social rights are accorded to all members of the polity' (*Stanford Encyclopedia of Philosophy*).
3. At the level between the nation-state and the world, we have intermediate identifications that may be associated with notions resembling citizenship, such as continental ones ('African unity', 'European values' . . .). A very visible expression of such an intermediate identification is the fact that on the cover of passports of citizens of the European Union, 'European Union' is at the top and the member state nationality appears further down.
4. Even explicit defenders of 'differentiated citizenship' would have to define a core of rights and duties that apply to all citizens and would have to explain why the special rights they demand for some are not affecting the core rights of others or to find reasons for the

extent they should be allowed to do so. Critics of the concept would deny the existence of core rights and duties applying to all. Such a critical sense of the term 'differentiated citizenship' can be found in Holston (2008: 7), who uses it to describe how, in Brazil, it 'generates a gradation of rights among [citizens] in which most rights are available only to particular kinds of citizens and exercised as the privilege of particular social categories'.

5. The preamble of the Constitution of the Federal Democratic Republic of Ethiopia shows this tension between universalist notions and addressing historical injustices affecting some more than others. It demands 'full respect of individual and people's fundamental freedoms and rights, to live together on the basis of equality and without any sexual, religious or cultural discrimination' and then includes the additional demand to rectify 'historically unjust relationships'.

6. In the UN jargon, these refugees would be IDPs (internally displaced persons) because their forced relocation has taken place within the borders of a nation-state.

7. Nib for Gurage; Anbessa and Wegagen for Tigray; Awash, Oromia International and Oromia Cooperative for the Oromo; Abay for the Amhara.

8. See Fulɓe and Uzbeks on sub-ethnicities; Schlee and Guichard (2013).

9. The sugar cane tops produced per hectare (21 tonnes) is theoretically enough to provide forage for 1 livestock unit (LU) over a year (1 LU = 500 kg) (Naseeven n.d.).

10. This selection is done by people who themselves are the result of a strict selection process. According to Data Dea (2019: 39), local administration is composed of members of the ruling party, chosen because of their loyalty to higher levels of government.

11. This resonates with Echi Christina Gabbert's observations (personal communication): in the peace meetings organized by zone officials, after violent incidents between Hamar and Arbore in 2016/17, speakers/elders who did not follow this pattern of model speakers were given a warning by the zone officials, and some had to refrain from speaking. The reason given was that their talk carried with it the potential to instigate violence or war. Actually, local patterns of peacemaking are based on 'saying it all', so to speak – putting everything on the table to identify all sources of resentment in order to be able to reconcile on that basis and prevent old resentments lingering that could endanger the peace agreement. The prohibition against certain speakers in effect stirred up more resentment because some of the speakers who were silenced were well respected and known as skilled peacemakers. To silence them was, to say the least, counterproductive and delayed the peace process. *Kebele* representatives who knew this suffered from their uncomfortable 'middle' position in the peace process, very much aware of the shortcomings of the external peacemakers but not free to act according to local understanding, or able to make themselves understood to the *woreda* and zone officials. The solution in the end was to (a) integrate knowledgeable elders not involved in party politics in the peacemaking and (b) organize customary peace meetings in addition to the official meetings.

References

Abbink, J., K. et al. 2014. 'Lands of the Future: Transforming Pastoral Lands and Livelihoods in Eastern Africa', *Max Planck Institute for Social Anthropology Working Papers* No. 154, Retrieved 31 July 2020 from https://www.eth.mpg.de/pubs/wps/pdf/mpi-eth-working-paper-0154.

Ameyu Godesso Roro. 2017. 'Transformation in Gumuz-Oromo Relations: Identity, Conflict and Social Order, Western Ethiopia', Ph.D. dissertation. Halle (Saale): Martin Luther University Halle-Wittenberg.

Ashami, M., M. Flood and J. Lydall (eds). 2018. 'In Pursuit of Afar Nomads: Glynn Flood's Work Journal and Letters from the Field, 1973–75', *Field Notes and Research Projects XXI*. Max Planck Institute for Social Anthropology, Department of Integration and Conflict. Retrieved 31 July 2020 from http://www.eth.mpg.de/pubs/series_fieldnotes/vol0021 .html.

Asnake Kefale. 2013. *Federalism and Ethnic Conflict in Ethiopia: A Comparative Regional Study*. London: Routledge.

Assefa Fiseha. 2018. 'Federalism and Development: The Ethiopian Dilemma', *International Journal on Minority and Group Rights* 25: 333–68.

Behnke, R., and C. Kerven. 2013. 'Counting the Costs: Replacing Pastoralism with Irrigated Agriculture in the Awash Valley', in A. Catley, J. Lind and I. Scoones (eds), *Pastoralism and Development in Africa: Dynamic Change at the Margins*. Abingdon and New York: Routledge, pp. 57–70.

Data Dea Barata. 2019. *Contesting Inequalities, Identities and Rights in Ethiopia*. London and New York: Routledge.

Dejene Gemechu Chala. 2012. 'Local Response to the Ethiopian Ethnic-Based Federalism: Conflict and Conflict Management among the Borana and Their Neighbours', Ph.D. dissertation. Halle (Saale): Martin Luther University Halle-Wittenberg.

Dessalegn Rahmato. 2011. *Land to Investors: Large-Scale Land Transfers in Ethiopia*. Addis Ababa: Forum for Social Studies.

Fekadu Adugna. 2009. 'Negotiating Identity: Politics of Identification among the Borana, Gabra and Garri around the Oromo-Somali Boundary in Southern Ethiopia', Ph.D. dissertation. Halle (Saale): Martin Luther University Halle-Wittenberg.

Gabbert, E.C. 2018. 'Future in Culture: Globalizing Environments in the Lowlands of Southern Ethiopia', in J. Abbink (ed.), *The Environmental Crunch in Africa: Growth Narratives vs. Local Realities*. Leiden: Palgrave, pp. 287–317.

Holston, J. 2008. *Insurgent Citizenship: Disjunctions of Democracy and Modernity in Brazil*. Princeton, NJ: Princeton University Press.

Kaleb Kassa Tadele. 2018. 'Changing Patterns of Conflict and Conflict Management in the Lower Omo Basin: The Daasanech and Their Neighbors, Ethiopia', Ph.D. dissertation. Halle (Saale): Martin Luther University Halle-Wittenberg.

LaTosky, S. 2015. 'Lip-Plates, "Harm" Debates, and the Cultural Rights of Mursi (Mun) Women', in C. Longman and T. Bradley (eds), *Interrogating Harmful Cultural Practices: Gender, Culture and Coercion*. London: Ashgate, pp. 169–91.

Max Planck Institute for Social Anthropology. 2017. *Report 2014–2016, Department 'Integration and Conflict'*. Retrieved 31 July 2020 from www.eth.mpg.de/4593872/Report _2016_3_Integration-and-Conflict.pdf.

Naseeven, M.R. n.d. 'Sugarcane Tops as Animal Feed', *FAO Corporate Document Repository*. Retrieved 20 March 2016 from http://www.fao.org/docrep/003/s8850e/S8850E10.htm.

Popp, W.M. 2001. 'Yem, Janjero oder Oromo? Die Konstruktion ethnischer Identität im sozialen Wandel', in A. Horstmann and G. Schlee (eds), *Integration durch Verschiedenheit*. Bielefeld: transcript, pp. 367–404.

Schlee, G. 1994. 'Islam and the Gada System as Conflict-Shaping Forces in Southern Oromia', in H.G. Marcus (ed.), *New Trends in Ethiopian Studies: Papers of the 12th International Conference of Ethiopian Studies, Michigan State University, 5–10 September 1994, Vol. II*. Lawrenceville, NJ: Red Sea Press, pp. 975–97.

———. 2008. *How Enemies Are Made*. Oxford and New York: Berghahn.

———. 2013. 'Why States Still Destroy Pastoralism and How They Can Learn That in Their Own Interest They Should Not', *Nomadic Peoples* 17(2): 6–19.

Schlee, G., and M. Guichard. 2013. 'Fulbe and Uzbeks Compared', in P. Finke and G. Schlee (eds), *CASCA: Centre for Anthropological Studies on Central Asia; Framing the Research, Initial Projects*. Halle (Saale): Max Planck Institute for Social Anthropology, pp. 25–62.

Schlee, G., with Abdullahi Shongolo. 2012a. *Islam and Ethnicity in Northern Kenya and Southern Ethiopia*. Woodbridge: James Currey.

Schlee, G., and Abdullahi Shongolo. 2012b. *Pastoralism and Politics in Northern Kenya and Southern Ethiopia*. Woodbridge: James Currey.

Stanford Encyclopedia of Philosophy. 2006/2017. 'Citizenship'. Retrieved 31 January 2019 from https:///plato.stanford.edu/entries/citizenship/.

Stevenson, E.G.J., and L. Buffavand. 2018. '"Do Our Bodies Know Their Ways?" Villagization, Food Insecurity, and Ill-Being in Ethiopia's Lower Omo Valley', *African Studies Review* 61(1): 109–33.

Taddesse Berisso. 2009. 'Changing Alliances of Guji-Oromo and their Neighbours: State Policies and Local Factors', in G. Schlee and E.E. Watson (eds), *Changing Identifications and Alliances in North-East Africa, Vol. I: Ethiopia and Kenya*. New York and Oxford: Berghahn, pp. 191–99.

Chapter 3

Global Trade, Local Realities

Why African States Undervalue Pastoralism

Peter D. Little

Introduction

The parched rangelands of the Horn of Africa are considered marginal in almost every sense of the term. Their geographies are remote from centres of power, environments are drought prone, main livelihood – pastoralism – is seen as backward, and their ethnic communities are viewed as wards of humanitarian aid and potential threats to governments. These drylands, however, produce a commodity, livestock, and support a trade that is anything but peripheral. They supply live animals and animal products for regional urban and international markets, elevating some of the countries in the region to global leaders in livestock trade. In recent years, more than four million live animals alone have been exported from Somalia (including Somaliland), a state that has been without a formal government for most of the past thirty years (Food Security Analysis Unit-Somalia 2018: 9). This achievement makes it one of the top exporters of live animals in the world, with approximately 50–60 per cent of these exports sourced informally from pastoral areas across international borders (Little 2013; Abdurehman 2014). Currently, annual exports of livestock and livestock products from the Horn of Africa exceed US $1.3 billion, a figure that does not include growing exports to regional markets, such as Addis Ababa and Nairobi (Stem 2016). Livestock trade represents one of the few economic success stories from a region often characterized as marginal and perpetually in political and economic crises (Catley, Lind and Scoones 2013; Abdurehman 2014; Little, Tiki and Debsu 2015). Ironically, this enterprise is undergirded by pastoralist production and informal cross-border trade, both livelihoods that regional governments often disdain.

The large majority of livestock for the region's export trade depends on pastoralism for its supply (Catley 2017). Despite this impressive fact, governments generally remain blinkered to the important economic role of pastoralism, at least in practice if not theory. In those few cases where official discourse acknowledges the contribution of pastoralism to the economy, policies and interventions on the ground usually contradict such positive recognition through appropriation of rangelands either for irrigation schemes, conservation projects, commercial ranching, and/or extractive industries. Pastoral lands are treated as 'vacant', unused, and/or unproductively utilized, in part to justify alternative land uses and investments.

Ethiopia represents a country in the region where the contradiction between a growing livestock trading sector, on the one hand, and policies that underappreciate or, at worse, undermine the production system (pastoralism) that supplies the trade, on the other, is especially apparent. Between 2011 and 2012, Ethiopia exported more than US$ 190 million worth of live animals, which is more than three-fold of what it exported in 2005 (Agricultural Growth Program-Livestock Market Development 2014: 37). The large majority of livestock and meat products (mainly sheep and goat meat) depends almost entirely on the pastoral lowlands for its supplies (Yacob and Catley 2010; Little, Tiki and Debsu 2015; Catley 2017). The government set the almost impossible goal of increasing the volume of meat exports by eleven fold from 2010 to 2015, which it never achieved but is indicative of how much the state perceives livestock as a source of export earnings (Ministry of Finance and Economic Development [MoFED] 2010: 17).

Drawing upon recent anthropological research on livestock trade and traders in southern Ethiopia[1] and a review of different policy papers and reports, this chapter suggests three main reasons for Ethiopia's failure to recognize pastoral economies. These are: (1) pastoralism counters modernist visions of Ethiopia's economy and society; (2) strong political and economic interests dictate the opening of pastoral lands to expropriation and investment, thereby undermining pastoralism and silencing its contributions to the economy; and (3) mobile populations, such as pastoralists, are viewed as political and administrative problems for the Ethiopian state. In short, it will be argued that efforts to undermine pastoralist production by settling them as farmers or agro-pastoralists are as much about politics as they are about economics.

The chapter begins with a discussion of the economic background to livestock trade and pastoralism in the region, with a focus on Ethiopia. It shows how policies and programmes that advocate economic growth and exports fail to recognize that growth in exports of livestock and livestock products are dependent on pastoralism. The chapter then discusses the local impacts of export market promotion on pastoral land use, including the expansion of private and communal enclosures for the benefit of export trade. Here it presents different agreements that traders pursue with pastoralists to reap profits and minimize grazing costs, often with support of local state officials. The chapter concludes with an assessment of some disturbing trends in inequality and poverty in Borana that are amplified by a fixation on export trade.

Economic Realities

Despite its status as the African country with the largest population of cattle, at an estimated 38.5 million head and sizeable populations of goats (9.6 million), sheep (17 million) and camels (1 million) (Ministry of Agriculture and Rural Development 2008: 1), Ethiopia's formal exports of live animals are considerably less than those of neighbouring Sudan and Somalia (including Somaliland). When the late Prime Minister Meles spoke of modernizing livestock-keeping among pastoralists in 2011 at a now famous speech on the country's National Pastoralist Day, he failed to acknowledge that pastoralism already was undergirding the country's livestock export sector (see Meles Zenawi 2011). These lands produce the livestock species Boran cattle and Persian Black head sheep, which are in very high demand in international markets, especially Saudi Arabia. Modern feedlot operations in and around Adama (about 120 km east of Addis Ababa) that hold market animals before they are exported and the abattoirs around Modjo (about 90 km south-east of Addis Ababa) that process meat for export are almost solely dependent on supplies from pastoralist communities.

The Ethiopian government makes it very clear in its planning documents that its ultimate goal is to settle pastoralists, preferably as irrigated farmers or intensive livestock producers. In a key development planning document, the goals for pastoral areas are noted to be 'to develop irrigation schemes and improve pasture land. In addition, settlement programs will be executed in order to enable pastoralists to lead a settled livelihood' (MoFED 2010: 24). It goes on to emphasize that pastoral settlement will be done on a 'voluntary basis' (ibid.), a questionable scenario that this chapter will show is not always practised (see also chapters by Asebe, Buffav and Fana).

There often is a gaping disconnect between foreign donor perceptions about the economic importance of pastoralism and what the Ethiopian government, often with donor funds, is actually doing on the ground. The authors of a recent USAID-sponsored assessment of water in pastoral areas note that:

> The healthy economic performance of the pastoral production system in some of the harshest landscapes in the country attests to its value . . . In Ethiopia, the livestock sector is a significant foreign exchange earner . . . The direct value of pastoralism is estimated to be $1.68 billion per annum

(SOS-Sahel Ethiopia, 2008) – and this does not reflect substantial unofficial trade in livestock and livestock products. (Nassef 2012: vii)

Positive assessments of the economic importance of pastoralism also are revealed in a major report of the African Union (AU) (see AU 2011) and in reports sponsored by other international development agencies, such as the UN Food and Agriculture Organization (FAO) and European Union (EU). The latter two agencies have funded a series of country-based studies that calculate the economic significance of pastoralism for different economies in the region, which in the case of Ethiopia shows that pastoral output (live animals and meats) accounts for approximately 20 per cent of the country's total international exports (Behnke and Fitaweke 2011: 36). In the case of the AU report, it is recommended that African governments invest in pastoral areas 'in a manner that is at least proportional to the economic importance of pastoralism' (AU 2011: 29). The AU report goes on to document that the economic contribution of pastoralism to different African governments is as high as 70 per cent of agricultural Gross Domestic Product (GDP) in livestock-dependent economies, such as Sudan (ibid.: 15).

The economic importance of pastoralism in Ethiopia and elsewhere in the Horn of Africa is even more significant when informal cross-border trade is taken into account. Estimates vary, but most sources show that the number of animals exported informally to neighbouring markets from Ethiopia is more than 4–5 times the official number of exports, which average annually about 200,000 live animals (cattle, sheep, goats and camels) (Yacob and Catley 2010: 21; also see Habtamu et al. 2016: 154). As noted earlier, informal exports of goats and sheep from eastern Ethiopia account for about 50–60 per cent of formal exports from Somaliland. Importantly, this cross-border trade facilitates the significant imports of food stuffs (especially rice, wheat flour and cooking oil) through Somaliland ports to food-deficit areas of eastern Ethiopia. In the case of exports of cattle from southern Ethiopia to Kenya, which are up to 40,000 in some years, virtually all are from informal cross-border trade (Little 2013: 390).

Among the different countries in the Horn of Africa, Ethiopia has been most vocal in its criticism of and its actions against cross-border trade. It has a law that restricts herders from grazing their animals within 15 kilometres of an international border, under the assumption that the animals are destined for illegal export (Habtamu et al. 2016: 167). Although it is not usually enforced, there are cases where animals have been confiscated and the owner arrested. To avoid suspicion, traders will disguise their market animals (mainly males) near borders by mixing them with those of a subsistence herd of mainly female animals.

The Ethiopian government has made minor modifications to its export regulations to allow minimal numbers of animals to be exported informally without the considerable and burdensome costs of taking out a letter of credit from the bank and registering the enterprise with the government (see Solomon et al. 2011). It has established what is called the Periphery Trade Directive. As Habtamu et al. (2016) describe, the regulation is for petty traders and for small amounts of trade (Ethiopian birr 10,000 per month, about $370 per month at 2018 exchange rates). For livestock traders working along the borders, it allows exports without fees and taxes of 'a maximum of 30 goats and sheep or three oxen or three camels' (Habtamu et al. 2016: 166). This volume is minuscule for a business that is measured in the hundreds of thousands of animals, and this probably explains why very few livestock traders have registered under the directive (ibid.).

Several times in my research, I heard border officials complain that cross-border trade by pastoralists was a 'contraband' activity that denies citizens and the federal government needed revenues. However, the consensus in favour of informal trade is not unanimous among merchants. For example, some of the licensed export traders in Ethiopia are against cross-border trade, feeling that they have gone to the trouble to register their businesses and pay additional fees so why should not others. One large export trader with his own feedlot at Adama complained that:

> Contraband trade hurts my business. Sellers can illegally take animals across the border and it hurts my business and the country's economy. We pay additional taxes and fees that contraband traders do not, so we cannot compete on price with contraband traders. (Field notes, March 2013)

In Ethiopia, national narratives about losses in potential foreign exchange earnings, tax evasion, and insecurity counter the realities of cross-border trade. In most cases, some taxes and fees are collected for livestock destined for informal export, with some traders having to pay 2–3 taxes and fees at markets and road checks before the animal(s) crosses the international border. Officials in the borderlands are often the ones who opt to relax or tighten up controls on cross-border trade, often against national regulations that make it almost impossible for traders to export legally. In many of the dryland border areas, such as the Kenya/Ethiopia and Somaliland/Ethiopia borders, administrators and customs officials live with the daily reality that trans-border trade, including trade in livestock, is the main commercial activity that drives the local economy. Previous work has shown the negative impacts on local businesses, consumer prices and food security in border areas when cross-border trade is stopped through punitive actions or a ban due to the outbreak of a livestock disease (see Little 2001, 2010). Because borders are far from capital cities and national bureaucracies, local administrative and state customs officials often work out their own informal arrangements to allow some level of cross-border livestock trade to operate, in order to collect needed revenues.[2] For example, at the border town of Moyale, Ethiopia/Kenya, there emerged by 2013–2014 an implicit understanding between border officials that traders who pay market fees will not be harassed and/or fined or arrested. Border officials even allow traders to openly convert their Ethiopian birr to Kenyan shillings on the street, which is illegal. One government official interviewed claimed he lets the currency exchanges take place because 'there are no banks to exchange currencies in the area'. In reality, the administrator allows it to occur because without the cross-border trade there would be no revenues to finance local government expenditures, including payment of staff salaries (Little et al. 2015).

So why does the Ethiopian government undervalue pastoralism and support actions that undermine it when the livelihood plays such a vital role in local and national economies, including the official export sector? The persistence of biases against pastoralists, especially Somali and Borana, has a very long history in Ethiopia, which I will not attempt to summarize here (see Markakis 2011). However, the goal of transforming pastoralism and pastoralists into so-called modern citizens took on a particular prominence during the late Prime Minister Meles Zenawi's regime (Mosley and Watson 2016). He viewed pastoralism as backward and the antithesis of the rapid modernization and economic transformation of the country that he so energetically pursued. In a speech on the country's national Pastoralist Day in 2011, the late Meles chastised those of us who study pastoralism for perpetuating their underdevelopment. He said 'there will be support for the pastoralists to combine agriculture with modern cattle herding . . . We want our people to have a modern life and we won't allow our people to be a study of ancient living for researchers and scientists' (Meles Zenawi 2011).

One of the major modern development efforts that the government pursued in the Borana area is a massive water development scheme that is to stretch west-to-east through the heart of Borana land for more than 120 kilometres. However, as of 2015 only about 20 kilometres of the water system had been completed. The effective goal of this costly investment is to promote settlement and irrigated agriculture. As Mgalula reports for the Borana area, 'the Ethiopian government has been actively promoting several large scale projects involving water wells and agriculture' (2016: 1). The ambitious water project funded by the government nicely complements the state's goal of modernizing the economy through large-scale infrastructure (Mosley and Watson 2016). Yet, despite its significant presence in Yabello and Dillo Woreda (districts), where we conducted research, it has been very difficult to gather information on the water scheme, and many officials are reluctant to discuss it. From observations, the project is based on a series of massive diesel-driven bore holes that pump water up from deep in the ground and through a series of storage tanks and networks of pipes to transport (gravity fed) the water to designated agricultural settlement areas. In visits to government offices in Yabello town, the capital of Borana Zone, reports about the project were not made available to us. As a result, there were lots of rumours swirling around the water project.

In Didi Hara Kebele, where we collected considerable household data and conducted numerous interviews, many houses had been resettled along the water delivery system, and cultivated fields had expanded. Interviews with herders indicated that most households only moved after considerable 'encouragement' and sanctions from local administration, including restricting access to food aid and emergency fodder until they moved out of seasonal grazing (*foora*) areas. They were advised to cluster their residences in villages and restrict settlement in the main grazing areas. A recent report referred to this spatial pattern as a linear settlement system where there was 'a kebele-level pastoralist settlement pattern along a defined line' (Stark et al. 2017: 38); in the case of Didi Hara, it was along the valley where irrigation was available for farming.[3] Similar to the villagization programmes of the Derg era[4] and those of the earlier Ujamaa experiment in Tanzania, the official rationale for planned settlements in Borana is that it is easier to provide health, education and other services to sedentary rather than mobile populations. The political counterargument is that planned settlement is a government technique for controlling pastoralists and forcing them to settle as farmers, a process that has marked pastoral settlement programmes around the world throughout history (see Salzman 1980; Khazanov 1994). In the limited interviews we were able to have with government officials about settlement and water projects among Borana, it was clear that a key goal of the linear settlement plan is to 'modernize' pastoralism and keep them from 'wandering' with their livestock (Field notes, February 2011). The narrative about 'wandering' from place to place was heard in many of our interviews with government employees and policymakers, especially among those from the Ethiopian highlands. Ironically, the Borana practise a form of pastoralism where the main residence is largely settled and the livestock are mobile and herded in camps usually by young males.

By 2015, the water project had ceased operations, at least temporarily. Rumours for why this happened included the following: the government had run out of cash, the project's engineering was faulty so the pipes were incapable of delivering water, and the project's boreholes were draining the aquifer and water supply was becoming a problem. My sense is that the first reason – lack of funds – was the main factor for the project's demise. It was unknown if the project would be restarted at a later date. As will be discussed in the next section, there are other ways that the government has undermined mobile pastoralism. These include allowing farms to expand in critical grazing areas and 'foot dragging' when asked by herders to restrict the expansion of farms and other types of land enclosures.

Settlements and Enclosures

The effects of increased trade and the state's misdirected policies towards pastoralism during the past 20 years have resulted in different land use changes in Borana. One is increased farming; the other is the expansion of land enclosures (*kaloo*) at community and individual levels (Solomon and Coppock 2004; Ayana and Oba 2008; Boru et al. 2015). I suggest that both of these trends are interrelated and partially stem from the increased commercialization of livestock trade.

To begin, the percentage of Borana who now claim to farm is more than 80 per cent, an increase of more than four-fold since 1990 (Coppock 1994; Ayana and Oba 2008; McPeak and Little 2018). McPeak and Little (2019) show that in many of the areas where farmers have claimed plots, they often are using much of the farm as pasture or simply leaving it fallow rather than cultivating it. In fact, in some of the drier areas of Borana, such as Dillo district, more than 50 per cent of land claimed and fenced off for farming is actually being used for livestock or left fallow. This strategy may reflect a technique to secure land. To quote McPeak and Little:

> under conditions of tenure insecurity the pursuit of farming by [Borana] herders paradoxically can be a strategy to secure access to land, especially when government favours the rights of farmers over those of pastoralists. By enclosing land for crop cultivation even when much of the farm is left uncultivated, provides a more secure claim to the land than open grazing lands, at least in the eyes of the administration. (2019: 1308)

Under contexts of tenure insecurity and a policy environment that favours farming, is it surprising that pastoral households are making claims to land under a pretence of farming? This is a pattern that has occurred elsewhere in East Africa under similar conditions of tenure insecurity (Little 1992; Little et al. 2001; Mwangi 2007; McCabe, Leslie and DeLuca 2010).

The second land use trend mentioned above, expansion of *kaloo* (enclosure), also reflects a mechanism for claiming land. *Kaloo* enclosures only became important in Borana during the 1970s, and only in the past 10–15 years did they become well established, often with encouragement of and funding from international Non-Governmental Organizations (NGOs), which used cash-for-work programmes to clear bush and fence off pastures. Before the 1980s, there were customary enclosures called *seera yabbii*, around 10 hectares, that were set aside for calves and lactating or sick cattle (Napier and Solomon 2011: 3). Their proliferation in some parts of Borana is noteworthy. For example, in Yabello and Dillo Woreda, more than 80 per cent of households have access either to a communal or private enclosure. About 60 per cent of Borana households who had access to a private or communal *kaloo* used them to hold 'market' animals for traders or themselves, and their own subsistence herds (Tiki 2015). The size of individual and communal *kaloo* varies in different areas. Based on data from six different districts in Borana, including Yabello and Dillo, the average size of communal and private *kaloo*, which mainly are owned by herders, is estimated at 61 and 2 hectares, respectively (McPeak and Little 2019: 1312).

There is little question that the recent growth in farming and land enclosures occurred around the same time. An interview with a local Borana herder depicts how closely related the expansion of both have been: 'Private pastures came with farming. Farming and private pastures expanded in the past 10 years. First enclosures are built around a large tract of land and only a small portion of it is used for farming and the rest is used as a private pasture' (Field notes, August 2013).[5] As will be discussed below, *kaloo* provide a convenient source of feed for the herds of traders purchasing animals in Borana.

Interviews with traders who operate in the area indicate frequent payments by them to individuals or groups of pastoralists for use of private or community *kaloo*. By making these transactions, they gain rights to graze their purchased animals before transporting them out of the area. Buyers often lease the pastures for periods from 2–3 weeks up to 3–4 months, where they can fatten their animals at relatively low cost. Traders indicate that they prefer to keep their market animals in the pastoral rangelands during wet seasons to take advantage of abundant grazing and water. Depending on the costs of feed at the time, fattening cattle for export at the feedlots in Adama can be very costly.

In some cases, the herder may also use the *kaloo* to fatten his own animals before selling to an export trader. Many young Borana males now are engaged in livestock trade at lower ends of the market chain, often buying a few animals at a time from herders in seasonal grazing areas and then fattening them on local pastures before selling to a trader. As Little et al. report: 'They move among remote settlements buying animals and responding to orders from large-scale traders. These bush traders are from pastoralist communities and often keep purchased animals for six months or more before selling them, especially if communal pastures are available' (2014: 395). These 'bush' traders, so to speak, have one foot in pastoralism and the other in trading and are critical to the export trade because they access distant areas that others do not.

From the perspective of a local trader who is supplying the export trade, it is important that the individual has access to local grazing to maintain the animals before he can finalize his sale to an export trader. The length of time the trader needs to keep purchased animals in local areas depends on a number of factors, including the exporter's contract with the importer, which stipulates the delivery date for animals, the number of animals being held in the feedlots in Adama and the condition of pasture in the pastoral rangelands. To keep costs down, traders prefer to graze and water animals in the communal areas and/or *kaloo* as long as possible, thereby avoiding the costs of maintaining them in feedlots in Adama.

Traders use other exchange mechanisms and strategies to secure the use of local pastures. In an interview with a trader from the Yabello area, the process of gaining access to local grazing was explained as follows:

> Some traders lease *kaloo* from individuals in exchange for a small number of animals, usually not more than 10. Buying [leasing] grazing rights started during the current government, but there is no law which says

you can sell grazing rights, and people do these things underground . . . They [community] say do not bring traders' animals; you are putting too much pressure on our pasture. But I have a good relationship with the community, so they do not complain much about my animals. For example, I buy a milk cow for a poor household in one community and then entrust about 5 bulls to that household. Then people say he is a good person, he helps poor people, and they do not complain about your cattle. After a year or so you add more animals. (Field notes, August 2013)[6]

There are other cases where traders themselves, often with support from the local administration, are able to access communal grazing lands on their own. In another interview, a Borana herder complained that corruption allows some large-scale traders to gain access to local pastures.

We have cases about the use of pastures, where money is involved. Traders bring goats from Goray [a market near the Ethiopia/Kenya border] and keep them for weeks in our pastures. Cattle traders also do the same, and this destroys our rangelands. In the past three years, the pasture was good and there has not been much complaint, but many people have even gone to the *woreda* and zone to appeal to authorities. For example, big traders like SHD, MLD and JM[7] have big private *kaloo* which they exclusively use for their livestock. People have openly complained about these traders, but they bribe the administration, who suppress the case. These traders stop buying [grazing leases] when there is a long dry season.

Not surprisingly, many Borana herders acknowledge and complain that enclosures are beginning to encroach on communal grazing areas. There are cases where fences around private enclosures have been removed and others where herders have gone to government officials to complain about privately fenced areas (McPeak and Little 2019). Individual herders express different opinions about the value of enclosures, although most find problems with private ones:

If *kaloo* [communal] is divided individually, the land for the pastoralists will be diminished; therefore, there should be no individual *kaloo*. Dividing *kaloo* among individuals may cause conflict. (Field notes, September 2014)

Kaloo is both bad and good. It is bad because enclosures are built everywhere and animals have nowhere to graze. It is good because *kaloo* can be developed through bush clearing. (Field notes, August 2013)[8]

At a meeting in December 2009, Borana customary leadership made it very clear that they were against private enclosures. Boku Tache, a Borana anthropologist from the area, quotes the position of leaders who attended the gathering:

> In our culture, rangeland is the property of the community as a whole and our customary law does not recognize and allow making and holding of private pasture reserves in any forms . . . Having consulted with community representatives from different districts in our Zone, government line departments and NGOs involved in pastoral development here, we hereby issue our directives that as of today December 7, 2009, there will be no private enclosures recognized in any part of our rangeland. Only the calf reserves enclosed for the purpose of supporting the more drought vulnerable herd classes (such as calves and weak cows), through public consensus, for communal utilization by *ardaa* [neighbourhood] and *reera* [large customary grazing unit with generally defined users], are recognized by our customary law. (Boku 2013: 41–42)

In practice, this edict has not been followed by livestock traders and the individuals and communities with whom they work. As noted earlier, traders often take advantage of *kaloo* by arranging to use them through cash or in-kind payments. A few large-scale traders who supply large volumes of cattle to exporters have obtained certificates from district officials, giving them rights to graze lands on communal pastures. Others spoke of negotiations with local officials to establish commercial ranches of several hundred hectares or more. One such trader, an Oromo merchant from the highlands of Ethiopia, spoke of obtaining permission to establish a ranch of more than 100 hectares (ha) in Yabello district. This merchant has an office right on the main street in Yabello town and boasts that more than 50 local traders supply cattle for him. In an interview with the individual in his office, he remarked:

> I have now gotten permission for a private commercial ranch of more than 100 hectares near Yabello town. It took a while to get the land and proposal approved from *woreda* officials. We put together a business plan, and *woreda* officials liked it and approved. We have started clearing the bush and will soon fence the area. (Field notes, August 2014)

When asked about whether or not there was local resentment from the community about fencing of communal pastures, he noted that by hiring workers from the affected community any problems would be avoided.

In contrast to the goal of establishing a commercial ranch, it is more common for a trader to lease ('purchase') grazing rights from individuals or groups of herders. This practice is done, in the words of one herder, 'underground' so that others do not know about any payments. Another pastoralist notes that 'traders often have connections to the administration, and they silence the community by bribing them' (Field notes, August 2014). Similar to what has occurred in neighbouring Somalia and in parts of Kenya, gradual fragmentation of communal lands through grazing enclosures and crop farming is occurring in Borana, and it correlates with a period of increased livestock trade and inequality. That the government is 'silent' when local protests about private enclosures are raised or, at worse, actively promotes them by allowing traders to carve out lands for commercial production confirms the government's position on the merits of pastoralism. In effect, the state wants to see pastoralism transformed into a modern production system based on either Western-style commercial ranching or settled agriculture. Yet, ironically, it is this division of communal rangelands and the associated constraints that it places on livestock mobility and production that threatens the supply of quality livestock, especially the Boran species of cattle on which the export trade depends.

Who Benefits from Export Trade

At a small café in Yabello town in March 2013, a large-scale trader who worked with an exporter/feedlot operator based in Adama bragged that he was 'still eating Enjera [Ethiopian bread] from money he made during the 2011 drought' (Field notes, March 2013). He went into considerable detail about how he was able to buy weak animals at 'throwaway' prices from herders desperate to unload their livestock before they perished. Because of the need to buy food during droughts, due to reduced availability of milk and other herd products, pastoralists are frequently compelled to sell weakened livestock at drought-reduced prices. For Borana and other East African pastoralists, the need to buy food is often the main reason they sell animals, and most traders are aware that this requirement is heightened during droughts (see Little, Tiki and Debsu 2014). In discussing the purchase and transport of cattle during the 2011 drought, the trader informant remarked that 'it was okay if I took 20 cattle and 2 or 3 died in transport to the feedlots at Adama' (Field notes, March 2013). The prices were so low and the potential returns so tempting that the loss of 10–15 per cent of purchased cattle was not perceived as a problem. The trader and his partner with the feedlot in Adama were able to stockpile feed and keep the Boran cattle alive in 2011. When the drought ended, he fattened them and watched the price of cattle soar by as much as three times what he had paid for them. The disaster had reduced supplies of cattle, leaving those traders with animals to sell in the post-drought period with potentially large profits. At one point in our conversation, the merchant stated that 'droughts are good for my business'.

Is this an isolated incident or are droughts generally good for livestock traders who buy from pastoral areas? In interviews with 67 individuals who buy/sell animals in Borana, more than 35 per cent of them noted that they benefit when droughts occur. The key factor is whether or not the individual has access to fodder and feed to maintain the animals. If they do, it means they own or have access to feedlots or enclosures with stored fodder. If they do not, a trader may confront the same problems of finding sufficient pasture and water to keep their animals alive as a herder does.

Yacob and Catley (2010) have shown how increased exports of livestock from Ethiopia and Somalia mainly have benefitted large-scale traders and producers, and thus widened the wealth gap between them and small-scale traders and pastoralists. The result is increased inequality and heightened vulnerability during droughts and other shocks for many traders and herders. Other research, including the recent CHAINS study (Little, Tiki and Debsu 2014, 2015), confirms that this is the case for the overseas export trade but less so for the informal cross-border trade discussed earlier (Little 2009, 2013). In this market, entry costs to participation are considerably less than for the overseas export trade, and because of its informal nature many small-scale traders and herders are involved. The overseas trade is highly selective in demanding bulls in the 4–7 years range and sheep and goats often between 18–24 months in age and weights of 18–24 kilogram depending on the specific market. In contrast, the informal cross-border trade to Kenya includes female animals as well as older animals destined for slaughter in Nairobi. A pastoralist without large numbers of cattle can participate in the cross-border trade but is unlikely to be able to supply many bulls for the overseas trade. While the major actors in the overseas export commerce buy and sell in the thousands of live animals, the cross-border trader usually operates in the range of 100–150 cattle per year (Little 2009, 2013).

Many herders are aware that most of the benefits in the export business accrue to traders and feedlot operators. It is estimated that herders receive only 45–50 per cent of the final sale price of an export bull in normal years but considerably less during droughts (Little, Tiki and Debsu 2014: 392). The remarks of one Borana herder who participates in the trade are informative: 'it is the sale of our Boran cattle that is responsible for the tall, new buildings in Adama, but we are not benefitting much' (Field notes, May 2012). The comment poetically makes the point that revenues from sales of Boran cattle allow Adama's traders and feedlot operators to invest in the town's growing real estate sector.

Discussion and Conclusion

This chapter has suggested that the ongoing fragmentation of the Borana landscape into farms and enclosures has moved in parallel with the growth in export trade and policies that favour cultivation. Wealthy, large-scale traders can make deals with communities to use their grazing rights or, in some cases, make deals with the local administration to gain large parcels of land for what is effectively commercial ranching. Herders, in turn, increasingly pursue cultivation both to produce food for their households as well as make claims to land in an environment of tenure insecurity. The chapter has highlighted a range of strategies that traders employ to gain access to local grazing, which they can use to avoid the costs of fattening animals at feedlots.

Informal cross-border trade is targeted and criminalized as contraband by the Ethiopian state, although it provides significant benefits for herders – through high prices and reduced market selectivity – and for small-scale traders, through minimal costs of entry. As the chapter demonstrates, a visible policy paradox is that certain export-oriented enterprises such as abattoirs depend on informality to profitably operate in the region. Moreover, because local administrations in the borderlands need the revenues, they also confront a contradictory juncture – to follow federal policies or adjust to local realities. Cross-border trade continues to exist because both traders and local governments are earning needed revenues from it and because the costs of policing it are too high and logistically troublesome to pursue. Thus, the common argument that cross-border trade in Ethiopia 'erodes government revenues . . . millions of dollars are lost in unpaid customs duties and value-added tax (VAT)' (Habtamu et al. 2016: 157) presents only one side of the story. Indeed, the evidence in this chapter suggests that the issue of lost public revenues through informal exports depends on the level of government that is considered. In the case of borderland administrations, they benefit from informal cross-border trade to the extent that disputes between government entities can occur over jurisdiction and rights to revenues from livestock trade.

Once again, the recent drought of 2016–2017 devastated livestock herds of south-eastern and southern Ethiopia, including Borana communities. The region is said to have lost an estimated 1.5 million livestock with the approximate value of US$350 million between November 2016 and April 2017 (Food and Agriculture Organization 2017: 1). While I do not have trader interview data from 2017–2018, it is suspected that large-scale traders with access to feed and fodder are likely to have benefitted from this recent disaster. The land use changes, especially the expansion of private farms and enclosures, which have been described in this chapter, constrain the main production technique, mobility, which herders use to cope with shocks like droughts. And studies from the region show that pastoralists who are more mobile fare better during droughts in terms of fewer livestock losses than those with less mobility (see McPeak, Little and Doss 2012). However, the state paradoxically continues to undermine pastoralist mobility, production and land rights even while emphasizing activities such as livestock and meat exports that are highly dependent on pastoralism. As the chapter has argued, the political goals of sedentarizing mobile herders and integrating them into a 'modern' economy override economic considerations, and that is the conundrum the future of pastoralism in Ethiopia confronts.

Peter D. Little is the Samuel Candler Dobbs Professor of Anthropology and Director of the Global Development Studies Program, Emory University, United States. He has conducted studies of political ecology, pastoralism, poverty and inequality, informality, development, and statelessness in Kenya, Somalia and Ethiopia. Currently, he is engaged in a comparative study of 'Changing Perceptions of Poverty and Well-being in Baringo County, Kenya and South Wollo, Ethiopia'.

Notes

I would like to thank Waktole Tiki and Dejene Negassa Debsu, who helped with many of the interviews and collection of data that are included in this chapter. The late Workneh Negatu, who will be sorely missed, played an important role in helping to administer and co-direct the Climate-Induced Vulnerability and Pastoralist Livestock Marketing Chains in Southern Ethiopia and Northeastern Kenya (CHAINS) Project and to navigate the bureaucratic channels of the collaborating institution, Addis Ababa University. I also would like to thank my colleagues at Emory University, Uriel Kitron and Carla Roncoli, and my long-time collaborator at Syracuse University, John McPeak, who over the years have provided valuable feedback on many of the ideas presented in the chapter. Finally, I acknowledge the funding support of the Innovation Lab for Adapting Livestock Systems to Climate Change Collaborative Research Program (USAID Grant No. EEM-A-00-10-00001), which at the time of the CHAINS project was administered by Colorado State University. The opinions expressed herein are those of the author and do not necessarily reflect the views of the above individuals and institutions, including the U.S. Agency for International Development (USAID).

1. Some of the information in this chapter was collected between 2012–2015 under the Climate-Induced Vulnerability and Pastoralist Livestock Marketing Chains in Southern Ethiopia and Northeastern Kenya (CHAINS) Project. It involved interviews with 67 livestock traders and annual data collection from 140 Borana households from Dikale (Yabello Woreda/district) and Quancharo (Dillo Woreda/district) communities. The author served as the Principal Investigator (PI) of the project and worked closely with Waktole Tiki and Dejene Negassa Debsu, who coordinated most of the interviews and household data collection. They were postdoctoral researchers on the CHAINS project at the time.
2. Other studies of cross-border trade in Africa show how border officials often modify official rules and norms in light of the realities on the ground (Titeca and De Herdt 2010; Van den Boogaard, Prichard and Jibao 2018). This practice demonstrates a case of what Olivier de Sardan refers to as 'practical norms' (Van den Boogaard, Prichard and Jibao 2018), whereby 'a particularly significant discrepancy exists between the official norms of the state and the public services on the one hand, and the behaviour of political elites and officials on the other' (Olivier de Sardan 2008: 1).
3. *Kebele* is a local administrative unit that corresponds to a small set of villages (often 4–5).
4. Refers to the militaristic socialist period of 1974–1991 under former soldier Mengistu Hailemariam. He ruled the country with a strong hand and often brutal tactics, especially near the end of his regime.
5. Interviews were conducted and translated by Dejene Negassa Debsu and Waktole Tiki.
6. Interviews were conducted and translated by Dejene Negassa Debsu and Waktole Tiki.
7. Pseudonyms using random initials were employed to protect the identity of individuals.
8. Interview was conducted and translated by Dejene Negassa Debsu.

References

Abdurehman Eid. 2014. 'Jostling for Trade: The Politics of Livestock Marketing on the Ethiopia-Somaliland Border', Working Paper 075. Future Agricultures Project, Institute of Development Studies, Sussex.

Agricultural Growth Program-Livestock Market Development. 2014. *End Market Analysis for Meat/Live Animals, Leather and Leather Products, Dairy Products Value Chains: Expanding Livestock Markets for the Small-Holder Producers*. Addis Ababa: USAID.

AU (African Union). 2011. *Pastoral Policy Framework in Africa: Securing, Protecting and Improving the Lives, Livelihoods and Rights of Pastoralist Communities*. Addis Ababa: AU.

Ayana Angassa, and G. Oba. 2008. 'Herder Perceptions on Impacts of Range Enclosures, Crop Farming, Fire Ban and Bush Encroachment on the Rangelands of Borana, Southern Ethiopia', *Human Ecology* 36(2): 201–15.

Behnke, R., and Fitaweke Metaferia. 2011. 'The Contribution of Livestock to the Ethiopian Economy – Part II', IGAD LPI Working Paper No. 02–11. Addis Ababa, Ethiopia: Intergovernmental Agency for Drought (IGAD)/UN Food Agriculture and Organization (FA)/European Union (EU).

Boku Tache. 2013. 'Rangeland Enclosures in Southern Oromia, Ethiopia: An Innovative Response or the Erosion of Common Property Resources?', in A. Catley, J. Lind and I. Scoones (eds), *Pastoralism and Development in Africa: Dynamic Change at the Margins*. Abingdon: Routledge, pp. 37–46.

Boru, D. et al. 2015. 'Effects of Family Size and Wealth on Size of Land Cultivated by Borana Pastoralists in Southern Ethiopia', *Human Ecology* 43: 15–28.

Catley, A. 2017. *Pathways to Resilience in Pastoralist Areas: A Synthesis of Research in the Horn of Africa*. Boston: Feinstein International Center, Tufts University.

Catley, A., J. Lind, and I. Scoones (eds). 2013. *Development at the Margins: Pathways of Change in the Horn of Africa*. London: Routledge.

Coppock, D.L. 1994. *The Borana Plateau of Southern Ethiopia: Synthesis of Pastoral Research, Development, and Change, 1980–91*. Addis Ababa: International Livestock Centre for Africa.

Food and Agriculture Organization (FAO). 2017. *Ethiopia: Drought Response Plan and Priorities in 2017*. Rome: FAO.

Food Security Analysis Unit (FSAU)-Somalia. 2018. *January Market Update*. Nairobi: FSAU-Somalia.

Habtamu Hailemeskel et al. 2016. 'Policy Research on Cross-Border Trade: Challenges and Prospects', in Mulugeta Getu, Tesfaheywet Zeryehun, Kibebew Kibret, Kassahun Mamo and Habtamu Hailemeskel (eds), *Proceedings of Research for Enhancing Pastoralists Livelihood through Resilience and Market Expansion Meeting*. Dire Dawa, Ethiopia: Haramaya University, pp. 151–72.

Khazanov, A. 1994. *Nomads and the Outside World*. Madison: University of Wisconsin Press.

Little, P.D. 1992. *The Elusive Granary: Herder, Farmer and State in Northern Kenya*. Cambridge: Cambridge University Press.

———. 2001. 'The Global Dimensions of Cross-Border Trade in the Somalia Borderlands', in Abdel Ghaffar M. Ahmed (ed.), *Globalisation, Democracy, and Development in Africa: Future Prospects*. Addis Ababa, Ethiopia: Organization for Social Science Research in Eastern and Southern Africa (OSSREA), pp. 179–200.

———. 2009. *Hidden Value on the Hoof: Cross-Border livestock Trade in Eastern Africa*. Policy Brief Number 2, Common Market for Eastern and Southern Africa (COMESA) and

Pastoral Areas Coordination, Analysis and Policy Support (PACAPS) Program, Tufts University, Medford, MA.

———. 2010. 'Unofficial Cross-Border Trade in Eastern Africa', in A. Sarris, T. Jayne and J. Morrison (eds), *Food Security in Africa: Market and Trade Policy for Staple Foods in Eastern and Southern Africa*. Cheltenham: Edwin Elgar Publishing, pp. 158–81.

———. 2013. 'Unofficial Trade When States are Weak: The Case of Cross-Border Livestock Trade in the Horn of Africa', in M. Bollig, J. Pauli and Hans-Peter Wotzka (eds), *African Pastoralism: Past, Present and Future – The Emergence, History and Contemporary Political Ecology of African Pastoralism*. New York and Oxford: Berghahn, pp. 387–410.

Little, P.D., W. Tiki and D.N. Debsu. 2014. 'How Pastoralists Perceive and Respond to Market Opportunities: The Case of the Horn of Africa', *Food Policy* 49: 389–97.

———. 2015. 'Formal or Informal, Legal or Illegal: Cross-Border Livestock Trade in the Horn of Africa', *Journal of Borderlands Studies* 30(1): 405–21.

Little, P.D., et al. 2001. 'Avoiding Disaster: Diversification and Risk Management among East African Herders', *Development and Change* 32(3): 401–33.

Markakis, J. 2011. *Ethiopia: The Last Two Frontiers*. Woodbridge and Rochester: James Currey.

McCabe, J.T., P. Leslie and L. DeLuca. 2010. 'Adopting Cultivation to Remain Pastoralists: The Diversification of Pastoral Livelihoods in Northern Tanzania', *Human Ecology* 38(3): 321–34.

McPeak, J., and P.D. Little. 2018. 'Mobile Peoples, Contested Borders: Land Use Conflicts and Resolution Mechanisms among Borana and Guji Communities, Southern Ethiopia', *World Development* 103: 119–32.

———. 2019. 'Land Use and Tenure Insecurity in the Drylands of Southern Ethiopia', *Journal of Development Studies* 55(6): 1307–24.

McPeak, J., P.D. Little and C. Doss. 2012. *Risk and Social Change in an African Rural Economy*. New York: Routledge.

Meles Zenawi. 2011. '13th Ethiopian Pastoralist Day Speech', 25 January. Retrieved 2 February 2018 from http://coolground.org/wp-content/uploads/2013/10/Meles-Zenawi-13th-Ethiopian-Pastoralist-Day-Speech-25-1-2011.pdf.

Mgalula, M. 2016. *Assessing Trends in Land Use Change in the Borana Rangeland Ethiopia as One Cause of Greenhouse Gas Emissions and Carbon Sequestration Variations*. Witzenhausen: Deutsches Institut für Tropische und Subtropische Landwirtschaft.

Mosley, J., and E. Watson. 2016. 'Frontier Transformations: Development Visions, Spaces and Processes in Northern Kenya and Southern Ethiopia', *Journal of Eastern African Studies* 10(3): 452–75.

Ministry of Agriculture and Rural Development (MoARD). 2008. *National Guidelines for Livestock Relief Interventions in Pastoralist Areas of Ethiopia*. Addis Ababa: MoARD.

Ministry of Finance and Economic Development (MoFED). 2010. *Growth and Transformation Plan (GTP), 2010/11–2014/15*. Addis Ababa: MoFED.

Mwangi, E. 2007. 'Subdividing the Commons: Distributional Conflict in the Transition from Collective to Individual Property Rights in Kenya's Maasailand', *World Development* 35: 815–34.

Napier, A., and Solomon Desta. 2011. *Review of Pastoral Rangeland Enclosures*, PLI Policy Project. Addis Ababa: Tufts University, Feinstein International Center.

Nassef, M., with Mulugeta Belayhun. 2012. *Water Development in Ethiopia's Pastoral Areas: A Synthesis of Existing Knowledge and Experience*. Addis Ababa: Save the Children-USA.

Olivier de Sardan, J.-P. 2008. 'Researching the Practical Norms of Real Governance in Africa', Discussion Paper No. 5. London: Overseas Development Institute.

Salzman, P. 1980. *When Nomads Settle: Processes of Sedentarization as Adaptation and Response*. New York: Praeger.

Solomon Desta, and D.L. Coppock. 2004. 'Pastoralism under Pressure: Tracking System Change in Southern Ethiopia', *Human Ecology* 32(4): 465–86.

Solomon Desta et al. 2011. *Assessment of Cross Border Informal Livestock Trade in Somali Region*. Addis Ababa: Food and Agriculture Organization.

SOS Sahel Ethiopia. 2008. *Pastoralism in Ethiopia: Its Total Economic Values and Development Challenges*. Addis Ababa: SOS Sahel.

Stark, J., K. Terasawa and Chalachew Niguse Agonafir. 2017. *Lessons Learned From The Peace Centers For Climate And Social Resilience: An Assessment In Borana Zone, Oromia National Regional State, Ethiopia*. Washington, DC: Chemonics, Inc.

Stem, C. 2016. 'Horn of Africa Livestock Export Trade: A Business at a Crossroads', *East Africa Business Journal*, 5 September. Retrieved 3 April 2018 from http://www.eabjournal.com/en/agriculture-east-africa-business-journal/584-horn-of-africa-livestock-export-trade-a-business-at-a-crossroads.html.

Tiki, W. 2015. *Livestock Marketing in the Horn of Africa: Shocks and Adaptations, a Summary Report*. Atlanta: CHAINS Project, Emory University.

Titeca, K., and T. de Herdt. 2010. 'Regulation, Cross-Border Trade and Practical Norms in West Nile, North-Western Uganda', *Africa* 80(4): 573–94.

Van den Boogaard, V., W. Prichard and S. Jibao. 2018. 'Norms, Networks, Power and Control: Understanding Informal Payments and Brokerage in Cross-Border Trade in Sierra Leone', *Journal of Borderlands Studies*, DOI: 10.1080/08865655.2018.1510333.

Yacob Aklilu, and A. Catley. 2010. *Livestock Exports from the Horn of Africa: An Analysis of Benefits by Pastoralist Wealth Group and Policy Implications*. Boston: Feinstein International Center, Tufts University.

Part II

Contested Identities and Territories

A History of Expropriation

Chapter 4

Modes of Dispossession of Indigenous Lands and Territories in Africa

Elifuraha I. Laltaika and Kelly M. Askew

Background and Context

Peoples from across the globe pursuing ways of life deemed 'traditional' or 'backward' by others have mobilized information, networks and strategies to create a global indigenous peoples' movement. Its origins can be traced to the early twentieth century, when leaders of indigenous communities began drawing international attention to the illegal seizure of their lands. In 1923, Chief Deskaheh of the Iroquois League (comprising Mohawk, Onandaga, Oneida, Cayuga, Seneca and Tuscarora peoples of Canada and north-eastern USA) travelled to Geneva in an attempt to address the League of Nations but was refused access. In 1924, Maori Chief Ratana of New Zealand travelled first to England then to Geneva to deliver a petition on land confiscations to King George V and the League of Nations and similarly was denied access. Both sought international support for their rights to live on their lands and pursue their customary livelihoods (Fontaine 2010). Though unsuccessful, their efforts did not pass unnoticed and inspired future generations to forge networks and alliances of indigenous peoples across national and ethnic lines. Following increased pressure from indigenous peoples, the Commission on Human Rights within the United Nations commissioned in 1971 a 'Study on the Problems of Discrimination against Indigenous Populations'. Finally released in 1984 as the Cobo Report,[1] it documented in painstaking detail the widespread oppression faced by indigenous peoples around the world and made recommendations on how to address it, including creating a body within the UN dedicated to protecting the rights of indigenous peoples.

The first successful appearance of indigenous peoples at the UN was a 1977 delegation of 250 people representing First Nations from Canada and the USA that demanded legal recognition of their treaties. In the 1980s, the indigenous peoples' movement expanded to include Aboriginal communities from Australia, Maori from New Zealand, and Inuit and Sámi from the Arctic regions. Over time, it grew to encompass an ever-widening collective of peoples from South America, the Pacific, South Asia, Southeast Asia, Eastern Europe, and eventually Africa (Deer 2010; Dahl 2012, 2013; Lightfoot 2016). 'Indigenous peoples' are recognized within the movement as having the following characteristics: they (1) seek to maintain a distinctive way of life (self-identification); (2) are viewed by other – typically majority – populations as being culturally different (external identification); (3) are affiliated with an ancestral homeland that they may or may no longer occupy; and (4) face political, social and/or economic marginalization in their nation-states.[2]

A contentious (and ongoing) debate about the term 'indigenous' exists. Some scholars vehemently reject the term 'indigenous' on the grounds that it resurrects colonial-era categorizations of certain peoples as inferior and primitive, or fulfils early anthropological depictions of 'natives' as static, traditionalist and essentially anti-modern (see, for instance, Kuper 2003a, 2003b, 2004; with responses from Kenrick and Lewis 2004 and Barnard 2006). Another strain of debate concerns whether or not the term is applicable in Africa because with the exceptions of South Africa, Namibia, Kenya, Angola and Algeria one cannot speak about white settler colonialism as a driver of marginalization of indigenous groups.[3] In this chapter, we follow usage of the term in African social justice circles, and specifically by the African Commission on Human and Peoples' Rights (ACHPR), the intergovernmental institution charged with promoting and protecting human rights in the continent. The ACHPR uses 'indigenous' to refer to marginalized groups pursuing specific livelihood strategies: 'The application of the term Indigenous Peoples . . . has today become a much wider internationally recognized term by which to understand and analyse certain forms of inequalities and suppression such as the ones suffered by many pastoralists and hunter-gatherer groups and others in Africa today' (ACHPR/IWGIA 2005: 86–87; and 2006).

It is this inequality and the active, often violent, discrimination exercised against them that facilitated the embrace of 'indigenous' identity among some African communities by connecting them and their experiences to other similarly positioned groups nationally and globally (Hodgson 2011). As has been noted in other contexts, 'Conditions can be identified under which it is advantageous for individual and collective actors to define wider identities which they share with others, for example to strengthen their own group or to widen their alliances when they feel insecure' (Schlee 2009: 1).

At the 2018 UN Permanent Forum on Indigenous Issues (UNPFII), the UN General Assembly President, Miroslav Lajčák, announced that indigenous peoples constitute 5 per cent of the world's population (an estimated 370 million) but 15 per cent of the world's poor, underlining the discrimination and disenfranchisement they meet across the globe. The ACHPR recognizes the existence of multiple indigenous peoples in Africa, including pastoralists (e.g. Maasai, Barabaig, Karamojong, Samburu, Turkana, Afar, Borana, Pokot, Tuareg, Wodaabe and Fulani), agro-pastoralists (Sukuma, Mursi/Mun, Anywaa) and hunter-gatherers (e.g. Batwa, Hadzabe, Ogiek and San) to name but a few (see Kipuri 2017 for an overview). In order to pursue their legally protected ways of life per the 2007 UN Declaration on the Rights of Indigenous Peoples (UNDRIP), these communities require access to the land and water resources of their ancestral territories. Yet while no African state voted against the UNDRIP when the UN General Assembly adopted it in 2007,[4] African states unilaterally insist that it does not apply to them for lack of indigenous populations, claiming that all Africans are equally indigenous.

The ACHPR identified multiple threats to indigenous lands, resources and livelihoods in Africa, foremost among them being powerful transnational corporations and conservation organizations – both typically aligned with political and economic elites:

> Dispossession of land and natural resources is a major human rights problem for indigenous peoples. They have in so many cases been pushed out of their traditional areas to give way for the economic interests of other more dominant groups and to large scale development initiatives that tend to destroy their lives and cultures rather than improve their situation. Establishment of protected areas and national parks have impoverished indigenous pastoralist and hunter-gatherer communities, made them vulnerable and unable to cope with environmental uncertainty and in many cases even displaced them. Large-scale extraction of natural resources such as logging, mining, dam construction, oil drilling and pipeline construction have had very negative impacts on the livelihoods of indigenous pastoralist and hunter-gatherer communities in Africa. So has the widespread expansion of areas under crop production. They have all resulted in loss of access to fundamental natural resources that are critical for the survival of both pastoral and hunter-gatherer communities such as grazing areas, permanent water sources and forest products. This is a serious violation of the African Charter (*Article 21,1* and *21,2*) which states clearly that every peoples [*sic*] have the right to natural resources, wealth and property . . . the right to existence (*Article 20,1*) . . . [and] the right to their economic, social and cultural development with due regard to their freedom and identity and in the equal enjoyment of the common heritage of mankind. (ACHPR/IWGIA 2005: 20–21)

Two decades later, the situation for indigenous African peoples continues to worsen, with an upsurge in violence, illegal evictions and human rights violations accompanying increased appropriation of their traditional lands, water and other natural resources (Barume 2010; Laher and Sing'Oei 2012; Pulitano 2012; Whitmore 2012; Stamatopoulou 2017; Mittal and Fraser 2018). While 'landgrabbing' in the Global South by *agribusiness interests* (see Hall, Scoones and Tsikata 2015) has attracted media attention, indigenous peoples in Africa suffer widespread dispossession of their land and resources from other drivers, including: (ii) *conservation* initiatives, (iii) *extractive industries*, (iv) *large-scale infrastructure* projects, and (v) increased *competition with cultivators* over ever-shrinking land resources. A sixth mode of dispossession stems from the (vi) *increasing numbers of internally displaced persons (IDPs) and refugees* across the continent. This affects indigenous communities in two ways: first, when indigenous peoples are evicted from their lands and meet rejection, violence and abuse in their search for new places to call home, and secondly, when their territories suffer an influx of IDPs or refugees fleeing conflict elsewhere.

In this chapter, we describe and analyse these six modes of land loss with cases from across the continent. We draw attention to the variegated nature of land and resource dispossession affecting indigenous communities, which has been effaced in the singular focus on large-scale agriculture. In an earlier paper, Laltaika called for the establishment of a robust oversight body to bolster the implementation of the UN Declaration (Laltaika 2015) and address increasing threats to indigenous land rights, livelihoods and existence. The need for such oversight and collaboration in the face of the above identified trends has never been more acute and urgent.

Agribusiness: The Most Prominent Mode of Dispossession

Indigenous peoples' land dispossession resulting from agribusiness in Africa has a long history. A well-documented example is the Tanzanian case of *National Agricultural and Food Corporation v. Mulbadau Village Council*, in which Barabaig pastoralists were evicted from 100,000 acres of ancestral pastureland in Hanang District in 1970 to launch the large-scale Tanzania Canada Wheat Program. Commenting on the court's remedy, Tenga et al. indicate that pastoralists lost because they 'failed to show legal allocation of land from prior land authorities' and 'failed to show the Court that they are natives of Tanzania! (Despite the public fact that Barabaig Pastoralists are found nowhere else on Earth, and in Court some had to get a translator!)' (2008: 55–56). Five decades have passed since eviction from their ancestral land, yet Barabaig communities are yet to recover from the negative after-effects, including landlessness, poverty and bloody conflicts between them and crop growers in areas to which they were forced to relocate because there was no court mandated restitution or allocation of alternative lands (Lane 1994, 1995, 2018; King 2013).

Although the reason for the eviction was business-related, based on the government's desire to cultivate wheat for sale in the face of an acute food shortage that was then prevailing, the eviction epitomizes earlier forms of land dispossession in which the government acquired community land for 'public interest', with the aim of implementing ostensibly broader national objectives (as opposed to leasing it to a private investor). This is partly because Tanzania was practising a policy of 'Socialism and Self-Reliance', on the basis of which it nationalized foreign-owned private properties, hence becoming unattractive to Foreign Direct Investment (FDI) (see Ebenroth and Peter 1996). Instead, the country designated government corporations to conduct business. However, following the 1985 shift to a neoliberal development policy that entailed reducing state involvement in the market (Ngugi 2005), a new wave of dispossession of indigenous lands emerged: the government placed community land under the control of private business corporations in the guise of FDI, resulting in direct encounters between communities and transnational corporations. The Southern Agricultural Growth Corridor of Tanzania (SAGCOT) is a case in point.

SAGCOT

Covering approximately one third of mainland Tanzania's total land area, including Morogoro, Iringa, Mbeya, Ruvuma, Lindi and Mtwara regions, SAGCOT links the Dar es Salaam port to Malawi, Zambia and the Democratic Republic of Congo. Introduced at the World Economic Forum for Africa held in Dar es Salaam in 2010, it is part of the broader UN General Assembly's 2008 proposal for the 'African Agricultural Growth Corridor' initiative (Paul and Steinbrecher 2013). Yara, a Norwegian fertilizer company, is credited with inventing and championing the idea of African Agricultural Growth Corridors, securing the support of major international development actors, including the World Bank and the Food and Agriculture Organization (FAO). Domestically, SAGCOT aligned well with the Tanzanian government's goals of instituting a smooth policy environment to attract foreign investment and boosting the country's agricultural sector. According to the SAGCOT Investment Blueprint (2011), the aim was to invest $ 2.1 billion over a twenty-year period for the purpose of tripling the area's agricultural input.

Impacts of SAGCOT on Indigenous Peoples

The distinctive lifestyles of indigenous peoples, and their incompatibility with proposals put forward for SAGCOT implementation, starkly reveal that indigenous peoples become losers in the land deals even during the mere planning stage of SAGCOT initiatives. As non-cultivators, indigenous pastoralists and hunter-gatherers are seen as unworthy of collaborating with the proposed investors by, for example, becoming contracted outgrowers. With the emphasis on the large-scale cultivation of crops like rice and sugar cane in SAGCOT-designated areas, indigenous livelihoods and land use gets further devalued.

It is along these lines that, while acknowledging that pastoralism is better suited to local conditions if left uninterrupted by outside forces, Paul and Steinbrecher warn that pressure on pastoralism due to misconceptions about it will increase. The authors summarize thus: 'Current patterns of land use often completely misunderstood may cease to be applicable across wide areas. This would threaten to eliminate the livelihoods of communities that would not want to collaborate with this externally imposed re-ordering' (2013: 10). More importantly, characterization of potential investment areas as constituting lands that are 'empty', 'underused', 'idle' or 'degraded' makes it evident that the idea behind African Agricultural Growth Corridor from the inception perpetuates common narratives that have been used repeatedly to dispossess indigenous peoples of their ancestral land. Accordingly, pastoralists and hunter-gatherers who use land sparingly have grounds for worrying about SACGOT implementation.

This has been borne out already in the case of the US$35 million Kilombero Plantation Ltd. (KPL) rice cultivation initiative within the SAGCOT area. Launched in 2010 as a public-private partnership between the Rufiji Basin Development Authority and Agrica, a UK-based agricultural investment company, it encompasses 5,818 hectares and has been the site of large-scale evictions of both pastoralists and small-scale farmers (Maganga et al. 2016). Another SAGCOT venture, the US$500 million Bagamoyo EcoEnergy (BEE) biofuel (sugar cane) project, involving a Swedish company Agro EcoEnergy and the Tanzanian government, has also seen widespread evictions. Spanning 24,000 hectares of a failed state-owned cattle ranch, the site is home to pastoralists, many of whom are Barabaig who were previously evicted in the 1970s from their homeland of Mount Hanang for the Canadian-Tanzanian wheat-growing scheme. While BEE acknowledges that people who have been utilizing the land since the closure of the RUZABA ranch in 1994 will have to be involuntarily resettled and admits to Barabaig and other pastoralists being among them, they insist that many of these people are 'invaders' because the land remained state-managed general land and they are thus not entitled to compensation. Moreover, BEE project documents state that 'The "*involuntary*" resettlement process, occurs all over the world and the choice is never "*whether they resettle or not*," but their active participation in "how" they resettle'; and furthermore that '"Involuntary" Land Acquisition is a global reality, not pertaining to Africa, Tanzania or the BEE project alone!' (Bagamoyo EcoEnergy 2015).

Conservation: The Second, and Most Widespread, Mode of Dispossession

While agribusiness has received the bulk of media attention in reports on land-grabbing in Africa and the Global South more generally, conservation goes

Table 4.1. Terrestrial areas protected to total surface area, percentage, United Republic of Tanzania.

Year	Terrestrial areas protected to total surface area, percentage	Source
1990	27.01 %	UNdata.org
2000	28.29 %	UNdata.org
2014	32.02 %	UNdata.org
2014	40 %	5th National Report on the Implementation of the Convention on Biological Diversity (United Republic of Tanzania (URT) 2014)

unrecognized as likely the greatest source of land alienation in the territories of indigenous peoples. Indigenous peoples are widely praised for their stewardship of land, water and natural resources such as forests and wildlife. The Global North seeks more forest cover for climate change mitigation and carbon emissions off-set, and pristine landscapes and exotic fauna for tourism and trophy hunting. It cannot produce these in its own territories, because of well-protected property rights and greatly reduced wildlife diversity. Hence, undue pressure arises on the Global South to compensate with their land and natural resources.

So, for instance, while the 1992 Convention on Biological Diversity proposed a target of 10 per cent of every biome to be protected, this 'targeted approach' has expanded in interpretation to be 10 per cent of every country's surface area (Mogelgaard 2006). Yet huge inequalities exist in attainment of this goal. In Tanzania, a country with significant indigenous populations – namely, Maasai and Barabaig pastoralists, Sukuma agro-pastoralists, and Hadzabe and Akiye hunter-gatherers – the amount of territory under protected status greatly exceeds this target (Table 4.1.).

Tanzania, moreover, was one of three countries highlighted in a December 2016 United Nations Environment Programme (UNEP) report documenting substantial increase in protected land within a six-month period of April–December 2016. If one adds the UNEP identified increase of an additional 6.3 per cent of Tanzania's total territory to the 2014 government figures, and assuming no additional increases between 2014 and April 2016, this means that no less than 46 per cent – *nearly half* – of the entire country is under protected status with restrictions on human activities.

Similar patterns of escalating amounts of land being relegated to conservation purposes can be identified in other nations of Africa, South America and the Pacific that have significant populations of indigenous peoples and for which UN data exists (Table 4.2.).

Table 4.2. Terrestrial areas protected to total surface area, percentage, in developing countries with significant indigenous populations.

Country	% land protected (1990)	% land protected (2000)	% land protected (2014)	Indigenous Communities (select)
New Caledonia	6.06	6.78	54.25	Kanak
Venezuela	39.98	53.82	53.86	Manapiare, Autana, Yanomami
French Guiana	0.00	5.55	52.46	Lokono, Téleuyu, Pahikweneh, Teko
Greenland	40.84	40.84	41.16	Inuit
Namibia	11.61	14.87	37.86	San, Nama, Ovahimba, Ovazemba
Nicaragua	15.42	36.73	37.11	Chorotega, Cacaopera, Ocanxiu, Náhuati
Belize	26.04	35.20	36.66	Mayan
Congo	1.68	5.25	35.24	Bakola, Batwa, Babongo, Baaka, Mikayas
New Zealand	24.66	28.45	32.53	Maori
Tanzania	27.01	28.29	32.02	Maasai, Barabaig, Hadzabe, Akiye
Guatemala	25.93	29.50	31.77	Achi', Akateco, Chalchiteco, Ch'orti, Chuj
Peru	4.78	7.35	31.44	Quechua, Aymara, Asháninka
Botswana	17.90	29.13	29.15	San, Balala, Nama
Brazil	6.69	14.15	28.44	Yanomani, Terena, Waorani, Xavante, Kayapo
Costa Rica	19.88	24.74	27.44	Huetar, Maleku, Bribri, Cabécar, Brunca
Ecuador	22.04	25.40	25.75	Kichwa, Shuar, Tsáchila, Chachi, Epera, Awa
Equatorial Guinea	7.19	19.21	25.04	Beyele, Bokuign
Bolivia	8.76	18.77	24.83	Quechua, Aymara, Chiquitano, Guarani
Colombia	19.54	19.88	23.06	Muisca, Totoró, Yanacona, Amorúa, Kokama
Panama	18.16	18.97	20.57	Ngäbe, Buglé, Guna Emberá, Wounaan
Gabon	5.36	6.43	20.49	Baka
Ethiopia	17.72	17.72	18.40	Oromo, Majang, Afar, Anuak, Borana
Central African Rep.	17.65	17.90	18.09	Batwa, Mbororo, Baka
Kenya	11.44	11.75	12.37	Maasai, Turkana, Pokot, Ogiek, Enderois
Dem. Rep. Congo	10.11	10.18	12.08	Mbuti, Baaka, Batwa

Source: IWGIA 2017, UN Data.

This expansion of protected areas in the Global South occurs largely at the behest of international conservation organizations that apply pressure on governments to conserve more. These include World Wildlife Fund, The Nature Conservancy, African Wildlife Foundation, World Vision, and Wildlife Conservation Society. This helps explain why – despite a target of 10 per cent of national territory under protection – we have countries like Tanzania with at least 46 per cent of its total territory protected (URT 2014; UNEP- World Conservation Monitoring Centre (WCMC) and International Union for Conservation of Nature (IUCN 2016)). It also sheds light on Venezuela, French Guiana and New Caledonia, which all have over 50 per cent of their total territory protected; Namibia, Nicaragua, Belize, Republic of Congo, New Zealand, Guatemala and Peru with 30–40 per cent of their total territories under protection; and Botswana, Brazil, Costa Rica, Ecuador, Bolivia, Colombia, Panama, Gabon, Ethiopia and Central African Republic with 15–30 per cent under protection. All of these countries have significant populations of indigenous peoples.[5]

By comparison, data for the ten highest CO_2 emitting countries reveal a rather different situation. Eight out of the ten have less than 20 per cent of their land in protected status, and four of the ten fall under the 10 per cent mark (Table 4.3.).

In sum, analysis of UN data showing percentages of land under protected status globally reveals that regions with significant populations of indigenous peoples committed on average an additional 200–400 per cent more land to conservation by 2014 than what had been protected in 1990, with Africa weighing

Table 4.3. Terrestrial areas protected to total surface area, percentage, highest CO_2 emitting countries.

CO_2 emissions ranking	Country	% land protected (1990)	% land protected (2000)	% land protected (2014)
1	China	13.56	15.51	17.03
2	United States	13.7	13.83	13.88
3	India	4.71	5.05	5.35
4	Russian Federation	5.01	10.83	11.36
5	Japan	18.09	18.66	19.35
6	Germany	19.61	28.68	37.4
7	Iran (Islamic Rep)	5.57	5.99	7.26
8	Saudi Arabia	7.58	31.27	31.27
9	South Korea	5.14	5.2	7.6
10	Canada	5.77	7.08	9.38

Source: CO_2 Emissions; UN Data.

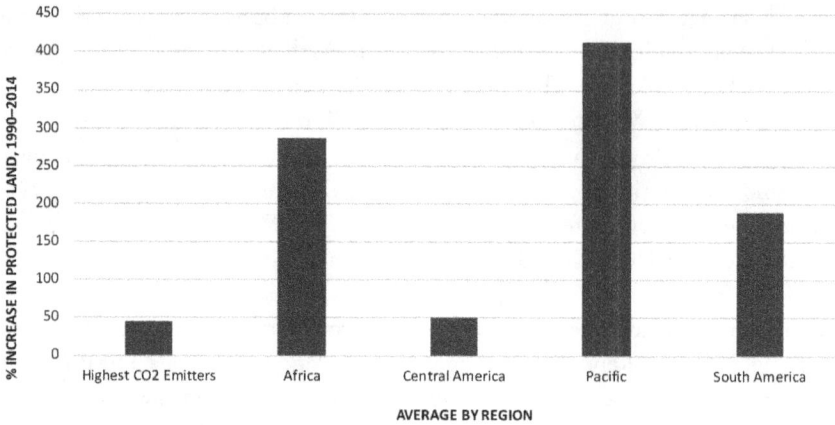

Figure 4.1. Percentage increase in land area protected by highest CO_2 emitting countries and by select regions, 1990–2014. Chart produced by Kelly Askew and Josh Errickson, CSCAR, University of Michigan.

in at 300 per cent. In contrast, the top ten CO_2 emitting countries (minus Saudi Arabia) committed on average only 50 per cent more land during the same time period (Figure 4.1.).[6]

The connection between indigenous populations and indigenous modes of environmental protection has been well-documented (Alcorn 1993; Stevens 1997). Less recognized is that their good stewardship is often their undoing when international conservation interests pressure governments to identify more land to protect from human activities. Indigenous territories tend overwhelmingly to be havens of diverse flora and fauna, absent of deforestation, and rich in resources from timber and honey to minerals and rare species. Yet rather than be rewarded for protecting their territories, they are frequently and increasingly evicted and persecuted because of the 'fortress conservation' approach to conservation, which views humans as impediments to be removed (Brockington 2002; Siurua 2006). A seemingly never-ending push for more land to be converted into pristine wilderness, absent of human activity except tourism or trophy hunting for privileged classes, consigns ever more populations of indigenous peoples to the literal as well as figurative sidelines of their former homelands.

Historical and recent events in Kenya and Tanzania bear this out. Under British colonial rule, Maasai and Samburu communities were disenfranchised from their pasture-rich homelands in Laikipia to make way for white settlers (Hughes 2006; Barume 2010; Laher and Sing'Oei 2012; Bond 2014). A county encompassing 9,694 square kilometres, 40.3 per cent of the land was divided amongst 48 settler parcels ranging in size from 7,000 to 100,000 acres and accorded 99-year leases. The Maasai residents were forcibly resettled in 1904/5 to a newly created Southern Masai Reserve – a destination that offered far inferior grazing land

and water resources. Others were relocated to the Northern Masai Reserve in the most arid part of Laikipia. In 1912, the Maasai filed a lawsuit to regain their original land, but lost (Hughes 2006). After independence, some settlers stayed while others left and transferred their colonial title deeds to elites in the postcolonial order. Lack of clarity over ownership encouraged Maasai and Samburu to reoccupy some underutilized and/or abandoned farms. The Eland Downs parcel, for example, encompassing 17,100 acres reverted *de facto* if not *de jure* to the local Samburu community, with thousands residing on it. Yet unbeknownst to them, the title deed had been assumed by former President Daniel arap Moi, who sold it in 2008 to the Nature Conservancy and the African Wildlife Foundation for conservation purposes. Eviction proceedings ensued in 2010, affecting some 3,000 Samburu families; their homes were burned down, their livestock confiscated, with incidences of rape, injuries and at least three deaths (Nichonghaile and Smith 2011; Letai 2011, 2015). The Samburu launched a lawsuit in 2011 to regain their land. Presumably to avoid the negative press, the Nature Conservancy and African Wildlife Foundation quietly transferred the title to the Kenya Wildlife Service to establish a new Laikipia National Park. This case of what some scholars call 'green-grabbing' – 'the appropriation of land and resources for environmental ends' (Fairhead, Leach and Scoones 2012) – remains tied up in court. Meanwhile, the original 99-year leases recently expired, and hope grows among pastoralist communities that they might be able to reclaim some of their lost land. No such outcomes have emerged as of yet. Instead, in 2017, following two years of failed rains and severe drought, desperate pastoralists started grazing their herds on parts of the private ranches. Swift condemnation followed of the 'ranch invasions', and pastoralists were cast in media reports as criminal bandits mired in intertribal warfare, or hired henchmen of local politicians. Tensions remain, and though some call for redistribution of the farms, little action has been taken to find a peaceful and sustainable solution to the gross inequities of Laikipia's land tenure regime and the histories of dispossession experienced by its indigenous populations.

A similar case concerns the ancestral homeland of Enderois pastoralists living around Lake Bogoria, Kenya. Part of their land, the Mochongoi Forest, was taken and gazetted as a protected forest reserve in 1973, despite a resident community of 400 families (Barume 2010: 100–5). The Enderois were evicted on the justification that the land was needed for tourism development. A lawsuit was filed in 1997 on behalf of the Endorois, and while they initially lost in 2000 in the Kenyan High Court, they subsequently won in 2010 at the African Commission on Human and Peoples' Rights (the African Commission) in a major victory for indigenous peoples everywhere. However, the African Commission issues only advisory opinions; its decisions are not binding. Following Kenya's lack of response, the African Commission in 2012 filed an application before the African Court on Human and Peoples' Rights (the African Court). In a landmark decision delivered on 26 May 2017 by the African Court, Kenya was found in violation of several rights contained in the African Charter on Human and Peoples' Rights (African Court 2017). The African Court ordered the Kenyan government 'to take all appropriate measures within reasonable time frame to remedy all the violations established and to inform the court of the measures taken within six (6) months from the date of this judgment' (ibid.: 68). The judgment, however, has yet to be implemented.

The area of Loliondo, Tanzania, which abuts the Serengeti National Park, has drawn considerable global attention and support from indigenous and human rights organizations around the globe. Resident Maasai in Loliondo suffered mass evictions and widespread human rights violations following the granting of different sections of their land to two foreign entities. In one case, 1,500 square kilometres (150,000 ha.) was leased to Ortelo Business Corporation (OBC), a royal Arab hunting outfit, beginning in 1992; in the other case, 51 square kilometres (12,617 acres) was leased in 2006 to US-based Thomson Safaris. In 2017, the government announced its intent to terminate the lease with OBC but has yet to do so. Brutal evictions and wide-scale destruction of Maasai villages in August 2017 led to Maasai filing suit against the Tanzanian government in September 2017 in the East African Court of Justice (Mittal and Fraser 2018). The lesser-known case of the Mkomazi National Park, also in Tanzania, follows the same narrative arc: ancestral land of the Maasai was appropriated for the purpose of a Rhinoceros Reserve, now called Mkomazi National Park. The Maasai were evicted in 1988 and filed a lawsuit in 1994. Paltry compensation was awarded to the few that testified and an order issued for alternative land to be provided, but the latter was never implemented (Mchome 2001; Tenga et al. 2008).

Conservation has been a primary, if not 'the' primary mode of dispossession of indigenous land, water and other resources in Africa and more broadly. Countless other supporting cases could be drawn from southern Africa involving San hunter-gatherers of Botswana and Namibia; from Uganda involving Ik and Karamojong (among others); from Ethiopia concerning Afar, Borana and peoples of the Lower Omo (among others). As one of the authors has noted elsewhere, 'the legal principle is consonant with faulty conservation practices – hinged on ignorance of indigenous peoples' connection to nature – of exclusion where human beings are viewed as inherently destructive to the environment. Therefore, unless wildlife conservation laws and their attendant perceptions are changed, indigenous peoples' right to self-determination will remain elusive' (Laltaika 2016: 232–33).

Extractive Industries: A Third Mode of Dispossession

Considerable attention now focuses on extractive industries as a mode of dispossession of indigenous resources. In his final (2013) report as the UN Special

Rapporteur on the Rights of Indigenous Peoples, James Anaya attributed this to the fact that a substantial amount of the remaining minerals and fossil fuels are found in indigenous peoples' lands and territories (Anaya 2013; see also Colchester 2003; Anongos 2012; Doyle and Whitmore 2014; Daley et al. 2018). In most African countries, legal frameworks that are relics of colonialism heighten hardships of indigenous peoples. Specifically, laws provide that sub-surface resources are excluded from land rights and that once discovered surface land rights come to an end, hence landowners must vacate it.

While some countries provide compensation, indigenous livelihoods such as pastoralism and hunting and gathering present unique challenges in the computation of payable compensation and in identifying the exact number of persons entitled to the payments. Indigenous pastoralists and hunter-gatherers use land communally or collectively. Moreover, land belonging to these communities may appear vacated during certain times of the year because of rotational grazing or seasonal food gathering, but that does not mean the land has been abandoned or is not in use. Accordingly, it is difficult to use 'Western benchmarks' embodied in the laws, such as basing compensation on 'unexhausted improvements', without occasioning injustices.

In Eritrea, a high-profile lawsuit has emerged concerning the Bisha copper mine owned and operated by Canadian-owned Nevsun Resources Ltd in the traditional territory of Kunama agro-pastoralists. Nevsun is accused of committing human rights violations against Kunama (and other) workers employed in their mining operations by forcing them to work in slavery-like conditions. Nevsun is facing historic legal proceedings in Canada – *Gize Yebeyo Araya, Kesete Tekle Fshazion and Mihretab Yemane Tekle v. Nevsun Resources Ltd. and Earth Rights International* – in which the Supreme Court of British Columbia has agreed to hear the case rather than refer it to Eritrean courts. It constitutes the first mass tort claim for modern slavery in Canadian judicial history. After Nevsun appealed at both provincial and federal levels, the Canadian Supreme Court ruled in February 2020 that the case can proceed. It will determine whether or not Nevsun violated the principle of 'Free, Prior and Informed Consent' (FPIC) in its interactions with the Kunama community, in addition to charges of crimes against humanity, slavery, forced labour and torture (IWGIA 2017; Kassam 2017, 'Nevsun Lawsuit').

Infrastructure Projects: A Fourth Mode of Dispossession

Large-scale infrastructure projects constitute a fourth mode of dispossession of indigenous lands, territories and water resources. These are typically state-led modernization projects of enormous cost and involve appropriation of territory in the name of 'public interest'. However, with aims to increase both development and political sovereignty, these giant projects often intersect with the three drivers of indigenous land dispossession explored above. Three examples from East Africa illustrate this.

The Gibe III Dam was constructed on the Omo River within the Southern Nations, Nationalities and Peoples Region (SNNPR) in Ethiopia. Built by Italian firm Salini Impregilo, it is only one of many dams being constructed in Ethiopia for hydropower generation. Indigenous communities along the Omo River include the Mursi (Mun), Bodi (Mela and Chirim), Hamar, Kara and Kwegu peoples, all heavily dependent on the river for watering livestock, farming and fishing purposes (LaTosky, this volume). Experts warn that the Gibe III dam will have serious environmental consequences further afield in obstructing the natural flooding of the river – which facilitates cultivation – and in drying up Lake Turkana, which is the river's final destination and a critical resource for indigenous communities in northern Kenya. A second driver for the dam project is to provide irrigation for commercial agriculture. Blocks are already being leased along the river for sugar, rice and cotton cultivation (Human Rights Watch 2017).[7]

The Lake Turkana Wind Power Project (LTWP) is an equivalent effort by the Kenyan government towards securing energy independence. A public-private investment costing an estimated €625 million ($858 million), it is the largest wind farm in all of Africa, with 365 turbines, and has come at the cost of the livelihoods and 66,000 hectares of ancestral land of Turkana, Samburu, Rendille and El Molo pastoralist communities (Power Technology n.d.; 'Kenya to Build Africa's Largest Windfarm' 2009; Danwatch 2016; 'Lake Turkana Wind Power Land Case On After Talks Collapse' 2017; Achiba 2019; Cormack 2019). LTWP is a Dutch-led consortium of multinational interests that include KP&P Africa, Aldwych International, Danish Investment Fund for Developing Countries, Vestas Wind Systems, Finnish Fund for Industrial Cooperation, Norwegian Investment Fund for Developing Countries, Siemens, Daher, and Google, with financing led largely by the African Development Bank. Delays in construction of the 438 kilometre-long transmission line to transport the energy to the national grid postponed the initial launch to July 2019, but it is now operational. Some Google shareholders, upon learning of the project's eviction and dispossession of indigenous peoples' land, launched a letter-writing campaign to protest Google's involvement in the project, but this did not have much impact. Of greater significance is the ongoing lawsuit in the Land and Environment Court in Meru, Kenya, in which Turkana and Samburu plaintiffs allege that their land was illegally acquired by the project without prior notice, public consultation or compensation. On 9 November 2016, the Kenyan High Court declined to stop the project and instead directed the parties to arbitration within a 90-day period. The case (*Environment and Land Case 163 of 2014*) has not been resolved, however, and is ongoing.

Finally, another nearby megaproject, the Lamu Port Southern Sudan-Ethiopia Transport Corridor (LAPSSET), is under construction: an oil pipeline traversing

South Sudan, Ethiopia and Kenya through which oil from South Sudan will be transported to a new port near Lamu for export. The recent discovery of oil in Turkana County means extraction will also likely occur there, which in turn means more land dispossession for Turkana pastoralists on top of that which has already occurred from the LTWP project. Moreover, Kenya's Vision 2030 development plan includes building three luxury resort cities in Isiolo, Turkana and Lamu to cater to LAPSSET personnel and increase the tourism potential of the north. This entails constructing a dam on the Ewaso Nyiro River, a water resource of critical importance to pastoralists (among others). These communities have voiced their concern about, and opposition to, these projects, anticipating long-term negative impact on their livelihoods, on wildlife and on the environment (IMPACT 2017) but to little effect.

These three cases highlight the intersectionality of economic and political interests in large-scale infrastructure projects and the alignment of multiple modes of dispossession. In the cases of the Gibe III Dam and the LTWP, both are presented as energy development projects; however, the first has linkages and motivations tied to commercial agriculture, while the second – by virtue of being a 'green energy' project – has linkages and motivations tied to conservation via climate change mitigation. The case of LAPSSET unambiguously intersects with the interests of extractive industries.

It should be recognized that investments in infrastructure, however, serve not merely economic or environmental ends but deeply political ones. Infrastructure is highly visible, whether it assumes the form of a dam, wind farm, roads, pipelines or powerlines stretching across vast landscapes. They render the state material and present – a force to reckon with. Secondly, the provisioning of energy, transportation, water and tourism opportunities are means through which nation-states engage their citizenry, develop regional ties with neighbouring states, assert their authority, collect revenue and attract foreign investors and tourists. Analysts who prematurely proclaimed the demise of the state during the era of globalization and neoliberal reform are having to accept that the state – not only in Africa but the world over – is aggressively reasserting itself. Some cast this as the 'return of the state'. Others would argue that it never left (Maganga and Jacob 2016). Finally, some assert that investments in remote, previously ignored regions should be celebrated. But unless accompanied by investments in healthcare, education, energy and water access and employment opportunities in indigenous communities – none of which are currently highlighted – they will benefit state and multinational corporate interests at the expense of local communities.

Competition with Cultivators: A Fifth Mode of Dispossession

It should come as no surprise that increasing competition between small-scale cultivators and indigenous peoples over land is ever more common and more deadly in light of all the above trends. It is estimated that 80 per cent of Africans depend on land-related activities to survive. Since survival is thus inextricably linked to land, defending one's access to land becomes a matter of self-preservation.

Conflicts between cultivators and pastoralists especially, but also cultivators and hunter-gatherers, are increasing in number and in violent outcomes across Africa. The literature on farmer–pastoralist conflict in Africa is vast (a few examples being Moritz 2006; Shettima and Tar 2008; Turner et al. 2011). In January 2018, more than 100 people died in Nigeria's Benue, Nasaraw and Taraba states because of conflicts between farmers and Fulani herders over access to land and water. Tensions and periodic flare-ups of violence continue to occur between farmers and Maasai pastoralists in Morogoro Region, Tanzania, where a number of deaths were reported between 2015 and 2016 (Benjaminsen, Maganga and Abdallah 2009; IWGIA 2015). Unsurprisingly, where increasing pressures on, and appropriation of, land and water resources for foreign interests or state-led projects result in less land for local residents, we see increased competition among groups pursuing different livelihood strategies.

Internally Displaced Persons: A Sixth Mode of Dispossession

Once indigenous lands and territories are expropriated through any of the above five modes of dispossession, displacement follows on scales ranging from a few individuals or households to entire communities spanning multiple villages across multiple districts. This is producing growing populations of internally displaced persons (IDPs), whose search for new land on which to pursue their livelihoods rarely finds welcome. The cascading effects of eviction and displacement, which necessarily results in the displaced having to seek refuge on the land of others, is more conflict and more displacement. Host communities may themselves be subject to similar threats of land appropriation, breeding suspicion and amplifying the divide between host and guest, resident and immigrant (Cassanelli 2015). This is exacerbated where indigenous peoples are concerned, since they typically meet with disrespect and a devaluing of their cultures, livelihoods and humanity by majority populations. The arrival of IDPs and/or refugees into others' territories generates competition over already strained resources. Conflicts over resources get misrepresented in public discourse as 'ethnic conflict' or 'intertribal conflict', connoting irrationality and primordialism without hope of resolution. This diverts attention away from the multinational corporate and state interests involved, and their culpability in land alienation.

From May 2006 to January 2007, expansion of Ruaha National Park resulted in mass evictions of Maasai pastoralists and Sukuma agro-pastoralists in the Usangu Plains of south-western Tanzania. Ruaha National Park is the largest national park in Tanzania, with an area of 20,226 square kilometres. Before the expansion, the park had an area of 10,300 square kilometres (URT 2015:

1), meaning that it doubled in size during the 2006–07 expansion. Pastoralists with 100 head of cattle or more were summarily evicted and forced to walk 1,000 kilometres with their cattle to Rufiji and Kilwa districts in the south-east of the country (Walsh 2012; Sirima and Backman 2013; Msigwa 2014). Over a decade later, they still suffer high levels of persecution by local residents and local government officials for being unwanted immigrants. And in a previously discussed case, Barabaig pastoralists evicted in the 1970s from their territory around Mount Hanang, Tanzania, and relocated to the coastal area of Bagamoyo district were subjected to new evictions and displacement four decades later because of land pressures from the Bagamoyo EcoEnergy (BEE) project and the desire for more contracted outgrowers (Maganga et al. 2016: 29). Land that pastoralists had been using for residences and pasture was given directly to BEE or reallocated to local farmers who had signed on as sugar cane outgrowers for the project.[8]

Another case involves the pastoralist Kunama community of Eritrea, who were displaced by the war between Eritrea and Ethiopia (1998–2000) and previously discussed in relation to the Nevsun copper mine. Because Kunama territory is located near the border, their allegiance to Eritrea was cast into doubt. Kunama thus experienced high rates of human rights abuses from their government, and an estimated 4,000 sought shelter in a refugee camp in Badme, Ethiopia (Minority Rights Group International 2017). Despite being unable to continue a pastoralist lifestyle, few Kunama express hope or willingness to resettle in Eritrea (IWGIA 2017: 15; 'Caught in the Middle' n.d.).

The reverse also occurs, when circumstances cause refugees or IDPs to stream into pastoralists' territories. This is occurring in Gambella region, Ethiopia, where an estimated 330,000 refugees from South Sudan have sought safe haven. Many are pastoralist Nuer fleeing political instability and violence with their herds. Local Anywaa agro-pastoralists in Gambella have had to accommodate and contend with this unexpected influx and face increasing conflicts over scarce water and pasture resources. The presence of Nuer refugees also exacerbates growing tensions between Anywaa communities and the Ethiopian government because of previous evictions of Anywaa from their ancestral territories and human rights abuses committed against them in a campaign to fight terrorism.[9]

With a number of ongoing active conflicts (namely in Burundi, Democratic Republic of Congo (DRC), South Sudan and Somalia), East Africa is home to seven of the ten largest refugee camps in the world (Table 4.4.).

It is also home to two of the five countries hosting the largest numbers of IDPs – Uganda (1.2 million) and Sudan (1.1 million) – as well as home to two of the five countries generating the largest numbers of IDPs – South Sudan (2.3 million) and Somalia (0.9 million).[10] The rise in the numbers of IDPs portends continuing and expanding problems of dislocation and violence, since the often-repeated claims of limitless, underutilized land in Africa is patently false.

Table 4.4. Ten largest refugee camps in the world (2019).

	Refugee Camp	Host Country	Population
1	Kutupalong/Cox's Bazar	Bangladesh	734,622
2	Bidi Bidi	Uganda	285,000
3	Dadaab	Kenya	210,472
4	Kakuma/Kalobeyei	Kenya	189,743
5	Nyarugusu	Tanzania	153,767
6	Jabalia	Gaza Strip	113,990
7	Nduta	Tanzania	92,075
8	Zaatari	Jordan	76,892
9	Pugnido	Ethiopia	51,433
10	Yida	South Sudan	43,968

Sources: Data compiled from multiple sources: UNHCR https://data2.unhcr.org/, UNOCHA https://reliefweb.int/, and StepUp.One https://stepup.one/identify-refugees/.

Conclusion

The cases discussed here expose the multiplying negative effects on indigenous communities when the interests of agribusiness, conservation, extractive industries and large-scale infrastructure projects converge. At ever growing risk are indigenous peoples' lands, territories, collective resources, sense of security and basic human rights.

The United Nations has three oversight mechanisms for indigenous issues: (1) the UN Special Rapporteur on the Rights of Indigenous Peoples; (2) the UN Permanent Forum on Indigenous Issues (UNPFII); and (3) the UN Expert Mechanism on the Rights of Indigenous Peoples within the Human Rights Council. These mechanisms need to align *their* agendas so as to better combat the multiple threats to indigenous peoples' existence. The mandates of these three entities sometimes conflict and overlap, hence the need for improved and consistent coordination efforts. Only with concerted collective action can the UNPFII and its partners within the UN and around the world shape a more positive future for indigenous peoples everywhere, but especially in Africa, which faces the highest level of threat.

In the absence of increased concern for, and protection of, the rights, livelihoods, land and resources of indigenous peoples in Africa, the trends outlined in this chapter will only intensify. That augurs a precarious future for us all. Sustainable development requires engaging indigenous communities as fully recognized and fully respected stakeholders in projects occurring in their territories. Our global community can learn from its past mistakes and chart a path of development that holds true to the principles and objectives articulated in the UN Declaration of the Rights of Indigenous Peoples. Moreover, the three UN

Mechanisms can individually, and in collaboration, ensure that member states, UN agencies and programmes implement their contents. While considered the most comprehensive international document relating to the rights of indigenous peoples, non-implementation of the UN Declaration will reduce it to a rhetorical proviso.

Elifuraha I. Laltaika is a former member of the UN Permanent Forum on Indigenous Issues (UNPFII) and a Senior Lecturer in Law at Tumaini University Makumira in Arusha, Tanzania. He recently served as a Harvard Law School Visiting Researcher. In addition to publishing in the area of indigenous peoples rights, he has consulted numerous institutions on the subject. He has trained high court judges, members of parliament, practising lawyers and staff of national human rights institutions in Tanzania on indigenous peoples' rights under International Law. Elifuraha holds a Doctorate in Law (S.J.D) from the University of Arizona.

Kelly M. Askew is a Professor of Anthropology and Afroamerican & African Studies at the University of Michigan, United States. She holds a Ph.D. in Anthropology from Harvard University and a BA in Music and Anthropology from Yale University and has worked for over three decades in Tanzania and Kenya. Her writings and documentary film projects focus on arts, aesthetics and politics, critical development studies and indigenous political movements, especially of Maasai pastoralists in East Africa.

Notes

1. Named after the commissioning author José Martínez Cobo.
2. See Iorns (1992:199) for the definition of 'indigenous' used in the Cobo Report.
3. While there are of course other African states with settler colonial pasts, such as Zimbabwe, Zambia and Mozambique, they do not have groups that currently participate in the global indigenous peoples' movement.
4. Of 53 sovereign African states in existence at the time of the vote on UNDRIP, 35 voted in favour, 3 abstained (Burundi, Kenya, Nigeria), and the remaining 15 states were absent and did not register a vote.
5. 'Significance' is measured here by inclusion in the annual report on indigenous peoples issued by the International Work Group on Indigenous Affairs (IWGIA) in Copenhagen, Denmark. Not all countries in the IWGIA report, however, are included here.
6. Saudi Arabia is ranked number 8 among top CO_2 emitting countries, according to the Global Carbon Atlas, but is excluded here because although it committed vast parts of The Empty Quarter, a vast desert, to protected status this is irrelevant for carbon offset.
7. For detailed studies on the impact of Gibe III, see section 'Underdeveloping South Omo' in this volume.
8. Interviews with Fukayosi villagers, Bagamoyo, September 2016.
9. 'Anuak vs. Nuer vs. Gambella', n.d. *Indigenous Africa*. Retrieved 3 October 2020 from https://indigenousafrica.org/anywaa-anuak-vs-nuer-vs-gambella/.

10. 'Global Trends: Forced Displacement in 2018,' UNHCR, https://www.unhcr.org/global trends2018/. Retrieved 1 April 2020.

References

Achiba, G.A. 2019. 'Navigating Contested Winds: Development Visions and Anti-Politics of Wind Energy in Northern Kenya', *Land* 8(1), doi:10.3390/land8010007.

African Commission on Human and Peoples' Rights (ACHPR) and International Work Group for Indigenous Affairs (IWGIA). 2005. *Report of the African Commission's Working Group of Experts on Indigenous Populations/Communities. Submitted in accordance with the 'Resolution on the Rights of Indigenous Populations/Communities in Africa'.* Banjul, The Gambia and Copenhagen, Denmark: ACHPR and IWGIA. Retrieved 23 September 2019 from https://www.iwgia.org/en/iwgia_files_publications_files/African_Commission_book .pdf.

African Commission on Human and Peoples' Rights (ACHPR) and International Work Group for Indigenous Affairs (IWGIA). 2006. *Indigenous Peoples in Africa: The Forgotten Peoples? The African Commission's Work on Indigenous Peoples in Africa.* Banjul, The Gambia and Copenhagen, Denmark: ACHPR and IWGIA. Retrieved 13 January 2018 from https://www .iwgia.org/images/publications/0112_AfricanCommissionSummaryversionENG_eb.pdf.

African Court on Human and Peoples' Rights. 2017. *African Commission on Human and Peoples' Rights v. Republic of Kenya, Application No. 006/2012, Judgment 26 May 2017.* Retrieved 23 June 2018 from http://www.african-court.org/en/images/Cases/Judgment/ Application%20006-2012%20-%20African%20Commission%20on%20Human%20 and%20Peoples%E2%80%99%20Rights%20v.%20the%20Republic%20of%20Kenya .pdf.

Alcorn, J.B. 1993. 'Indigenous Peoples and Conservation', *Conservation Biology* 7(2): 424–26.

Anaya, J. 2013. 'Extractive Industries and Indigenous Peoples: Report of the Special Rapporteur on the Rights of Indigenous Peoples', *Report A/HRC/24/41.* Retrieved 11 August 2020 from http://unsr.jamesanaya.org/?p=948.

Anongos, A. 2012. *Pitfalls and Pipelines: Indigenous Peoples and Extractive Industries.* Baguio City, Philippines: Tebtebba Foundation.

Bagamoyo EcoEnergy Ltd. (BEE). 2015. 'Land Grabbing Definition Perpetuated in the BEE Project', 31 March. Retrieved 16 May 2018 from http://www.ecoenergy.co.tz/news/deta ils/?tx_news_pi1[news]=13&tx_news_pi1[controller]=News&tx_news_pi1[action]=detail &cHash=eab3af2bffc470d6c9e61816c5e9eb1d.

Barnard, A. 2006. 'Kalahari Revisionism, Vienna and the "Indigenous Peoples" Debate', *Social Anthropology* 14(1): 1–16.

Barume, A.K. 2010. 'Land Rights of Indigenous Peoples in Africa', *IWGIA Document* 115. Copenhagen: International Work Group for Indigenous Affairs (IWGIA).

Benjaminsen, T., F.P. Maganga and J.M. Abdallah. 2009. 'The Kilosa Killings: Political Ecology of a Farmer-Herder Conflict in Tanzania', *Development and Change* 40(3): 423–45.

Bond, J. 2014. 'Conflict, Development and Security at the Agro-Pastoral-Wildlife Nexus: A Case of Laikipia County, Kenya', *Journal of Development Studies* 50(7): 991–1008.

Brockington, D. 2002. *Fortress Conservation: The Preservation of the Mkomazi Game Reserve.* Bloomington, IN: Indiana University Press.

Cassanelli, L. 2015. 'Hosts and Guests: A Historical Interpretation of Land Conflicts in Southern and Central Somalia', *Rift Valley Research Paper* 2. London and Nairobi: Rift Valley Institute.

'Caught in the Middle: Kunama Refugees', n.d. *Indigenous Africa*. Retrieved 3 October 2020 from https://indigenousafrica.org/caught-in-the-middle-kunama-refuge-postes/.

'CO$_2$ Emissions'. 2016. *Global Carbon Atlas: Global Carbon Project*. Retrieved 15 January 2018 from http://www.globalcarbonatlas.org/en/CO2-emissions.

Colchester, M. (ed.). 2003. *Extracting Promises: Indigenous Peoples, Extractive Industries and the World Bank*. Baguio City, Philippines: Tebtebba Foundation.

Cormack, Z. 2019. 'Kenya's Huge Wind Power Project Might Be Great for the Environment but Not for Local Communities', *Quartz Africa*, September 3, 2019. Retrieved 4 September 2019 from https://qz.com/africa/1700925/kenyas-huge-wind-power-project-in-turkana-hurts-local-people/.

Dahl, J. 2012. *The Indigenous Space and Marginalized Peoples in the United Nations*. New York: Palgrave Macmillan.

———. 2013. 'The United Nations and the Indigenous Space', in J. Dahl and E. Fihl (eds), *A Comparative Ethnography of Alternative Spaces*. New York: Palgrave Macmillan, pp. 19–40.

Daley, E. et al. 2018. 'Gender, Land and Mining in Pastoralist Tanzania', *WOLTS Research Report No. 2. Mokoro Ltd. and HakiMadini*. Retrieved 11 November 2018 from http://mokoro.co.uk/wp-content/uploads/Gender_Land_and_Mining_in_Pastoralist_Tanzania_WOLTS_Research_Report_No.2_June_2018.pdf.

Danwatch. 2016. *A People in the Way of Progress: Prostitution, Alcoholism and a Lawsuit on Illegal Land Acquisition in the Lake Turkana Wind Power Project*. Retrieved 17 November 2016 from https://old.danwatch.dk/en/undersogelse/a-people-in-the-way-of-progress/?chapter=1.

Deer, K. 2010. 'From Development to Implementation: An Ongoing Journey', in J. Hartley, P. Joffe and J. Preston (eds), *Realizing the UN Declaration on the Rights of Indigenous Peoples: Triumph, Hope, and Action*. Saskatoon, SK, Canada: Purich, pp. 12–28.

Doyle, C., and A. Whitmore. 2014. *Indigenous Peoples and the Extractive Sector: Towards a Rights-Respecting Engagement*. Baguio City, Philippines: Tebtebba Foundation.

Ebenroth, C.T., and C.M. Peter. 1996. 'Protection of Investments in Tanzania: Some New Issues from Zanzibar', *African Journal of International and Comparative Law* 8(4): 842–70.

Fairhead, J., M. Leach and I. Scoones. 2012. 'Green-Grabbing: A New Appropriation of Nature?', *Journal of Peasant Studies* 39(2): 237–61.

Fontaine, P. 2010. 'A Living Instrument', in J. Hartley, P. Joffe and J. Preston (eds), *Realizing the UN Declaration on the Rights of Indigenous Peoples: Triumph, Hope, and Action*. Saskatoon, SK, Canada: Purich, pp. 8–11.

Hall, R., I. Scoones and D. Tsikata (eds). 2015. *Africa's Land Rush: Rural Livelihoods and Agrarian Change*. Suffolk: James Currey.

Hodgson, D. 2011. *Being Maasai, Becoming Indigenous: Postcolonial Politics in a Neoliberal World*. Bloomington: Indiana University Press.

Hughes, L. 2006. *Moving the Maasai: A Colonial Misadventure*. Basingstoke: Palgrave Macmillan.

Human Rights Watch. 2017. 'Ethiopia: Dams, Plantations a Threat to Kenyans', 14 February. Retrieved 16 May 2018 from https://www.hrw.org/news/2017/02/14/ethiopia-dams-plantations-threat-kenyans.

IMPACT (Indigenous Movement for Peace Advancement and Conflict Transformation). 2017. 'Activity Report on the LAPSSET and Megadam Community Meetings Held on 9th and 10th March 2017 at Kimanjo and Archers Post Respectively', *Ref. KAR 4/13/3/2017*. Nanyuki, Kenya: IMPACT, 21 March 2017.

Indigenous Africa. n.d. Retrieved 30 September 2020 from https://indigenousafrica.org.

Iorns, C.J. 1992. 'Indigenous Peoples and Self Determination: Challenging State Sovereignty', *Case Western Reserve Journal of International Law* 24(2): 199–348.

IWGIA (International Work Group for Indigenous Affairs). 2015. 'Ethnic Violence in Morogoro Region in Tanzania', *IWGIA Briefing Note*, March 2015. Retrieved 18 November 2016 from https://www.iwgia.org/en/.

―――. 2017. *The Indigenous World 2017*. Copenhagen: IWGIA. Retrieved 30 April 2017 from https://www.iwgia.org/en/indigenous-world.

Kassam, A. 2017. 'Canadian Firm to Face Historic Legal Case Over Alleged Labor Abuses in Eritrea', *The Guardian*, 23 November. Retrieved 23 June 2018 from https://www.theguardian.com/global-development/2017/nov/23/canadian-mining-firm-historic-legal-case-alleged-labour-abuses-eritrea-nevsun-resources.

Kenrick, J., and J. Lewis. 2004. 'Indigenous Peoples' Rights and the Politics of the Term "Indigenous"', *Anthropology Today* 20(2): 4–9.

'Kenya to Build Africa's Largest Windfarm', *The Guardian*, 27 July 2009. Retrieved 4 February 2019 from https://www.theguardian.com/environment/2009/jul/27/kenya-wind-farm.

King, N.A.S. 2013. 'Conflict Management among the Farmers and Pastoralists in Tanzania', *International SAMANM Journal of Business and Social Sciences* 1(2): 40–50. Retrieved 15 September 2014 from https://www.researchgate.net/publication/311934623_Conflict_Management_among_the_Farmers_and_Pastoralists_in_Tanzania.

Kipuri, N. 2017. 'Indigenous Peoples' Rights, Conflict and Peace Building: Experiences from East Africa', in E. Stamatopoulou (ed.), *Indigenous Peoples' Rights and Unreported Struggles: Conflict and Peace*. New York: Columbia University Institute for the Study of Human Rights, pp. 68–79.

Kuper, A. 2003a. 'The Return of the Native', *Current Anthropology* 44: 389–402.

―――. 2003b. 'The Return of the Native', *New Humanist* 118(3): 5–8.

―――. 2004. 'Reply', *Current Anthropology* 45: 265–66.

Laher, R.L., and K. Sing'Oei (eds). 2012. *Indigenous People in Africa: Contestations, Empowerment and Group Rights*. Pretoria: African Institute of South Africa.

'Lake Turkana Wind Power Land Case On After Talks Collapse', *Business Daily*, 7 June 2017. Retrieved 4 February 2019 from https://www.businessdailyafrica.com/corporate/companies/Lake-Turkana-Wind-Power-land-case-on-after-talks-collapse/4003102-3960154-fvibhx/index.html.

Laltaika, E.I. 2015. 'Proposing an Oversight Mechanism to Bolster Implementation of the United Nations Declaration on the Rights of Indigenous Peoples', presented to the Expert Group Meeting, Secretariat of the Permanent Forum on Indigenous Issues, Division for Social Policy and Development, Department of Economic and Social Affairs, United Nations, 27–29 January 2015. Retrieved 12 January 2018 from http://www.un.org/esa/socdev/unpfii/documents/EGM/2015/Experts-papers/Elifurah-Laltaika.pdf.

―――. 2016. 'Extractive Industries, Human Rights, and the Environment in Tanzania: A Framework for Legal, Policy and Institutional Reforms', Doctor of Laws (S.J.D.) dissertation. Tucson: University of Arizona.

Lane, C. 1994. 'Pastures Lost: Alienation of Barabaig Land in the Context of Land Policy and Legislation in Tanzania', *Nomadic Peoples* 34/35: 81–94.

―――. 1995. 'Update on the Barabaig Land Cases', presented to the *'Land Issues in Tanzania'-seminar*, Britain-Tanzania Society, 13 May 1995.

―――. 2018. *Barabaig: Life, Love and Death on Tanzania's Hanang Plains*. London: River Books.

Letai, J. 2011. 'Land Deals in Kenya: The Genesis of Land Deals in Kenya and Its Implication on Pastoral Livelihoods: A Case Study of Laikipia District, 2011'. Retrieved 18 November 2016 from http://landportal.info/sites/default/files/land_deals_in_kenya-initial_report_for_laikipia_district2.pdf.

———. 2015. 'Land Deals & Pastoralist Livelihoods in Laikipia County, Kenya', in R. Hall, I. Scoones and D. Tsikata (eds), *Africa's Land Rush: Rural Livelihoods and Agrarian Change*.

Lightfoot, S. 2016. *Global Indigenous Politics: A Subtle Revolution*. Abingdon and New York: Routledge, Taylor & Francis.

Maganga, F., and T. Jacob. 2016. 'Defying the Looming Resource Curse with Indigenization? Insights from Two Coal Mines in Tanzania', *African Review* 43(2): 139–60.

Maganga, F. et al. 2016. 'Dispossession through Formalization: Tanzania and the G8 Land Agenda in Africa', *Asian Journal of African Studies* 40: 3–49.

Mchome, S. 2001. *Eviction and the Rights of People in Conservation Areas in Tanzania*. Dar-Es-Salaam: University of Dar es Salaam, Faculty of Law.

Minority Rights Group International. 2017. 'Eritrea–Kunama and Nara'. Retrieved 1 November 2017 from http://minorityrights.org/minorities/kunama-and-nara/.

Mittal, A., and E. Fraser. 2018. *Losing the Serengeti: The Maasai Land That Was to Run Forever*. Oakland, CA: The Oakland Institute. Retrieved 10 May 2018 from https://www.oaklandinstitute.org/tanzania-safari-businesses-maasai-losing-serengeti.

Mogelgaard, K. 2006. 'How Much Land Should Be Protected for Biodiversity?', Population Reference Bureau. Retrieved 15 January 2018 from http://www.prb.org/Publications/Articles/2006/HowMuchLandShouldBeProtectedforBiodiversity.aspx.

Moritz, M. 2006. 'The Politics of Permanent Conflict: Farmer-Herder Conflicts in Northern Cameroon', *Canadian Journal of African Studies* 40(1): 101–26.

Msigwa, G.B. 2014. 'Changing Livelihoods and Adaptive Capacity of Agro-Pastoralists Evicted from Ihefu in Tanzania', Ph.D. thesis, Sokoine University of Agriculture.

'Nevsun Lawsuit (re Bisha mine, Eritrea)'. 2020. *Business and Human Rights Resource Centre*. Retrieved 1 April 2020 from https://www.business-humanrights.org/en/nevsun-lawsuit-re-bisha-mine-eritrea.

Ngugi, J.M. 2005. 'Policing Neo-Liberal Reforms: The Rule of Law as an Enabling and Restrictive Discourse', *Journal of International Law* 26(3): 513–97. Retrieved 11 August 2014 from http://scholarship.law.upenn.edu/cgi/viewcontent.cgi?article=1217&context=jil.

Nichonghaile, C., and D. Smith. 2011. 'Kenya's Samburu People "Violently Evicted" after US Charities Buy Land', *The Guardian*, 14 December.

Paul, H., and R. Steinbrecher. 2013. 'African Agricultural Growth Corridors and the New Alliance for Food Security and Nutrition: Who Benefits, Who Loses?', *Econexus Report*. Retrieved 22 January 2018 from http://www.inter-reseaux.org/IMG/pdf/African_Agricultural_Growth_Corridors___New_Alliance_-_EcoNexus_June_2013.pdf.

Power Technology. n.d. 'Lake Turkana Wind Power Project, Loyangalani'. Retrieved 4 February 2019 from http://www.power-technology.com/projects/lake-turkana-wind-power-project-loyangalani/.

Pulitano, E. (ed.). 2012. *Indigenous Rights in the Age of the UN Declaration*. Cambridge: Cambridge University Press.

SAGCOT. 2011. *SAGCOT Investment Blueprint*. Retrieved 13 May 2018 from http://sagcot.co.tz/?mdocs-file=1023.

Schlee, G. 2009. 'Introduction', in G. Schlee and E. Watson (eds), *Changing Identifications and Alliances in North-East Africa, Vol. 1 Ethiopia and Kenya*. New York and Oxford: Berghahn, pp. 1–13.

Shettima, A.G., and U.A. Tar. 2008. 'Farmer-Pastoralist Conflict in West Africa: Exploring the Causes and Consequences', *Information, Society and Justice* 1(2): 163–84.

Sirima, A., and K.F. Backman. 2013. 'Communities' Displacement from National Park and Tourism Development in the Usangu Plains, Tanzania', *Current Issues in Tourism* 16(7–8): 719–35.

Siurua, H. 2006. 'Nature above People: Rolston and "Fortress" Conservation in the South', *Ethics & the Environment* 11(1): 71–96.

Stamatopoulou, E. (ed.). 2017. *Indigenous Peoples' Rights and Unreported Struggles: Conflict and Peace.* New York: Columbia University, Institute for the Study of Human Rights.

Stevens, S. (ed.). 1997. *Conservation through Cultural Survival: Indigenous Peoples and Protected Areas.* Washington, DC: Island Press.

Tenga, R. et al. 2008. 'A Study on Options for Pastoralists to Secure Their Livelihoods in Tanzania: Current Policy, Legal and Economic Issues', vol. 1, *Main Report.* Retrieved 27 March 2020 from https://www.tnrf.org/files/E-INFO-RLTF_VOL1_MAIN-REPORT _A_Study_on_options_for_pastoralism_to_secure_their_livelihoods_in_Tanzania_ 2008.pdf.

Turner, M.D. et al. 2011. 'Livelihood Transitions and the Changing Nature of Farmer-Herder Conflict in Sahelian West Africa', *Journal of Development Studies* 47(2): 183–206.

United Nations (UN) Data. 'Terrestrial Areas Protected to Total Surface Area, Percentage'. Retrieved 15 January 2018 from http://data.un.org/Data.aspx?q=terrestrial+areas+pro tected+to+total+surface+area&d=MDG&f=seriesRowID%3a784.

United Nations Environment (UNEP)-World Conservation Monitoring Centre (WCMC) and International Union for Conservation of Nature (IUCN). 2016. *World Database on Protected Areas: Update on Global Statistics, December 2016* (Cambridge, UK and Gland, Switzerland, p.1). Retrieved 15 January 2018 from https://www.protectedplanet.net/c/ protected-planet-report-2016/december-2016--global-update.

United Republic of Tanzania (URT). 2014. *Fifth National Report on the Implementation of the Convention on Biological Diversity.* Vice President's Office, Division of the Environment (March 2014). Retrieved 15 January 2018 from https://www.cbd.int/doc/world/tz/tz-nr-05-en.pdf.

———. 2015. *Report on Ruaha National Park Boundary Dispute with Villages of Mbarali and Chunya Districts.* Dar es Salaam: Ministry of Natural Resources and Tourism, United Republic of Tanzania. April 2015.

Walsh, M. 2012. 'The Not-So-Great Ruaha and Hidden Histories of an Environmental Panic in Tanzania', *Journal of Eastern African Studies* 6(2): 303–35.

Whitmore, A. (ed.). 2012. *Pitfalls and Pipelines: Indigenous Peoples and Extractive Industries.* Baguio City, Philippines: Tebtebba Foundation.

Chapter 5

Land and the State in Ethiopia

John Markakis

'Ethiopia is a mountainous land' runs the typical introduction to the country, referring to the massive plateau at its centre that stands at an average elevation of 2,000–2,500 metres above sea level and boasts of peaks soaring above 4,000 metres. Yet, this accounts for only half of this state's domain of 1,127,127 square kilometres. The hot arid lands below 1,500 metres make up the other half. The cool plateau and the hot lowlands that surround it are dramatically different physical environments and host societies with sharply different modes of livelihood and cultures.

The Great Rift cleaves the Ethiopian massif into two uneven sections, usually referred to as the northern and southern plateaus. Flat land is not plentiful on the northern plateau, the Abyssinian homeland, and much of it is found on flat-topped mountains and hills called *amba*. Precipitation in the highlands is normally plentiful. It is also the agent of catastrophic soil erosion when it falls with torrential force on the unprotected, tilled flanks of mountains and hills and carries away the topsoil that is the Nile's gift to Egypt. The southern plateau has a lot more flat and less eroded land.

Land remains the most valuable resource in Ethiopia and is the object of perennial competition and political conflict. Control of land is the means of maintaining the state and controlling a peasant society, and every regime that has ruled this country has sought to control this resource by manipulating the system of land tenure (Dessalegn 2009). A major portion of the land is the domain of traditional pastoralists and shifting cultivators, and it has been the subject of manipulation by every regime in the modern history of this country. This chapter reviews the shifting policies of the Ethiopian state in this region and their impact on its inhabitants.

High- and Lowlands

More than half of Ethiopia's land lies in the arid lowland periphery, where rainfall is scarce and highly erratic. Aridity occurs where rainfall is insufficient to replenish loss of moisture. According to this criterion, the entire coastal zone of the Horn is arid, as is all of Somaliland and Djibouti, southern Somalia (save for the inter-riverain valley), three quarters of Eritrea and Kenya, and more than half of Sudan and Ethiopia. This means that crop cultivation using locally available technology cannot be relied on to sustain a sizeable human population in the lowland region. The arid lowlands were and remain the habitat of mobile pastoralists and subsistence agro-pastoralists, who combine shifting cultivation with animal husbandry. By far the most populous country in the Horn, Ethiopia has the largest pastoralist population, estimated at some 10 per cent of the total, and reputedly the largest livestock population in Africa, a significant portion of which is raised in the lowlands.

The implementation of traditional pastoralist production strategies is premised on the double imperative of extensive use of land and unfettered freedom of movement. The best protection against the unreliability of rainfall is freedom of movement over extensive territory, with at least one permanent water supply. Aspects of the traditional pastoralist mode of production would prove incompatible with the capitalist economy that has prevailed in Ethiopia and the Horn recently. Communal ownership of land and free movement of humans and animals across it is one of the reasons; additional reasons are that the pastoralist economy is not governed by the laws of the capitalist market, does not engage in commodity exchange and does not provide the state with directly taxable surplus. Furthermore, for reasons of security and administration, the modern state cannot tolerate free population movement across its territory and borders. Accordingly, state-promoted development strategies for the lowlands are invariably premised on sedentarization of people and commercialization of the pastoralist economy.

Until the second half of the twentieth century, high- and lowlands coexisted autonomously with tenuous contact and did not impinge on each other, save superficially. In the second half of the century, however, the contrast between highland and lowland societies widened and sharpened, as the Ethiopian state was centralized and political power was concentrated on the plateau. The state pursued a process of modernization that began the transformation of the highland economy, society and culture and at the same time promoted the integration of diverse highland communities within the domain of the Ethiopian Empire. This process had scarce impact on the lowlands, where communities continued to follow their traditional mode of life. Thus, over time, the contrast between the plateau and the lowlands grew, and the pattern of a powerful dominant centre and a powerless dominated periphery was set (Markakis 2011). Inevitably, this disparity would define the increasingly complicated relationship that evolved more recently, and land has been at the crux of it.

Land and the State in Ethiopia's Modern History

Land scarcity in the northern plateau has played a pivotal role in the modern history of Ethiopia. It was a major factor in the massive expansion of the Christian kingdom of Abyssinia that took place in the late nineteenth century and brought the southern plateau and the lowlands into the Ethiopian Empire. A steady stream of northerners flocked to the southern plateau in its wake, to colonize and rule the conquered territories. They were compensated with the land and labour of the native people, who were turned into tenants of the alien landholders. Given the lack of irrigation technology, the arid lowland zone was considered barren and its climate unhealthy, obstacles that prevented the migrants from the north from spilling over the escarpment onto the lowland periphery (Markakis 1974).

The expansion did not solve the problem. Land surveys in the mid-1960s showed that 90 per cent of land holdings in three northern provinces (Tigray, Semien, Begemdir) measured less than one hectare, and half of them measured less than half a hectare. The problem was gruesomely highlighted by mass famine in mid-century, prompting the imperial regime in the 1950s to launch a project of resettlement from north to south. In its last years, the Haile Selassie regime, heeding the advice of international agencies, moved to scrap the archaic, immensely complex, imperial land tenure system in favour of private property. Famine triggered the end of Haile Selassie's 44-year reign in 1974, and the private property initiative ended with it.

The problem of land preoccupied the successor military regime known as the Derg (the Committee), whose solution was revolutionary: nationalization instead of privatization. Launched with the slogan 'Land to the Tiller', what it did in fact was to make the state the sole arbitrator of matters regarding the disposition and use of land. The 1975 Land Reform expropriated the landlords and gave the peasants usufruct rights over the land, distributed among them in equal shares, and was very popular with the peasants in the south, who were freed of onerous landlord exactions. This did not solve the problem of falling agricultural productivity in relation to population growth. In the early 1980s, drought once again hit the same blighted region of the north and was followed by a biblical famine that took an estimated one million lives. The disaster prompted the military regime to launch a massive resettlement programme to move land-hungry peasants from the north to the south.

At the outset, the resettlement proceeded gradually, and about 100,000 people were moved by 1983. It was then, in the midst of famine, that a drive was unleashed to drain the worse-affected areas of excess population. In a crash programme, more in the nature of evacuation than planned resettlement, some 700,000 people were moved to the southern plateau and the lowlands of western Ethiopia within two years, 1984 and 1985. About 60,000 were settled in four sites in the Gambella region, where the proportion of settlers to natives reached 40 per cent, the highest in the country. In Beni Shangul Gumuz, a long-term incursion of highlanders from the adjacent Amhara region into the elevated western Metekel district accelerated under the Derg. State farms were established with workers brought from the highlands; an irrigation scheme was built on the Bambasi River for the use of highlanders; and 10,000 settlers occupied two sites in the Beles River basin, where some 250,000 hectares were earmarked for them, displacing about 18,000 Gumuz natives. Ultimately, this ambitious project proved a costly failure and did not outlive the regime, whose collapse in 1991 was followed by the spontaneous abandonment of resettlement sites.

This was also the fate of another Derg project: villagization. Began as a security project in Bale province during the 1977–78 war with Somalia, and extended, for the same reason, to Hararghe province in 1984, it was then implemented throughout the country. Bullied by local administrators, peasants were forced to dismantle their huts and use the material to build new ones on sites laid out in grid fashion along roads. Detailed but flawed guidelines were issued for every aspect of the programme – from village sizes that proved too large, to house dimensions that proved too small – making no concession for the immense diversity of Ethiopia's countryside (Human Rights Watch 1991; Clapham 2002; Taddesse 2002). According to a former regime official, 'the main goal was the control of and regimentation of society, not development' (Dawit 1989: 307). Not surprisingly, agricultural production suffered. By the end of the decade, peasants were already abandoning the new villages, and few survived the regime's collapse in 1991.

It was the search for energy that initially drew the centre's attention to the lowlands. This goes back to the mid-1940s, when US companies began exploring for petroleum in the south-eastern Somali-inhabited region, where gas deposits were discovered in 1973, and also began explorations in Gambella. These activities were halted by regime change in 1974.

Lowland Agricultural Development Policies in the Twentieth Century

Ethiopia, aka 'the water tower of East Africa', is amply endowed with another source of energy, which is water. Twelve major rivers comprise the drainage system of the plateau, descending the escarpment to cross the lowlands. The Awash River that flows close to Addis Ababa and along the railway line from Djibouti offered the potential of irrigated cultivation in the vast Awash Valley using technology that was available in the mid-twentieth century. The land was inhabited by subsistence cultivators and pastoralists, who were easily displaced by *force majeure*, and the valley would become the development prototype for the lowlands and a harbinger of their future.

Development in the form of commercial agriculture was introduced in the early 1950s, when the Gille Oromo pastoralists were evicted from their lands on the Upper Valley to make room for a Dutch firm to establish Wonji Sugar Estate and a processing factory. The company was exempted from taxation in all goods it imported and was assured of a virtual monopoly of the national market through the imposition of a high tariff on imported sugar. The Estate's relationship with its workers was such that it required the presence of a police contingent to keep them in line (Human Rights Watch 1991; Clapham 2002; Taddesse 2002). Ten years later, a hydroelectric project, the Koka Dam reservoir, was inaugurated in the same region. Meanwhile, the Gille community disintegrated and virtually disappeared.

Established in 1962 to promote commercial cultivation, the Awash Valley Authority (AVA) introduced the 'investor' concept. Mitchell Cotts, a British firm with extensive interests in Africa, was first to secure a vast concession in the Lower Valley for irrigated cotton cultivation. By 1975, irrigation covered one-quarter of the estimated potentially cultivable area of the valley, and cotton occupied 87 per cent of it. When cotton prices doubled in the early 1970s, investor profits increased hugely. It did not last long, however, because the 1975 Land Reform nationalized all land, banned private land ownership and expropriated the landlords without compensation.

Pastoralists and Agricultural Development in the Twentieth Century

The Land Reform marked the first time that pastoralism was accorded official recognition in Ethiopia, appropriately with reference to land. 'Nomadic People shall have possessory rights over the lands they customarily use for grazing or other purposes related to agriculture', it declared. The plight of the lowlands was also noted in the Derg's 1976 Programme of the National Democratic Revolution: 'Nationalities on border areas and those scattered over various regions have been subjected to special subjugation for a long time', it said, and promised that 'special attention will be given to raise the political, economic and cultural life of these nationalities. All necessary steps to equalize these nationalities with the other nationalities of Ethiopia will be taken'. Replacing the derogatory term *zelan* (nomad) with *arbto ader* (livestock producer) in official pronouncements was a flattering touch.

The first official study of pastoralism in Ethiopia was undertaken in the early 1980s under the auspices of the Ministry of Agriculture, and it produced several well-researched volumes on *The Nomadic Areas of Ethiopia* (Fekadu et al. 1984). Settlement was a key issue the study was requested to consider, and it was expected to identify potential sites and design development models for it. The study came to the opposite conclusion, however, and stated it forthrightly, to wit: 'The strategy of transforming the sector into settled agriculture cannot be a proper development approach except in particular cases' (Vol. 3: 74).

The Land Reform wrecked the commercial agriculture sector that had grown under the imperial regime in the Awash River Valley. Most of the large plantations became state farms, and the rest was parcelled among the clansmen in plots of 2.5 hectares per household. A settlement programme was launched to turn the pastoralists into cultivators, and a Public Settlement Authority was formed in 1977 to oversee the programme. It was replaced in 1980 by a Settlement Department in the Ministry of Agriculture, which was taken over by the Relief and Rehabilitation Commission (RRC) later. A number of settlement schemes were established, and by 1983 over 10,000 hectares were occupied by some 7,000 Afar settlers. Sixty per cent of production was cotton, the rest maize and irrigated pasture. Funding was made available to provide the settlements with infrastructure and road links.

The settlement farms were run by appointed managers with minimal settler participation. Many settlers worked only part time in their farms, and others hired highlanders to work for them. Heavily subsidized with inputs and services, the settlement farms were far from profitable. This did not affect the settlers themselves, who were paid a fixed stipend regardless of profit. The programme, particularly its emphasis on cultivation, was faulted by every study made of it. 'A production system totally divorced from the pastoralist traditional way of life seems to be the one major factor that has been a hindrance to its success,' was the verdict of *The Nomadic Areas of Ethiopia*. 'As it stands, it would be hard to recommend any part of it for further expansion of rain-fed crop production', it concluded (Vol. 3: 82). Summing up the experience of the settlement policy towards the close of the Derg era, one observer described it as 'a special type of state farm' and a 'welfare programme' (Abdulhamid 1989: 105).

For Afar pastoralists, the dawn of modernization was an unmitigated disaster. The most serious damage to livestock production was caused by the loss of vast areas of fertile grazing land on the eastern side of the Awash River. All the land taken by irrigated farming was previously intensively used by pastoralists on a seasonal basis. Needless to say, there was no compensation for this loss. The AVA claimed to own the land and gave concession rights to investors on land the Afar claimed as their own.

Land loss resulted in overload of the remaining grazing areas, with overstocking and overgrazing as the result. Even more damaging was the blocking of livestock access to the Awash River by the plantations that stretched along its eastern flank. The AVA had scarce knowledge of Afar society and the dynamics of mobile pastoralism, and they gave no thought to dealing with this problem by providing alternative access routes. Farms were planted across major access routes to the river, obliging the herders to trek great distances to find open access, or forcing them to invade the farms, causing damage to fencing, crops and irrigation canals while losing animals drowned in the muddy canals. Such incidents became routine and poisoned relations between planters and herders.

Afar pastoralists depend on flooding to regenerate the areas they call '*kalo*', which provide dry season pasture close to the river. The taming of the Awash River with a hydroelectric dam and water reservoirs in the Upper Valley, and the manipulation of its flow for irrigation in the Middle and Lower valleys, had a lasting impact on the moisture and vegetation regimes throughout the region. The dams on the Upper Valley reduced flooding and distorted its pattern, affecting pasture growth throughout the entire valley. Flooding was further reduced and distorted in the Middle and Lower valleys by water diversion into irrigation canals, field bunding, and the blocking of distributaries to control flooding into planted areas.

Irrigated cultivation on a massive scale also had serious health implications. Herbicides and biocides used in the plantations contaminated canal water used by people and animals. Plantation crop residue and weeds foraged by animals were likewise contaminated. Malaria, a familiar scourge in the region called *da-hanaso* ('milk sickness'), because it comes with the rains when animals give a lot of milk, now became a major health problem and remains the leading cause of death in the Afar region.

The scale on which the plantation economy operated was far beyond the scope of the local economy, and there was no synergy between them. Theoretically, large-scale commercial production creates employment opportunities for the local population. In this case, there were scarcely any Afar with the skills or education needed for well-paid jobs, and few had the motivation for low-paid seasonal work. The former went to qualified highlanders, and the latter to destitute Oromo peasants from Wolo and Shoa, who did the seasonal weeding and cotton picking for pitiful wages. The plantation economy brought with it the first signs of urbanization in the Awash Valley, and there were more than 20,000 highlanders in the valley in the early 1970s. However, Afar were not attracted to the hamlets that appeared in the Middle and Lower valleys, and they were dominated by highland shopkeepers and Oromo labourers.

The rapid decline of the local economy was tragically revealed in the catastrophic drought and the famine that followed in 1972–74, known as *Unda Abar* ('Great Famine'). The estimated livestock loss for the Afar region was 70 per cent of cattle, 37 per cent of camels and 40 per cent of flock animals. Isolated in their inhospitable territory, a large part of what was still then *terra incognita* outside state control, the Afar died in the thousands without aid ever reaching them.

A decade later, the famine that devastated north-eastern Ethiopia was another blow. A report by the Ethiopian Red Cross noted the malaise felt by the people:

The Afar feel their way of life has failed in terms of the viability of their pastoral economy, politically in the maintenance of their regional autonomy and in competition with their regional adversaries ... The traditionally self-reliant Afar that defied any external encroachment or subjugation, now find themselves dependent and willing to receive any assistance and protection against stronger opponents and for this they are willing to accept a less lofty position. (Ethiopian Red Cross 1988: 4)

Loss of land and displacement exacerbated conflict over diminishing resources between the Afar and their neighbours. On the approaches to the escarpment of the northern plateau, they clashed with the Karrayu Oromo, who themselves had been devastated by the sugar cane plantations on the Metahara plain between the Kessem and Awash rivers. On the opposite side of the valley, the century-old struggle with the Issa Somali drive intensified. Afar–Issa Somali clashes in the area crossed by the railway line forced Addis Ababa to intervene, and it repeatedly tried to draw a line to separate them, but in vain.

Lowland Development Policies in the Twenty-First Century

The coming to power in 1991 of the Ethiopian Peoples' Revolutionary Democratic Front (EPRDF) promised fundamental reforms of the political system through democratization, and decentralization of the state through the adoption of federalism. The first, it was promised, would transform people's relationship to the state, while the second would redress the iniquitous centre-periphery balance of power.

Federalism raised the profile of the lowlanders. For the first time, ethnic communities were congregated in their own federal state (*kilil*) and district (*woreda*), with a degree of self-administration and recognition of their distinct identity and way of life. Self-administration restored some of the autonomy they had lost, and the recognition of their languages was the first step towards restoring the dignity of their cultures. These were major and quite unanticipated gains for which Ethiopians in the southern plateau and lowland periphery were beholden to the new regime. Federalism also produced resources allocated to the *kilil* by the federal government, and these became the object of competition among local elite factions and the substance of lowland politics.

A highland insurgent movement, the EPRDF had scarce knowledge of the lowlands when it came to power. Meles Zenawi admitted later, 'we went in there blind'. An EPRDF official explained: 'These are clan-based societies, unlike our peasantry, and we did not know if our political experience suited them'.[1] There had been tenuous contact with some lowland groups opposed to the Derg who were considered allies in the common struggle, but none of them were regarded sufficiently politically mature for membership in the EPRDF.

In its political approach to the lowlands, the EPRDF showed a lack of imagination that contrasted sharply with the talent for political inventiveness it displayed elsewhere. Overcoming an initial wariness of clan-based communities, it resorted to the same political formula it used on the highlands. A bewildering series of Peoples Democratic Organizations were formed to represent ethnic groups. They produced neither political stability nor administrative effectiveness, nor did they make good use of the federal subsidies, the carrot the regime offered them. They were shells within which the lowlanders carried on with their ethnic and clan rivalries. They merged and split and changed names and leaders repeatedly in the years that followed. At the same time, the federal government began grooming a corps of lowland elite it called 'regional intellectuals'. Young lowlanders with secondary education were sent to the Civil Service College in Addis Ababa and to institutions of higher education elsewhere in Ethiopia, from where they returned with degrees to be appointed to senior positions in the *kilil* administration. More often than not, these novices were backed by highlander deputies with the required skills and experience.

The EPRDF came to power in 1991 with the motto 'Land to the Tiller' it inherited from the radical student movement that had led the opposition to the Haile Selassie regime. Despite considerable pressure from Western donors, it refused to reverse the land reform of the Derg and kept the land under state ownership and control. During its first decade in power, it struggled mightily to bring about a green revolution in the highland peasant sector and end the food production deficit that had plagued the country for generations. It was the first time modern agricultural practices were introduced to the Ethiopian peasantry, with the state mobilizing an army of trained agricultural agents to work with the tillers. It was a determined effort by a ruling party that considered the peasantry its solid political base.

Run from the centre, the so-called Agricultural Development Led Industrialization programme was heavily politicized and increasingly prone to coercion. A flawed design assumed that one size fits all and was applied without concession to the highly diversified Ethiopian countryside. As a result, it had modest success in some areas and no impact on others. A variety of inputs – fertilizer, improved seeds, pesticides and so on – were imported. Initially subsidized by the state from depleting resources, the burden was later shifted to the peasants to carry through loans. The overall result was meagre, and food aid from abroad remained a structural component of the economy, while famine continued its periodic visits to the country. By the turn of the past century, the ruling party had lost faith in the peasantry.

The EPRDF had initially cancelled the resettlement and villagization programmes of the military regime 'until conditions are ripe for such programmes'. Conditions apparently had ripened by the beginning of the twenty-first century, when a three-year voluntary resettlement programme aiming to move 2.2 million people was announced. This time, political considerations ruled out shifting people across *kilil* boundaries, and the programme was carried out within the Amhara, Tigray, Oromia and Debub (southern) federal states. About 180,000 households were resettled in more than 100 purpose-built villages by the beginning of 2005. The strategy envisaged that after five years of implementation, 67 per cent of the Afar and Somali regions would be settled, and 75 per cent of Beni Shangul Gumuz and Gambella pastoralists and agro-pastoralists would take part in villagization. Villagization began in conjunction with the land lease policy introduced in the lowlands during the second decade of the century.

The resolutions of the July 1991 Addis Ababa Conference that set up the transitional government led by the EPRDF pledged to 'give special consideration to hitherto neglected and forgotten areas' (art. 16), and the 1995 Ethiopian Constitution required both the federal and regional states (*kilil*) 'to provide special assistance to nations, nationalities and peoples least advantaged in economic and social development' (art. 89/4). Pastoralist rights to land for grazing and cultivation as well as the right 'not to be displaced from their own lands' were also enshrined in the Constitution (art. 40/5). The EPRDF's initial Statement on Economic Policy referred to nomadic regions as areas with special problems and promised 'to issue policies based on studies in order to alleviate the particular problems of these regions' (Transitional Government of Ethiopia 1991: 23). No studies or policies were produced, and the issue was not mentioned again, save for a brief Statement on Pastoral Development Policy issued by the Ministry of Federal Affairs a dozen years later, which referred vaguely to sedentarization and agro-pastoralism.

By the turn of the twenty-first century, the EPRDF had shifted from its original radical Marxist posture to an accommodation with capitalism; a requirement for obtaining economic and political support from Western patrons. Even so, it sought, with some success, to fend off the tight embrace of the free market by protecting state assets from privatization and retaining a strong role of the state in production, distribution and regulation: neatly packaged in the concept of the 'developmental state'. Among other things, this endorsed the leading role assumed by the state in the 'development' of the lowland periphery.

In the first decade of the present century, Ethiopia entered a phase of so-called 'accelerated and sustainable development', planned and managed by the state and financed by foreign loans and private capital. The Growth and Transformation Plan (2010–20) was conceived on a grand scale with the goal of raising the country to middle development status by 2030. The plan involved the development of major water sources for the twofold purpose of energy production and irrigation agriculture along the banks of the Awash, Wabi Shebele, Genale, Dawa, Akobo, Weyib, Omo and Abay rivers.

The lack of domestic capital and expertise obliged Ethiopia to rely on foreign enterprise to take the initiative. It proved an opportune time. The fallout of the global food crisis of 2008 and rising prices created the opportunity for transnational capital to cash in by investing in food production in areas of 'the Global South', where land, water and labour are cheap, taxes are low and regulations lax. Food-importing rich countries looked abroad for opportunities to invest in food production, and sparsely populated, capital-starved sub-Saharan Africa was a prime choice. Energy-producing countries were also attracted to the region for investment in crop production for conversion to biofuels. Low production costs in Africa and high consumer prices in rich countries promised large profits and lured capital from many parts of the world, including Asia, the Middle East, Europe and the United States, in a massive trend critics called an international 'land grab' and the 'second scramble for Africa'.

By the end of the first decade of the present century, Ethiopia had become a major participant in this global scheme. According to the director of the Agricultural Investment Support Agency set up in 2009 to expedite the process, there is no limit to the amount of land available for leasing in Ethiopia. 'We have 74.5 million hectares of cultivable land of which only about 15 million is cultivated by small scale farmers,' he said. 'Two million hectares were already leased by 2009 and three million more were made available for investment in the following two years' (Reuters Report, Addis Ababa, 6 November 2009).

It was the lowland periphery of Ethiopia that offered optimum conditions for this scheme, including sparsely populated land that could be cleared of its inhabitants; immense potential for irrigation, which could restore fertility in the arid terrain; and flat topography, which allowed for expansive mechanized cultivation. In 1997, the federal government had taken direct control of the four lowland *kilil* – Afar, Somali, Gambella and Beni Shangul Gumuz – now dubbed 'emerging regions', offering them federal assistance in terms of skilled manpower, training and equipment. Technical and managerial assistance teams of federal civil servants were dispatched by the Prime Minister's Office. At the same time, the EPRDF intervened to stabilize the political process through the single-party per *kilil* formula – merging squabbling political factions into one party – which it applied everywhere, and the Ministry of Federal Affairs was created to take the 'emerging regions' under its wing. Thus, the dominant centre-dominated lowland periphery relationship reverted to its historical form.

A development plan for the lowlands – Equitable and Accelerated Development – was part of the Growth and Transformation Plan. Its focus was on agricultural transformation through irrigation, modern technology and investor capital. The 1995 Constitution gave the *kilil* authority to administer land, provided they acted in accordance with federal law, and the Federal Rural Land Administration Proclamation (1997) confirmed the authority of the *kilil* over the 'assignment of holding rights and the execution of distribution of holdings'. Nevertheless, the Council of Ministers decreed (Proclamation 29/2001.EC) that plots of over 5,000 hectares were to be administered by federal authorities and included in a land bank available to investors. Five *kilil* were asked to identify parcels of land of 5,000 hectares and above suitable for large-scale commercial agriculture. A total of 3.31 million hectares were identified in 2009 in Afar, Debub, Gambella, Beni Shangul Gumuz and Oromia.

The issue of leasing land touched the very core of the federal arrangement, since the main advantage of decentralization from the viewpoint of the periphery was to give local communities a measure of control over their land, and to prevent it being taken over by Addis Ababa fiat as in the past. Early on, aspiring investors were directed to the *kilil* investment bureaux, but after a period of confusion and indecision, the process was taken in hand by the Natural Resources Management branch of the Ministry of Agriculture and Rural Development, whose own capacity for the task was assessed as 'very limited'.[2] Land offered for leasing was classified 'available' because it was classified 'uninhabited', 'idle' or 'wasteland', implying it neither belongs to nor is used by anyone. Accordingly, there is no obligation on the part of the government or the investor to pay compensation.

Afar

The Awash Valley was once more the pioneer in this phase of 'development', and the Afar were the people who paid a heavy price. The plantation economy in the Awash Valley that had flourished in the late imperial era and expanded under the Derg collapsed entirely in the 1990s. State farms, settlement schemes, community projects and other ventures dependent on state management simply dissolved.

It was not until the turn of the century that the EPRDF was able to turn its attention to the Awash Valley with a grandiose scheme. The Tendaho Dam and Sugar Project was designed to occupy nearly all the irrigable land in the Middle and Lower valleys for sugar production. At the time, three existing plants in Ethiopia produced some 267,000 tons of sugar yearly, and the country's domestic consumption was predicted to reach 400,000 tons by 2010. The projected output of the new scheme was expected to meet domestic demand and also export sugar in the Horn. To reach this goal, the scheme would occupy 85,000 hectares in the Middle and Lower valleys: 65,000 for cultivation and the rest for infrastructure, factories and supporting services.

This expanse included not only the land of existing state cotton plantations in the valley and vast grazing areas but – inconsistently, given the EPRDF's penchant for agro-pastoralism – all the land cultivated by Afar Aussa in the Lower Valley. According to the report of an Indian firm of consultants who prepared the feasibility study, 'the irrigation scheme will therefore occupy much of the most productive grazing in Afambo, Assaita and Dubti districts'.[3] Construction of a giant dam began in 2007 near Logia town to harness Awash River. A similar but smaller project is under construction in the south-west with a dam on the Kessem River, a tributary of Awash River.

The devastating impact on the ecology of the valley and its inhabitant were bluntly predicted in the study. It acknowledged that in this largely desiccated and denuded land 'a forested area of 15,000 hectares will be cleared, plus 19,000 hectares of bush and shrub land'. An accompanying environmental impact assessment made the following chilling predictions:

> The impact of the project on the existing wildlife species is significant because most of the land in the area will be allotted to the irrigation scheme and vegetation will be cleared . . . It is not simple to suggest a solution to this problem . . . The project site is in one of the most malarial parts of the region . . . malaria is and will be the major cause of death in the project area . . . The dam poses a vital threat to the lakes that form the Awash River . . . the lakes, they will dry out.[4]

The area to be occupied by the dam and reservoir was described as 'desert area and has no significant cultural, economic & agricultural importance to the Afar'. The loss of pastureland was not deemed harmful. 'Even though a big area of pasture land will be expropriated for irrigation development, the conditions for livestock appreciably will be improved due to the irrigated pasture, range improvement and services provided to the pastoralists.' To compensate the herders for this massive dispossession it recommended a mere 1,800 hectares be allotted for 'pastoralist development'.

The report did not attempt to veil the fact that the scheme spelled death for the Afar economy and way of life. It did put the familiar gloss on it, in terms of the future benefits it would bring to the people of the region: infrastructure, training, employment and so on. In the meantime, the mass of displaced and stockless people would be gathered in resettlement camps. 'Resettlement sites to be provided with access roads, schools, health units, mosques, veterinary health posts, flourmills, watering points, etc., before displacement'; all familiar promises routinely made and unfailingly reneged on in the past.

'Though the task of covering such a large area of land with sugarcane in three years is challenging, it can [be] made possible by efficient management and perfect planning,' was the blithe conclusion of the original study by the Indian consultancy.[5] Unfortunately, neither prerequisite materialized. The plan's ambitious goals and targets were seriously affected by the inordinate delay in the completion of the infrastructure and plant. In 2017, several years past the planned date of completion, neither of the two projects was operational and not a single kilogram of sugar had been produced.

The reasons for this are many. The grandiose size of the Growth and Transformation Plan and the unrealistic targets it set are now said to be far beyond the country's economic, technological and administrative capacity to deliver. The government's choice to entrust a major role in planning, construction and administration to federal and *kilil* state agencies had negative consequences, given the lack of capacity for the task at both levels. State agencies, ministry divisions and departments, and ministries themselves, bid for contracts directly or set up parastatal structures for this purpose. The Ministry of Defence became the biggest local contractor using state assets. Soon after coming to power, the original parties that formed the EPRDF set up their own business ventures, which flourished on state contracts and gradually expanded into production, transportation and construction; a practice imitated by EPRDF-affiliated political parties that appeared afterwards at the *kilil* level. Obviously well placed to win state contracts, these parties were also able to get unsecured bank loans. The Ethiopian Sugar Development Corporation itself was staffed with inexperienced young graduates, and senior posts were filled with persons with political connections who were frequently recycled: the Kessem Project had four managers in five years.

The result was a feeding frenzy involving Ethiopian state and private capital, as well as foreign state and private counterparts. Eleven Indian contractors were involved in Tendaho. Chinese contractors were brought in to finish Kessem, after a company owned by the Ethiopian Ministry of Defence walked out of the project without returning the funds it received or incurring any liability, legal or financial. Within a few years, the Ethiopian 'economic miracle' had produced a new hierarchy of power and privilege spawned by the 'developmental state'. It also produced corruption on a monumental scale, which did more than anything else to dim the lustre of the 'miracle' and people's confidence in the EPRDF regime. An editorial in a local paper noted, 'the construction of around ten sugar factories . . . is saddled by a plethora of shortcomings that have dented the government's credibility in the eyes of the public'.[6] With eleven sugar projects at various stages of preparation, the country depended on imported sugar as late as the end of 2017. Meanwhile, the fate of the Afar was sealed. Their future lies in seasonal work at starvation wages in the sugar cane fields.

Gambella

The chaotic interval that followed the overthrow of the military regime in 1991 was particularly violent in Gambella, where it is remembered as *girgir* ('turmoil'). When the Ethiopian soldiers abandoned the area, pent-up Anywaa resentment of highlander settlements in their midst found release through attacks on settler villages. The initial incident was an assault on the village of Ukuna, which had a mixed population of some 3,000 settlers and 770 Anywaa. The village was burned down, and as many as 100 highlanders lost their lives. This signalled the start of an exodus of settlers that eventually left only a small number of them in the region.

The Anywaa then turned on the Nuer pastoralists, who had been moving into Gambella to avoid the civil war in South Sudan for years, pushing the Anywaa before them and settling on their land. The Nuer had gained local ascendancy under the Derg, and their incursion accelerated during its reign. Under the EPRDF, the situation was reversed, as the Anywaa gained supremacy in the *kilil* and used it to isolate the Nuer politically. For the next dozen years, the two clashed violently while the federal government tried to find a political arrangement that would satisfy both sides. It was not until the mid-2000s that a solution was found that gave parity in the state government to the Anywaa, Nuer and a smaller ethnic group, the Majang, and a semblance of normality returned. However, intermittent clashes on the ground continued, as the pressure on land intensified with outsiders moving in.

The Gambella plain with its many rivers and rich alluvial soils was beginning to attract attention, and investors eager to open the land to commercial exploitation lined up with applications in hand. Among the first was the MIDROC Ethiopia Technology Group conglomerate with plans for half a million hectares. A subsidiary, Saudi Star Agricultural Development, began rice production on 10,000 hectares on the banks of the Alwero River. Others soon followed, including BHO Bioproducts, an Anglo-Indian company that planted rice and cotton on 27,000 hectares.

By far the largest venture was undertaken by an Indian-owned company with a lease on 300,000 hectares and was unveiled in 2010 on the Baro River. The ninety-year lease gave the Karuturi Global company free land for six years, after which it would pay 15 birr ($0.90) per hectare yearly. The cost of local labour was estimated at $50 monthly per hectare, while the company's projected annual profit in ten years was $100,000. 'This strategy will build capitalism,' boasted Omot Obot Ogom, the *kilil* president. The leased land was declared 'uncultivated', despite the fact that the Baro River has been the mainstay of Anywaa agriculture since time immemorial. The Anywaa practice a diverse production system that utilizes available resources – forests, grasslands, riverbanks – and combines crop production, fishing and hunting. The pivot upon which the system depends is the annual flooding of the river. The Anywaa mode of production adapts and exploits the river's flood pattern without interfering with it, while the technology introduced by Karuturi aimed to tame the river and change its pattern. It proved a costly mistake.

The project began by clearing the forest along the riverbanks to make room for large-scale mechanized cultivation. It then sought to divert the floodwater by constructing flood control dykes, which were repeatedly breached, flooding the cultivated area, drowning crops and destroying expensive imported machinery, which had proved useless anyway in waterlogged land. Typically, state officials and company experts ignored the Anywaa and made no effort to draw on local knowledge gained over centuries.

In 2011, the company planted 12,000 hectares with corn, only to see it inundated shortly before harvest time; a disaster it claimed was caused by a freak-ish and unpredictable whim of nature. In fact, it was widely believed to be the natural consequence of widespread deforestation. Until then, forest-covered land absorbed much of the floodwaters, allowing the Anywaa to plant local flood-re-sistant varieties of maize and sorghum adapted to the wet ecological condition. The flood's annual renewal of the soil's organic content removes the 'problem of exhausting soil fertility', allowing the land to be 'continuously cultivated forever unless the river changes its course' (Kurimoto 1996: 44–45). During the dry season, the fertilized soil retains enough moisture to allow for a second planting, a process known as 'flood-retreat cultivation'.

Karuturi brought in flood control experts from India and Holland to deal with the problem. Their advice was to redouble the effort to tame the Baro River and change its course, using the same methods. It backfired spectacularly the next year when the fortified dykes first diverted the flood towards Anywaa-cultivated land, causing much damage, then the flood breached the dykes and spread over the company's fields. The reversal that cost Karuturi some $15 million not only derailed the company's plans to expand cultivation to 45,000 hectares; it led to the collapse of its share prices, forcing the company to declare bankruptcy in 2015.

South Omo

In South Omo, the collapse of state authority in 1991 was the signal for a free-for-all among several ethnic groups, just as the region was flooded with automatic weapons left by the dismantled Ethiopian army. In 1993, elders of twelve ethnic communities reached an agreement that secured a fragile peace. Land use rights were the focal point of the agreement, which stipulated that rights over land concerned use, not ownership, and all groups and their animals have the right to land they need for survival.

It was the spectacular physical setting of the Omo River Valley and the flam-boyant culture of its people that first raised interest as a potential tourist attrac-tion. A major portion of it had already been reserved under previous regimes for national parks, wildlife reserves and controlled hunting zones. The reserved area amounted to more than 18,000 km^2 in South Omo Zone – the total area of which is 22,360 km^2; that is, over three-quarters. Its potential for tourism could be exploited only if herders and livestock were excluded from the designated areas, or their activities inside were restricted. This became a bone of contention between the local population and officials responsible for these areas, occasionally leading to violence.

The rivers that cross the zone are another resource with potential for devel-opment to which Addis Ababa turned its attention in recent years. The focus is the Omo-Gibe basin, whose hydroelectric energy potential is second only to that of the Blue Nile. The country's biggest supplier of electricity, fed from a dam known as Gilgil Gibe I, began operations in 2004. Gibe II, a second power plant fed from this dam, was completed in 2010. It was believed that neither of these would have a significant impact on the hydrology of the Lower Omo. By contrast, Gibe III sited on the Omo River 300 kilometres south-west of Addis Ababa, whose potential surpassed Gibe I and Gibe II, raised great concern in that respect. It was advertised as the second largest dam in Africa and expected to double Ethiopia's generating capacity. Up to 50 per cent of its output would be exported to neighbouring countries. The Italian government provided part of the funding for the project, the contract for which was awarded to an Italian company without bidding, as was the contract for the initial ecological impact assessment, which made no mention of the dam's potential impact on the ecology of the Omo River floodplain (see Turton, this volume).

Concern voiced abroad about the negative impact on the downriver ecology prompted Ethiopia's Environmental Protection Authority to carry out its own assessment two years after construction began in 2006. Referring to the Lower Omo, it recommended an annual 'controlled flood' over a ten-day period 'to fully compensate all adverse effects'. This assessment was roundly condemned abroad as 'grossly inadequate'.[7] The African Development Bank, which had provided part of the initial funding and was considering additional support, was then obliged to produce its own assessment. Critics abroad found this one 'fatally flawed in terms of its logic, in terms of its thoroughness, in terms of its conclusions'.[8] Nevertheless, a Chinese firm was awarded the contract for a fourth dam on the Omo River on the northern border of South Omo Zone.

Those who know the area warn of a potentially devastating impact on people whose livelihood depends entirely on the river's floodwaters. Seasonal flooding sustains pastures for their livestock and prepares the land for crops that make up a good portion of their diet. Already significantly reduced, Lake Turkana, which is fed by the Omo River, is threatened with extinction, as are the people who live on its shore.

Gibe III also provides water for projects undertaken by the Ethiopian Sugar Development Corporation (ESDC) in South Omo. The Kuraz Sugar Development Project (KSDP), enclosing 150,000 hectares of land with plans to expand it to 175,000 hectares, is the mega development scheme for the area. Kuraz I commenced planting in 2014 and was expected to go into production in 2016, while Kuraz II and III were scheduled to begin production in 2017. None of these targets have been met, and no sugar had been produced in South Omo by the end of 2018.

About twenty firms – state and private, Ethiopian and foreign – have been involved in consultancy and construction work in the KSDP project. They engaged some 30,000 workers, nearly all of them highlanders, whose number is estimated to rise to 700,000 when it is fully operational. As in the case of the Awash Valley, such a massive intrusion will change the demographic balance of the region, whose native population does not exceed 500,000. In the Salamago district, where the project is located, the imported workforce outnumbers the native population by ten to one. Most of the sixteen ethnic groups who live there are miniscule in size and face an existential threat to their identity and culture.

The local input in the resettlement and villagization process was provided by the native intelligentsia that has been groomed into an auxiliary elite recruited into the EPRDF-affiliated local political party and local administration. They persuaded the local people to abandon their homes and land to be herded into villages provided by the ESDC. If persuasion was not enough, force was provided by the police, company security personnel and, when needed, the federal army. Each household was allotted half a hectare to grow maize.

Land in South Omo was leased also to Ethiopian and foreign agribusiness companies for commercial plantations. This land was declared vacant, and native rights to it were converted to corporate leases. It began with the acquisition of 30,000 hectares, by a North Korean investor, that were sold to an Italian 'alternative energy company' for oil palm and jatropha cultivation in southern Ethiopia. Three private cotton plantations in the Woyto Valley: Omo Sheleko, Nassa and Sagla grow cotton on an area of over 11,000 hectares. Overall, these three plantations dispossessed more than 7,000 individuals.

Beni Shangul Gumuz

Like elsewhere in the lowlands, the crisis associated with the change of regime in Addis Ababa in 1991 triggered violence in Beni Shangul Gumuz, as the Gumuz gave vent to their resentment of the resettlement programme by attacking settler villages and killing scores of highlanders. Likewise, the following years were marked by intense competition among the ethnic groups, including the highlanders, who comprise nearly one-third of the population, for political power in the *kilil*. A *modus vivendi* was reached by the end of the decade with a power-sharing formula and the rise to the *kilil* presidency of a Gumuz politician.

Beni Shangul Gumuz prospects for development improved greatly when the plans for the Grand Ethiopian Renaissance Dam on the Blue Nile that crosses the *kilil*, dividing it in two segments, were announced. Construction began in 2011 on what is projected to be the largest dam in Africa, with a huge potential for the future of the wider region.

As the first decade of the twenty-first century came to a close, the opportunity for development appeared in the form of edible crops and biofuel production promoted by the EPRDF, which also had the enthusiastic support of the local elite. 'The region has huge available plots,' enthused the president of the region

(*Addis Fortune*, 28 January 2008), and the Ministry of Agriculture earmarked one million hectares for leasing. According to the Regional Bureau of Agriculture, the overall area of arable land in the *kilil* is about 911,877 hectares, of which less than half is cultivated.

An early start was made in Metekel zone by highlanders leasing land for commercial farms and mining ventures. By 2001, eleven such enterprises were registered with 38,000 hectares (Wolde Selassie 2002: 121). The leasing process accelerated quickly, and by the middle of the second decade of the present century, 600,254 hectares were covered, putting Beni Shangul Gumuz in the lead, followed by Oromiya and Gambella with 458,292 and 399,491 hectares respectively. However, only a fraction of the leased area was under cultivation, something that holds true for the entire lowland periphery. For example, one investor in Beni Shangul Gumuz, the Ethiopian Plc, holding a lease on 5,000 hectares secured in 2009, cultivated only 900 hectares of cotton after three seasons. About two-thirds of the land was leased in small and medium plots, while two Arab investors held leases of 100,000 hectares each.

Summary

Because of its arid climate, the lowland periphery had not been affected by the historic expansion of the Ethiopian state that started in the late eighteenth century. It is only now, with new capital and technology, that the expansion process is nearing completion with the expropriation of lands in the lowlands.

Because it concerns the age-old struggle over land that has marked Ethiopia's history, the latest development is the subject of intense debate. The debate raises issues – economic, social, moral and political – that are not always easy to address separately. Since the beginning of the twenty-first century, the state has opted for the large-scale, mechanized model to break the shackles of subsistence agriculture and eradicate the ever-present threat of famine.

The new approach depends on the private sector to provide the capital and advanced technology. As an inducement, Ethiopia offers land and labour at a cost that is among the lowest in the world, and at a time when the global market sees superprofits for investment in foodstuff and biofuel production. Investor response has been enthusiastic and Ethiopia has emerged overnight among the leaders in this field in Africa. While domestic capital is involved, the bulk of the investment is expected to come from abroad.

Foreign capital has focused on production of edible and biofuel crops destined for export, which is also the preference of the country's rulers. According to the Ethiopian Investment Guide of 2012, companies that export half or three-quarters of their production are entitled to greater incentives compared to those that supply the domestic market. For a country with a perennial food shortage problem, this struck observers as perverse. The official thinking on this was explained by a minister of agriculture, who said: 'If we have the money, we can buy food anywhere'.

The preferred mode of production requires large spreads of land, which are not easily available on the highlands, where smallholder farming prevails and land tenure rights are not easily manipulated under the federal system of government. By contrast, subsistence cultivators and pastoralists in the periphery use land extensively – and, from the economist's point of view, wastefully. Furthermore, since their rights to the land have never been recognized by the state, they are easily dispossessed, and the cost of leased land for the investor is nominal because the inhabitants receive no compensation for it. Instead, they are promised that the new model of agricultural cultivation will bring significant benefits for the local communities, employment opportunities in the plantations and factories being the most important.

From the investor's point of view, however, mechanization reduces the need for human labour and lowers its cost. As a rule, seasonal labour is paid less than the World Bank $1.25 per day poverty threshold. Ethiopia has no minimum wage law. A bundle of infrastructural benefits for the dispossessed communities are promised: roads, bridges, electricity, schools, hospitals and so on. These are perceived as goodwill presents from the investors, rather than community contractual rights, and are honoured more in the breach than in the observance.

The consequences for the land in the periphery could be dire. The environmental cost of highly intensive farming – devastated soils, dry aquifers and ruined ecology from chemical infestation – are already obvious in the highland region near Addis Ababa, where horticulture for export has flourished for some time. The protection of the environment is entrusted to the Environmental Protection Authority. However, the agency appears to regard itself as the facilitator of investment, and its findings have been challenged at home and abroad.

The breakneck speed with which the programme was implemented raised issues of social welfare and morality that concern the people who live on the land. They face a cataclysmic upheaval of their world. They are compelled to switch from subsistence cultivation to industrial agriculture, from being owners of the land to become tenants and hired labourers on it, from being food producers to food consumers, to leave their scattered homesteads and congregate in villages designed for them by the state, to abandon ancillary activities – food gathering, hunting, fishing, beekeeping – that enrich their diet and are integrated into their culture in order to survive in the margins of a production system that will produce food and energy not for them but for strangers in other lands.

John Markakis is a political historian who has devoted a professional lifetime to the study of the Horn of Africa. His latest work, *Ethiopia: The Last Two Frontiers* (2011), is a study of the manifold contrasts between Ethiopia's high- and lowlands.

Notes

1. Personal interview.
2. See Swedish International Development Agency (2009), 'Ethiopia: Study on Institutional Structure and Human Resources Development Needs in Sector of Land Administration', *Final Report* 8.
3. Draft Final Report (2005), 'Sugarcane Production Agronomy and Farm Machinery' (Section 007), Addis Ababa, prepared by Water Works Design and Supervision Enterprise and Water Power Consultancy Service (India) LTD, and Hora Agroindustry PLC. Addis Ababa.
4. Interim Report (2005), *Environmental Impact Assessment*, Addis Ababa, p. 29.
5. Draft Final Report (2005), Addis Ababa, p. 36.
6. *Reporter*, Addis Ababa, 16 July 2017.
7. International Rivers Press Release, 7 March 2009.
8. Richard Leakey interview, BBC Amharic Service, 14 April 2009.

References

Abdulhamid Bedri Kello. 1989. 'Settling Semi-Nomadic Pastoralists in the Awash Valley', *Ethiopian Journal of Development Research* 11(1): 105.

Clapham, C. 2002. 'Controlling Space in Ethiopia', in W. James, L.D. Donham, E. Kurimoto and A. Triulzi (eds), *Remapping Ethiopia: Socialism and After*. Oxford: James Currey, pp. 9–32.

Dawit Wolde Giorgis. 1989. *Red Tears: War, Famine and Revolution in Ethiopia*. Lawrenceville, NJ: Red Sea Press.

Dessalegn Rahmato. 2009. *The Peasant and the State: Studies in Agrarian Change in Ethiopia: 1950s–2000s*. Addis Ababa: Addis Ababa University Press.

Ethiopian Red Cross. 1988. 'Even after Good Rains, Afar Pastoralists Remain Vulnerable', *Report*. Addis Ababa.

Fekadu Gedamu et al. 1984. *The Nomadic Areas of Ethiopia*. Addis Ababa: Ministry of Agriculture.

Human Rights Watch (HRW). 1991. 'Evil Days: 30 Years of War and Famine in Ethiopia'. New York, Washington and London: *Africa Watch Report*.

Kurimoto, E. 1996. 'People of the River: Subsistence Economy of the Anywaa (Anuak) of Western Ethiopia', in S. Sato and E. Kurimoto (eds), *Essays on Northeast African Studies*. Osaka: National Museum of Museum of Ethnology, pp. 29–57.

Markakis, J. 1974. *Ethiopia: Anatomy of a Traditional Polity*. Oxford: Clarendon Press.

———. 2011. *Ethiopia: The Last Two Frontiers*. Woodbridge and Rochester: James Currey.

Taddesse Berisso. 2002. 'Modernist Dreams and Human Suffering: Villagization among the Guji Oromo', in W. James, L.D. Donham, E. Kurimoto and A. Triulzi (eds), *Remapping Ethiopia: Socialism and After*. Oxford: James Curry, pp. 117–32.

Transitional Government of Ethiopia. 1991. 'Ethiopian People's Revolutionary Democratic Government Economic Policy'. Addis Ababa.

Wolde Selassie Abbute Deboch. 2002. 'Gumuz and Highland Resettlers: Differing Strategies of Livelihood and Ethnic Relations in Metekel, Northwestern Ethiopia', Ph.D. dissertation. Göttingen: University of Göttingen.

Chapter 6

Persistent Expropriation of Pastoral Lands

The Afar Case

Maknun Ashami and Jean Lydall

The Famine of 1973 was caused in great part by development allowed
and encouraged by a government elite working in corrupt liaison with
international capitalists. If the present type of development continues
unchecked, the full utilization of the 200,000 irrigable hectares in the
Awash Valley will leave many millions of hectares of desert and semi-
desert totally under-utilized – for the only people or culture capable of
exploiting such land will no longer exist.

—G. Flood, 'Nomadism and Its Future: The Afar'

This radical assessment of the Afar plight was written by Glynn Flood in November 1974 while doing anthropological fieldwork among the Afar pastoralists in
the lower Awash Valley of Ethiopia. Flood estimated that the Awash River was
then 'the life-source for some 150,000 Afar pastoralists and their animals (cattle,
camels, goats and sheep) in the southern two-thirds of Afar territory' (1975a: 5).
His essay 'Nomadism and Its Future: The Afar', published by *RAINews* in January 1975, is as pertinent today as it was then.

The Impact of Agro-industrial Development on Afar Pastoralism

This chapter reviews the economic and political history of the Afar in the Middle and Lower Awash Valley, with an aim to investigate how commercial agro-
industrial projects and corresponding development policies of different govern-

ments have impacted the livelihood of Afar pastoralists, and how the Afar, both ruling elites and regular pastoralists, have responded.

Tensions between the state and pastoralists are widespread throughout Africa, and the Afar case is no exception. This example is particularly interesting because it spans three political regimes with radically different approaches to governance, and yet in each instance the needs of the Afar pastoralists were and are effectively subordinated to the interests of agro-industrial development. It also shows how the predicament of the Afar pastoralists was, and continues to be, aggravated by the policies of their own local elites.

We concentrate at length on the period starting in the 1960s, when capital-intensive agriculture was introduced to the Lower Awash Valley during Haile Selassie's regime, up to June 1975, when the military forces of the Derg attacked the Afar, and the Awsa Sultan and his entourage fled in exile to Saudi Arabia. Maknun's doctoral dissertation, 'The Political Economy of the Afar Region of Ethiopia: A Dynamic Periphery' (Ashami 1985), was devoted to this period, and Glynn Flood's Afar work journal and field notes cover the pivotal years 1973–75 (see Ashami, Flood and Lydall 2018).[1]

We then deal more briefly with the Marxist-Socialist period, when land was nationalized and irrigation projects were turned into state farms, followed by the present era, where large-scale commercial farming and fast-track development have been promoted by the current Federal Democratic Republic.

The Afar and the Awsa Sultanate

The Afar are known by different names: the Arabs call them Danakil, and the Amhara and Oromo call them Adal, but they call themselves Afar. The name Danakil first occurs in the thirteenth-century writing of the Arab geographer Ibn Said (Ibn Said 1970, quoted in Lewis 1998: 155).

The Afar, who speak a Lowland East Cushitic language closely related to Saho, Somali and Oromo, live in Ethiopia, Eritrea and Djibouti, in an area known as the Afar Triangle, which lies in the East African Rift. The Afar region is bordered by the Ethiopian escarpment to the west, the Red Sea to the north-east, the Buri peninsula to the north, and the Addis Ababa–Djibouti railway to the south. Dominated by the Danakil Desert (lowest point 155 metres below sea level), the region is characterized by extreme heat (25°–48°C) and aridity (100–200 millilitres per annum). The Awash River and its tributaries, fed with water from the rain-rich Ethiopian Highlands, flows through the southern part of the region and spreads out in the Awsa Delta before ending in a chain of desert salt lakes.

For hundreds of years, the Awash Valley, including the Awsa Delta, provided the Afar with valuable grazing land, watering points and cultivation sites, figuring prominently in their history as the only area where food crops could be grown, and an elaborate irrigation system was established long before modern irrigation schemes were introduced.

In the middle of the seventeenth century, the Aidahiso ruling lineage within the Moodayto confederation of clans dislodged the Afar Islamic Imamate that ruled the Awsa Delta and established the Awsa Sultanate under Wazir Kadafo. Sultan Kadafo inherited the administrative system of the Islamic Imamate, which was based on state officials called *malak* (sing.)/*malokti* (pl.), who were in charge of collecting taxes. The *malokti*'s responsibilities included: organization and co-ordination of controlled flooding and irrigation of pasture areas; controlling and limiting entry of outsiders and coordination of access by resident herds; organization and coordination of the treatment of cattle diseases and the isolation of infected animals. In addition, there was a special official, known as Baari Malak, for the Awsean peasantry residing in the Awsa Delta. Prior to the nineteenth century, the *malokti* collected taxes from the Awsean peasantry and the agro-pastoralists of the Moodayto clan (the ruling clan) in the north and central areas of the delta. This system was later extended beyond the delta to include management of forests, grazing areas, agriculture and livestock. Many *malokti* were recruited from non-Moodayto groups. In the 1970s, under the *malak* system, there were three regional management units for livestock – two in the delta and one in Kalo (the periphery) – and a separate unit for timber.

Traditionally, the Afar were divided into five sultanates: Awsa, Tadjoura, Rahayto, Biru and Gobad, which differed in size, degree of centralization and economic activities (agriculture, fishing, salt trade and, above all, pastoralism). Individuals were (and still are) affiliated to particular sultanates by way of their patrilineage and clan (see Ashami 1985: 40). Social and political institutions were based on territory and clan affiliation, with the sultans and clan leaders controlling the distribution of land rights and water, dealing with legal disputes and managing external relations. Many clans are found dispersed throughout the sultanates, thus providing valuable cross-cutting ties.

In the past, the sultans depended on revenues from trade and taxation imposed on salt extracted from Lake Assa. However, the decline of Red Sea trade and the establishment of colonial trading centres on the coast led the Awsa Sultanate to raise revenues from agriculture and livestock. Tax was imposed on livestock at the turn of the twentieth century, and pastoralists who utilized dry season grazing areas had to pay the relevant *malak* one cow, called *kalo saga*, per herd and season.

Livestock (cattle, camels, goats, sheep and donkeys) belonged to individuals or to the sultanate. In 1973, Cossins estimated the number of cattle belonging to the Awsa Sultanate at between 20,000 and 25,000, and possibly double that number of camels, goats and sheep (Cossins 1973). In 1975, Flood collected details of 26 camel and 40 cattle herds belonging to the sultanate (GFFNW: 431–32).[2] The Dambeela tribe, which inhabits the Bayahale (also written Boyale) area, where Flood had his field site, was estimated to own more than 20,000 head of cattle. The sultanate's herds were cared for on a usufruct basis, according to a custom called *agle*. Privately owned animals were also often loaned out to others in this way, as Flood noted:

> *Agle* constitutes one of the binding forces of Afar society. The potential threat that a man can take from you his animals is a great source of power. Even if you have *agle* with someone else and can take back from him then you are being forced to break yet another social relation . . . The man who has your animals shares the capital increase with you – he gets male young, perishable, slaughtered, and you get female young, allowed to live. (GFFNW: 441)

Agro-industrial Development in the Awash Valley

At the beginning of the 1960s, the Awsa Sultanate, under Sultan Alimirah, was still an autonomous region without central government presence. Since the 1950s, the central Ethiopian government had tried to undermine the sultan's influence, but without success. Formerly, Imperial Ethiopia had allowed traditional authorities to run their regions, depending on them to maintain peace. Alimirah's personal connections with the royal family made it difficult for the central government to have its way. Although the Awsa *Awraja* (district) was nominally under the authority of the Wollo province, Wollo was also a royal province with Crown Prince Asfa Wassen as its governor. He and his wife were close friends of Sultan Alimirah, who helped them acquire two thousand hectares of land, known as Barga Farm, in the Awsa Delta, and adjacent to his own Sahile farm of similar dimensions, in order to grow cotton under the management of the Tendaho Plantation Share Company (TPSC). In 1962, the central government established the Awash Valley Authority (AVA) with the explicit aim of administering the valley's resources and directing its development. The AVA was granted the right to encourage foreign investment, and land was handed out to foreign and non-Afar Ethiopian concessionaires. Because the government did not recognize the Afar's right to own land, Sultan Alimirah rejected the AVA's authority:

> We are loyal to our government, and we paid Giber (Tax) for generations. We fought for the land as we fought for the country because the land is ours, just as the country is ours. No man with official paper from Addis Ababa is going to take that right away from us.[3]

The British Mitchell Cotts Group initiated the TPSC, the first cotton plantation in the Awash Valley and Ethiopia. J.K. Dick, chairman of the Mitchell Cotts Group, wrote about his initial meeting with Alimirah, the Sultan of Awsa:

Subsequent T.V. pictures of the men on the moon would give a close idea of the sort of landscape we were confronted with. Our Land Rover driver had erected our table, and four chairs and Arthur Gaitskell and I, plus Alimirah, and Yayo, duly sat down. The purpose of this absolutely vital meeting was to establish whether or not we would be welcome in the Danakil Territory, whether people would work for us, whether an influx of casual labour at the height of the cotton-picking season would be acceptable, and whether or not we ought to model ourselves on the Gezira scheme or pay wages in cash. This last point was crucial . . . We got a very good reception from Alimirah who explained that in his view this could be an excellent development for his people, that they should be paid in cash and that he would support us in any way he could. (From Dick's biography, quoted in Ashami 1985: 151)

The Mitchell Cotts Group signed an agreement with the Ethiopian government that envisaged a three-tier cooperation among TPSC, AVA and 'outgrowers' (local people who would cultivate cotton for TPSC to process in their ginneries). The TPSC was to provide 'such assistance as would be necessary to support the cultivation of cotton by outgrowers to a minimum quantity of 9,000 tons per annum' (Ashami 1985: 155). Sultan Alimirah advised TPSC to make their plantations at Dubti and Ditbahari, areas that were 'not important to the Afkeek-Maada (tribal section), the political power base of the Awsa Sultanate, which retained exclusive control of the delta, but (were important) to two politically less important groups' (ibid.: 153). 'These were the numerically large Dambeela clan who resided in Bayahale near Dubti, and Arbta (a segment of the ruling Moo-dayto clan), some of whom were residents of Dubti, but the majority of whom were migrant herders' (ibid.: 161).

In the delta region, the sultan's family, the crown prince and a few others developed large cotton farms with substantial TPSC support, while hundreds of agro-pastoralists cultivated small farms of maize for sale to migrant workers (ibid.: 195). Meanwhile, in Dubti and Bayahale, as well as in the Middle Awash Valley, uncounted thousands of pastoralists suffered a critical loss of dry season grazing without gaining compensation, either in the form of irrigated pastures or as a share in cotton profits. Furthermore, the plantations blocked easy access to the Awash River for watering purposes.[4]

In exchange for TPSC assistance, the sultanate supplied fifty Afar guards to provide security for their plantations, especially protection from trespass by nomadic cattle (ibid.: 157). This, of course, increased the pastoralists' resentment. The political leaders of the most affected groups put pressure on the sultan to negotiate with AVA and TPSC to provide them with irrigated pastures. Although an agreement was made among Afar leaders, TPSC and AVA to irrigate the Bayahale grazing area, TPSC decided in 1968 to embank the Ferite canal and put a weir across the Bayahale to stop unwanted flooding of their plantations, thereby effectively eliminating any flooding of the Bayahale grazing areas (ibid.: 164).

When N.J. Cossins made a 'Study of the New Cotton Wealth of the Old Afar Sultanate of Awsa', some pastoralist elders told him:

> 'We allowed them to come here,' they say, 'because Amoyta (the Sultan) said be patient they will help develop your land, but nothing happened.' 'Now', they add, 'if the company (TPSC) tries to get more land, we will fight. If the Amoyta says don't fight no one will hear him for there is no patience anymore.' (Cossins 1973: 155)

The AVA attempted to solve the pastoralist problem by settling a few of them as cotton farmers at Amibara in the Middle Awash Valley. But, as Flood pointed out,

> the existing settlement schemes in the Valley have the obvious appearance of mere appendages to a massive development of capitalist agriculture. What else is a settlement scheme involving 214 families each on 2.5 hectare plots, in comparison with 50,000 hectares of 'developed' land? . . . AVA's need to make a success of the scheme *on paper*, explains why the 'settlers' were given ridiculously high wages for practically no work on 'their' farms. (Flood 1975b: 18)

These 'settlers' used their money to restock their and their relative's herds, which indicates how they were still fundamentally pastoralists (see Ashami 1985: 144–45).

In 1967, the growing community of Afar capitalist farmers, anxious to protect their new-found cotton wealth, decided to cut their dependence on TPSC and sought alternative finance from the Addis Ababa Bank (Ashami 1985: 169). The sultan used some of his wealth to educate a new elite to manage the cotton farms. He also set up a blocked account for drought emergency at the Addis Ababa Bank.

The sultan updated the sultanate to better manage the new cotton enterprise by appointing members of the newly educated elite to positions of authority. The governorship of the district, which had been held by *Fitawari* Hamadi Yayo, the first minister of the sultanate and a close ally of Emperor Haile Selassie, passed to Hanfare Alimirah, one of the sultan's sons. Likewise, Alwan Yayo, the senior *malak* responsible for the agricultural section, was replaced by Haji Hanfare, who also held the position of deputy sultan.

The Awsa Farmers Cooperative (AFC) unofficially came into existence with the objectives of expanding irrigated land in the interests of the emerging farmers, and thereby limiting the growth of existing foreign and government projects;

replacing existing highland tenants by Afar; and following a long-term policy of self-reliance that would involve provision of agricultural inputs, aerial spray services and acquisition of cotton-processing plants (Ashami 1985: 170). The AFC decided that large farmers should share 40 per cent of their profits with the clan members to whom the land belonged.

The AFC encouraged hundreds of Afar and some non-Afar (Arabs, Sudanese and highlanders) to convert pastureland in the Bayahale area into farms that would provide cotton for TPSC and maize for thousands of migrant workers. By the end of 1972, AFC farms had hemmed in the TPSC Ditbahari plantation. The expansion of AFC farms worsened the situation of the pastoralists, and in an attempt to ease their plight, the sultan settled four hundred nomad families on a thousand hectares in the Ferite area, adjacent to the TPSC Dubti plantation.

Growing Discord between Afar and Haile Selassie's Government

In the early 1970s, tensions between the central government and the Awsa Sultanate intensified. The sultanate's economic power, generated by cotton, and the sultan's close political relations with the Middle East – in particular Egypt, where students had been sent and an Afar language radio programme established – worried Prime Minister Aklilu Habte Wold. On his annual pilgrimages to Mecca, which were always cleared by the emperor's office, the sultan met other Muslim leaders. Independent of Ethiopian officials, he also cultivated friendships with foreign embassies, particularly those of Britain and the United States. The sultan made several visits to foreign countries: the Gezira plantation in Sudan sponsored by the Mitchell Cotts Group; a visit to the United States sponsored by the State Department; a private visit to the United Kingdom; and visits to West Germany and Kenya.

In 1971, a bomb was planted in a busy market in Asaita, the capital of Awsa, killing several people and injuring many. The sultan's security force reacted violently, attacking highlanders whom they saw as the enemy. Both the Afar and the Mitchell Cotts Group thought the bomb was planted deliberately to draw the Afar into military confrontation with the highlanders, and thereby to justify the government sending in the army. To avoid this, the sultan decided to hand over seventeen of his soldiers to the police, along with his nephew, who was the sultanate's head of security. These men were sent to jail in Dessie, the capital of Wollo. A year later, they were set free. The confrontation inevitably intensified tensions between the Afar pastoralists and hundreds of thousands of migrant highlanders who worked on the cotton plantations.

In 1972, under pressure from AVA and the irrigation-scheme farmers, the amount of water released from the Koka hydroelectric dam between March and

October was increased to allow 25,000 ha of land to be cultivated in addition to the 45,800 ha already under cultivation (see Kloos 1982: 29; Ashami 1985: 120). As Flood remarked:

> The Awash has been tamed and regularized for the farmers, but the effects of this reduction in the river's potential to flood has an obvious effect throughout the Valley. The irrigation process, too, takes much water from the river and allows it to drain away or evaporate in the fields, where it is lost to the herdsmen. Less water reaches the inland delta of the Awash nowadays, so that vegetation balances have been disturbed and the desert is allowed to encroach. (Flood 1975a: 7)

Moreover, in 1972–73 the rains failed and a disastrous famine hit the province of Wollo, including the Afar region. Almost 30,000 people perished, and many thousand head of livestock as well. At the same time, the cotton plantations had bumper crops. Alone, the Awsa cotton farms (including those of the sultan and crown prince) sold 27,457 quintals of cotton to TPSC in 1972–73, compared to 13,230 quintals in 1971–72 (Ashami 1985: 159).

When the rains finally came in August 1973, Flood remarked on the tragic irony in a letter to his friend Barrie Machin:

> It rained too, so there's plenty of grass, and Ol Man Awash burst its banks on August 3 and there's mud all over the desert, green, and the Afar are putting their houses on stilts. Grass is plentiful. It's a pity that most of the animals are dead. Still, can't have everything. Mother Nature is doing her bit again, with typhoid knocking off the wise guys who stuck out the cholera. Between 1 & 2000 people died in Asaita (population probably around 5000 before). But the number of people in town hasn't changed much, because the hungry ones are still flocking in. The faces change. There have been mass burials. No burials. The jackals & hyenas are looking good. (GFJL: 246–47)[5]

H.E. Voelkner, a consultant to the AVA, cautiously blamed irrigated farming for the devastating effects of the drought:

> The effect of the latest drought (1972–73) may not have been as devastating had the river been allowed to flood as in its unregulated past, and had the normally flooded area been available as grazing area to the Afar pastoralists. (Voelkner 1974: 335)

Flood, elaborating on the importance of flooded grazing, wrote:

In the pastoral economy, flooded grazing was absolutely essential during the dry season ... Above all, each group needs access both to land which drains quickly after flooding and to land which drains slowly, if it is to survive a dry season which can last from mid-September to late-June. The land which has been taken for early development is mostly land close to the river in areas which flooded easily and took a long time to drain. Consequently the pastoralists have lost the land which is of greatest importance to them – that land which gave good grazing during the hottest and driest part of the year from February to June. (Flood 1975a: 7)

As regards the famine, Flood suggested its effects were less in Awsa than elsewhere because of the sultan's help:

The Great Famine of 1972/3, which killed an inestimable number of people in Wallo Province, including the Awash Valley, was noticeably less in evidence in Awsa than elsewhere – although population density is higher than in the rest of the Valley, and although many thousands of Afar from other regions flooded into Awsa to seek help. This is because the leader of the Afar of Awsa, Alimirah, used the profits from farming accumulated in earlier years to save the people. (Flood 1975a: 8)

Two months after writing this, Flood learned from the people of the camp where he was doing fieldwork that, contrary to what he previously understood, they did not get assistance from the sultan during the drought:

17 January 1975
Last night talked with Ali about the bad times. The two years before I came were the worst with animals and people dying of starvation. No animals have died of starvation since I joined them (October 1973). At first they ate cotton, but then they also turned to H.E.'s (His Excellency, the sultan's) private pastures where they fought with his people. There was fighting between the people and *amoyta askar* (sultan's militia), and the sultan's people took and slaughtered the animals people tried to put on their pastures. They ate the meat. Ali was for a time in prison, in the hands of the highlanders and had to be brought food by Fatuma (a kinswoman). The ordinary people received no help from H.E. and were in fact heavily put down by his people. These people out here in no way like Ali Mirah. If Derg comes for him they will do nothing, they say. 'His people will fight – we will not.' (GFJL: 203–4)

In his work journal, Flood often mentioned how the pastoralists let their animals eat the cotton in the plantations. This was an obvious action for them to take, given that the cotton grew on their former pastures, which were no longer available to feed their herds. The plantation owners inevitably did their best to prevent the destruction of their crops. It was because his cattle entered a large cotton farm that Hummad, Flood's friend and host, lost his life:

> Learnt more about Hummad's death – he was searching for his cows which had gone into the cotton. Down towards Boqayto he was got by the *bi‘ida* (oryx) which had been allowed to run free, outside its compound. (GFJL: 149)

Ostensibly, the oryx that the farmer kept in captivity killed Hummad by accident, just as Hummad's cattle, which ate the cotton, supposedly trespassed by chance.

The Fall of the Old Regime, Rise of the Derg and Exile of Sultan Alimirah

In the wake of the great famine, representatives of the armed forces formed the Provisional Military Administrative Council, also known as the Derg, which took over power in July 1974 and formally deposed Haile Selassie on 12 September 1974.[6] At first Sultan Alimirah pledged support for the Derg, no doubt because they had appointed Major Mohamed Yassin, an Afar, then governor of Assab *Awraja* in Eritrea, to act as its agent and security advisor for the Afar region as a whole. Flood indicated that the appointed chairman of the Derg, Lt. General Aman Andom, respected the sultan:

> *εidi saaka* (end of Ramadan, 18 October) was a big big affair this year. Solidarity show. Aman Andom's coming was a time for him to praise Afar and H.E. (the sultan). Hanfare bowed to Andom, but Andom bowed to H.E. (GFJL: 180)

Andom's days were, however, already numbered:

> On Saturday evening (23.11.1974) the Derg killed – executed – about 60 of the prisoners from the Old Regime . . . Aman Andom, who has been a figurehead of the PMAC for some weeks (I nearly said months) was also shot, along with 3 others from within the Derg. (GFJL: 310–11)

These killings shattered whatever confidence Sultan Alimirah might have had in the military government. With the sultan's approval, the Afar Liberation Front (ALF) and the Afar students' organization, the Afar National Liberation Movement (ANLM), were founded in August 1974, and now (in November) he decided to send 60 students, via the Eritrean Liberation Front (ELF), to Somalia for military training (Ashami 1985: 219). The Derg, likewise, began to assert pressure on the sultan, as noted by Flood on16 January 1975:

> The derg (6 vehicles) came to Asaita yesterday for talks with amoyta (the sultan), and were very well received by the Oromo. They had plenty of guns. (GFJL: 203)

Meanwhile, relations between the pastoralist community and the sultan were increasingly strained. On 28 January 1975, Flood wrote:

> They tell me that there has been a little trouble with the region's goats eating cotton in Ditbahari. Helim took our goats there because there is a shortage of grass in this area, enough to seriously reduce the milk supply. They went to eat company cotton (Kobbani – TPSC) and were surprised to be met by *amoyti askara* (sultan's militia) who chased them off and, so Helim says, slaughtered four of his goats, tho' Fatuma says two. (GFJL: 210)

At the beginning of March, the Derg launched sweeping social and economic reforms, most importantly land reform, to put an end to the feudal system. The possessory rights clause in the land reform proclamation (see PMAC 1975) gave nomads the rights to grazing lands, but they were vague and ambiguous. The government announced they would nationalize all commercial farms, including one at Badhu (Middle Awash Valley), which the sultan had financed and was run by Afar elders, but excluding the Awsa farms.

On 10 March, Flood recorded that:

> *Zamača* (students sent to teach the rural population about the new reforms) have been here c. 15 days and there have been fights with Afar. They are frightened of Afar. Lokke tells of fighting in the bar – a drunk who said 'why are you playing billiards whilst we starve.' . . . The Oromo held a big demo in favour of land reform and the Afar watched scornfully. The noise of the demonstration brought thousands to Asaita for Afar defence. Some [Oromo] have gone back to their own land. Afar fully armed. (GFJL: 233)

Initially, the sultan responded to the new reforms by avowing the Afar were already socialists, as Flood wrote on 14 March 1975:

> H.E. on television to say Afar were in favour of Socialism and were 'defending the land against enemies and foreigners'. Also on the radio not

so long ago saying Afar were the first socialists in Ethiopia: – eat together. (GFJL: 234)

At the beginning of May 1975, instead of complying to a summons from the Derg to go to Addis Ababa, the sultan sent a sixty-seven member delegation of Afar chiefs, carefully selected to reflect all Afar regions of Ethiopia, Eritrea and Djibouti, to request the Badhu farm be restored to its owners and support for the exiled son of Sultan Mohamed Yayo be halted. The delegation was told, however, that they could not stand in for Alimirah, who should come and talk with the government about matters of national security.

Alimirah refused to go to Addis Ababa or to meet a delegation sent to Asaita. The impasse was exacerbated by an announcement broadcast on the Afar language programme from Addis Ababa that land in the Awsa area was to be divided into two types: land to be taken over by the Ministry of National Resources Development, which meant the establishment of state farms, and land to be taken over and distributed by the AVA.

In an ALF appeal to the Islamic world that was broadcast from Jeddah, Saudi Arabia, Sultan Alimirah gave the following account of his final meeting with the Derg:

On 28 May 1975, the Military Junta sent another delegation requesting a meeting between ourselves and a government delegation. I received them in my residence on 1 June 1975. The delegation was composed of fifteen members, including three members of the Ruling Council. They requested that I assemble the Country's chiefs and notables, and having done this we all met in a large space in front of my residence. Suddenly, we were surrounded by two hundred soldiers who were pointing their guns at myself and the notables from all sides. Major Wandered of the Ethiopian delegation spoke in an offending manner which gave the impression of extremism. The idea of gathering us in one place was meant to kill us all, but they were surprised that they too were soon surrounded from all sides by the Afar defence force in turn pointing their weapons at the soldiers. They then realised their failure, and demanded from me to disperse the Afar defence force. I told them that their actions contradict the understanding between us. That this was proof of a pre-meditated conspiracy, we knew about it. You should now leave in peace until we meet again. The Ethiopians left the meeting with their heads down. They soon became engaged in an immoral act (operation), as is their custom, by attacking unarmed civilians without any warning. (Ashami 1985: 224)

The sultan promised the delegation he would leave for the Ethiopian capital the following day. On Tuesday, 3 June 1975, reports in Addis Ababa asserted that peace had been made between the Afar leaders, when in fact violent fighting had broken out between the sultan's militia and the highland labourers. That same evening, the sultan and his entourage decided to leave the country in secrecy. As Alimirah told Aramis Houmed Soulé: 'We left Asaita late in the evening in a convoy of more than ten cars. By the grace of God, they didn't notice anything'[7] (Soulé 2011: 107–16).

The government dispatched tanks in the direction of Awsa, and by Monday evening the tanks had taken up positions near Asaita and along the desert road between Asaita and Sardo, probably aimed at preventing the sultan's escape, but they were too late. The tank force was later reinforced with jet aircraft, causing many Afar to cross to Djibouti. Meanwhile, on the morning of 3 June, the sultan's men blew up the main Doobi bridge along the Assab–Addis Ababa highway, some 160 kilometres west of Assab, thereby cutting off oil supplies to the Ethiopian capital.

Back in Asaita, violent fighting between the Afar, on the one side, and government forces, Oromo and other highlanders, on the other, led to hundreds of people being killed or wounded, with casualties on both sides. As Alimirah's son Hanfare explained to Aramis Houmed Soulé (Soulé 2011: 141–65), '(t)he military turned their arms against the civilian population of the villages. During one day (3 June 1975) in the village of Asa'eyta alone, they gathered and summarily executed 1600 persons, one of whom was a British citizen, married to a French woman, and who was in the area doing his doctoral research.'[8] The British citizen was Glynn Flood, who had gone to Asaita to retrieve his field equipment, notebooks and recordings.

Nationalization of Land under the Derg

The Derg replaced Sultan Alimirah with the son of Sultan Mohamed Yayo, but he had no power, since the *malak* system of administration had been replaced by the Derg's centralized one. The ANLM split from the ALF to join the Derg, and its members were appointed as administrators in various Afar districts, while some became fighters in Ethiopia's wars in the east and north. Because the Derg was too busy elsewhere to maintain peace and order in the Afar region, the ANLM established its own militia, known as Ugoguma, to carry out security functions.

As planned, the Derg nationalized all rural land, turning the plantations of foreigners and highlanders into state farms, but leaving the Afar farms, besides Badhu, untouched. The cotton farm of the former crown prince presumably was taken over by the Afar clansmen to whom the land originally belonged. The sultan's farm remained his in name, but without financial backing his clansmen could not run it on a commercial basis. As in former days, the agro-pastoralists of the delta reverted to growing subsistence crops, and grazing livestock. As for the sultan's herds, they remained his in name while being used by the pastoralists who herded them.

Constantly involved in wars with different groups, the Derg had no time, interest or ability to deliver development to the Afar region. According to a Food and Agriculture Organization (FAO) group, which visited the Lower Awash in 1977, there was only confusion, and they were not able to determine how the agricultural developments were being managed (see Bonnemaison 1977). There was, however, a noticeable increase in the number of Afar working as farm labourers. They replaced the highland labourers (predominantly Oromo), hundreds of whom had been killed in the 1975 June conflict, while the rest had retreated to the highlands to claim land under the new land reform. Relief settlement schemes, which after the 1972/73 drought had been set up along the main roads to provide food for work, became more or less permanent settlements for pastoralists who had become destitute, not least of all because of the loss of crucial dry season grazing. Many of these people became farm labourers, earning an income that they shared with relatives who still herded animals. Thus, for the first time, Afar pastoralists became a source of cheap labour for the cotton and banana plantations (see Kloos 1982: 38).

The vast majority of the Afar subsisted as pastoralists. As before, they continued to let their livestock enter the plantations to eat the crops. This was not only a way of feeding their hungry animals but also a demonstration against the expanding state and concessionary farms. In the 1980s, the government was obliged to abandon banana production because of such defiance. The introduction of a compensation fund to appease the pastoralists, according to Bekele and Padmanabhan (2008: 12), 'did not put an end to the grievances, however, as the power of the pastoralists emanate from their great numbers, which was increasing over time'.

After the Derg's Defeat: Ethnic-Based Federal Government and Fast-Track Development

The year 1991 was a milestone in the history of Ethiopia. The reign of the military Derg came to an end. Its leader left the country and sought asylum in Zimbabwe. New elites were preparing to fill the vacuum, having militarily defeated the Derg. Early in 1991, a US-sponsored conference took place in London to ensure a smooth transfer of power. Among those who attended were representatives of the Derg, the Tigray People's Liberation Front (TPLF), the Oromo Liberation Front (OLF), the Afar Liberation Front (ALF) (represented by Hanfare Alimirah) and the Eritrean People's Liberation Front (EPLF). They agreed to form a new government in Addis Ababa, minus the EPLF, who were soon to form a new government in Eritrea. In June 1991, all political organizations in Ethiopia, excluding the Derg and the Ethiopian Workers' Party, attended a new conference. In their deliberations, they agreed to the formation of a federal government based on ethnicity and the recognition of a right to self-determination of nationalities.

Ethiopia was to be made up of fourteen regions, but in 1995 these were reduced to nine national regional states and two special administrative localities. Hence, the Afar National Regional State (ANRS) was created, and in 2007 a new capital was established at Semera to replace Asaita. According to the official ANRS website, the state is currently made up of 5 administrative zones, 28 *woreda* (districts) and 28 towns.[9] The 2007 Ethiopian Population and Housing Census estimated there was a total population of 1,390,273 in the Afar region, and a rural population of 1,205,138, of whom 401,764 were categorized as 'pastoralists . . . who are wandering from place to place in search of grass and water for their animals' as opposed to people living in 'conventional or non-conventional housing' (Samia 2008: 5). In Zone 1, which covers the Middle and Lower Awash Valley, there was an estimated rural population of 327,904, of whom 173,066 were 'pastoralists'. As the census did not gather data on economic occupation, we do not know how the others made their living, but according to the current Ethiopian government's ANRS web page, 90 per cent of the state's population leads 'a pastoral life by rearing camels, cattle, goats, sheep and donkeys'.[10] We suspect that the 'pastoral life' embraces agro-pastoralists as well as nomadic pastoralists. Firehiwot and Yonas (2015) estimated the number of livestock at 10,179,277, while Behnke and Kerven (2013) reported that 'over a third of all Awash Valley irrigable land is under irrigation'. These statistics indicate that pastoralism is far from dead in the Afar region, and this in spite of continued expropriation of valuable flood-fed grazing land for the benefit of large-scale irrigation projects.

The ALF, led by Sultan Alimirah, embarked on reorganizing the war-torn region of Afar. The primary issues they tackled were security and restoration of land expropriated by the Derg. With the help of the new government, they secured a victory when it was decided that the Middle Awash Agricultural Development Enterprise (MAADE), which replaced the former AVA, would hand over 6,547 hectares of land, together with its entire irrigation infrastructure, to the Afar elders (see Bekele and Padmanabhan 2008: 12). This land included the Badhu farm, which the sultanate had funded in the early 1970s, but which the AVA had then taken over, only for the Afar to gain it back through a court order, before finally being expropriated as a state farm under the Derg. Although the restoration of the farm was important, the Afar of the Middle Awash were unable to maintain it properly, having little expertise in farming and no way of acquiring necessary credit and technical assistance. In the end, the elders opted for sharecropping with highlander investors (see Abdurahman 2002; Bekele and Padmanabhan 2008; Mulugeta and Firehiwot 2014: 97).

Generally speaking, the establishment of the ANRS has led to major improvements in the fields of health and education, and the development of *Afaraff* (Afar language) as the working language of the regional government. However, the launching of two major sugar development schemes (Tendaho and Kessem), and parallel villagization programmes, seriously threaten the livelihood of pastoralists by expropriating vast areas of nomadic land and removing pastoralists from their traditional habitats.

The Kessem Sugar Development Project is located in the Middle Awash (Zone 3) at Fentalle, 50 kilometres from the Metahara Sugar Factory. The 20,000 hectares of land allocated for the production of sugar cane were formerly dry season pastures used by Afar pastoralists. The Kessem Dam, with a capacity of 500 million cubic meters of water, providing water for irrigation and a sugar factory, also takes over land from the pastoralists. According to the Ethiopian Sugar website (published 18 January 2017), irrigable land has reached 2,946 hectares.[11] The sugar factory should at first produce 153,000 tons of sugar and 12,500 cubic meters of ethanol, and in the long run 260,000 tons of sugar and 30,000 cubic meters of ethanol annually. The ethanol will be used to produce 26 megawatts of electricity per annum.

The Tendaho Sugar Development Project (TSDP) is located in the Lower Awash around Dubti, Asaita and Afambo (Zone 1) on land where the TPSC and AFC formerly had their cotton plantations, which the Derg later turned into state farms. Originally, of course, the land provided important dry season pastures for Afar pastoralists. According to the Ethiopian Sugar website (published 18 January 2017), TSDP was allocated 50,000 hectares: 25,000 hectares to be cultivated by TSDP staff, and 25,000 hectares by Afar pastoralists as outgrowers.[12] Over 20,866 hectares of land was already irrigated with water from the Tendaho Dam, which has a capacity of more than 1.8 billion cubic meters. In the long run, the Tendaho Sugar Factory, which is already in operation, should produce more than 3 million quintals of sugar and 31,000 cubic meters of ethanol, and generate 60 megawatts of electricity annually.

We have no information regarding the number of Afar pastoralists who have been or will be given land to grow sugar as outgrowers. Nor do we know how many pastoralists are interested in becoming outgrowers. There is no information on the size and number of families removed from the land to pave the way for the dams, factories and sugar plantations. We do know, however, that many thousands of Afar have been removed from their regular habitation and grazing areas in the lower plains. Firehiwot and Yonas (2015: 101) report that, '[a]ccording to most informants at the field, particularly the pastoral inhabitants of the *woreda*, the sugar development project has been perceived negatively. To them, it was an initiative that confiscated their land and led to the impoverishment of the local inhabitants than an agent of prosperity [*sic*]'. More recently (2018), there are rumours that the Indian contractors of the Tendaho Sugar Factory have abandoned the undertaking, and there are eyewitness accounts claiming that no sugar has been planted.

The government started a villagization programme involving 18 centres covering 18,000 hectares of land, and they promised the provision of schools, health centres, clean water, grinding mill and mosques. The provision of mosques was unique to this part of Ethiopia, but after a couple of years the government (or the Ethiopian Sugar Corporation) stopped funding their construction.

Compensation amounting to 243 million birr has been transferred from the federal government to the ANRS for distribution to affected agro-pastoralists. However, most observers agree that the programme was not properly managed. The ANRS staff admitted its failure and disbanded the Tendaho-Kessem Coordination Secretariat, a regional government office responsible for the distribution of compensation funds (see Mulugeta and Firehiwot 2014: 106–7). Another contentious issue is the absence of pastures in the resettlement areas. Not surprisingly, the government wants the pastoralists to give up their animals. But pastoralists have no desire to give up their livestock and independent way of life. Those who agreed to move to the settlements did so primarily because of the promise of social services. In practice, however, the provision of social services was either inadequate or simply not available (see Firehiwot and Yonas 2015).

Despite their rhetoric of granting greater autonomy and self-determination to the ANRS, the federal government actually imposes strict controls, doing so by way of the ruling party in the ANRS, the Afar National Democratic Party (ANDP), some of whose leadership were part of the TPLF prior to 1991. For the first time in the history of the Afar, the central government has a military presence in the valley under the pretext of keeping peace between Afar and Issa Somali. (The Afar and Issa are age-old rivals for grazing land and water, both in Ethiopia and Djibouti.) The Afar, however, believe the army is there to protect the Issa alone. The government's conflict with Eritrea means that Ethiopia depends on Djibouti for its port, and on the Somali for access to sea trade.[13] To improve its bargaining position, the Ethiopian government has recently bought a 19 per cent stake in the port of Berbera.[14] This may explain why the government seems to favour the Issa, to whom it recently handed over three *kebele* (neighbourhoods) in the Middle Awash Valley.

Unlike any previous Afar leadership, the regional government elite has the same attitude as the central government towards the pastoralists, refusing them their right to grazing land and insisting they become sedentary.

Conclusion

Whatever the regime, the Afar have always been confronted by negative attitudes towards their pastoral way of life. Government elites have regarded, and continue to regard, pastoralists as backward, and their mode of herding livestock as non-productive, and therefore consider their land as disposable. It is remarkable to note the similarities between the feudal set of assumptions that puts regions and peoples under feudal obligation, the revolutionary ideology that establishes all land may be held by, and at the disposal of, the state, and finally a neoliberal philosophy that grants the state the right to allocate land for capitalist development. Although the Derg and EPRDF governments acknowledged the pastoralists' right to possess the land that their families had used for hundreds of years, in practice they ignored this right. Rather, each government favoured agro-industrial projects, allowing foreigners, highland Ethiopians and/or the state to cultivate large areas of irrigable land – even though that land was crucial to the pastoralists as dry season pasture – and supported projects to settle pastoralists as sedentary farmers or farm labourers. The pastoralists, however, consistently preferred their pastoral way of life, it being the only viable and sustainable way of making a living in the region, and one which gave them freedom of movement, and economic and political autonomy. Those Afar pastoralists who resorted to relief settlements and seasonal work on plantations did so because of desperate need, not out of preference.

Under the Imperial regime, Sultan Alimirah welcomed the cotton plantations, happy to bring the Afar into the modern world. At first, the Mitchell Cotts Group helped him establish his own cotton farm and encouraged other Afar to cultivate cotton as outgrowers. For the sake of Afar independence, Alimirah was keen to get as much irrigable land as possible into Afar hands. When the Afar farmers met with opposition from the AVA, they established their own independent cooperative, the AFC. As on non-Afar farms, the Afar farmers used seasonal wage labourers, mainly Oromo from the highlands. In spite of taking up farming, Sultan Alimirah and hundreds of small Afar farmers did not abandon pastoralism but kept their herds, and, in the sultan's case, retained dry season pastures. In their role as farmers, however, their interests came into conflict with those of the pastoralist majority, who had lost crucial grazing land and access to watering points. In principle, the large Afar farmers shared 40 per cent of their profits with hundreds of clan members to whom the land belonged, but money could neither replace the pastures that the livestock needed for survival nor provide an alternative living for their owners.

From the very beginning, the pastoralists reacted to the expropriation of vital pastures by letting their hungry livestock enter the commercial farms to eat the crops. This led the plantation management to guard the farms with fences and armed guards. Sultan Alimirah used his militia to guard not only his own farm but also those of TPSC and the crown prince. The pastoralists also came into conflict with thousands of highland labourers, mainly Oromo, who earned their living on the plantations at the expense of the pastoralists who could no longer graze their livestock on the selfsame land.

Under the Derg, all privately owned plantations, other than those of the Afar, were nationalized. The Afar cotton farms, however, collapsed because of lack of funding and equipment, which may have been an advantage for the pastoralists, but the loss of the sultan to bargain for their interests was probably a greater disadvantage. Under the present government, the huge dams and vast sugar plantations seriously threaten the pastoralist way of life and have already impoverished innumerable Afar.

What is remarkable is how, in spite of losing crucial flood-fed grazing areas, the great majority of Afar still survive, for better or worse, as pastoralists and agro-pastoralists. Investigations by Bekele and Padmanabhan (2008: 27) indicate that '[l]ivestock remains to be the best, if not the only, sustainable livelihood option under these ecological conditions'. Had Glynn Flood not lost his life during the Derg's oppressive assault on the Afar in June 1975, he would surely have continued his research with Afar pastoralists and found out how 'the only people or culture capable of exploiting' 'many millions of hectares of desert and semi-desert' have proved resilient in the face of relentless large-scale irrigation projects, various development programmes of alternate regimes and a persistent expropriation of valuable pastures.[15]

Maknun Ashami's first degree was in Economics. In 1985, he gained a PhD in social and political sciences from the University of Cambridge with his dissertation 'The Political Economy of the Afar Region of Ethiopia: A Dynamic Periphery'. He worked as research officer and editor of the Refugee Participation Network newsletter (forerunner of Forced Migration Review) at Oxford University. Since 1998, he has taught development studies at Birkbeck, University of London and carried out consultancy work in UK, Europe and Africa. His research interests include: the state and pastoralism, migration, war and conflict.

Jean Lydall is an anthropologist and ethnographic filmmaker. She studied anthropology at the London School of Economics and did and continues to do research and make films in Hamar, Southern Ethiopia. Together with Maknun Ashami and Michèle Flood, she archived Glynn Flood's ethnographic estate at the Max Planck Institute for Social Anthropology and produced *In Pursuit of Afar Nomads: Glynn Flood's Work Journal and Letters from the Field, 1973–75*. Her film, *Family Subsistence in the Hills of Hamar*, is part of the *Guardians of Productive Landscapes* series, within the *Lands of the Future* Initiative.

Notes

1. Flood's ethnographic estate is archived at the Max Planck Institute for Social Anthropology, Halle (Saale).
2. GFFNW refers to the Glynn Flood Field Notes and Writings, which are archived at the Max Planck Institute for Social Anthropology, Halle (Saale). See also Ashami, Flood and Lydall (2018).
3. Interview with Sultan Alimirah, Awash Valley Authority, Master Plan, 1974, Annex II, p. 2. See Asmarom et al. (1974: 37).
4. See Markakis, this volume.

5. GFJL refers to the Glynn Flood Journal and Letters, which are archived at the Max Planck Institute for Social Anthropology, Halle (Saale). See Ashami, Flood and Lydall (2018).
6. For an account of the revolution, see Halliday and Molyneus (1981).
7. Our translation of French to English.
8. Translation by Michèle Flood.
9. See www.ethiopia.gov.et/afar-regional-state. Retrieved 28 May 2018.
10. See www.ethiopia.gov.et/afar-regional-state, p. 2. Retrieved 28 May 2018.
11. See http://ethiopiansugar.com/index.php/en/factories/kessem-sugar-factory. Retrieved 28 May 2018.
12. See http://ethiopiansugar.com/index.php/en/factories/tendaho-sugar-factory. Retrieved 28 May 2018.
13. The conflict has now been resolved because of Ethiopia's acceptance of the terms proposed by the International Commission – which should open up Eritrea as a site for Ethiopian export and import trade – and to the peacemaking between the new Ethiopian prime minister Abiy Ahmed and the Eritrean president Isaias Afwerki on 9 July 2018.
14. See http://capitalethiopia.com/2018/03/05/ethiopia-buys-19-stake-berbera-port/. Retrieved 28 May 2018.
15. Persistent expropriation of land can also be seen as 'accumulation by dispossession', which Fana Gebresenbet suggests may be disguised by villagization (see Chapter 9, this volume). Asebe Regassa links land expropriation with state consolidation and livelihood changes (see Chapter 8, this volume).

References

Abdurahman, A. 2002. 'The Paradox of Sharecropping in the Middle Awash Valley of Ethiopia', *12th International Annual Conference on Ethiopian Economy*. Addis Ababa. Ethiopia.
Ashami, M., M. Flood and J. Lydall (eds). 2018. 'In Pursuit of Afar Nomads: Glynn Flood's Work Journal and Letters from the Field, 1973–75', *Field Notes and Research Projects XXI*. Max Planck Institute for Social Anthropology, Department of Integration and Conflict. Retrieved 31 July 2020 from http://www.eth.mpg.de/pubs/series_fieldnotes/vol0021 .html.
Ashami, M.G. 1985. 'The Political Economy of the Afar Region of Ethiopia: A Dynamic Periphery', Ph.D. dissertation. Cambridge: Cambridge University. Printed as *Field Notes and Research Projects XXII*. Max Planck Institute for Social Anthropology, Department of Integration and Conflict. Retrieved 31 July 2020 from https://www.eth.mpg.de/pubs/ series_fieldnotes/vol0022.html.
Asmarom Legesse, V.R. Fadal and K. Krishna. 1974. 'A Report by Consultants to the Ministry of Agriculture, for the Awash Valley Authority's Master Plan for Regional Development of the Awash River Basin'. Addis Ababa: Imperial Ethiopian Government.
Behnke, R., and C. Kerven. 2013. 'Counting the Costs: Replacing Pastoralism with Irrigated Agriculture in the Awash Valley', in A. Catley, J. Lind and I. Scoones (eds), *Pastoralism and Development in Africa: Dynamic Change at the Margins*. London and New York: Routledge, pp. 57–70.
Bekele Hundie, and M.A. Padmanabhan. 2008. 'The Transformation of the Afar Commons in Ethiopia: State Coercion, Diversification, and Property Rights of Pastoralists', *CAPRI Working Paper* No. 87. International Food Policy Research Institute (IFPRI). Retrieved 20 August 2020 from www.ifpri.org/publication/transformation-afar-commons-ethiopia.

Bonnemaison, P. 1977. 'Report on a Field Visit to the Lower Awash Valley', jointly prepared by FAO Project staff. Rome: FAO.

Cossins, N.J. 1973. 'Green Heart of a Dying Land: A Study of the New Cotton Wealth of the Old Afar Sultanate of Aussa', prepared for Sir Alexander Gibbs and Co. and Hunting Technical Services. Addis Ababa.

Firehiwot Sintayehu, and Yonas Ashine. 2015. 'The Ethiopia State and Pastoralism: Appraisal of Pastoral Policies in the Afar National Regional State', in Yohannes Aberra and Mahmud Abdulahi (eds), *The Intricate Road to Development: Government Development Strategies in the Pastoral Areas of the Horn of Africa*. Addis Ababa: IPSS, Addis Ababa University, pp. 72–106.

Flood, G. 1975a. 'Nomadism and Its Future: The Afar', *RAINews* 6: 5–9.

———. 1975b. 'Development in Ethiopia', *RAINews* 9: 18–19.

Halliday, F., and M. Molyneus. 1981. *The Ethiopian Revolution*. London: Verso.

Ibn Said. 1970. *Kitabal Geographia*, edited with introduction by Ismael Alcarabi. Beruit: Al Maktabat Al Atijanrinyan.

Kloos, H. 1982. 'Development, Drought and Famine in the Awash Valley in Ethiopia', *African Studies Review* 25(4): 21–48.

Legum, C., and B. Lee. 1977. *The Continued Conflict in the Horn of Africa*. London: Rex Collings.

Lewis, I.M. 1998. *Peoples of the Horn of Africa: Somali, Afar and Saho*. London: Haan Associates.

Mulugeta Gebrehiwot, and Firehiwot Sintayehu. 2014. 'Land Use, Pastoralism and Transformation Challenges in the Afar Regional State of Ethiopia', in Mulugeta Gebrehiwot (ed.), *A Delicate Balance: Land Use, Minority Rights and Social Stability in the Horn of Africa*. Addis Ababa: IPSS, Addis Ababa University, pp. 92–116.

PMAC (Provisional Military Administration Council). 1975. 'Proclamation to Provide for the Public Ownership of Rural Lands', *Proclamation No. 31*. Addis Ababa: Ethiopian Herald.

Samia Zekaria. 2008. *Population and Housing Census 2007 Report, Afar Region*. Addis Ababa: Population Census Commission. Retrieved 20 Aug 2020 as Afar_Statistical.pdf from https://catalog.ihsn.org/index.php/catalog/3583/related-materials.

Soulé, A.H. 2011. *Deux vies dans L'histoire de la Corne de L'Afrique: Les sultans 'afar Maḥammad Ḥanfaré (r. 1861–1902) and 'Ali-Mirah Ḥanfaré (r. 1944–2011)*. Addis Ababa: Centre Français des Études Éthiopiennes. Retrieved 28 May 2018 from https://books.openedition.org/cfee/950.

Voelkner, H.E. 1974. 'The Social Feasibility of Settling Semi-Nomadic Afar on Irrigated Agriculture in the Awash Valley', *Informal Technical Report UNDP/FAO/ETH72/006 No. 23*, prepared on behalf of the State Rivers and Water Supply Commission for the Food and Agriculture Organization. Rome: FAO (FAO Access no. 35717).

Part III
Power, Politics and Reactions to State-Building

Chapter 7

Anatomy of a White Elephant

Investment Failure and Land Conflicts on Ethiopia's Oromia–Somali Frontier

Jonah Wedekind

Introduction

White elephant projects are defined as investments 'whose cost of upkeep is not in line with how useful or valuable the item is'. From an investor's perspective, such projects are 'so expensive to operate and maintain that it is extremely difficult to actually make a profit'.[1] From a social anthropologist's perspective, white elephant projects instead signify large-scale investments that serve high modernist visions of planned development and progress but fail to meet their intended purpose or backfire with political, economic and ecological after-effects.

In Ethiopia, one such white elephant project was the case of Flora EcoPower (FEP). The company first gained attention when it contracted thousands of farmers as outgrowers in East Hararghe, constructed an oil mill south of Harar, and set up plantations on the Oromia–Somali frontier to produce and process castor for biodiesel.[2] High-ranking government officials, including the late Prime Minister Meles Zenawi, supported the project and attended its inauguration. The project was celebrated as a pioneering agro-industrial investment, in line with the state's development strategy of 'agrarian transformation', part of which aimed to develop Ethiopia's Biofuel Programme, which sought to put 'degraded' and 'unused' land in 'marginal' peripheries to productive use (Nalepa, Short Gianotti and Bauer 2017). But despite the high (modernist) hopes vested in FEP and similar biodiesel projects, all of them failed (Dawit 2013).

Here, I provide an anatomy of FEP's history from start-up to failure (2005– 15). I was able to reconstruct this trajectory through an extended case study, conducted between 2013 and 2015, based on interviews with (former) government officials, investment managers and local communities involved in the project (see Table 7.1.). Empirical details and insights were gained through exceptional, authorized access to internal communiqués between FEP and the government (see Footnotes). I illustrate how Ethiopia's ruling elites facilitated FEP's project to advance state-building, gain socio-economic control over Hararghe and subdue territorial disputes in the borderlands of the Oromia and Somali Regional States. Yet, this mode of extending the reach of the state by transforming agrarian and agro-pastoralist livelihoods through large-scale farmland investments in Hararghe was a risky strategy – one that backfired with unintended economic and political consequences for state and society, some aspects of which only revealed themselves a decade later.

Frontiers, Frictions and Failures

The case of FEP complements research on Ethiopia that finds that farmland investments can serve as a lever to prise open frontiers – not only as a means of making visible and governing peripheral peoples, and of controlling access to and use of land, but also as a means of advancing state-building and initiating capital accumulation (Fana 2016; Fana and Asebe this volume). Beyond this, the case shows that state control of frontier space and society is a contingent achievement that can unravel and be undone over time (Watts 2017) – particularly if state-facilitated investments 'fail to land somewhere and create something of value', or if they leave behind broken promises of development and compensation (Li 2014: 597). Where states force frontier society and space in the thrall of large-scale investments, the worst of outcomes can be dystopian 'global neighbourhoods' (Gabbert 2018), involving multinational companies, government cadres and local communities with diverging interests and perspectives that collide to create 'frictions' that shape the particular course of an investment project and the context of the frontier (Tsing 2005). As an outcome, such frictions may leave various kinds of social, economic and ecological wreckage in their wake. Investment failures not only pose political risks to the state's capacity to consolidate control over access to and use of frontier space, society and resources; they can also have boomerang effects and lead to backlashes against the authorities that initially enabled the investments (Li 2015).

　　Much attention has been paid to the influx of farmland investments in the Global South and associated 'land grabs' justified on grounds of 'unused' lands (Li 2014). The failures of many investment projects and their specific long-term histories are, however, scarcely documented in the research literature (Edelman, Oya and Borras 2013). This study of FEP demonstrates why many investment projects that start out with investors pursuing productive enterprises – supported by state planners driven by the modernist 'will to improve' the livelihoods of peripheral peoples through their integration into such projects (Li 2007) – nonetheless fail spectacularly. The risks involved in making frontier investment projects productive and profitable often tempt investors to switch to speculative business strategies, while local actors may in turn pursue rent-seeking activities to try to feed (i.e. survive) off of dysfunctional projects. This conjures up an 'economy of appearances' (Tsing 2000)[3] in which land, often initially appropriated by force or by law in the name of increasing productivity, in fact lies idle – much to the detriment of local communities. But the tenacity of farming and/or agro-pastoralist communities may allow them – precariously – to outlast such projects and reoccupy or reuse the land in question. After the initial land grab and eventual failure of the investor thus may follow a variety of micro land conflicts between local communities and state authorities (Li 2018).

In Ethiopia, a backlash to state-facilitated farmland investments emerged in the years prior to Abiy Ahmed's ascent to power in April 2018. Previously silent forms of resistance by affected communities against investment projects and the government officials enforcing them (Tsegaye 2015) had gained in potency since the land rush took off – pushing land conflicts from the peripheries to the centre of political discourse in Ethiopia. A catalyst was the Oromo (or *qeerroo*)[4] protests, triggered in 2014 in reaction to the Addis Ababa and Surrounding Oromia Special Zone Integrated Master Plan. Although the plan's proposal to expand the federal city's territorial boundaries into the surrounding Oromia Region was dropped, protests spread across the country. They displayed discontent over top-down land administration, dispossession and displacement and the failures of investment projects. Grievances were vented vividly and violently in 2016, with protesters attacking properties of agro-industrial companies. As protests persisted, the federal government imposed two States of Emergency (in October 2016 and February 2018) but was eventually forced to promise reforms and a change in leadership.

The case of FEP is relevant here. It represents a forerunner to many subsequent failures of and resistances to farmland investments in Ethiopia. FEP first made negative headlines by clearing land within the Babile Elephant Sanctuary. This was contested by local communities, who had lost access to parkland, while conservationists challenged the encroachment on elephant rangelands (Yirmed and Negusu 2008), making FEP basically synonymous with the Elephant Sanctuary conflict.[5] For a number of reasons – which I explore here – FEP created many more problems that ultimately resulted in its failure. Previous reviews of FEP concluded that 'the project is exceptional both in its size and the extent of its failure' (Lavers 2012a: 807–9). Despite strikingly similar biodiesel project failures elsewhere in Ethiopia (Chinigò 2015a), others argue that there still remains potential for such biofuel investments in the future (Loos and Hoppe 2015). However, with the benefit of hindsight, I suggest that FEP's case is not only paradigmatic of the crisis of large-scale farmland investments in Ethiopia but also represents a precursor to the social contestation that eventually emerged in the wake of this crisis.

Castor and Context

In May 2006, representatives of the family business Hovev Agriculture Ltd arrived in Ethiopia to explore investment opportunities and apply their experience of running frontier agribusinesses. The Hovevs, once one of the largest Israeli producers of fruits and vegetables and employers of mostly Palestinian workers in Gush Katif on the Gaza Strip, had to withdraw from their land holdings after business prospects dwindled with Israel's 'disengagement' from the settlement in August 2005. While agribusinesses were compensated for relinquishing their land holdings and encouraged to resettle to other agricultural sites in Israel,[6] the Hovevs shifted their gaze to Ethiopia, where land and labour were comparatively cheap. One Hovev representative claimed, 'it is impossible to find labourers who will work for what they paid in Gush Katif. Also, water and land in Ethiopia are free . . . in Israel agriculture is dying off'.[7] Their interest in Ethiopia was timely; it was just as the Ethiopian state began attracting foreign direct investment (FDI) in land, following a shift in development strategy from a smallholder towards a dualist agricultural system. The strategy pursued an agrarian transformation from a predominantly agricultural towards a diversified agro-industrial economy, funnelling investments into lowland peripheries to put supposedly 'unused' land under production while at the same time increasing and commercializing the agricultural output of relatively 'unproductive' smallholder farmers in the highlands (Lavers 2012b).

The Hovevs noticed the biofuel boom that had begun to take hold in Ethiopia and saw a business opportunity. Biodiesel crops like jatropha and castor were booming globally, valued as 'flex crops' for their variable ecological qualities and multiple uses in energy, pharmaceutical and cosmetic industries (Borras et al. 2016). In Europe, the Renewable Energy Directive pushed for renewable energies like biofuels to make up at least 20 per cent of the energy consumption of EU members by 2020. Subsidies – under the General System of Preferences, the Everything But Arms initiative or the Africa–EU Energy Partnership programme – promoted FDI in farmland for biofuels in Africa (Kesicki and Tomei 2012). In Ethiopia, biofuel investments were promoted nationally under the 2007 Biofuel Development and Utilization Strategy, which sought less dependence on fossil fuel imports and envisioned the agro-industrial production of biofuels, both for consumption and export. Next to state-led production of sugar cane for bioethanol by the Ethiopian Sugar Corporation, investment-driven production and processing of biodiesel crops was central to the Biofuel Strategy. Biodiesel investments were promoted to commercialize both large-scale and smallholder agricultural production and link up with agro-industrial processing. The ecological qualities of biodiesel crops as 'drought resistant' and 'soil enriching' were considered suitable for improving the productivity of 'degraded' and economically 'underutilized' land in geographically 'marginal' areas of Ethiopia (Nalepa, Gianotti and Bauer 2017).

The Hovevs identified the Hararghe highlands in Oromia Region, descending to the Shebelle plains of Somali Region, as a suitable setting for castor production. Castor (*ricinus communis*) is indigenous to Hararghe, where the oil crop is known by the vernacular names of *qobbo* (Afan Oromo) or *gulo* (Amharic) (Azene 2007: 444). Hararghe's farmers cultivate castor with sorghum, groundnuts and *khat* to complement crop rotation, as organic pesticide and for fencing. Already in the late 1960s, Hararghe's agroclimatic conditions had been considered suitable for castor production, processing and export (Miller, Shaner and Burton 1969).

The Hovevs's identification of Hararghe for investment overlapped with the state's identification of land suitable for biofuel crops in marginal and degraded areas of Oromia Region, although land in Hararghe was not yet registered in the Federal Land Bank for lease to biofuel investors (Interview F). When the Hovevs applied for land in 2006, it was still standard procedure for regional states to allocate large-scale land leases to foreign investors, before this process was centralized at the federal level in 2009 (Lavers 2012b). The Hovevs proceeded to apply for an investment permit from Oromia Investment Commission, to establish Flora EcoPower Ethiopia PLC, and then travelled to Harar with a task force of regional officials to enquire about possibilities of leasing farmland in East Hararghe. The enquiry was met with hesitance by local officials, who argued that 'unused' farmland was hardly available. A former Fadis Woreda official recalled,

> FEP came here in 2006 with top guys from Oromia *kilil* [Region]. They asked for 10,000 ha. I showed them around and said, 'Look, we don't have sufficient land in Fadis. It is densely used by farmers'. But they insisted, 'If you don't have land, we need at least 10,000 farmers with 1 ha each so we can invest on 10,000 ha'. I told them, 'It will be hard to convince our farmers'. But my regional superiors said, 'Go ahead'. (Interview A)

In Hararghe, the Hovevs were confronted with a diversity of agrarian and agro-pastoralist property, production and trade relations that were historically embedded there. Most of the *gossa* (clans) inhabiting the Hararghe highlands identify as Oromo. They lay claim to the overarching Afran Qallo federations and territories, including the Alaa, Baabille and Obooraa groups, and the Dagaa subgroups of Jarso, Noole and Hume. While they share an agro-pastoral patrilineal background, most groups practised sedentary agriculture on the Harar plateau by the late nineteenth century, developing sophisticated intercropping systems in the face of land scarcity and droughts (Ezekiel 2010). Hararghe's highland farmers engaged in long-standing social and economic interactions – but also in property and resource conflicts – with agro-pastoral groups in the lowlands (Braukämper 1983). The latter include groups that share joint Oromo-Somali identities, such as the Ghirri-Jarso and Ghirri-Baabille, known for 'using Oromo farming techniques but possessing Somali social institutions' (Ezekiel 2004: 36), as well as lowland nomadic pastoralists from the Somali Issa clans (Markakis 2003). Exchange between the highlands and lowlands is frequent, as (agro-)pastoralists traverse the borderlands from Somali Region's Fik and Degehabur zones into Oromia Region's East/West Hararghe zones on seasonal livestock feeding and trade routes between the commercial hubs of Dire Dawa, Harar, Babille and Jijiga.

To demarcate the territories under the administration of the Oromia and Somali Regional States, a border referendum was held in 2004. Its contested process and outcome drove a wedge between the shared identities and relations of Oromo farmers and Somali pastoralists, particularly as most borderland *kebele* fell under Oromia Region's administration, enraging Somali Region's political elites (Hagmann and Khalif 2008). The referendum was to settle contested claims over *kebele* and land jurisdiction along the entire regional frontier (Asnake 2010), but instead the borderland territories of East/West Hararghe – where FEP planned to operate – became subject to ethnicized conflicts (Jeylan and Fekadu 2015). As FEP began its operations on the Oromia side, the Ethiopian National Defence Force dispatched the *Liyu* police to combat 'oppositional forces', including the Ogaden National Liberation Front (ONLF) on the Somali side, in response to deadly attacks on border checkpoints and a Chinese oil exploration site in Degehabur Zone in April 2007 (Hagmann 2014).

Plantations and Outgrowers

Faced with the diverse land access and use practices in Hararghe, FEP and government officials worked out two overarching property and production arrangements for plantation and outgrowers in Hararghe's highlands and lowlands.

Firstly, under the plantation arrangement, which FEP called a 'government land option', 8,000 hectares of scattered plots ranging from 100–3,500 hectares were labelled as 'unused bushland' and leased to FEP. Most plots were located in the lowlands of East Hararghe, in Midega Tola and Fadis Woreda. The first plots were ready for land 'clearance' and 'preparation' in March 2007. On paper, the lease agreement signed with the Oromia Investment Commission in January 2007 included further land concessions of 40,000 hectares, meaning that additional land would become accessible in West Hararghe should FEP expand.

Land 'clearance' involved the transformation of 'bush' into farmland. FEP cleared thousands of hectares of forest/woodlands, thereby eroding the basis for agroforestry (Yirmed and Negusu 2008) that had previously complemented the production of sorghum and groundnuts (Poschen 1986). Land 'preparation' entailed the mobilization of 'daily labour' in the vicinity of plantation plots. Labour was mobilized by government development agents (DAs) and supervised by FEP agronomists to prepare and work on the plantation land for 15 Ethiopian birr (ETB) for 8 hours/day.[8] Given high population to land ratios and lack of alternative wage-work opportunities in Hararghe (Tesfaye et al. 2004), mobilization became self-sustaining once word of job opportunities spread (Interview FEP1). Employment increased from ca. 1,000 to 4,300 labourers in the preparation phase of 2007.[9] The presence and fate of agro-pastoralists in plantation areas was not documented in communiqués between FEP and the government, nor in media or academic reports. This was a peculiar omission, given that (agro-)-pastoralists often defy state-imposed ethnic-federal territories, regional borders and formal property regimes (Schlee 2013), particularly along the contested borderlands of the Oromia and Somali Regions (Fekadu 2011). *Woreda* and zone officials remarked that (agro-)pastoralists often resisted FEP's 'land clearance' by sending livestock to feed on crop residues, potentially damaging plantations. A typical explanation for this was that 'pastoralists were told to move elsewhere or settle down and work for FEP. This was sporadic, not systematic. If they disturbed land clearance, the government intervened', either through negotiations between local officials, elders and pastoralists or, if conflicts could not be resolved, through coercion by regional police forces (Interview D). In contrast, FEP's management complained about the 'constant camel inundations of plantations and the tribal warfare down in Midega, where it is impossible to teach herders to farm in modern ways, and local government guys are entangled in tribal affairs' and supposedly neglect to protect FEP's property (Interview FEP2). Agro-pastoralists presented their experience quite differently, explaining that while FEP's plantation plots disrupted their seasonal trade routes and feeding grounds, they lacked the means and status to have their problems heard and addressed by officials (Interview E).

The plantations created facts on the ground, marking the state's authority over territory, property and resources. DAs and extension workers (EWs) were instructed by the zone administrators to strengthen and expand the patchy administrative control over *kebele* along the lowland frontier. This allowed co-optation and coercion of each *Aba Gandaa* (village leader) and local *Jaarsolii Biyyaa* (elected elders) into endorsing 'land clearance' and defusing potential conflicts through the customary process of reconciliation (*Jaarsummaa*). Defining and mapping plantations as 'government land' also served to formalize state ownership of land where customary land access and use was previously prevalent.

The 'bushlands' identified for clearance were often referred to as *bosona* (jungle) by government officials and DA/EWs (Interview F), an Afan Oromo term also used in Oromo People's Democratic Organization (OPDO) propaganda to refer to the territories of opposition organizations (labelled 'terrorists' for the past decade) such as the Oromo Liberation Front (OLF) (Zitelmann 1999). Clearance of *bosona* could be interpreted as clearing the bushlands of opposition to the OPDO/EPRDF ruling coalition. Similarly, the plantations served as a territorial strategy for the ruling elites of Oromia Regional State (i.e. high-ranking OPDO cadres) vis-à-vis the former president of the Somali Regional State, Abdi Mohammed Omar, aka Abdi Iley (Hagmann 2014), as they struggled to solidify the ethnic-regional-based administration over the contested borderlands following the 2004 border referendum. Prior to FEP's arrival, Oromia regional police presence near plantations along the borderlands was bolstered to ensure security and undermine the incursions of 'oppositional forces' (Interviews C, D).

Secondly, under the outgrower scheme, called 'community farming' by FEP, land was placed into production by contracting farmers. As of March 2007, 'cooperative agreements' (contracts) were signed between FEP and the first groups of farmers from participating 'peasant associations' (*kebele*). Accordingly, 'associated growers' (contract farmers) were mobilized by DAs and represented and signed up by their *kebele* chairmen. Once approved at *woreda* level, the contracts were passed up the chain of command and registered at Oromia's Cooperative Promotion Commission.[10] Outgrower farming was organized into three categories, which FEP called 'options'. Option 1 applied to most of the farmers who were contracted. The contract read: 'growers in this category will use their land holding, which is at present cultivated with other crops, for castor cultivation.' The company provided inputs (seeds, fertilizers) and purchased the harvest at 40 ETB per quintal (qt). Apart from groundnuts (which enhance castor yields when intercropped), farmers were obliged to eliminate the production of other crops (e.g. sorghum and *khat*).

Option 2 applied to a smaller number of farmers – those who could prove usufruct rights to land holdings that were not under cultivation when FEP arrived (e.g. because of seasonal/shifting cultivation). FEP would propose to rent such land from the rightful farmers. While the latter could engage in household production, they had to agree to 'provide the available land and labour as may be required for seeding, weeding and harvesting', while the former would provide inputs and purchase the harvest.

Option 3 served as a compromise in cases of disputes. Farmers often claimed customary/ancestral rights to land that the state and company simply saw as 'land which is not cultivated at present [and] has bush which requires land clearing'. The claimants would be given 'the option to provide the land to FEP for castor cultivation' or to 'work on these plots as mentioned in Options 1 and 2'. In return, they would 'receive a daily salary for works performed as and when required' by FEP. Similar to the 'government land option', FEP would 'use the land for its own need without sharing the income' for three years, after which the contract could be renegotiated.

Initially, only 700 farmers took part in the outgrower scheme, but FEP planned to 'select a minimum of 7,000 growers . . . holding no less than 1 hectare' each.[11]

By November 2007, reports show that 5,295 farmers jointly holding only 3,213 hectares were contracted from Fadis, Babile and Midega Tola Woreda.[12] Follow-up reports from March 2008 recorded the project's expansion to a further 11 *woreda* in East Hararghe, where FEP distributed castor seeds to 13,838 farmers.[13] FEP also notified regional officials of planned expansions to seven additional *woreda* in West Hararghe, estimating that 'the cultivated area in 2008 in West and East Hararghe will be more than 17,000 ha, [from] over 60,000 landholds in community farming'.[14] The numbers show that the planned 1 hectare per farmer ratio was always implausible. Unsurprisingly so, given that government records show that average land holding sizes in East/West Hararghe were well below 1 hectare (CSA 2009).

Projections and Production

Given initial scepticism amongst farmers, FEP's agronomists and government DA/EWs mobilized *kebele* officials and farmers to attend so-called 'participatory demonstration and training' meetings, where the supposed household benefits of producing castor were presented and farming procedures explained (Interview FEP3). It was claimed that FEP's castor variety could yield 40–50 qt/ha annually, while FEP would pay an average of 40 ETB per quintal of castor. East Hararghe's Agricultural Office recorded sorghum prices of around 150–200 ETB per quintal for 2005–6 and estimated that on average households would produce 10–12 qt/ha of sorghum in 2006–7.[15] Based on these projections, FEP's agronomists concluded that contract farmers could expect an annual income of 2,000 ETB minimum (plus start-up bonuses, fertilizer subsidies and insurance guarantees), whereas sorghum farmers would earn only 1,800 ETB maximum in 2007–8 (Interviews A, B, C). As we shall see, these projections would prove not only inaccurate but detrimental to local producers.

These simplistic calculations did not factor in the impacts that a mass switch from sorghum to castor production could have on local food market prices. They were also based on the assumption that Hararghe's farmers were overwhelmingly engaged in subsistence agriculture. In other words, FEP failed to consider that production systems in Hararghe are based on intricate practices of intercropping the multipurpose crop sorghum with the cash crop *khat* along with groundnuts, maize and vegetables. They also ignored pre-existing commodity market relations between Hararghe's farmers and *khat* and groundnut traders from which local households derived incomes that sustained their livelihoods (Ezekiel 2010).

For the state, FEP's outgrower scheme was politically and economically suitable. Hararghe's highland farmers are historically notorious for subverting bureaucratic state control over access to and use of land and the taxation of their produce (Ezekiel 2004). Vernacular land markets (e.g. land borrowing within the community) were vibrant in Hararghe, occurring under the radar of state authorities and managed under the customary authority of elders, while *guza* labour sharing (a reciprocal form of sharecropping) was crucial to sustain community cohesion and welfare (Belaineh 2006). Such practices contributed to household reproduction and land access in the midst of low land holding to population ratios that indicated 'latent landlessness' in Hararghe (Belay and Manig 2004). The new property and production arrangements under FEP, however, disrupted and inhibited informal land use practices. Under Option 1, land use for most crops other than for castor was limited; under Option 2, land rentals were formalized; and under Option 3, informal property claims by farmers were registered.

Mobilization of contract farmers also enhanced legibility and control over the activities of peripheral farming households and village elders for local state authorities. At the time, Oromia Regional State ordered the expansion of the quasi-governmental sub-*kebele* structures (*gott*) in East Hararghe, under which government DA/EWs organized farmers into development groups (*garee misooma*) (Interviews G, J; Zitelmann 2005; Emmenegger 2016). Comparable to 'one-to-five' and 'model farmer' systems of bureaucratic control elsewhere in Ethiopia (Lefort 2012; Planel 2014), OPDO-affiliated *garee*, *gott* and *kebele* leaders regularly reported any negligence, resistance to or breach of contracts by farmers or their elders not only to FEP agronomists and governmental DA/EWs but also to higher-level authorities at *woreda* and zone levels (Interviews A, C). This created widespread suspicion.

Having invested 30 million ETB seed capital to found FEP and acquire investment permits in Ethiopia, the Hovevs qualified for a loan of 15 million ETB from the Ethiopian Nib International Bank to finance the construction of their oil mill.[16] Ethiopian political elites were impressed with the construction of the oil mill on 15 hectares of land in Fadis, 25 kilometres south of FEP's headquarters in Harar. Capable of processing 500 tonnes of castor and yielding 110 tonnes of oil equivalent (toe) per day, FEP's publicly stated aim was an annual production rate of 700,000 toe by 2011.[17] The oil would be taken from storage and transported by train from Dire Dawa to the port in Djibouti for export, while any surplus produced would feed Ethiopia's biofuel programme.

In early 2007, Prime Minister Meles Zenawi (who held the office until his death in 2012) and high-ranking politicians including Abadula Gemeda, at the time president of the Oromia Region, visited Fadis to attend the inauguration of FEP's oil mill construction. The latter emphasized the importance of investments in Hararghe, an 'undeveloped area . . . prone to drought and famine', affirming that 'investments that are largely changing the livelihood of the community, such as this, deserve closer support from both the government and the public'.[18] Giving the Prime Minister a tour of the facilities, a company manager explained, 'FEP's philosophy is to integrate ourselves in the local community.'[19] The Hovevs likewise expressed confidence in the 'strong cooperation system with governmental representatives' as they publicly proclaimed their 'vision to create an end-to-end bio-energy supply chain' with the goal of gaining 'control of the world-wide growing of crops for oil'.[20] On paper, the Hovevs's assets in Ethiopia appeared impressive; in reality, they lacked operational capital to put their plans into practice. Their website hinted that they would pursue 'joint ventures and partnerships' with transnational investment funds.[21] In other words, to capitalize on the global biofuel boom, they would spin off company assets to financial backers. In a reverse merger, the Hovevs were joined by the Swiss British Fiduciary Trust Centre as a majority shareholder and backed by strategic investors from Germany, who co-founded FEP Holding AG to fund FEP Ethiopia PLC with €13 million of operational capital in late 2006.[22] As the parent company, the Holding's financial operations were registered in Munich, Germany,[23] and listed on the Frankfurt Stock Exchange Open Market by February 2007. The Hovevs held minority shares in the Holding but maintained influential positions on its supervisory board, remaining in command of the subsidiary FEP Ethiopia PLC and in control of agricultural operations in Hararghe.

Reality and Resistance

Within months of starting operations in East Hararghe's lowlands, it emerged that over 80 per cent of ca. 12,000 hectares of land under FEP's plantation plots fell inside boundaries of Babile Elephant Sanctuary. The parkland, it turned out, was actually under federal, not regional state jurisdiction, and no prior Environmental Impact Assessment (EIA) had been conducted in accordance with existing laws (Yirmed and Negusu 2008). Land clearance was resisted by local communities, while park managers and conservationists lobbied the government, NGOs and the press to review FEP's actions. Conflict resolution began in mid-2008, as an EIA was ordered (Lisanework et al. 2008), and a task force consisting of government officials from the federal, regional (Oromia and Somali), zone, district and local levels, village elders, NGOs and park managers worked out a compromise to re-demarcate the park's boundaries and protect elephant range-lands (WSD and EWCA 2010).

Nonetheless, most of FEP's plantations remained unaffected by re-demarcation. Former park managers remarked that regional '*kilil* officials applied formal pressure and informal threats' to ensure that FEP only faced minor land losses (Interviews H, I). However, the bad press FEP received over the conflict had a knock-on effect on FEP's shares from 2008–9, despite the company's attempts to maintain that the environment had not been affected. Stock market performance further deteriorated as castor oil prices fell by 28 per cent from a five-year high of €1,250/mt (metric tonne) in November 2008 to €900/mt in May 2009 (GIZ 2011: 31).

FEP's production, processing and export rates in 2008 were consistently below the projections that they had publicly released (Interviews ACA1, ACA2).

Castor output by farmers often only ranged between 4 and 8 qt/ha, and company agronomists and government DA/EWs quickly realized that castor output was far below what FEP had promised (Interviews FEP1, FEP3, C). In addition, the currency inflation of the ETB and global food price hikes led to a sharp rise in local cereal and edible oil prices in 2008 (Assefa 2014). As a consequence, rising prices and demand for sorghum and groundnuts in East Hararghe made it illogical for contract farmers to continue producing castor, without FEP significantly adapting its payment scheme.[24] Farmers began to resist castor production and break contractual rules as their households came under pressure, often resuming cultivation of sorghum, groundnuts and *khat*. They argued that the qualities of sorghum were more valuable to them than castor because of its reliable yields and multipurpose uses (household food, fire, fodder) (Interview M). Groundnuts also became more valuable as edible oil prices increased, and local traders sought to supply the local edible oil mill in Hamaressa and other small-scale processing points, while *khat* remained lucrative in the highlands because of comparatively stable and high prices.

Farmers also began taking advantage of the sheer size of community farming, which resulted in lax supervision by FEP's understaffed agronomists (Interviews FEP1, C). Forms of subversion included manipulating castor harvest weights to receive higher payments, secretly growing other crops behind fences of castor, applying FEP's fertilizer and pesticides for other crops or selling it, or registering multiple times as contract farmers under different names to cash in on start-up bonuses and input credits (Interview FEP3). Community farming quickly spiralled out of control as agronomists struggled to maintain the cooperation not only of contract farmers, their elders or *kebele* chairmen and DA/EWs but also *woreda* officials, who refused FEP's requests to push farmers to abide by contracts (Interviews A, B). Despite zone officials' attempts to mediate between different parties, FEP ceased its operations in Fadis in April 2008.[25] Rather than assess the reasons for low outputs and improve relations with farmers and local officials, FEP's *modus operandi* became increasingly aggressive, often relying on the support of regional officials to apply pressure on local officials (Interviews A, C). FEP's agricultural management began rapidly expanding the scale of operations in West Hararghe. Highlighting company assets and releasing PR statements of fantastical yield projections seemed to be the business strategy pursued by FEP's agricultural management in Ethiopia to appease existing shareholders and attract new ones for FEP Holding AG.

For 2008, financial operations in Munich recorded losses of €16.7 million.[26] FEP quickly ran out of operational capital and by early 2009 struggled to pay contract farmers, labourers and agronomists. The parent company refused to provide further capital for 2009, given dire global biodiesel markets, disgruntled board members and shareholders, and deteriorating relations between the Hovevs and financial operators in Munich. Faced with the imminent collapse of their project, the Hovevs abruptly left Ethiopia in mid-2009, leaving behind a wreckage.

The Beginning of the End

Farmers who worked to contract were hard hit by the project's failure, in conjunction with the inflation of food costs and currency values during 2008–9. Zone officials acknowledged that hundreds of contract farmers became reliant on the government Productive Safety Net Programme in order to assure household subsistence (Interview J). This came amidst high demands for food aid in Hararghe due to price hikes and droughts (Devereux and Sabates-Wheeler 2008). The role that the state played in FEP's failure eroded trust between farmers and government officials. As a result, many *woreda* and zone officials had to leave their positions and, following *gimgema* (cadre evaluation/critique) sessions in 2009–10, were either demoted or promoted depending on their role in the project (Interviews A, B, C).

The *gott, garee* and *misooma* structures that had complemented the mobilization and supervision of contract farmers temporarily broke down in parts of the Hararghe highlands. In 2010, local officials were tasked with implementing a new rural sub-*kebele* supervision system called *seelii* (party cells), which was, however, merely a new name for a rural control apparatus staffed with OPDO/EPRDF party members (Interviews G, J). In the Hararghe lowlands, some village elders attempted to reassert autonomous control over access to and use of land. Along the Oromia–Somali regional borderlands some *kebele* in Midega Tola effectively went rogue, marginalizing the influence of DA/EWs and OPDO cadres and undermining and ignoring orders from higher-level offices (Interviews K, L).

As FEP's plantation system broke down, idle investment land was officially to be kept free from 'land invaders' (*meret werariwoch*) by *woreda* officials (Interviews D, FEP2). Nonetheless, property and resource struggles emerged over deserted plots that were temporarily reoccupied by farmers and agro-pastoralists for sorghum cultivation and/or herding. While some farmers managed to accrue land this way, others were left dispossessed and forced to search for wage work in neighbouring towns (Interview N). Some deserted plots in Babile's Erer Valley were leased by East Hararghe Zone's Investment Office to domestic investors for livestock rearing, fruit and vegetable farming. Struggles to accrue leftover company assets (machinery, factory parts, etc.) also ensued between different actors seeking compensation for or profit from the company's failure. A Workers' Union of former FEP agronomists was organized to legally challenge FEP's (absent) managers for outstanding wages and compensations, but also to ensure that leftover company assets were secured or confiscated by regional police forces (Interview FEP4). Some individuals tried to take advantage of the situation, stealing and selling machinery, factory parts and castor beans that had been left behind (Interview C).

The Failed Resurrection

FEP Holding AG underwent restructuring after its subsidiary's failure in Ethiopia. During the annual general meeting in Munich in December 2009, FEP was renamed Acazis AG (henceforth Acazis), its board of directors was dismissed and replaced, and a new CEO was chosen. Remaining shareholders agreed to recapitalize Acazis with ca. €17 million to cover the negative balance, leaving it with ca. €1.3 million restart capital[27] and relisting the company on the Frankfurt Open Stock Market. A new strategic investor, namely Luxemburg-based Athanor Equities, acquired a majority stake in the company. Seeing potential in recovering castor oil market prices and the assets Acazis still held in Ethiopia, the investors sent a crisis manager to Ethiopia in 2010 to 'resurrect' the project.[28] Acazis's management began to pay off debts (bank loans, wages, taxes) to re-establish trust with the Ethiopian authorities and secure what remained of FEP assets (land, factory, machinery).

Acazis's business strategy, however, remained in flux between 2011 and 2015. The management abandoned biodiesel processing and shifted to castor bean production for export to international agro-chemical firms, coupled with groundnut production and edible oil processing for the national market. This seemed sensible, as the Ethiopian state banned the export and encouraged production of edible oil crops/seeds in May 2011 because of edible oil shortages and inflated prices. Acazis's engineers reconfigured the castor oil mill to process edible oils. Although contract farming was to be restarted at a smaller scale for castor and groundnut production, it quickly became apparent that neither Hararghe's farmers nor local officials were willing to participate (Interview ACA2). Attempts to begin groundnut production also angered local traders, who bought from farmers and sold to the local Hamaressa edible oil factory. Thus, plans to produce groundnuts ended prematurely, even though Acazis already rebranded itself as an edible oil company.[29]

To restart operations, Acazis sought the support of federal offices and officials, often bypassing regional and local levels for two main reasons: administrative powers related to large-scale farmland investment projects had been centralized at the federal administrative level in 2009, and Acazis's new management was met with distrust by local officials after relations had broken down under FEP (Interviews ACA1, ACA2). Acazis's management attempted to use their connections at federal level to coerce local officials into vacating parts of the 'illegally occupied' 8,000 hectares of plantation land in the East Hararghe lowlands (Interview FEP1). Despite attempts by company agronomists to restart castor production between 2011 and 2013 on 1,200 hectares, output remained low and hardly any produce was exported or sold.[30] The new managers spread the blame for the poor results, citing their own agronomists' supposed 'laziness and lack of professionalism', the 'clannishness and mafia structures' of local authorities, and 'tribal warfare between farmers and agro-pastoralists' in the lowlands (Interviews FEP2, ACA1).

At the end of 2013, Acazis's management abandoned any serious efforts at producing castor. While the plantation sites seemingly remained cultivated with castor plants, at closer inspection I observed that agricultural production was haphazardly maintained for fictitious reasons. That is, to give the impression that the company was using leased land productively, when in fact it held on to the land mainly as a speculative asset. Acazis's management did so aware that the federal and regional states had begun cracking down on 'unproductive' investors as of 2013 (Interview ACA2), cancelling investment licences and confiscating the land of investors whom the ruling party called 'rent-seekers' – referring to investors who failed to use their land productively and attempted to profit from it by other means. Acazis, like its forerunner FEP, prioritized gaining shareholder capital over actually producing castor, as agricultural output and export profits fell below projected targets. This suggests that Acazis was undercapitalized and sought to sell off company assets or attract investors/shareholders – a 'value grabbing' strategy based on virtually profiting from property without actually producing much (Andreucci et al. 2017).

Given the lack of productive profits after the restart and tired of its PR departments' empty promises, shareholders were unwilling to provide further capital increases in 2015. Acazis AG Holding's share certificates were rated as some of the worst performing ones, and a delisting from the stock market became inevitable.[31] The agricultural management in Ethiopia again ran out of operational capital. Attempts to sell the oil mill failed repeatedly, and after years of inactivity the oil mill properties were eventually confiscated by court order for failure to pay back outstanding debts to Nib Bank and salaries to FEP's Workers' Union, *woreda* unions such as the Afran Qallo Farmers' Cooperative and other individuals.[32] Acazis was effectively bankrupt, and chances of a restart looked bleak as castor prices plummeted by approximately 27 per cent from late 2015 to early 2016.[33] Finally, the insolvency of Acazis AG Holding in Germany in 2015 also spelled the end of the story of FEP/Acazis in Hararghe.[34]

Conclusion

Shortly after FEP/Acazis's failure in 2015, rural towns across the Hararghe highlands became a hotbed for protests, while in the lowlands along the Oromia–Somali frontier, disputes between the Somali and Oromia Regional States intensified, leading to ethnicized conflict and mass population displacement (Lefort 2017). During these clashes, FEP/Acazis's confiscated oil factory was 'ravaged by fighting' in the borderlands, with operations of other investment projects similarly 'affected by anti-government demonstrations which had broken out in Oromia'.[35] Even without asserting a direct link between FEP/Acazis's failure and the outbreaks of protests and clashes in Hararghe, it is impossible to dismiss the sheer size of the project and the amount of people it adversely and lastingly affected. It marked an unprecedented interruption in the livelihoods of local farmers and agro-pastoralists, and its failure still lingers in the memory of those affected. As I showed, it played a decisive and divisive role in the deteriorating relationship between the federal and regional states and Hararghe's rural communities over a single decade (2005–15). While former political elites temporarily enabled state-building in Hararghe through the proxy of a large-scale, capital-intensive investment project, state control over frontier space and society in fact remained contested throughout the investment duration and was partly reversed after its failure.

The story of FEP/Acazis is typical for a white elephant project, but despite its impressive scale, scope and dramatic unfolding, it is by no means atypical for Ethiopia (see Chinigò 2015a; Gill 2016; Kamski 2016). Instead, it serves to point out the elephant in the room: failures of state-enforced large-scale farmland and agro-industrial investment projects in Ethiopia have become not the exception but the norm (Dessalegn 2014). The contestation of such projects in Ethiopia, moreover, has arguably been partly responsible for setting in motion the recent political changes within and reforms of the EPRDF government. The political forces now in ascendancy within the newly formed ruling Prosperity Party may want to bear this in mind should they try to plan future land investment projects on behalf of Hararghe's communities, and thus attempt to coercively gain control over frontier territories and resources that are already being used productively by farmers and agro-pastoralists.

Table 7.1. Interviews.

Respondent	Occupation/Office	Place	Date
A	Former Official, Fadis Woreda Admin.	Harar	July 2014
B	Former Official, East Hararghe Zone Investment Office	Harar	October 2013, July 2014
C	Former Official, East Hararghe Zone Admin.	Addis Ababa	October 2014
D	Official, Midega Tola Woreda Land Admin.	Midega Tola	September 2014
E	Group of Agro-pastoralists	Babile, Erer Valley	July 2014
F	Official, Oromia Regional Land Admin.	Addis Ababa	October 2013
G	Official, Oromia Regional Agricultural Office	Addis Ababa	October 2013

H	Former Park Ranger, Babile Elephant Sanctuary	Babile	September 2014
I	Former Park Manager, Babile Elephant Sanctuary	Addis Ababa	November 2014
J	Official, E. Hararghe Social Affairs Admin.	Harar	June 2014
K	Kebele Chairman in a Midega Tola Woreda	Midega Tola	July 2014
L	Village Elders in Erer Valley	Babile	July 2014
M	Group of Contract Farmers	Midega Tola	July 2014
N	Group of Plantation Workers	Fadis	July 2014
FEP1	Project Manager, FEP/Acazis	Harar	October 2013, 2014
FEP2	Project Manager, FEP/Acazis	Dire Dawa	September 2014
FEP3	Group of Former FEP Agronomist	Harar and Babile	October 2013, 2014
FEP4	Group of FEP Worker's Union Members	Harar	October 2013, 2014
ACA1	CEO, Acazis	Dire Dawa	September 2014
ACA2	General Manager, Acazis	Addis Ababa	November 2014

Jonah Wedekind is a political ecologist working on large-scale biofuel investment projects in Ethiopia at Humboldt-Universität zu Berlin, Germany. His research interests include agrarian and environmental transformations, property relations and anthropologies of the state. He was a Marie Curie Early Stage Career fellow within the EU research project ENTITLE – The European Network for Political Ecology (2013–2016) and is a co-editor of undisciplinedenvironments.org and ethiopia-insight.com. Formative years spent in Ethiopia as a third-generation expatriate of linguists and human rights workers resulted in his deep-rooted interest in Ethiopian Studies.

Notes

This research was funded by the People Programme (Marie Curie Actions) of the EU's 7th Framework Programme, REA Grant No. 289374 – 'ENTITLE'.
Research assistance was provided by Ashenafi F.H. Research invitations were extended by Bekele Hunde and Fekadu Beyene. Research authorization was granted by the Agricultural Investment Land Administration Agency. I thank William Davison and Julian Tadesse for comments on earlier drafts. I am indebted to Hararghe's communities for entrusting me with their version of the above story.

1. Investopedia, s.v. 'White Elephant'. Retrieved 13 February 2018 from www.investopedia .com/terms/w/whiteelephant.asp.
2. Biodiesel crops here refer to spurge plants (e.g. jatropha, castor), while biofuels includes the aforementioned plus bioethanol from sugar cane molasses.

3. An economic space created by investors who dramatize the performance of their investment and 'speculate on a product that may or may not exist' as 'a necessary aid to gathering investment funds' (Tsing 2000: 118, 141).

4. In Afan Oromo, '*qeerroo* means bachelor or unmarried man of fighting age' (Mohammed 2015: 240).

5. The commendable but narrow conservationist focus on the Elephant Sanctuary conflict is the reason for my exaggerated use of elephant themes in this article, inspired by Turton's (2002) 'The Mursi and the Elephant Question'.

6. Nir Hasson, 'Gush Katif Farmers To Be Dealt a Knockout by Disengagement Plan', *Haaretz*, 15 April 2005. Retrieved 31 July 2018 from www.haaretz.com/1.4850548.

7. Amiram Barkat, 'Katif Evacuees Making the (African) Desert Bloom', *Haaretz*, 4 June 2006. Retrieved 31 July 2018 from www.haaretz.com/1.4911003.

8. On 1 January 2006, 1 US dollar (USD) = 8,72 ETB. By 31 December 2007, 1 USD = 9,25 ETB. All ETB exchange rates mentioned apply to this range from 2006–2007.

9. FEP, 'FEP(Eth)Plc – Activity Summary: Phase 2: April – end of August 2007', East Hararghe Zone Investment Office, Harar, 21 November 2007.

10. Each contract established an 'agricultural cooperative society' in accordance with Ethiopia's *Cooperative Societies Proclamation No. 147/1998*.

11. FEP, 'Cooperative Agreement', Oromia Investment Commission: Addis Ababa, March 2007.

12. FEP, 'FEP(Eth)Plc Activity Summary (for 2007): Comparison of Farm Lands across Districts', East Hararghe Zone Investment Office, Harar, 21 November 2007.

13. FEP, 'Seeds Distribution Status in East Hararghe', East Hararghe Zone Investment Bureau, Harar, 23 April 2008.

14. FEP, 'FEP Has Expanded Its Operations in Oromiya', Oromia Cooperative Promotion Commission, Addis Ababa, 25 March 2008.

15. EHZ, 'Estimates of Annual Income Share from Annual Crop Production of Agricultural Sector for year 2006/2007: Fadis District', East Hararghe Zone, Harar, 2007.

16. NIB International Bank S.C., 'Compensation to Oromia Investment Commission for Flora's 15 Ha in Fechatu', East Hararghe Zone Finance and Economic Office, Harar, 9 May 2007.

17. FEP, 'Company: Biodiesel', 2006. Retrieved 31 July 2018 from web.archive.org/web/20070519200706/http://www.floraecopower.com/Eng/Activities/Overview.asp.

18. Girmaye Kebede, 'Biodiesel Factory Inaugurated', *Ethiopian Herald*, 4 December 2007, Addis Ababa.

19. For a video of Meles's visit, see François Achour, *Flora EcoPower Oil Mill in Fechatu Harar, Ethiopia*, 23 December 2012. Retrieved 31 July 2018 from youtu.be/8Ci7b 22AoIM?t=5m13s.

20. FEP, 'About', 2006. Retrieved 31 July 2018 from web.archive.org/web/20070623091035/, http://www.floraecopower.com/Eng/About/Company.asp.

21. FEP, 'Activities', 2006. Retrieved 31 July 2018 from web.archive.org/web/200710 21031616/http://www.floraecopower.com/Eng/Company/Activities.asp.

22. FEP Holding AG, '*Bilanz zum 31. Dezember 2006*', 31 December 2006, Munich.

23. Deutsches Handelsregister, 'Neue Firma: Flora EcoPower AG', *Amtsgericht München* HRB 159323, 15 November 2006, Munich.

24. FEP merely raised payments from 40 to 50 ETB.

25. FEP, 'Remarkable Incidents in the Relation between FEP and Fedis District's Administrator (From March 2007 up to Now)', East Hararghe Zone Administration, Harar, date unknown.

26. FEP, 'Gewinn- und Verlustrechnung für die Zeit vom 1. Januar bis 31. Dezember 2008', 31 December 2009, Munich.
27. FEP, 'Einladung – Ordentliche Hauptversammlung der FEP Aktionäre', 15 December 2009, Munich.
28. Solomon Bekele, 'Interview: Resurrection Time', *Capital*, 20 February 2011, Addis Ababa.
29. Acazis, 'Acazis AG Subsidiary, Acazis Agro Industry Plc Ethiopia Signs Contract to Start Edible Oil Production in Ethiopia', 3 December 2012, Gilching.
30. Acazis, 'Über das Geschäftsjahr 2012 – Bericht von Patrick E. Bigger', 20 December 2013, Munich.
31. O. Ristau, 'Harte Nüsse für die Anleger', *Euro am Sonntag*, 1 August 2015, Munich.
32. Oromia General Courthouse, 'Auction Advertisement – Oil Processing Company, Fechatu', 13 February 2016, Addis Ababa.
33. OPW Ingredients, 'OPW Trendcheck April 2016 – Castor Oil and Castor Oil Derivatives', 25 March 2016.
34. O. Ristau, 'Patrick Bigger scheitert mit Geschäft in Afrika', *Handelszeitung*, 5 August 2015, Zurich.
35. Africa Intelligence, 'Game Over for Flora EcoPower', *Indian Ocean Newsletter*, 22 September 2017.

References

Andreucci, D. et al. 2017. '"Value Grabbing": A Political Ecology of Rent', *Capitalism Nature Socialism* 28(3): 28–47.
Asnake Kefale. 2010. 'Federal Restructuring in Ethiopia: Renegotiating Identity and Borders along the Oromo-Somali Ethnic Frontiers', *Development and Change* 41(4): 615–35.
Assefa Admassie. 2014. 'The Political Economy of Food Price Policy in Ethiopia', in P. Pinstrup-Andersen (ed.), *Food Price Policy in an Era of Market Instability: A Political Economy Analysis*. Oxford: Oxford University Press, pp. 134–52.
Azene Bekele-Tesemma. 2007. *Useful Trees and Shrubs of Ethiopia: Identification, Propagation, and Management for 17 Agroclimatic Zones*. Nairobi: RELMA / ICRAF.
Belaineh Legesse. 2006. 'Risk Perceptions, Risk Minimizing and Coping Strategies of Smallholder Farmers in The Eastern Highlands of Ethiopia', in K. Havnevik, Tekeste Negash and Atakilt Beyene (eds), *Of Global Concern: Rural Livelihood Dynamics and Natural Resource Governance*. Stockholm: Sida Studies, pp. 47–79.
Belay Kassa, and W. Manig. 2004. 'Access to Rural Land in Eastern Ethiopia: Mismatch between Policy and Reality', *Journal of Agriculture and Rural Development in the Tropics and Subtropics* 105(2): 123–38.
Borras, S.M. et al. 2016. 'The Rise of Flex Crops and Commodities: Implications for Research', *Journal of Peasant Studies* 43(1): 93–115.
Braukämper, U. 1975. 'Natürliche und anthropogene Katastrophen in Südost-Äthiopien: Geschichtliche Hintergründe einer Gegenwartskrise', *Paideuma* 21: 61–133.
———. 1983. 'Notes on the Islamicization and the Muslim Shrines of the Harar Plateau', *Archaeology and History*. Second International Congress of Somali Studies. Hamburg: Helmut Buske.
Chinigò, D. 2015a. 'Historicising Agrarian Transformation Agricultural Commercialisation and Social Differentiation in Wolaita, Southern Ethiopia', *Journal of Eastern African Studies* 9(2): 193–211.

CSA (Central Statistical Agency). 2009. 'Agricultural Sample Survey 2008–2009, Report on Land Utilization: Private Peasant Holdings', *CSA Statistical Bulletin*, vol. 4. Addis Ababa: CSA, p. 446.

Dawit Alemu. 2013. *Scoping Report on the Status of Biofuel Developments in Ethiopia*. London: Overseas Development Institute (ODI).

Dessalegn Rahmato. 2014. 'The Perils of Development from Above: Land Deals in Ethiopia', *African Identities* 12(1): 26–44.

Devereux, S., and R. Sabates-Wheeler. 2008. 'Ethiopia's Productive Safety Net Programme (PSNP)', *Assessment Report*, December. Brighton: Institute of Development Studies.

Edelman, M., C. Oya and S.M. Borras. 2013. 'Global Land Grabs: Historical Process, Theoretical and Methodological Implications and Current Trajectories', *Third World Quarterly* 34(9): 1517–31.

Emmenegger, R. 2016. 'Decentralization and the Local Developmental State: Peasant Mobilization in Oromiya, Ethiopia', *Africa* 86(2): 263–87.

Ezekiel Gebissa. 2004. *Leaf of Allah: Khat & Agricultural Transformation in Harerge, Ethiopia 1875–1991*. Ohio: Ohio State University Press.

———. 2010. 'Leadership from Below: Farmers and Sustainable Agriculture in Ethiopia', in B.W. Redekop (ed.), *Leadership for Environmental Sustainability*. New York: Routledge, pp. 158–69.

Fana Gebresenbet. 2016. 'Land Acquisitions, the Politics of Dispossession, and State-Remaking in Gambella, Western Ethiopia', *Africa Spectrum* 51(1): 5–28.

Fekadu Adugna. 2011. 'Overlapping Nationalist Projects and Contested Spaces: The Oromo–Somali Borderlands in Southern Ethiopia', *Journal of Eastern African Studies* 5(4): 773–87.

Gabbert, E.C. 2018. 'Future in Culture: Globalizing Environments in the Lowlands of Southern Ethiopia', in J. Abbink (ed.), *The Environmental Crunch in Africa: Growth Narratives vs. Local Realities*. Leiden: Palgrave, pp. 287–317.

Gill, B. 2016. 'Can the River Speak? Epistemological Confrontation in the Rise and Fall of the Land Grab in Gambella, Ethiopia', *Environment and Planning A* 48(4): 699–717.

GIZ (Gesellschaft für Internationale Zusammenarbeit). 2011. *Nachwachsende Rohstoffe für die stoffliche Nutzung – Auswirkungen für Entwicklungs- und Schwellenländer*. Eschborn: Bundesministerium für Wirtschaftliche Zusammenarbeit und Entwicklung (BMZ).

Hagmann, T. 2014. *Talking Peace in the Ogaden: The Search for an End to Conflict in the Somali Regional State in Ethiopia*. Nairobi: Rift Valley Institute.

Hagmann, T., and M.H. Khalif. 2008. 'State and Politics in Ethiopia's Somali Region since 1991', *Bildhaan: An International Journal of Somali Studies* 6(1): 6.

Jeylan Wolyie Hussein, and Fekadu Beyene. 2015. 'Dynamics of Institutionalized Competition in the Geography of Inter-ethnic Rivalry: The Case of the Jarso and the Girhi in Eastern Ethiopia', *International Area Studies Review* 18(2): 138–63.

Kamski, B. 2016. 'The Kuraz Sugar Development Project (KSDP) in Ethiopia: Between "Sweet Visions" and Mounting Challenges', *Journal of Eastern African Studies* 10(3): 568–80.

Kesicki, F., and J. Tomei. 2012. 'Will Peak Oil Cause a Rush for Land in Africa?', in T. Allan et al. (eds), *Handbook of Land and Water Grabs in Africa: Foreign Direct Investment and Food and Water Security*. London: Routledge, pp. 273–85.

Lavers, T. 2012a. 'Patterns of Agrarian Transformation in Ethiopia: State-Mediated Commercialisation and the "Land Grab"', *Journal of Peasant Studies* 39(3–4): 795–822.

———. 2012b. '"Land Grab" as Development Strategy? The Political Economy of Agricultural Investment in Ethiopia', *Journal of Peasant Studies* 39(1): 105–32.

Lefort, R. 2012. 'Free Market Economy, "Developmental State" and Party-State Hegemony in Ethiopia: The Case of the "Model Farmers"', *Journal of Modern African Studies* 50(4): 681–706.

———. 2017. '"Ethnic Clashes" in Ethiopia: Setting the Record Straight', *Open Democracy*, 22 October. Retrieved 31 July 2018 from https://www.opendemocracy.net/ren-lefort/ethnic-clashes-in-ethiopia-setting-record-straight.

Li, T.M. 2007. *The Will to Improve: Governmentality, Development and the Practice of Politics*. Durham, NC, and London: Duke University Press.

———. 2014. 'What Is Land? Assembling a Resource for Global Investment', *Transactions of the Institute of British Geographers* 39(4): 589–602.

———. 2015. 'Transnational Farmland Investment: A Risky Business', *Journal of Agrarian Change* 15(4): 560–68.

———. 2018. 'After the Land Grab: Infrastructural Violence and the "Mafia System" in Indonesia's Oil Palm Plantation Zones', *Geoforum* 96: 328–37.

Lisanework Nigatu, Heluf Gebrekidan and Muktar Mohammed. 2008. 'Environmental Impact Assessment of the Castor Bean Production Project of the Flora Eco Power Company in East Hararghe Zone'. Alemaya: Haramaya University.

Loos, T.K., and M. Hoppe. 2015. 'Castor Oil as a High Value Raw Material Export Commodity for Smallholder Farmers – Linking Ethiopian Producers to German Companies', *Tropentag 'Management of Land Use Systems for Enhanced Food Security: Conflicts, Controversies and Resolutions'*, September 16–18, Berlin.

Markakis, J. 2003. 'Anatomy of a Conflict: Afar & Ise Ethiopia', *Review of African Political Economy* 30(97): 445–53.

Miller, C.J., W.W. Shaner and R.E. Burton. 1969. 'Development of Agriculture and Agro-Industry in Ethiopia: Strategy and Programs' Commissioned Study for the Technical Agency Imperial Ethiopian Government'. Stanford, CA: Stanford Research Institute.

Mohammed Hassen. 2015. *The Oromo and the Christian Kingdom of Ethiopia 1300–1700*. Rochester: James Currey.

Nalepa, R.A., A.G.S. Gianotti and D.M. Bauer. 2017. 'Marginal Land and the Global Land Rush: A Spatial Exploration of Contested Lands and State-Directed Development in Contemporary Ethiopia', *Geoforum* 82: 237–51.

Planel, S. 2014. 'A View of a "Bureaucratic" Developmental State: Local Governance and Agricultural Extension in Rural Ethiopia', *Journal of Eastern African Studies* 8(3): 420–37.

Poschen, P. 1986. 'An Evaluation of the Acacia Albida-Based Agroforestry Practices in the Hararghe Highlands of Eastern Ethiopia', *Agroforestry Systems* 4: 129–43.

Schlee, G. 2013. 'Territorializing Ethnicity: The Imposition of a Model of Statehood on Pastoralists in Northern Kenya and Southern Ethiopia', *Ethnic and Racial Studies* 36(5): 857–74.

Tesfaye Lemma Tefera, S. Perret and J.F. Kirsten 2004. 'Diversity in Livelihoods and Farmers' Strategies in the Hararghe Highlands, Eastern Ethiopia', *International Journal of Agricultural Sustainability* 2(2): 133–46.

Tsegaye Moreda. 2015. 'Listening to Their Silence? The Political Reaction of Affected Communities to Large-Scale Land Acquisitions: Insights from Ethiopia', *Journal of Peasant Studies* 42(3–4): 517–39.

Tsing, A. 2000. 'Inside the Economy of Appearances', *Public Culture* 12(1): 115–44.

———. 2005. *Friction: An Ethnography of Global Connection*. Princeton, NJ: Princeton University Press.

Turton, D. 2002. 'The Mursi and the Elephant Question', in D. Chatty and M. Colchester (eds), *Conservation and Mobile Indigenous Peoples: Displacement, Forced Settlement and Development*. Oxford: Berghahn, pp. 97–118.

Watts, M.J. 2017. 'Frontiers: Authority, Precarity, and Insurgency at the Edge of the State', *World Development* 101: 477–88.

WSD (Wildlife for Sustainable Development) and EWCA (Ethiopian Wildlife Conservation Authority). 2010. 'Revised Boundary of Babile Elephant Sanctuary', June 2010. Addis Ababa: Wildlife for Sustainable Development and Ethiopian Wildlife Conservation Authority.

Yirmed Demeke, and Negusu Aklilu. 2008. 'Agrofuel Development in Ethiopia: Rhetoric, Reality and Recommendations', in T. Heckett and Negusu Aklilu (eds), *Agrofuel Development in Ethiopia: Rhetoric, Reality and Recommendations*. Addis Ababa: Forum for Environment, pp. 83–113.

Zitelmann, T. 1999. 'Des Teufels Lustgarten: Themen und Tabus der politischen Anthropologie Nordostafrikas', habilitation thesis. Berlin: Free University.

———. 2005. 'Blühende Landschaften in Äthiopien: Entwicklung als Versprechen, Macht und Mythus', in K. Lange and K. Geisenhainer (eds), *Bewegliche Horizonte: Festschrift zum 60. Geburtstag von Bernhard Streck*. Leipzig: Leipziger Universitätsverlag, pp. 139–52.

Chapter 8

From Cattle Herding to Charcoal Burning

Land Expropriation, State Consolidation and Livelihood Changes in Abaya Valley, Southern Ethiopia

Asebe Regassa

Since the 1960s, successive Ethiopian regimes have embarked upon a broad policy of transforming the pastoralist frontiers into areas of mechanized agriculture by adopting high-modernist development discourses and practices. In the process, the three regimes (imperial, military and Ethiopian Peoples' Revolutionary Democratic Front – EPRDF), now Prosperity Party (PP), transferred lands in pastoralist and agro-pastoralist areas of the country to private and state-affiliated companies, mostly by evicting the local communities. Likewise, in 2010, over 18,000 hectares of land in Abaya Valley, West Guji zone, were given to Abaya Galana Agro Industry (a private investor) for the purpose of cultivating sugar cane and other commercial crops. For the implementation of the project, the federal government initiated a medium-level dam construction on the Gidabo River in 2010, which was inaugurated on 3 February 2019 with the presence of the Prime Minister, and has resettled over 450 households. Although the dam was initially designed to have a 240 cubic metre carrying capacity, it was reduced to 62.5 cubic metres.

In this chapter, I investigate how local people used charcoal production to compensate for their dwindling cattle-herding opportunities, which had become difficult as a result of restricted access to grazing grounds and water sources following the transfer of land to Abaya Galana Agro Industries. I also critically analyse the local communities' responses to the Gidabo dam project, having collected ethnographic data during different intervals of fieldwork since early 2014.

I argue that large-scale agribusiness projects in Ethiopia's pastoralist frontiers are primarily enabled by emptying land through villagization programmes. Likewise, by expropriating the resources upon which the indigenous communities sustain their livelihoods, the state extends its power into the margins of the nation. This process eventually leads to a shift in property regimes from communal land ownership to the utilization of private enclosures, to which local communities respond systematically and contextually by changing their notions of property ownership and also shifting their livelihood.

Introduction

In 2015, during a field trip to the Abaya Valley in southern Ethiopia, I observed two contrasting developments that reflect broader contradictions found in Ethiopia's development narratives. On the one hand, the Gidabo dam construction site, funded by the federal government to enhance a private sugar cane irrigation project, was evidence of a broader 'developmental' state narrative that has been set in action – that is, modernizing the economy and boosting foreign exchange to promote the overall growth of the country's economy. According to the dam project manager, the reservoir has a potential to irrigate about 15,000 hectares of land in addition to the 18,000 hectares already given to Abaya Galana Agro Industry (hereafter 'the corporate investor'). On the other hand, the government has displaced over 450 Guji agro-pastoralist households for the purpose of transferring the land to the agro-industry project, and the project is expected to result in the further removal of over 600 households after the completion of the dam. The major objective of the corporate investor is to cultivate sugar cane and to establish a sugar factory in the area in addition to growing other commercial crops such as cotton for domestic and foreign markets.

As an agro-pastoralist community, the Guji in the Abaya Valley – located some 35 kilometres to the west of Dilla town (Gedeo zone) – have long been the main suppliers of livestock and livestock products to Dilla and other neighbouring towns and villages (McClellan 1988; Asebe 2010). Because of restrictions on accessing their customary grazing land, water grounds and farmlands following the expropriation of their farmland by the corporate investor in 2010, Guji communities are now in the process of augmenting their means of livelihood by producing charcoal (through 'charcoal burning', whereby wood is carbonized in a pile or kiln). In addition, those restrictions have compelled them to enclose formerly communal hills to burn charcoal as a private enterprise. It is possible that burning charcoal may eventually lead them to adopt another form of land use, such as farming, once the trees and shrubs have been cleared, but unpredictable rainfall from year to year remains a major challenge. In fact, local governmental authorities assert that the government has prohibited charcoal burning, and even charcoal trading has been forbidden as part of the country's policy of promoting green economic development. Nevertheless, the restriction on accessing grazing and water grounds, on the one hand, and criminalization of charcoal production, on the other, have left the local communities in limbo.

Exclusion through Land Expropriation

Land expropriation is one of the mechanisms used by governments and other development actors to exclude local communities from accessing resources (Li 2014). Exclusion, involving discursive support for the physical restriction of resource users from spaces, entails the exercise of power, narratives and technologies as both justifications and enforcement strategies. The situation in the Abaya Valley can be understood within the framework of Ethiopia's broader agrarian political economy that successive regimes have promoted despite underlying differences in ideologies. The central commonality across the regimes has been to seek control over land in order to create both political and economic capital. The government's aggressive engagement in large-scale agribusiness projects on the pastoralist frontiers has radically changed aspects of natural resource ownership, utilization and management, which has prompted local communities to systematically respond to, negotiate and interpret externally imposed models (Gill 2016; Millar 2016). In the Lower Omo region, for example, the government presents a modernist notion that conceptualizes pastoralist territories as underutilized, vacant spaces and resorts to narratives of modernization and economic transformation to legitimize expropriation of Mun (Mursi) and Mela and Chirim (Bodi) lands for the Kuraz Sugar Development Project (Buffavand 2016, and this volume) and has started implementing a mechanized wheat farm.

Practices and regulations pertaining to utilization, control and ownership of resources are reconfigured through changing agrarian politics and reshaped by different actors in their pursuit to claim access/control over resources (Ribot and Peluso 2003). Such reconfiguration of access to and ownership of land as 'property' creates what Li (2014) considers 'regimes of exclusion'. Unlike notions of property as 'access', which help us to conceptualize people's abilities and rights to derive benefit from resources, 'exclusion' takes us to the core of understanding land as a material resource that is excludable, partitioned and 'improved' (Li 2014). Many academic studies of large-scale agribusiness schemes in Africa seek to examine the nexus between recent waves of land deals and their impacts on local communities (Lavers 2012; Makki 2012). However, it is imperative to understand how exclusion through land expropriation (i.e. the process of dispossessing people from their land) is legitimized, justified and enforced through deployment of particular technologies, political discourses and actions. Indeed, these new waves of enclosure, and more generally the commodification of pastoralist lands, have radically changed meanings, values, ownership rights and governance of formerly communal land in pastoralist regions, including those in Ethiopia (Lavers 2012; Makki 2012; Korf, Hagmann and Emmenegger 2015; Tsegaye and Spoor

2015). However, as one elder participant in this study succinctly argued, while current land expropriations may have changed in terms of style and discourse, they represent a continuation of past Ethiopian regimes' strategies of state expansion and resource exploitation. The elder further argued:

> In the past, we lived on our land and cultivated for the feudal lords, or paid our cattle, honey and many things as tribute to the emperor through local lords. Now, they displaced us and took our land. But all are the same. They all claim land belongs to the government. Of course, the current is the worst. We are denied the use of our ancestral land. (Anonymous informant, November 2016; translated from Afan Oromo by author)[1]

This Guji elder recalled land expropriation under the imperial regime in the agriculturally suitable midland areas where the Guji reside. Both the highland and midland Guji territories became eligible for utilization through the land apportionment law that went into effect in 1910 in many parts of Oromia (Tesema 2002). The current waves of land acquisition in Oromia National Regional State and other parts of the country also can be directly related to the historical trajectories of state-building through expansion of a predatory state system long established in the country. As Borras et al. (2013) and Edelman and León (2013) strongly assert, historicizing land expropriation helps us to understand complex trajectories of agrarian politics, state-society relations and changes in agrarian political economy. Husen (2018) argues that successive regimes in Ethiopia have designed strategies and policies of land expropriation both as mechanisms of controlling people and their resources and as instruments of accumulating wealth – which in turn gives the state political leverage over agrarian society.

In presenting the empirical case of the corporate investor in West Guji zone of Oromia National Regional State, this chapter sets forth two arguments that have not received much attention in scholarly works on large-scale land deals in the country and beyond. Firstly, the chapter contends that while large-scale land expropriations by the government and corporate investors have changed access and property regimes with regard to land and other land-based resources by disrupting customary rules, local communities also create alternative strategies through which they claim and control access to other land-based resources and in this process reconfigure property rights. Secondly, unlike recent literature that links land grabs in the country to the 'land rush' that ensued during the post-2007/08 global food and fuel crisis, and unlike others who associate such land grabs with the current government's 'developmental state' paradigm, this chapter asserts that such a phenomenon is rather a continuation of state-building and resource expropriation that has long been part of the formation of the modern Ethiopian state. Even if one acknowledges that the post-2007/08 global food and fuel crisis provided an impetus for the federal government to embark upon a process of designing policies and strategies that pertain to land expropriation (Assefa 2013; Makki 2014), it remains essential to pay attention to regional contexts, such as in Oromia. These areas have become the resource frontiers for successive Ethiopian regimes, thus demonstrating that land expropriation cannot be disentangled from state-building projects. In other words, continued land appropriation represents the ongoing, unfinished project of the consolidation of state power.

With an aim to show how large-scale land expropriation reconfigures regimes of access and property, grounding current waves of enclosure and dispossession in the country's history of agrarian relations, this chapter is structured in four subsequent sections. The first section explores the literature on access and property regimes with a focus on land expropriation – the act of dispossessing people from their customary land. In the second section, the empirical context is discussed in detail, paying attention to broader narratives in the government's representation of pastoralist lands, the process of land expropriation and the government's justification for their actions, while also considering various strategies of claiming access to resources by the Guji communities. The third section connects the past to the present with regard to state-building and land expropriation in Oromia and establishes a broader argument aimed at historicizing enclosure and dispossession. However, it discerns distinct differences in the political and economic models adopted by successive regimes (the imperial regime, 1880s–1974; the socialist military regime, 1974–91; and the EPRDF/PP government, 1991–). The final section focuses on changes in access and property regimes within the context of state-invoked dispossession.

Land Grabbing and the Reconfiguration of Regimes of Access and Property

Despite the literature boom, or what Oya (2013) calls the 'literature rush' in keeping with the global 'land rush' after 2007/08, only a few scholars have tried to connect the current waves of large-scale enclosure and dispossession with questions of property rights, social and political relations, authority, and citizenship rights that are central to state formation in Africa (Lund and Boone 2013). Addressing property rights and access is essential because it entails issues of recognition and entitlement to land ownership, utilization and development (Lund 2011; Edelman and León 2013). Ribot and Peluso's conceptualization of access and property as 'the ability to derive benefit from something' and 'the right to benefit from something' (Ribot and Peluso 2003: 156) is illustrative of power constellations constituted in the interplay among the various actors vying for environmental resources. By restricting customary users from accessing resources and instead granting those resources to corporate investors, governments seek to raise tax revenues and to prime the land for the extraction of value (Schlee 2013). In doing so, governments exert control over the political and economic life at the margins.

As governments confer power on individuals, groups or institutions to deter others from accessing resources, land expropriation thus produces asymmetrical power relations – empowering some, disempowering others. In this regard, referring to the dynamic nature of access regimes, Ribot and Peluso (2003: 158) further argue that 'different political-economic circumstances change the terms of access and may therefore change the specific individuals or groups most able to benefit from a set of resources'. In contexts such as Ethiopia – where land remains the major source of political and economic power for the state, serves as social prestige for customary chiefs, sustains livelihoods, and is regarded as a sacred space and a crucial element in the history of indigenous communities – ownership status and regulations that set conditions for entry, utilization, management and control of natural resources are important variables with important political, economic and cultural implications (Dessalegn 2009; Markakis 2011).

Informed by broader notions of state-building, colonial and postcolonial states established control over land and other natural resources in Africa by nullifying the customary rights of indigenous communities (Adams and McShane 1996; Harawira 2005; Saugestad 2005). For example, in addition to creating racial and class boundaries and asymmetrical power relations between colonial elites and native African communities, enclosures pursued for nature conservation, plantation and mining projects have also disconnected local people from their cultural, spiritual and economic spaces and enabled the colonial and postcolonial states to exert power over the people (Turton 1987; Brockington, Duffy and Igoe 2008). Accordingly, control over productive land and other natural resources continues to be the backbone of postcolonial African state-building projects, as it gives the government the leverage to exploit resources, exercise political power and render society more transparent, and more beholden, to the state (Scott 1998; Harawira 2005).

The act of taking away land from colonial subjects, which Carl Schmitt (1950) conceptualizes as *Landnahme* (land appropriation), was a political project of social reordering within the ideological realms of European conceptions of the world order. Such a dichotomy between the West and the Rest produced a presumption that the 'civilized' West was granted a moral responsibility to reconfigure the social ordering of the 'uncivilized Others'. In such a political and ideological project, colonial expansion and annexation of land in the New World were used as instruments to exert power over colonial subjects (Minca and Rowan 2015). In contexts such as Ethiopia, land-grabbing – a concept I use interchangeably with land appropriation in this chapter – is conceptualized as a practice of expropriating land from customary landholders for the purpose of building the commercial economy, with little or no compensation, and without having consulted with or sought the knowledge of local communities, practices that lead to structural and discursive change in property regimes (Baglioni and Gibbon 2013).

Land appropriation and reconfiguration of access and property regimes in modern Ethiopia were strongly entangled with the creation of the modern Ethiopian empire in the late nineteenth century through a form of military conquest that some scholars refer to as internal colonization (Seyoum 2001; Donham 2002; Markakis 2011; Korf, Hagmann and Emmenegger 2015). Following Emperor Menelik's conquest and subsequent empire-building projects that resulted in the introduction of a feudal system of land tenure, economic exploitation and cultural and political domination in the conquered regions fundamentally created hierarchically ordered relationships between northern settlers and southern native communities (Holcomb and Sisai 1990; Mohammed 1996; Donham 2002). All of the successive regimes in modern Ethiopia (from imperial to military/socialist to EPRDF) have been engaged in expropriating land from peasants and pastoralists within broader notions of modernizing the economy through large-scale agricultural schemes (Hagmann and Alemmaya 2008; Markakis 2011; Makki 2014). During the imperial regime, peasants in the conquered highland regions, or what Markakis (2011) considers the first frontiers, were dispossessed of their rights over the land and reduced to tenancy – working for feudal lords, the Orthodox Church and other state-related institutions. They were recruited as wage labour on the state farms under the socialist regime (Dessalegn 2009) and displaced for the sake of transferring land to foreign and domestic investors and state 'development' projects under the EPDRF 'developmental' state (Lavers 2012).

To return to my two main arguments: first, the ongoing land appropriation in Ethiopia, particularly in Oromia, should be understood within the historical trajectories of state-building and an agrarian political economy that successive regimes upheld as a means to use land as an economic commodity and a political instrument (Husen 2018). Despite changes in political ideology over the last fifty years, state control over land, dispossession of peasants and pastoralists, and policies of emulating foreign development models have been common practices (Clapham 2006; Dessalegn 2009). Second, taking a specific empirical case from southern Oromia, I argue that large-scale agribusiness projects are mechanisms of exclusion, separating local people from their customary resource bases. I further argue that the processes of exclusion act to reconfigure property regimes pertaining to ownership, utilization and control of natural resources. Such reconfiguration is entailed by the expropriation of land through the enforcement of state-formulated regulations related to land, which in turn reinforces the necessity of local communities to design alternative strategies of accessing resources. I also argue that the process of emptying land through the physical and discursive exclusion of resource users enables agribusiness investors such as Abaya Galana

Agro Industries to gain land. As Li (2014) argues, this exclusion requires adding knowledge and technological values to land, and then using such values as a mechanism through which to label existing land-use systems as 'backward' and the land as 'underutilized'. In the particular case of the Abaya Valley, high-energy technologies are deployed for constructing dams, bulldozing forests by caterpillar machines, and ploughing and cultivating with tractors instead of ox ploughs or hoes. Such 'improvements' legitimize the exclusion of traditional resource users, who, according to government authorities and development 'experts', have never added value to the land, which given the modification of landscapes over hundreds and thousands of years is clearly not the case.

The Ethiopian government follows a 'carrot and stick' approach with regard to people and territories along its pastoral frontiers. On the one hand, it affirms the narratives of 'improving' the lives of local people and the economy of the country at large. This notion of 'improvement' resonates with the state's perception of the territory as underutilized, as wasteland, and as empty space, and further resonates with the state's normative perception of poverty from a monetary perspective, quite contrary to local people's understanding of their territory, well-being and wealth. For the Guji, wealth and well-being are comprehensively explained in terms of their psychological, economic, social, cultural and cosmological dimensions (see Asebe 2010). On the other hand, the government often resorts to coercive strategies of displacing local communities and suppressing all (local) resistance (Asebe, Yetebarek and Korf 2018). Under such circumstances, local communities evade the state by designing covert approaches to access resources for their livelihoods, and in the process they develop a different access and property regime that contradicts both the customary rules and state-imposed regulations for land ownership. By cutting trees at night for charcoal production, the people both challenge the state's environmental conservation discourses and adopt a survival mechanism to supplement their dwindling livestock economy. This is the focus of the next section, which examines the specific case of local communities' shifting from cattle herding to charcoal burning for commercial purposes.

The Context: Land Expropriation in Abaya Valley

The Guji Oromo in the West Guji zone has experienced an unprecedented level of 'development' interventions over the last eight years, even more so than during their incorporation into the Ethiopian state in the late nineteenth century. State encroachment on Guji's customary lands had begun during the imperial regime when local feudal lords began expropriating resources of the pastoralist Guji Oromo, mainly livestock and honey, in the form of taxation (Taddesse 1994). Because of its location close to Lake Abaya to the west and drained by the Gidabo River that flows into the lake, the Abaya Valley provided year-round farming, grazing land and access to water for Guji pastoralists' livestock until 2010. From the 1970s, the Guji began irrigating maize and root crops along the banks of the river, and thus the valley became a major source of their livelihoods both through farming and animal husbandry (Asebe 2010). The people used crops for subsistence, while livestock and livestock products were traded with neighbouring communities, such as the Gedeo and Sidama, who in turn provided the Guji with *ensete* and coffee (McClellan 1988; Asebe 2010).

Despite the valley's economic significance for the Guji and their neighbours, the new plantation managers and local government authorities have reconfigured the entire valley by re-engineering nature, human settlement and human-environment interactions. As a result of the federal government leasing the land to agro-industry, the traditional practices of resource utilization and governance in the valley have changed. In 2010, the federal government began building a dam on the Gidabo River that will, upon completion, be fully used for irrigation purposes. The corporate investor cleared all the land given to it, bulldozing big trees that were previously used for cultural purposes and beekeeping, and started planting sugar cane only on less than 10 per cent of the land, using both rain-fed and traditional irrigation methods. As the construction of the dam has progressed, some 450 Guji households have been resettled to a newly established Sariiti village on the outskirts of the sugar cane plantation. As a result, the people have been denied access to their customary grazing land, home, farms and water grounds. A local Guji elder described the process of land expropriation:

> The local government authorities and the investor came to our village and told us that the land is needed for development purpose. They said, the investor will provide you with all that you need – social services such as roads, health centres, schools, tractors, water and many other promises. Later, the man [the owner of the agro-industry] and government authorities from Abaya district demarcated the entire valley for the investment. We were eventually removed from the area with the only option of settling at the outskirts of the investment scheme. (Informant, Edema Ayano, Sariiti village, September 2017)

Local residents state that the government authorities often claim that the land had been underutilized and thus did not meaningfully contribute to national economic development. 'The investor will develop and improve the land' – this has been the common justification given by government authorities, including the then Oromia National Regional State president Abadula Gemeda, according to my informants. This accords with what Li (2007, 2014) identified as the discourse of 'improving' the lives of local people by adding technologically derived value to the land, often used as the justification for, and legitimization of, exclusion. One of the elders narrated his experiences as follows:

Under the previous regimes, we were forced to pay fattened bulls and goats, honey and other goods/commodities to the provincial administrators. They did not take our land. Now, this government completely transferred our land to this investor. The investor first came with district officials and told us the land is enough for him and us. They first demarcated portions of the land for him and left some farmland and grazing ground for us. But when we claimed that was not enough for us, the investor became aggressive. He didn't want to listen to us. He told us that all the land, including that left for us for farm and grazing, belongs to him. He said, 'I got the land from the government. You can go and ask the government.' We sent five elders to the Oromia regional president [during Abadula's time in office]. They decided in favour of the investor and forcefully removed all of us from the place and gave the entire land to the investor. As you see now, we don't have any farmland, and our cattle don't get grass and water. Some young people took the cattle far to Lake Abaya, and others work for the investor. Women and elderly men burn charcoal to sustain the lives of their families. Life has become so terrible here. (Anonymous informant, November 2016)

The local people did not passively accept the government's decision to transfer their lands to the corporate investor. Although they suspected the government authorities' complicity with the corporate investor, they first opted to appeal to the Oromia National Regional State administration, but the regional government found against their appeal. To make matters worse, community representatives were arrested by district officials upon their return from Addis Ababa and accused of mobilizing people to oppose government investment policies and strategies. Since 2017, when reforms began in Oromia with regard to investment, the corporate investor has occupied the entire 18,000 hectares of land.

In response to the Oromia-wide popular uprising that has been under way since 2014, during which protests have encompassed a wide range of issues, including land expropriation in the region, the Oromia National Regional State government – according to information provided by them – has apportioned about 6,000 hectares of land to local communities. Nevertheless, the Command Post, established by the central government to oversee the 'state of emergency' (February–June 2018), also has been given the power to reverse such appropriation of 'investment' land by locals. During the parliamentary session in which this power of reversal was declared, MPs from the Oromo People's Democratic Organization (OPDO) (one of the coalition parties in EPRDF) reacted by demanding an explanation. They argued that putting land issues under the Command Post was tantamount to endorsing further land appropriation in Oromia.

As a result of dispossession and restriction of local communities from accessing resources, the local people in Abaya valley have been relegated to areas not suitable for livestock and farming. While residing at the outskirt of the plantation scheme, the people only have access to hill trees for charcoal production. My ethnographic research in the Abaya Valley over the last four years reveals a significant engagement of local people, mainly women and elderly men, in charcoal burning to supplement declining returns from cattle herding and local cultivation as well as the uncertainty of yields. The enclosure of land by the corporate investor has prompted many of the households to engage in charcoal production as a mechanism of sustaining their life, while others have had to work for the corporate investor to earn income through wages. However, with the simultaneous decline in forest cover and the discrimination in employment practices of the corporate investor, uncertainty has marred the lives of local communities.

Research among displaced Guji communities sheds some light on the complex interplay between the state-backed, privately owned agribusiness project and the exclusion of local communities from access, utilization, control and management of natural resources. During my first field visit to the Gidabo dam construction site on 15 February 2015, the coordinator of the dam project explained that the project represents a significant advancement and achievement because of its diversion of the Gidabo River for irrigation projects. The dam diverts the river into two major canals (one to the north to be used by a corporate investor in Sidama Regional State; the other to the south for a sugar cane planation, which is the focus of this chapter). Proceeding further south, I observed the weekly market in Arero village taking place under five remaining big *Odaa* trees; the others had been bulldozed. Traditionally, Arero was a common marketplace for the Guji, Gedeo and Sidama. A Guji elderly woman recalled that Guji land was once a land of abundance, fertility and peace and that Arero had been a symbolic space for peaceful social interaction, particularly for women.

The land transfer to the corporate investor, however, has resulted in significant changes both to the environment and the livelihoods of the local people. For example, according to information from local communities, the number of cattle of some households shrunk on average from 250 to 30–50 from 2010 to 2017. This radical herd reduction has been a result of many interconnected factors, among which lack of pasture and water as a result of the enclosure of communal lands is prominent. The area was also severely hit by drought in 2010, 2012 and 2016. While drought-related disasters have been common challenges to pastoralist and agro-pastoralist communities in East Africa (Oba 2013), the exclusion of the Guji from their customary land has reduced their resilience in the face of such challenges. Therefore, although the herd reduction can be attributed in part to drought, it can still be viewed through a political ecology lens that reveals how resource deprivation impoverishes local communities. In addition to shortages of pasture that led to the death of livestock, the shortage of food has prompted local people to sell off their cattle and smaller ruminants to buy food.

As Krätli (2015) argues, pastoralist and agro-pastoralist communities over the years have developed strategies for adapting to climatic variability and adjusting their livelihood to changing environmental conditions. However, their exclusion from seasonal grazing land and water points has deprived Guji agro-pastoralists not only of resource utilization but of exercising their knowledge of how to adapt to climatic variability. Similar impacts of large-scale agribusiness projects have occurred in other parts of Ethiopia over the last five decades (Schlee 2013; Abbink et al. 2014). A Guji elder listed some of the changes that have been introduced because of the 'development' project:

> Unlike in the past when people came here to buy different stuff for a cheap price, now things are completely changed after this man [the corporate investor] took our land. Our cattle do not have enough grass and water. Cows do not give milk. We are witnessing complete destruction of our sacred trees, water ground and pasture areas. The river is drying out. The *kaloo* [pasture land reserved for calves, milk cows and weak cattle] is now taken by the investor. Our children are not getting milk. (Anonymous informant, April 2015)

Another elder desperately explained to me the environmental and economic consequences of the agribusiness project:

> In the past, our elders told us not to cut trees such as the *Odaa* trees that you see here. We also transferred the same knowledge and values to our children. However, these investors do not care about the sacred values of the trees. These trees are shades for people and livestock as you see now. People gather here for markets. The *Odaa* trees are also special ritual grounds and we consider them sacred. Two years ago, the investor bulldozed all the trees except these remaining five. These were left after we protested. This company took our land and now we can't farm and our cattle don't get grass and water. (Anonymous informant, February 2015)

Because the dam has not been completed, the corporate investor has not fully begun cultivating the fields; nonetheless, vacating the land is under way. After driving more than an hour across the open field now under the control of the corporate investor, I arrived at Sariiti village, where I had lunch with local residents. A few neighbours joined us for coffee and shared their stories with us. The lunchtime created an important opportunity for me to socialize with the local people and share their experiences, observe their living conditions and hear their stories. My first impression upon entering the village was the obvious engagement of the people in charcoal production. According to local informants, at least one family member of each resettled household produces charcoal. In support of this impression was my observation of several sacks/bags of charcoal piled in front of each house in the village ready for traders to pick them up. Local residents in the resettlement area stated that they had never before cut trees to produce charcoal, although some residents close to Dilla town had practised it on a small scale.

I was told that charcoal production has now become not only a means of income for local residents but also a business activity for traders, who distribute it to Dilla town and beyond. Sociologically, while a few youth travel far from home with livestock, many elderly men, women and a significant number of the youth are engaged in charcoal production. The economics of the 'charcoal rush' can also be conceptualized as providing both subsistence options for local communities and an opportunity for urban-based businessmen/women. The construction of a road by Abaya Galana Agro Industry has enhanced easy transportation of charcoal by trucks and motorbikes. However, it should be emphasized that the Guji in the Abaya Valley only learned charcoal burning and the economic value of charcoal from the corporate investor – who bulldozed big trees and burned them to make charcoal.

Because cattle have moved as far away as the Lake Abaya area, which is almost a full day's travel by foot, children do not normally have access to milk and so have become weak and underweight. Charcoal has, therefore, become the only source of family income except for those who found employment as security guards in the new sugar cane plantation. Charcoal making has become dominant both in terms of income generation and in the number of people engaged in the practice compared to employment in the agro-industry. For example, a person can produce four sacks/bags a month, each selling for 240 Ethiopian birr (equivalent to US dollars 8.8 per the exchange rate as of this writing), giving the producer a total of 1,920 (US dollars 70.5), whereas those employed by the investor get a maximum of 800 Ethiopian birr (US dollars 29.4) as a monthly salary. In this regard, charcoal burning and employment in Abaya Galana Agro industries have become strategies of family income diversification alongside livestock husbandry for those families who can engage their children in different categories of activities. Because land is not privately owned among the Guji, they use lands under state control or communal lands for charcoal production, but they are trying to turn the land into private enclosures, not through formal land distribution among themselves, but, rather, each individual fences off part of the hill where government officials from the district do not visit (though village authorities are complicit with the local people, as they are also victims of the land appropriation).

During my follow-up fieldwork in November 2017, I observed that the bush land where people cut trees for charcoal was devastated and nearly barren. As part of the 'charcoal rush', people have been forced to travel further south and west in search of mature trees to be chopped for charcoal burning, but state restrictions on this practice remain a major challenge. A few days before my visit to the area, a person had been convicted and sentenced to five years in jail as a result of confronting local militia while cutting trees for charcoal production. Nevertheless, local communities continue to defy the court decision and government authorities' hard power, resisting in various ways. On the one hand, they are ready to fight against state authorities because charcoal production has now become a matter of life and death. They claim that since their land has been taken from them for the purpose of 'investment', the state should not restrict charcoal production until it can provide alternative livelihood strategies. In this context, charcoal burning can be considered both as a strategy for generating income and a mechanism for capturing a resource – a different type of resource – in defiance of the government's expropriation of their farms and grazing lands.

As part of the charcoal rush, utilitarian notions of human–environment interactions and ideas of commodifying nature have become prominent preoccupations. In the past, cutting trees without the knowledge and permission of clan chiefs was socially prohibited. Transgressors of locally accepted values and regulations would be sanctioned in accordance with established punishments, such as enacting payments of goats or sheep. It was particularly prohibited to cut down trees that grew in sacred spaces. Although the changes in the values of human–environmental relations are a continuation of much older processes such as the introduction of Christianity, the modern market economy and modern administrative systems, they have been exacerbated as a result of the land expropriation that has dismantled families, dispossessed people of their land and prompted the local communities to engage in charcoal production as a subsistence strategy.

In the past, elders held a special place in the community and were empowered to set rules with respect to utilizing communal grazing lands and water grounds and distributing farmland to clan members (Asebe 2012). For the Guji pastoral community, with only relatively recent experiences of agro-pastoralism and farming, natural resources were communally shared among clan members and governed by traditional institutions that had spiritual meaning and by authorities with the social capital to sanction transgressors of customary rules. All clan members had access to pasture and water grounds but were also responsible for complying with rules enacted by the *Gadaa*[2] and *Qaalluu*[3] elders.

Nevertheless, 'development' interventions through large-scale agribusiness projects have radically changed ideas regarding local property rights and access to natural resources. According to Ethiopia's Land Expropriation Proclamation No. 455/2005, rural land can be expropriated for public purposes with proper compensation. In contrast to the customary rules regarding access to natural resources, this proclamation provided the government with the power to expropriate the rights of local communities and to transfer those rights to investors.

Dispossession as a Project of State-Building in Ethiopia

In this chapter, I have argued that land expropriation in the Abaya Valley, although in part a response to the post-2007/08 global rise in food and fuel prices, also reflects a continuation of attempts by successive Ethiopian regimes to control land as a political and economic resource. This section describes the nexus between historical processes of land appropriation and the state's strategies of expansion towards pastoralist frontiers. The formation of the modern Ethiopian empire in the late nineteenth century was effected through successive military conquests of the territories in the south-western, southern and eastern parts of present-day Ethiopia by the Abyssinian highland Christian kingdoms (Teshale 1995; Bahru 2002). Like colonial states in other African countries, the modern Ethiopian state has been built through successive processes of resource expropriation, dispossession of indigenous communities and the creation of hierarchical social relations into ethnically and racially ordered relationships between conquering and conquered groups (Ullendorf 1965; Donham 2002; Markakis 2011; Habecker 2012). In the state-building projects of successive regimes, beginning in the late nineteenth century, control over land has remained a defining feature of state power and an instrument of patronage, control and the amassing of economic wealth, which raises the question of survival for peasants and pastoralists (Dessalegn 2009).

Trajectories in land appropriation in Ethiopia can be broadly categorized into three different phases, all of which indicate processes of state-building. The first phase began following the conquest in the late nineteenth century, the effects of which were felt into the early 1960s. During that time, feudal lords and the Orthodox Church confiscated smallholder peasant farmlands in the conquered highlands, mainly by expropriating the peasants' property rights and limiting their ability to draw benefits from their resources (Bahru 2002; Dessalegn 2009). The feudal regime's political economy depended on the control of land, the extraction of meagre resources from the peasantry, the creation of a patronage system, and an 'arranged marriage' between church and state (Bahru 2002). Feudal relations in Ethiopia relied on peasants being kept on rather than displaced from their lands in order to produce a surplus available for export. During this period, land expropriation was legalized through different proclamations and land regulations that enabled feudal lords, the church and military officers to accumulate wealth in the form of 'primitive accumulation' (Holcomb and Sisai 1990; Donham 2002; Husen 2018). After the 1940s, Haile Selassie's regime declared a land grant proclamation for the patriots, ex-soldiers, exiles and families of deceased patriots in 1942. The regime also legalized land sale in the region (Tesema 2002).

The second phase of land expropriation, between the 1960s and 1991, took two forms. Firstly, a new paradigm of transforming the country's agriculture through the establishment of modernized and mechanical large-scale state farms, carried out under both imperial and military regimes, dispossessed peasants and pastoralists in different parts of the country. Secondly, particularly under the military regime, peasants were corralled into villages and allocated land to produce a surplus for the state. Building on the narrative of agrarian transformation, which Christopher Clapham (2006) describes as the 'politics of emulation', the imperial regime and the socialist/military Derg embarked on land appropriation from smallholders and pastoralists to establish large-scale state farms such as the Chilalo Agricultural Development Unit (CADU), Wolaita Agricultural Development Unit (WADU), Awash Valley Agricultural Authority, Godey Agricultural Irrigation Project and many others (Ayele 2005; Clapham 2006). Although I lumped together the two regimes (the last years of the imperial regime and the entire period of the military regime) for convenience, this phase is characterized by an early stage of land transference to multinational corporations with an aim towards establishing large-scale agricultural projects (1960s–1974), and the establishment of state farms through state socialism (1974–91) (Clapham 2006). The large-scale agricultural schemes under both regimes resulted in the displacement of local communities from their ancestral lands.

The third phase, which is currently practised, began in earnest around 2003 as part of EPRDF's new 'neoliberal' philosophy of agrarian political economy, although it grew out of EPRDF's gradual transition from an Agricultural Development-Led Industrialization (ADLI) (from 1991–2003) to a market-led economy. Around 2003, the expansion of floriculture for foreign markets increased the transfer of arable land in the central part of Oromia to flower industries (Markakis 2011; Lavers 2012; Makki 2012). Eventually, given the post-2007/08 global rise in food and fuel prices, the government made a major policy shift from smallholder agriculture (policy principles enshrined in ADLI) to leasing out land to investors, particularly in the pastoralist and agro-pastoralist frontier lands (Asebe, Yetebarek and Korf 2018). Accordingly, large tracts of fertile land have been leased out to domestic and foreign companies in Gambella, Benishangul-Gumuz and South Omo both for economic and state-building purposes (Markakis 2011; Gill 2016). From the government's perspective, such land expropriation in the margins of the state is presumably understood as 'improving' the life of local communities (Li 2007) and 'enhancing' national economic development (Schlee 2013), although it undermines local realities, livelihood strategies and human–environment connectedness (Scott 1998). The current phase, however, is unique in that peasant land is being expropriated and the peasants themselves are driven away from it. In the wake of this displacement, the Guji are now concentrated in the remaining common lands that are neither fertile nor wide enough to sustain the Guji's livelihood needs.

Despite differences in their political economic narratives, the three regimes engaged in one or more forms of land expropriation in the peripheries. The common denominator for all three regimes is the continuity of land expropriation, with land as a source of political, economic and social power for the state.

As I stated earlier, land expropriation from peasants and pastoralists enhanced the state's consolidation of power. Under the imperial regime, the government's control of rural lands gave it the power to control society (Asebe, Yetebarek and Korf 2018). In pastoralist territories, state control of land has made both the areas and the people vulnerable – with taxation more easily enforced and resources more easily extracted (Ayele 2005; Korf et al. 2015). Certain empirical data from the Abaya Valley also substantiate this general argument. Until 2008, there was no formal state presence found in various villages of the Abaya Valley. Social organizations and community relationships were established on the basis of strong clan structures. Access to resources (farmland, water, grazing areas and forest resources) was regulated through customary practices. However, in 2008, in preparation for transferring land to Abaya Galana Agro Industries, the government established new villages (*kebele*) and assigned village administrators. According to local informants, district officials could institute policies, strategies and programmes directly through newly introduced arrangements called *caasaa gandaa* (village structures). It also came out in focus group discussions that local people who opposed the land expropriation were easily identified and arrested by the *caasaa gandaa*. The establishment of the villages and introduction of state structures to the valley became possible, as they did in many pastoralist areas, as a result of the villagization programme that collected agro-pastoralist communities into sedentary villages. Thus, while agribusiness projects necessitated the villagization programmes for the purpose of emptying land, villagization in turn enhanced the state consolidation of power by making the local people more visible with respect to taxation, administration and control.

Conclusion

Land expropriation in pastoralist and agro-pastoralist frontiers in Ethiopia is promoted by narratives emphasizing the modernization of 'underutilized' land and 'backward' societies. At the same time, these expropriations are signs of the consolidation of state power and steps towards the accumulation of wealth in the physically less accessible peripheries. While land continues to be a strong socio-economic, cultural and political resource for both the society and the state, expropriation underpins the fundamental notion that power relations between state and society are hierarchical, with the former using control over land as an instrument of controlling the latter (Husen 2018). Nevertheless, these top-down approaches – alienating people from their customary lands; the reconfiguration of regimes of governance; the utilization of natural resources – are prompting people to resort to diverse and novel strategies of capturing and using resources. The empirical evidence from the Abaya Valley reveals local community responses and how they show agency by designing new mechanisms to access resources. Because of their exclusion from farmland, water points and pasturelands, the people seal off territories that government authorities have reserved as protected bush lands and use them for charcoal production. The local communities' tenacity in cutting trees for charcoal production, despite the coercive and discursive enforcement of environmental regulations, indicates that land expropriation may lead to changes in the livelihood strategies of local people, and also to their reconfiguration of notions of property ownership and resource utilization.

Two different forms of property regimes are unfolding in the Abaya Valley. First, local communities are converting communal lands into private enclosures for charcoal production, and human–environment relations are understood from more utilitarian perspectives instead of through values embedded within the cultural and spiritual cosmologies of the people. The Guji Oromo's use of charcoal burning as a mechanism of complementing their dwindling cattle-rearing practices is not only a coping strategy in the context of livelihood uncertainty but also a form of establishing territoriality and authority over the land. They have captured the land previously defined as communal land and sought to enclose it for private charcoal production. Although communal, the government still claims control over this land; however, the local people have established authority over it by enclosing the territory for charcoal production, which is environmentally destructive and unsustainable as an investment. Second, the government's transfer of land to Abaya Galana Agro Industry through a lease system has also introduced a new property regime that gives the state the ultimate authority over the land while the corporate investor exercises its rights of quasi-ownership until the lease term expires. In light of the above two property regimes, it is sound to conclude that the government's land expropriation under the broader narrative of transforming the economy of the country and improving the lives of the local community has conversely resulted in economic impoverishment, social crisis and environmental destruction in the study area.

Asebe Regassa is an Associate Professor at the Institute of Indigenous Studies, Dilla University, Ethiopia. His research interests include pastoralism and frontier dynamics, indigenous peoples' rights, conflict and peace-building, nature conservation and human-environment relations. Dr Regassa has extensively published articles and book chapters on the above themes. He was also a postdoctoral fellow at Zürich University, Switzerland through a Swiss Government Excellence scholarship.

Notes

1. All quotations from informants were translated from Afan Oromo by the author.
2. The *Gadaa* system is a political and sociocultural age- and generation-grading institution that governs the ways of life of the Oromo. It is based on democratic principles of power transfers every eight years.
3. *Qaalluu* is a religious institution that is believed to enable a connection between the people and their supernatural authority. It is central to conflict resolution in Guji society.

References

Abbink, J. et al. 2014. 'Lands of the Future: Transforming Pastoral Lands and Livelihoods in Eastern Africa', *Max Planck Institute for Social Anthropology Working Paper* No. 154. Retrieved 8 November 2019 from https://www.eth.mpg.de/pubs/wps/pdf/mpi-eth-working-paper-0154.

Adams, J., and T. McShane. 1996. *The Myth of Wild Africa: Conservation without Illusion*. Los Angeles: University of California Press.

Asebe Regassa. 2010. *Ethnicity and Inter-Ethnic Relations: The 'Ethiopian Experiment' and the Case of the Guji and Gedeo*. Saarbrücken: VDM Verlag.

———. 2012. 'Contesting Views on a Protected Area Conservation and Development in Ethiopia', *Social Sciences* 1(1): 24–43.

Asebe Regassa, Yetebarek Hizekiel and B. Korf. 2018. '"Civilizing" the Pastoral Frontier: Land Grabbing, Dispossession and Coercive Agrarian Development in Ethiopia', *Journal of Peasant Studies*.

Assefa Fiseha. 2013. 'Ethiopia's Experiment in Accommodating Diversity: 20 Years' Balance Sheet', *Ethiopian Journal of Federal Studies* 1(1): 103–54.

Ayele Gebre-Mariam. 2005. 'The Critical Issue of Land Ownership: Violent Conflict between Abdalla Tolomogge and Awlihan in Godey Zone, Somali Region of Ethiopia', *WP 1 "Governance and Conflict Transformation" Working Paper* No. 2. Addis Ababa: Ogaden Welfare Development Association; Bern: Swisspeace.

Baglioni, E., and P. Gibbon. 2013. 'Land Grabbing, Large- and Small-Scale Farming: What Can Evidence and Policy from 20th Century Africa Contribute to the Debate?', *Third World Quarterly* 34(9): 1558–81.

Bahru Zewde. 2002. *The History of Modern Ethiopia*. Addis Ababa: Addis Ababa University Press.

Borras Jr., S., J.C. Franco and C. Wang. 2013. 'The Challenge of Global Governance of Land Grabbing: Changing International Agricultural Context and Competing Political Views and Strategies', *Globalizations* 10(1): 161–79.

Brockington, D., R. Duffy and J. Igoe. 2008. *Nature Unbound: Conservation, Capitalism and the Future of Protected Areas*. London and Sterling: Earthscan.

Buffavand, L. 2016. '"The Land Does Not Like Them": Contesting Dispossession in Cosmological Terms in Mela, South-West Ethiopia', *Journal of Eastern African Studies* 10(3): 476–93.

Clapham, C. 2006. 'Ethiopian Development: The Politics of Emulation', *Common Wealth and Comparative Politics* 44(1): 137–50.

Dessalegn Rahmato. 2009. *The Peasant and the State: Studies in Agrarian Change in Ethiopia 1950s–2000s*. Addis Ababa: Addis Ababa University Press.

Donham, D. 2002. 'Old Abyssinia and the New Ethiopian Empire: Themes in Social History', in D. Donham and W. James (eds), *The Southern Marches of Imperial Ethiopia: Essays in History and Social Anthropology*. Oxford: James Currey, pp. 3–50.

Edelman, M., and A. León. 2013. 'Cycles of Land Grabbing in Central America: An Argument for History and a Case Study in the Bajo Aguán, Honduras', *Third World Quarterly* 34(9): 1697–722.

Gill, B. 2016. 'Can the River Speak? Epistemological Confrontation in the Rise and Fall of the Land Grab in Gambella', *Ethiopia Environment and Planning A 2016* 48(4): 699–717.

Habecker, S. 2012. 'Not Black, but Habasha: Ethiopian and Eritrean Immigrants in American Society', *Ethnic and Racial Studies* 35(7): 1200–19.

Hagmann, T., and Alemmaya Mulugeta. 2008. 'Pastoral Conflicts and State-Building in the Ethiopian Lowlands', *Africa Spectrum* 43(1): 19–37.

Harawira, M. 2005. *The New Imperial Order: Indigenous Responses to Globalization*. New Zealand: Huia.

Holcomb, B., and Sisai Ibsa. 1990. *Invention of Ethiopia: The Making of Dependent Colonial State in Northeast Africa*. New York: Red Sea Press.

Husen Ahmed Tura. 2018. 'Land Rights and Land Grabbing in Oromia, Ethiopia', *Land Use Policy* 70: 247–55.

Korf, B., T. Hagmann and R. Emmenegger. 2015. 'Re-Spacing African Drylands: Territorialization, Sedentarization and Indigenous Commodification in Ethiopia's Pastoral Frontier', *Journal of Peasant Studies* 42(5): 881–901.

Krätli, S. 2015. *Valuing Variability: New Perspectives on Climate Resilient Dryland Development*. London: International Institute for Environment and Development.

Lavers, T. 2012. 'Patterns of Agrarian Transformation in Ethiopia: State Mediated Commercialization and the "Land Grab"', *Journal of Peasant Studies* 39(3–4): 795–822.

Li, T.M. 2007. *The Will to Improve: Governmentality, Development, and the Practice of Politics*. Durham, NC: Duke University Press.

———. 2014. 'What is Land? Assembling a Resource for Global Investment', *Transactions of the Institute of British Geographers* 39(4): 589–602.

Lund, C. 2011. 'Property and Citizenship: Conceptually Connecting Land Rights and Belonging in Africa', *Africa Spectrum* 46(3): 71–75.

Lund, C., and C. Boone. 2013. 'Introduction: Land Politics in Africa – Constituting Authority Over Territory, Property and Persons', *Africa* 83: 1–13.

Makki, F. 2012. 'Power and Property: Commercialization, Enclosures, and the Transformation of Agrarian Relations in Ethiopia', *Journal of Peasant Studies* 39(1): 84–104.

———. 2014. 'Development by Dispossession: *Terra Nullius* and the Social-Ecology of New Enclosures in Ethiopia', *Rural Sociology* 79(1): 79–103.

Markakis, J. 2011. *Ethiopia: The Last Two Frontiers*. Rochester and Woodbridge: James Currey.

McClellan, C. 1988. *State Transformation and National Integration: Gedeo and the Ethiopian Empire, 1895–1935*. East Lansing: Michigan State University Press.

Millar, G. 2016. 'Knowledge and Control in the Contemporary Land Rush: Making Local Land Legible and Corporate Power Applicable in Rural Sierra Leone', *Journal of Agrarian Change* 16(2): 206–24.

Minca, C., and R. Rowan. 2015. *On Schmitt and Space*. London: Routledge.

Mohammed Hassen. 1996. 'The Development of Oromo Nationalism', in P.T.W. Baxter, J. Hultin and A. Triulzi (eds), *Being and Becoming Oromo: Historical and Anthropological Enquiries*. Uppsala: Nordic Africa Institute, pp. 67–80.

Oba, G. 2013. *Nomads in the Shadows of Empires: Contests, Conflicts and Legacies on the Southern Ethiopia-Northern Kenya Frontier*. Leiden: Brill.

Oya, C. 2013. 'The Land Rush and Classic Agrarian Questions of Capital and Labour: A Systematic Scoping Review of the Socioeconomic Impact of Land Grabs in Africa', *Third World Quarterly* 34(9): 1532–57.

Ribot, J.C., and N.L. Peluso. 2003. 'A Theory of Access', *Rural Sociology* 68(2): 153–81.

Saugestad, S. 2005. 'Improving Their Lives: State Policies and San Resistance in Botswana', *Before Farming* 4(1): 1–11.

Schlee, G. 2013. 'Why States Still Destroy Pastoralism and How They Can Learn That in Their Own Interest They Should Not', *Nomadic Peoples* 17(2): 6–19.

Schmitt, C. 1950. *Der Nomos der Erde im Völkerrecht des Jus Publicum Europaeum*. Berlin: Duncker and Humblot.

Scott, J. 1998. *Seeing Like a State: How Certain Schemes to Improve Human Conditions Have Failed*. New Haven, CT: Yale University Press.

Seyoum Hameso. 2001. *Ethnicity in Africa: Towards a Positive Approach*. Lincoln, NE: iUniverse.

Taddesse Berisso. 1994. 'Warfare among the Guji-Oromo of Southern Ethiopia', in Bahru Zewde, R. Pankhurst and Taddesse Beyene (eds), *Proceedings of the Eleventh International Conference of Ethiopian Studies. Volume II*. Addis Ababa: Institute of Ethiopian Studies, Addis Ababa University, pp. 309–23.

Tesema Ta'a. 2002. '"Bribing the Land": An Appraisal of the Farming Systems of the Maccaa Oromo in Wallagga', *Northeast African Studies*, New Series 9(3): 97–113.

Teshale Tibebu. 1995. *The Making of Modern Ethiopia: 1896–1974*. Trenton, NJ: Red Sea Press.

Tsegaye Moreda, and M. Spoor. 2015. 'The Politics of Large-Scale Land Acquisitions in Ethiopia: State and Corporate Elites and Subaltern Villagers', *Canadian Journal of Development Studies* 36(2): 224–40.

Turton, D. 1987. 'The Mursi and National Park Development in the Lower Omo Valley', in D. Anderson and R. Grove (eds), *Conservation in Africa: Peoples, Policies and Practice*. Cambridge: Cambridge University Press, pp. 169–86.

Ullendorff, E. 1965. *The Ethiopians: An Introduction to Country and People*. Oxford: Oxford University Press.

Chapter 9

Villagization in Ethiopia's Lowlands

Development vs. Facilitating Control and Dispossession

Fana Gebresenbet

Background

Villagization is a strategy used to concentrate agro-pastoralists in residential areas, apart from their fields, and is justified by the provision of social services. This chapter will explore other factors and aims that underlay the villagization process in Ethiopia in early 2010s. One key area of investigation focuses on how villagization relates to land deals (often called 'land grabbing') that are promoted by the government in agro-pastoral lowlands. It is proposed here that despite the differences in processes, objectives and outcomes of the two schemes (land deals and villagization), they are nonetheless two sides of the same coin, in that both advance two goals of the Ethiopian government – the clearly stated goal of development and the unstated goal to control agro-pastoralists.

Villagization is not a recent introduction to the portfolio of Ethiopian government schemes intended to influence and mould state-society as well as production relations. Villagization during the imperial era (till 1974) pales in comparison to that of the 1980s, whether with respect to the extent of population affected, brutality of the process, idealization of village life, high modernist dreams of planners and implementers, and the resultant social, economic and human costs.

The Derg – the military government that ruled Ethiopia between 1974 and 1991–commenced a compulsory villagization programme, starting with the establishment of 'security villages' in insurgency-prone Bale, Arsi and Hararghe provinces, with plans for such a scheme included in the 1975 land reform (Tesfaye 1995). The aim was to villagize Ethiopia's entire rural population over the course of a decade in three phases: first the cereal-producing highlands, then the perennial crop-producing areas (such as for coffee and *enset*), and finally the agro-pastoral areas. These villages were to be contrasted with the previous ones; because development was the main goal, they were called 'development villages' (ibid.). These 'development villages' followed high modernist dreams of mechanized farming and standardization (Scott 1998).[1] Before the planned end to the programme in 1989, some 40 to 50 per cent of the rural population was villagized at a colossal cost (for details see Human Rights Watch [HRW] 1991; Tesfaye 1995; Scott 1998; Taddesse 2002). The programme failed miserably, especially considering that by its end only 4 per cent of farmers were collectivized, even though collectivization was its ultimate objective (HRW 1991).[2]

The Derg's ambition had been preceded by experiments undertaken by socialist comrades in Tanzania and Russia. Indeed, as Scott (1998: 247) stresses, the 'pattern of compulsory villagization in Ethiopia uncannily resembles that of Russia in its coerciveness and Tanzania in its ostensible rationale'. Ethiopian government officials visited Tanzania before embarking on the preparations of standardized plans (HRW 1991; Scott 1998), and they attributed Tanzania's failure to 'a lack of resolve – i.e. force' (HRW 1991: 229). Although there were differences in degree, both Ethiopia's and Tanzania's schemes failed, which Scott (1998) attributed to ignorance of practical ecological knowledge. The ignorance was underpinned by the state's grand simplification of social life and production relations. The stated objectives of improving the human condition and 'modernization' were negated by the government's unstated objectives of population control and surplus appropriation (Clapham 1988, 2002; Tesfaye 1995; Scott 1998; Taddesse 2002). Clapham (2002: 20) argues that '(v)illagization was . . . the most visible expression of the "capture" of the peasantry, within residential perimeters accessible to wheeled transport, where they could be taxed, conscripted, and prevented from smuggling their produce to illegal open markets'.

By the time of the 1991 regime change, which brought the Ethiopian Peoples' Revolutionary Democratic Front (EPRDF) to power, agro-pastoralists were mostly unaffected by state-led villagization (Tesfaye 1995). It was only in the early 2010s that the Ethiopian government was able to engage in a similar social engineering exercise in its vast lowlands. Moreover, unlike the Derg's efforts, villagization in current times is confined to the lowlands and is based on the constitutional obligation of helping the historically least advantaged people catch up to those who are more advantaged (see Article 89(4) of FDRE 1995). The label of 'least advantaged' is measured against differences in socio-economic development indicators in the highlands and lowlands, while it also serves to construct the agro-pastoralists and shifting cultivators as poor and in need of government handouts.

The EPRDF-led government is framing villagization as an inherent component of development in the agro-pastoral lowlands. Framed as development, villagization is presented as a benign project of improvement of the life conditions of pastoralists while simultaneously it is enabling expansion of state control and dispossessive accumulation processes.

This chapter aims to explicate the link between land deals and villagization by investigating the sociopolitical implications of villagization based on extensive field research in Gambella and South Omo since 2012. This chapter situates the villagization programme within contemporary development discourse and practice by critically examining both its officially stated and veiled purposes. Excluding this background section, the chapter has four sections. The first provides an overview of the extent of implementation, actors and 'success' of the programme in Gambella Regional State and Salamago Woreda (*woreda* = district, the second lowest administrative level) of South Omo Zone, South Nations, Nationalities and Peoples Regional State. The second examines the government's rationale for engaging in this costly exercise. The third provides a detailed analysis of the four main purposes of villagization: easing service delivery, de/reskilling, creating legible and governable units, and disguising the effect of dispossessions that occur because of land deals. The last section concludes with a perspective on Ethiopia's history of state–society interaction and state consolidation.

The Villagization Experience in Gambella and Salamago

Villagization became central to government actions carried out in the lowlands in the first half of the 2010s.[3] Although there is no essential linkage between the two, during this period villagization and land deals were co-occurring phenomena in the lowlands. The entire rural populations of Gambella and Benishangul-Gumuz – regions most affected by land deals (earmarking some 40 and 27 per cent of their territory for commercial farming, respectively) – were scheduled to be villagized, compared to less than 10 per cent of Somali region's population, for example, where land deals are much less extensive. In South Omo, villagization commenced in Salamago Woreda coterminous with the peak of activities related to the establishment of sugar cane plantations (SNNPRS 2012). The government dismissed this co-occurrence as a coincidence, not a design to 'push' people off of their land and lease the land to investors. According to the government, the aim of villagization is to

> ensure the food security and fundamentally change the livelihood of the . . . dispersed population currently vulnerable to natural and manmade disasters and not accessing development and good governance, by congregating [households] in villages, delivering infrastructure, social and economic services and making the population utilise modern technologies. (GPNRS 2014: 3; see also GPNRS 2010b, 2010c)

The programme intends to bring dispersed households to a nucleated village and to provide this village centre with various social services, with the aim of sedentarizing the population (GPNRS 2010c). It is through the provision of these social services that the government intends to meet the two key objectives of the programme: ensuring food security and bringing about a fundamental change in the livelihood of the community. This stated aim is very similar to the aim of the Derg's villagization programme (see Taddesse 2002: 118).

Each village expects to be provided with various social services, which could be labelled, following Li (1999: 302), as a 'modernity package'. The modernity package includes a school, a health post, rural roads, a veterinary clinic, water points, grinding mill houses and a *kebele* (lowest administrative unit) office. The rationale in selecting these services is based on the five priority poverty-reduction sectors: water, health, agriculture, good governance and education, to which is usually added the construction of roads.[4] Moreover, until the village community makes the first harvest, each household will be provided with food rations. Furthermore, the villagization programme calls for each household to be provided with a half hectare of land for residence and another three or four hectares for agriculture in Gambella (GPNRS 2010a, 2010b), while only a total of 1.25 hectares (0.75 hectare for sugar cane outgrower farms, 0.25 hectare for maize, and 0.25 hectare for residence) is provided in Salamago.[5]

In the three implementation years (2010/11–2012/2013 fiscal years), 37,602 households were resettled out of the planned 45,000 (a success rate of 83.56 per cent) in Gambella. This was praised as a resounding success, and the less than 100 per cent success rate was attributed to poor data quality during planning, not lack of implementation capacity. These villages are not evenly distributed in the region's zones or *woreda* (administrative district). Of the 95 villages established overall, 35 are in Anywaa Zone, followed closely by 33 in Nuer Zone, despite the fact that the Nuer are more populous. The remaining 27 are distributed between Majang Zone (17) and Itang Special Woreda (10). This implies that Nuer villages are more populated (households per village) than Anywaa villages.

The cumulative performance for Salamago Woreda indicates a 75 per cent success rate: 2,949 (1,370 being female headed households, FHH) of the 3,945 households (1,777 FHH) joined the established villages between 2011/12 and 2016/17 fiscal years. However, less than 50 per cent of those who officially joined the village live there, as only 1,375 (671 FHH) built houses. Of the 2,673 households (about 90 per cent of those who officially joined the villages) who started farming, only 1,244 permanently live in the villages. Put differently, more than half (about 53 per cent) of those cultivating the maize fields are not living in the new villages but continue to live in old villages or near Hana town, the *woreda* capital. In addition to gaining the plots, many are claiming land certificates, and 1,082 received them by July 2016, which automatically qualifies the recipient as a sugar cane outgrower. The remaining were in the process of obtaining a certificate, and more importantly getting closer to accessing the promised money as an outgrower (although to date it has proved to be no more than a mirage). The above disparity in the numbers from Salamago indicates that 'joining' a village means different things to different actors. The local community is strategizing and actively making choices to maximize the benefits potentially garnered from the scheme and to minimize the social/economic costs.[6]

We see some difference in the implementing actors too. In the case of Gambella, it is the federal government, through the Equitable Development Support Directorate (EDSD) of the now defunct Ministry of Federal and Pastoral Development Affairs (MoFPDA),[7] which took the lead. In South Omo, the regional government takes the lead in mobilization and expertise, but the Ethiopian Sugar Corporation covered expenses. As such, while the villagization in Gambella is conceived as part of the broader project of helping the 'developing' regions to catch up, in South Omo it remains a regional issue. Despite this difference in implementation actor and financier, the thinking and practice is identical.

Unveiling the Political Objectives of Villagization: Governability, Control and Disguising Dispossessions

The government argues that it is determined, especially since 2010, to bridge the chasm between the 'developed' (Amhara, Oromia, SNNP and Tigray) and 'developing' (Afar, Benishangul-Gumuz, Gambella and Somali) regional states that make up the Ethiopian federation. It is argued that the vision of building a single political and economic community could not be realized without addressing the serious differences in socio-economic indicators between Ethiopians inhabiting the highlands and those inhabiting the lowlands. The highlands are inhabited by agrarian communities with modernized socio-economic infrastructure and more political influence than the agro-pastoral communities residing in the lowland peripheries. The director of the Southern Region at the EDSD, Mr. Kori Abdalla, argues that villagization aims 'to ensure equitable development, to narrow the gap between pastoral and agricultural communities in the country. In the past, much [more] has been done on food security, meaning agriculture, than livestock'.[8] Seen from this vantage point, the need to address the highland–lowland gulf in socio-economic levels of development is understandable. Ostensibly, villagization is an expression of the solidarity shown by the ruling elite towards the lowlanders and the fulfilment of the constitutional obligation to address inherited imbalances in development. In discourse and practice, however, the expertise, knowledge and cultural diversity of the lowlanders are completely ignored.

The most obvious outcome of villagization is to create a compact, nucleated settlement. This enables the achievement of a range of other stated and unstated aims. There is no exclusivity; rather, one serves as a foundation for the other, and one is achieved through the other. This section focuses on the overt and covert purposes of the programme, specifically: service delivery; de/reskilling; creating legible, governable units; and the disguising of dispossessions.

Service Delivery

Clearly, among the most important professed benefits of villagization is improving service delivery in hitherto hard-to-service areas. The government has time and again stressed that its single most important objective in pursuing this politically and economically very costly programme is congregating households into nucleated villages, thereby making service delivery easier and cheaper. With apparent good intentions, a return of some sort on this investment, at least after some time lag, is anticipated. If costs (political, financial and social) are prohibitive, a rational government would refrain from a project until the situation changes and costs go down (or expected returns increase). Based on this understanding, to the extent that dispersed and seasonally changing settlement patterns reduce the cost-effectiveness of service delivery, it is clear that having congregated and permanent settlements increases efficiency of service delivery. This, however, does not mean that there are no other alternatives to providing services to dispersed and agro-pastoral populations.[9]

The promised social services are not the sole ends sought by the government. Promises also serve as strings to pull households into the villages, in addition to the subtle and, if needed, blatant coercive action of pushing.[10] Nor have the promises been fully kept. Households are made to join villages before social infrastructures are in place, according to informants on the ground:

> We were told that there will be school for our children, clinic, water pumps, grinding mills to ease the workload of our women . . . etc. Some of us were convinced to come here to utilize those services. First we were told that we will join the villages after the services are readied, after some time we were rushed to go to this barren land with no services. Some of the promise has been kept, but we are very sad. How can a government, a father, go against his word? Is the government a liar? (Anywaa elder, Abol village, 3 July 2015)

> A few years ago, the government and Sugar people [officials/experts working for the Ethiopian Sugar Corporation] promised us everything. Promised to give us everything we asked, as long as we joined the villages. We ask for ambulance, the Sugar [Corporation] sends it. We ask for something today. It comes after a week or month. Now nobody listens to us. Everything is deteriorated. No school, no clinic, no water, no support to have better housing structures. (Mela elder, Hana town, 14 October 2017)

Necessary resources for various services (teachers and textbooks for schools and pharmaceuticals for clinics, for example) are lacking. Services, if available, are of poor quality. Moreover, there is an awareness that livelihoods and food security have deteriorated (World Bank 2014; Stevenson and Buffavand 2018). This general condition is recognized by the Ethiopian government (Ethiopian Human Rights Commission 2013), studies (Zinabu 2014; Cham 2015), INGO research reports (HRW 2012a; OI 2013) and donors (World Bank 2014). What this implies is contested: to government officials, it is only attributed to inadvertent gaps in implementation capacity, while others present this as evidence of ill intentions of the government.

De- and Reskilling

Villagization also has the advantage of allowing the government to 'rationalize' land use. This, as much as service delivery, is at the core of the scheme.[11] The intention is to convert the modes of livelihood (shifting cultivation, agro-pastoralism) practised in the lowlands into settled forms of agriculture. This entails firmly anchoring residences and farming plots.

The government does not hide its aims of changing the lifestyle/livelihood strategy of the lowlanders. It does not see anything worth nurturing in the local livelihood systems and knowledge (see Meles 2011). What the government intends to bring about is a complete displacement of mobile forms of agriculture and animal husbandry, and in their place, the application of settled forms: shifting agriculture to be replaced by smallholder farming, agro-pastoralism to be supplanted by smallholder farming and ranching (GPNRS 2010b; SNNPRS 2012). A member of the Economic Affairs Standing Committee of the SNNP Regional Council, in October 2012, emphasized the 'civilizing' and skilling mission in the following manner:

> I am part of the team which visited the sugar scheme in South Omo representing the council. The propaganda of the foreigners should not be trusted. The sugar work helps the community live a better life. I was unhappy because the government did not reach and help them before now. If you think about it we were all like them some centuries ago. Now, it is their time: thanks to God and the government. We cannot simply let them live a simple life, wandering following their cattle, naked. We should help them get skills, produce better and have surplus food and other resources.

This requires the villagized lowlanders to acquire new skill sets in place of the old. The government was working on the assumption that the community had been relying on survival skills for their livelihoods. The Government Communication Affairs Office (GCAO 2015: 146; emphasis mine) exemplifies this position: 'The paradox is . . . human rights advocates would have been the first to criticize the government should it fail to provide . . . basic necessities to remote and detached social groupings, burdened by *worries of mere survival*'. Shifting cultivation and agro-pastoralism are seen only as 'low-yield system(s) of production that barely meet . . . basic sustenance needs' (ibid.: 118). Therefore, the government does not see its mission as promoting a new skill set to replace the old; rather, the new skill set will conquer 'wildernesses'. The community is not going to be deskilled, and there will be no reskilling; this is a skilling campaign, since the government does not recognize that a skill set preceded its intervention (for a detailed presentation of the skill set of pastoralists, see Abbink et al. 2014; Gabbert 2018).

Unfortunately, reskilling occurs not only following the demise of local knowledge but also the destruction of existing wealth and expertise. Deskilling and destocking represent an impoverishment in agro-pastoral settings, but as is often the case, such inputs will either be ignored (since the state labels such people as poor from the outset) or not taken into account, because the state does not recognize the existence or relevance of local knowledge, existing wealth or expertise. Lower levels of marketable surplus and tax generation, as in pastoral areas, will mean that the state does not *see* the local economy, let alone augment it (Scott 2009).

Creating Governable, Legible Units

A third purpose, a veiled one, relates to what Scott called legibility and Foucault called governmentality.[12] Governability is about conducting conduct (Foucault 1991). The conduct that is being conducted through villagization is all-encompassing and includes the manner of settlement, livelihoods and ways of practising agriculture and social and cultural life in general. The relations, links and attachments of lowlanders to various 'things' are being governed in paternalistic ways (Gabbert and Thubauville 2010; Abbink et al. 2014).[13] No aspect of social, cultural or economic life is safe from this governing attempt. The government aims to reconfigure such relations, links and attachments with regard to how people go about their daily lives, engage in agriculture, maintain their health, settle in certain areas and so on, arguably for the benefit of the lowlanders themselves but without genuinely consulting them. Villagization, thus, is an attempt to rationalize the lowlanders' relations with one another, the state, and the natural environment.

A complex, illegible community is difficult to govern; villagization contributes to making society legible and governable. It is well established that successive Ethiopian governments did not interfere in the social life of the lowlands in the past, not for lack of interest but because the lowland population was not a *proper subject* to be governed. The state did not *understand* the social and cultural order of the lowlanders and could not reduce their social and economic complexity.[14] As argued in the two preceding subsections, villagization now intends to demolish the old and build a new mode of life. This is mainly done to match the desires of the (federal) government. This new village life could more easily and economically be penetrated by the state's servicing and controlling tentacles (the *kebele* and police stations, schools, clinics, veterinary clinics, development agents and so on). As to the villagization scheme and promises of creating jobs in the formal/ sugar sector, a young Mela man stated:

> The government wants us to be subservient. We are a happy, free people enjoying the bounty of our cattle, land and the river. We are not used to government. Now we are forced to come to these villages and work for the Sugar [Corporation]. The government does not want us to be free. It does not want us to be happy. It wants to control us: what we do, where we live . . . we are not happy. (FGD, Village 1, Tewolde and Fana, January 2013)

In government circles, there is widespread agreement as to the importance of congregated settlements in servicing the people of the lowlands. The same factors and arguments apply to the state's attempt to make basic conditions of life in the lowlands subject to policy – it is by subjecting certain aspects of life to state-implemented policies that the lot of an ordinary individual from the lowlands is expected to improve. These policies cover education, health, agriculture, animal health, transportation and so on (i.e. the modernity packages). It is therefore by meeting the objectives of such policies that this veiled aim will be realized. However, failure to deliver on the promised modernity package in most village centres has reduced the expected success of the social engineering exercise.

Villagization potentially affects the governability of the lowlands – if the stated objectives are met – through the following three channels. First, it is obvious that having a permanent place of residence in nucleated villages makes agro-pastoralists an easy object to be nurtured, governed, disciplined and controlled. Second, each village will be subject to state control through administrative *kebele* and police stations.[15] This makes the task of governing the lowlander a lot easier. In effect, what we are beginning to see is the Ethiopian state making its presence in the lowlands increasingly felt: through the *kebele* and police stations, which represent an entrenchment of the state's coercive powers; through service delivery, which also necessitates the deployment of civil servants; and through symbols (ranging from the Ethiopian flag to photos of the late prime minister Meles).[16]

Third, the building of state institutions will contribute towards the ongoing exercise of social engineering. Similar to Li (1999: 301) with regard to Indonesia's resettlement programme since the 1950s, Ethiopia's villagization programme is a 'complete attempt at social engineering, governability in gross form'. This exercise is not aimed solely at helping the lowlanders but also at converting their culture, values and attitudes into what is perceived to be appropriate and correct by the centre. What is occurring in Ethiopia's lowlands is similar to what David Scott (1999: 26, italics in original) said of colonial governability, deemed as *not merely coincident with colonialism*. Colonial governability is about 'disabling old forms of life by systematically breaking down their conditions, and with constructing in their place new conditions so as to enable – indeed so as to *oblige* – new forms of life to come into being'. The 'modernity packages' demolish the cultural base and, if successfully delivered, also contribute to eroding the legitimacy of indigenous processes and building up the legitimacy of state institutions. Augmented by the symbols described above, villagization contributes to creating new subjectivities, oriented away from traditional leaders and towards the state (official), or, following Markakis (2011), the subordinate elite. All of these concerted efforts are intended to lay the foundation for turning lowlanders into proper subjects for state governance.

Disguising Dispossessions

The undeclared purpose of villagization is related to dispossessions generated by land deals. The federal and regional governments stress, in fact, that land deals and villagization are unrelated, which contrasts with the widely held view that villagization is a sugar-coated term for the forced displacement of local people to make way for large-scale agricultural investments (see HRW 2012a; OI 2013; for diaspora activism along similar lines, see various opinion pieces from the Solidarity Movement for a New Ethiopia). Rather than debating the authenticity of the government's stated intentions versus what is believed on the ground, the aim herein is to draw a conceptual association between the two.

Land investments are not undertaken in an economically sound and technocratic manner; rather, these are mainly enabled by political interventions of wealth transfer from the poor to the wealthier class. As such, land deals constitute a form of primitive/original accumulation, what David Harvey (2003) rebranded as accumulation by dispossession (for a more detailed discussion, see Fana 2016). The defining feature of this process is 'the use of extra-economic coercion to expropriate means of subsistence, production or common social wealth for capital accumulation' (Levien 2011: 457).

Dispossessions occur through coercion, and the state's agency is primarily expressed through enforcement of dispossessions (Levien 2011). It is state power manifested as disciplining action (Negi and Auerbach 2009), which lowers barriers to the drive for accumulation (Levien 2011). Accumulation by dispossession is a 'decidedly *political* process through which the state's coercive power is deployed to make a key condition of production . . . available for capital in a context where increasing demand confronts the barrier to accumulation' (Levien 2011: 457; italics in original). Such processes are pursued through the 'appropriation and co-optation of pre-existing cultural and social achievements as well as [their] confrontation and supersession' (Harvey 2003: 146). As such, accumulation by dispossession is an inherently violent process (Harvey 2003).

The current international political situation, given the extent of Ethiopia's dependence on foreign aid and repeated cases of international advocacy against government actions, puts a limit to the violence that could be involved in such processes. Contemporary rounds of dispossession will not be 'written in the annals of mankind in blood and fire', as Marx (1982: 875) said. In Ethiopia's lowlands, this can partly be attributed to the ambivalence with which the local people view villagization. Villagization promises the widespread delivery of modernity packages to serve as foundations for a 'modern' life. This can be attractive, even to the extent that some members of the community favour village life.[17] Moreover, had local people been simply displaced from their land, as the Afar and Karrayu were half a century earlier (Kloos 1982; Buli 2006), without any mitigation strategies, the violence involved in the dispossessions would have been much 'louder' for everyone to hear. Indeed, villagization, as Mulugeta (2014) argues, could be perceived as a mitigation strategy to lessen the negative consequences of the land deals.

Thus, villagization conceals the impact of the dispossessions occurring through land deals. The 'camouflage', so to speak, would be the promise of service delivery and of creating suitable conditions for local people to live a better, more stable, secure and modern life. The consequence of not meeting service delivery promises is then tantamount to removing the 'silencer', thus laying the violence bare for everyone to see.

That villagization is helping conceal the violent nature of accumulation by dispossession through land deals is not to say that no violence is involved in the process of villagizing the community. Indeed, as HRW (2012a, 2012b) and other reports/news articles and interviews with members of the local community reveal, the programme's implementation has been punctuated by violent incidents (see also contributions by Asebe, Buffavand and LaTosky in this volume). Members of the local community who did not volunteer to join the new villages were *made* to volunteer, if needed through brute force (more so in Gambella than South Omo). Redwan Husen, Ethiopia's former communication minister, responding to pressure from international NGOs on villagization, in particular in Gambella and South Omo, stated that there was only 'salutary pressure' or 'semi-coercion' 'born out of haste to radically improve their living condition'. He went on to add that when the locals complained about it (directly to the government), without questioning the intention of the programme, a rural and urban good governance package was implemented and the 'salutary pressure' stopped (quoted in GCAO 2015: 123–25).

What Was Villagization Really About?
As stated in the previous sub-sections, the villagization programme aimed to stimulate development (through service delivery and reskilling), create legible units

of governance in the lowlands, and make land deals more palatable. The stated objectives relating to 'developing' the local community were presented as the primary end, and significant amounts of expertise, effort and time were devoted to it by staff of the EDSD and regional governments. Combined with subtle/blatant coercion, this led to some joining the villages. To ensure that these households remained in the villages and that more followed suit, the Ethiopian Sugar Corporation (in Salamago) and the federal government (in Gambella) invested sizeable resources in constructing various social and physical infrastructures. This peak in government attention and commitment coincided with the peak in land deals and land-clearing activities. Similarly, a drop in new land deals a few years later is coterminous with a drop in government attention to service delivery and reskilling. This has been noticed by members of the local community; for example, in Salamago there is a widespread feeling that the ESC is now less attentive to the needs of the Mela (see also Buffavand this volume). For example, services once provided by the ESC (including ambulances) and promises to build better housing structures have fallen through the cracks.[18] One elder stressed:

> The villages were created only to distract us . . . when the land (for sugar plantations) was being taken away, we could not wholly focus on that. The government wanted us to settle as well. I now think that the government tricked us to give away our land with little resistance by confining us in these villages . . . If that was not the case, why doesn't the government support us now. Now that they took our land, they don't care what we think. (Interview, Hana town, 14 October 2017)

I had the opportunity to get back to village sites in Salamago in August 2018, nearly seven years after my first visit to the same sites. In seven years, the village sites had taken on an abandoned appearance and been reclaimed by grasses and bushes. Moreover, the various service centres, including water points, grinding mill house and the *kebele* store, which were (partly) operational in 2012, were in ruins. Therefore, to the local community the objective of stimulating development only served as a false front and a distraction. From the government's perspective, there is a recognition that the development aims of villagization have not been fully met. Thus, more human, financial and material resources are committed to this end. As such, to government officials and experts, the stated objectives were not merely a charade. Inability to meet the stated objective translated into lower success in creating a legible and governable unit through interference in settlement matters. By reducing the violence involved in land alienations, however, villagization made land deals more thinkable for the political elite and more bearable for the local community. This is not to say that the local community was treated well or that the violence was negligible. Rather, the argument here is that had there been no villagization, the alternative would have been full proletarianization. Moreover, the involved violence was not out in the open for everyone to see, particularly foreign pressure groups and donors. The disguising of dispossessions is a relatively short-term and easy-to-meet goal, compared to the social engineering necessary to create legible and controllable units.

If one is to draw some conclusion from the foregoing discussion, it would not be a very optimistic one. Equitable development is not on the horizon, and what the state does only brings marginalization closer to home. The benefits that the environment offers, which the local community know and value deeply, are either ignored or openly trampled upon. This is not an irreversible process, however, and the differences in the worldviews of lowlanders and the state and its experts are not insurmountable. Going beyond the current scenario to a scenario that values the local community – its knowledge and expertise – and the local environment is technically possible but politically unlikely.

As Appadurai (2013) argues, anthropology should become a future-oriented science and seek to understand how individuals and communities create their futures. In this process, the 'capacity to aspire' is a crucial resource that the weak and marginalized lack. The capacity to aspire – as a 'social and collective capacity' that is locally specific – is a 'navigational capacity', through which poor people can effectively change the "terms of recognition" within which they are generally trapped' (ibid.: 289–90). Lacking in this capacity will detract from the potency to make good on their full potential. If we are to be optimistic and hope that the lowlanders become makers of their worlds (Gabbert 2018), the task will be balancing the power differential through empowerment that improves their participation and voice in future projects in their locality. The Ethiopian state by its very nature is repressive, and even if it is to democratize, the waves will reach and be felt in the lowland frontiers last. As such, the task of empowering the lowlanders and balancing the power differential while the state pursues its resource interests is not easy or straightforward. Therefore, the troubled current political, socio-economic and livelihood situation in the lowlands is more likely to persist.

Concluding Remarks on the Objectives of Villagization

If the task at hand is addressing the gap between 'developed' and 'developing' regions, then the issue is one of redistribution and equity. The necessity of redistribution is less debatable, but how to define it and how to go about it are points of fierce contestation. When it comes to adopting mechanisms to bring about equitable development, the Ethiopian government does not *see* anything worth salvaging from the socio-economic, livelihood, institutional and political practices of the diverse cultures and of the lowlanders, let alone the potential of their knowledge (see Gabbert 2018). Rather, the adopted approach is to completely replace the institutions, values, practical knowledge and livelihood mechanisms of shifting cultivators or agro-pastoralists with those brought from the highlands and the imposition of settled forms of agriculture. The rationale for this total disregard of practical knowledge is the attitude that such mechanisms are no more than survival skills, and not skills that could be used to build a surplus-oriented economy.

This intention of replacing ways of life, livelihoods and production practices in the name of rationalization, or development, reflects contemptuous attitudes towards the lowlanders' lifestyle. These are not necessarily reflections on the performance of local livelihoods or the choices made by people on how to live their lives. For example, the Anywaa were previously surplus producers at a time when their socio-political organization was functional, before they were uprooted by state institutional encroachments (Kurimoto 1996). Yet this is conveniently ignored in enforcing a new way of doing agriculture. The cultural values of Ethiopia's political elite support the reification of such meanings and views on agro-pastoralism and shifting cultivation, and as such buttress the continuation of the extant 'cultural political economy' (Jessop 2010).

The rhetoric that paints pastoralists as poor and vulnerable has often become manifest only after the basis for their subsistence economy, land, has been taken away (Abbink et al. 2014). Thus, the 'rationalization' argument is not based on technical truth but advanced for the self-serving ends of promoting land deals (Galaty 2011). Power relations and peripherality also partly explain why the ruling elites of the region agreed to the implementation of the programme with little or no resistance.

Although it arrived in the guise of 'improving the lots of the local community', in the eyes of the local community, the main aim of villagization was to draw the new villagers' attention away from the land alienations that were taking place. Villagization made land acquisitions more thinkable and practicable and in effect enabled land deals, although the two should not necessarily happen together. The four objectives that the scheme serves – service delivery, reskilling agro-pastoralists, creating legible, governable units, and disguising dispossessions – were co-occurring and necessary in the early stages of implementation. Less than a decade after commencement of the scheme, however, the political objective of concealing the dispossessions through land deals and making the land deals doable was met more than the other objectives. Regional and federal government officials and experts are continuing to work on servicing and reskilling aspects of villagization. There is more work being done but at a much slower pace and to less of a degree than in the earlier years of the decade. Developing the agro-pastoralists is still on the government's agenda.

The conception of development and the state's role in the process has remained unchanged in Ethiopia's peripheries. Development is expected to occur through the active role of the government and is premised on the irrelevance and denigration of local environmental knowledge and the production techniques of the lowlanders. The intention is not to augment but rather to displace and subsequently replace old and rich knowledge and expertise that should have been harnessed as opportunities. What started off as a strategy of addressing historical imbalances ends up further entrenching the state's power and disempowering and marginalizing the local community. Cultural diversity is either ignored completely, or if it is recognized, its sacrifice is regarded as acceptable and inevitable for the sake of developing the lowlanders themselves and the country. In the end, however, development through villagization does not meet its stated targets but rather contributes to concealing the resource interests of the state.

A proper recognition and incorporation of local values and norms in these interventions would at the very least reduce social and environmental costs, and at the most contribute towards the stated aim of improving the lives of the local communities. It is by helping to create a win-win situation that the local community could be induced into actively taking part in creating the future they have reason to value. Otherwise, the local community is reduced to the status of a subject, and the true aims of 'development' are thwarted.

Fana Gebresenbet is an Assistant Professor at the Institute for Peace and Security Studies of Addis Ababa University. He wrote his PhD on 'The Political Economy of Land Investments: Dispossession, Resistance and Territory-Making in Gambella, Western Ethiopia'. He has been researching state-building and development in Ethiopia's lowlands for more than a decade.

Notes

Part of the fieldwork informing this paper was financed by support from the Africa Peacebuilding Network of the Social Sciences Research Network, with funds provided by the Carnegie Corporation of New York.

1. High modernism refers to an unshakeable confidence in scientific knowledge and technology, which are seen as the most effective means towards ordering life, while at the same time disregarding other desires and knowledge.
2. For the self-organized villagization experience of the Majang, combined with conversion to Christianity, as an avenue to material modernity, equality with neighbouring ethnic groups and increasing negotiation powers, see Sato (2002).
3. The figures provided in this section are from Gambella's regional and South Omo's zonal governments. The figures mainly are produced for government services, and as such might not accurately reflect the reality on the ground.
4. Interview: senior expert, President Office, Gambella region, 23 June 2014.
5. Interviews: development agent, Salamago Woreda; expert, Agriculture and Natural Resources Bureau, Salamago Woreda, 4 August 2016.
6. The grim realities of implementation of these 'development' projects in Salamago are well covered by Buffavand (2016 and this volume) and Stevenson and Buffavand (2018). While my work is mainly based on interviews and discussions with state officials and experts, theirs is based on extended anthropological studies among the Mela. As such, the works should be complementary.

7. As of October 2018, activities of this Directorate fall under the mandate of the Ministry of Peace.

8. Interview: Addis Ababa, 13 April 2018.

9. The African Union's (2010: 28) Policy Framework for Pastoralism in Africa lists some alternatives: 'In education these include distance learning and alternative basic education approaches; in health, community case management and community health worker systems have been proven to be effective; for basic veterinary care, community-based animal health workers can be used.' Chambers et al. (2013) indicate that innovative approaches should be adopted to effectively deliver services in such low population density areas, including aiming for higher adaptability and mobility of providers and service points; improving connectivity between providers and users; and promoting practical hybrids between public and private, formal and informal. On adaptations of pastoral mobility (modern mobility) to access services in urban sectors, see Galaty (this volume).

10. Food rations could also be one such string (Interview: Anywaa working for an NGO, 10 December 2013).

11. Interview, director, EDSD, MoFPDA, 14 March 2018.

12. Legibility is simultaneously a condition for, and product of, state action. As a process, it leads to reducing local specificities and complexities through a range of interventions by the state and capital to enable control and extraction (Scott 1998).

13. These 'things' include land, water, livelihood, forest (common) resources, culture and vulnerability to extreme weather events (drought, flooding).

14. This could easily be noticed in the complexity and illegibility of the agricultural practices of the Anywaa in long-ago times (see Kurimoto 1996).

15. These could as well be called, following Hammond (2002: 95), 'infrastructures of state control'. Save for obvious differences in context and aim, villagization is a project of control similar to the programme promoted during the Derg era (Clapham 2002; Taddesse 2002).

16. In various new villages in Gambella, the model house – first built under the supervision of villagization coordinators as a demonstration to teach how to build *tukul* (small round houses, made of wood and mud, with a thatched roofing) – is converted into a *kebele* office, with a flag hoisted in front of it. Pictures of the late prime minister are found in all government offices, accompanied by a quote about the urgent need to eradicate poverty.

17. Some local people argue that the villages are 'backward' and the government should have promoted the creation of urban centres (see Dereje 2013).

18. Interview, an elder in Hana town, 14 October 2017.

References

Abbink, J. et al. 2014. 'Lands of the Future: Transforming Pastoral Lands and Livelihoods in Eastern Africa', *Max Planck Institute for Social Anthropology Working Paper* No. 154. Retrieved 21 March 2018 from http://www.eth.mpg.de/cms/de/publications/working_papers/.

African Union. 2010. *Policy Framework for Pastoralism in Africa: Securing, Protecting and Improving the Lives, Livelihoods and Rights of Pastoralist Communities*. Department of Rural Economy and Agriculture, African Union, Addis Ababa, Ethiopia. Retrieved 21 March 2018 from http://www.achpr.org/files/instruments/policy-framework-pastoralism/policy_framework_for_pastoralism.pdf.

Appadurai, A. 2013. *The Future as Cultural Fact: Essays on the Global Condition*. London: Verso.

Buffavand, L. 2016. '"The Land Does Not Like Them": Contesting Dispossession in Cosmological Terms in Mela, South-West Ethiopia', *Journal of Eastern African Studies* 10(3): 476–93.

Buli Edjeta. 2006. *The Socio-Economic Dimensions of Development-Induced Impoverishment: The Case of the Karrayu Oromo of the Upper Awash Valley*, Social Anthropology Dissertation Series vol. 12. Addis Ababa: Addis Ababa University.

Cham, O. 2015. 'Human Rights Issues in Development-Induced Displacement: A Look into Villagization Program in Anywaa Zone, Gambella Regional State', M.A. thesis. Department of Governance and Development Studies, Jimma University, Ethiopia.

Chambers, V., L. Wild and M. Foresti. 2013. 'Innovations in Service Delivery: International Experience in Low-Density Countries', *Overseas Development Institute Report*. Retrieved 21 March 2018 from https://www.odi.org/sites/odi.org.uk/files/odi-assets/publications-opinion-files/9442.pdf.

Clapham, C. 1988. *Transformation and Continuity in Revolutionary Ethiopia*. Cambridge: Cambridge University Press.

———. 2002. 'Controlling Space in Ethiopia', in W. James, D. Donham, E. Kurimoto and A. Triulzi (eds), *Remapping Ethiopia: Socialism and After*. Oxford: James Currey, pp. 9–32.

Dereje Feyissa. 2013. '"Centering the Periphery"? The Federal Experience at the Margins of the Ethiopian State', *Ethiopian Journal of Federal Studies* 1(1): 155–92.

Ethiopian Human Rights Commission. 2013. *The Status of Human Rights in Ethiopian Villagization Programs*. Addis Ababa.

Fana Gebresenbet. 2016. 'The Political Economy of Land Investments: Dispossession, Resistance and Territory-Making in Gambella, Western Ethiopia', Ph.D. dissertation. University of Leipzig and Addis Ababa University.

Federal Democratic Republic of Ethiopia (FDRE). 1995. *The Constitution of the Federal Democratic Republic of Ethiopia*. Addis Ababa, Ethiopia.

Foucault, M. 1991. 'Governmentality', in G. Burchell, C. Gordon and P. Miller (eds), *The Foucault Effect: Studies in Governmentality with Two Lectures by and Interview with Michel Foucault*. Chicago: Chicago University Press, pp. 87–104.

Gabbert, E.C. 2018. 'Future in Culture: Globalizing Environments in the Lowlands of Southern Ethiopia', in J. Abbink (ed.), *The Environmental Crunch in Africa: Growth Narratives vs. Local Realities*. London: Palgrave Macmillan, pp. 287–315.

Gabbert, E.C., and S. Thubauville. 2010. *To Live with Others: Essays on Cultural Neighbourhood in Southern Ethiopia*. Cologne: Köppe.

Galaty, J.G. 2011. '(Non) Rational Choice', *paper presented at the Workshop Organized on the Occasion of the 60th Birthday of Günther Schlee, Roundtable on Rational Choice and Challenges, 10–12 July 2011*. Max Planck Institute for Social Anthropology, Halle (Saale).

Gambella Peoples' National Regional State (GPNRS). 2010a. 'The Organisation, Power and Duty of Gambella Peoples' National Regional State's Executive Branch' (in Amharic), *Proclamation No. 95/2011*. Gambella, Ethiopia.

———. 2010b. *Villagization Program Action Plan (2003 EFY)*, August. Gambella.

———. 2010c. 'Villagisation Programme's Implementation Directives', *Agriculture and Rural Development Bureau* (in Amharic), July. Gambella.

———. 2014. *2013/14 Budget Year Nine Month's Implementation Report for the Villagisation Programme* (in Amharic). Gambella, Ethiopia.

Government Communications Affairs Office (of Ethiopia; GCAO). 2015. *The Ethiopian Human Rights Landscape in the Context of Right-Based Approach to Development*. Retrieved 21 September 2015 from http://www.gcao.gov.et/documents/10157/107515/The+Ethiopian+Human+Rights+Landscape++in+the+Context+of+Right-Based+Approach.

Hammond, J. 2002. 'Garrison Towns and the Control of Space in Revolutionary Tigray', in W. James, D. Donham, E. Kurimoto and A. Triulzi (eds), *Remapping Ethiopia: Socialism and After*. Oxford: James Currey, pp. 90–115.

Harvey, D. 2003. *The New Imperialism*. Oxford: Oxford University Press.

Human Rights Watch (HRW). 1991. 'Evil Days: 30 Years of War and Famine in Ethiopia', *Africa Watch Report*. Retrieved 23 May 2014 from http://www.hrw.org/sites/default/files/reports/Ethiopia919.pdf.

———. 2012a. 'Forced Displacement and Villagization in Ethiopia's Gambella Region'. Retrieved 22 January 2014 from http://www.hrw.org/reports/2012/01/16/waiting-here-death.

———. 2012b. 'What Will Happen If Hunger Comes? Abuses against the Indigenous Peoples of Ethiopia's Lower Omo Valley'. Retrieved 22 January 2014 from http://www.hrw.org/reports/2012/06/18/what-will-happen-if-hunger-comes-0.

Jessop, B. 2010. 'Cultural Political Economy and Critical Policy Studies', *Critical Policy Studies* 3(3–4): 336–56.

Kloos, H. 1982. 'Development, Drought and Famine in the Awash Valley of Ethiopia', *African Studies Review* 25(4): 21–48.

Kurimoto, E. 1996. 'People of the River: Subsistence Economy of the Anywaa (Anyak) of Western Ethiopia', in S. Sato and E. Kurimoto (eds), *Essays in Northeast African Studies*, Senri Ethnological Studies No. 43. Osaka: National Museum of Ethnology, pp. 29–57.

Levien, M. 2011. 'Special Economic Zones and Accumulation by Dispossession in India', *Journal of Agrarian Change* 11(4): 454–83.

Li, T.M. 1999. 'Compromising Power: Development, Culture, and Rule in Indonesia', *Cultural Anthropology* 14(3): 295–322.

Markakis, J. 2011. *Ethiopia: The Last Two Frontiers*. Woodbridge and Rochester: James Currey.

Marx, K. 1982. *Capital: A Critique of Political Economy*, vol. 1. Middlesex: Penguin Books.

Meles Zenawi. 2011. 'Speech at the 13th Annual Pastoralist Day of Ethiopia', Jinka, South Omo, Ethiopia, 25 January 2011. Retrieved 14 January 2014 from http://www.mursi.org/pdf/Meles%20Jinka%20speech.pdf.

Mulugeta Gebrehiwot Berhe. 2014. 'Conclusion', in Mulugeta Gebrehiwot Berhe (ed.), *A Delicate Balance: Land Use, Minority Rights and Social Stability in the Horn of Africa*. Addis Ababa: Institute for Peace and Security Studies, Addis Ababa University, pp. 309–14.

Negi, R., and M. Auerbach. 2009. 'The Contemporary Significance of Primitive Accumulation', *Human Geography* 2(3): 89–90.

Oakland Institute (OI). 2013. 'Development Aid to Ethiopia: Overlooking Violence, Marginalization, and Political Repression'. Retrieved 23 January 2014 from http://www.oaklandinstitute.org/sites/oaklandinstitute.org/files/OI_Brief_Development_Aid_Ethiopia.pdf.

Sato, R. 2002. 'Evangelical Christianity and Ethnic Consciousness in Majangir', in W. James, D. Donham, E. Kurimoto and A. Triulzi (eds), *Remapping Ethiopia: Socialism and After*. Oxford: James Currey, pp. 185–97.

Scott, D. 1999. *Refashioning Futures: Criticism after Postcoloniality*. Princeton, NJ: Princeton University Press.

Scott, J. 1998. *Seeing Like a State: How Certain Schemes to Improve the Human Condition Have Failed*. New Haven, CT: Yale University Press.

———. 2009. *The Art of Not Being Governed: An Anarchist History of Upland Southeast Asia*. New Haven and London: Yale University Press.

Southern Nations, Nationalities and Peoples Regional State (SNNPRS). 2012. 'Government, Pastoral Affairs Bureau, S. Omo Zone, Salamago Woreda and Kaffa Zone, Decha

Woreda', *Villagization Plan of 2005* (E.C). Submitted to Kuraz Sugar Development Project Nehassie 2004, Hawassa.

Stevenson, E.G.J., and L. Buffavand. 2018. '"Do Our Bodies Know Their Ways?" Villagization, Food Insecurity, and Ill-Being in Ethiopia's Lower Omo Valley', *African Studies Review* 61(1): 109–33.

Taddesse Berisso. 2002. 'Modernist Dreams and Human Suffering: Villagization among the Guji Oromo', in W. James, D. Donham, E. Kurimoto and A. Triulzi (eds), *Remapping Ethiopia: Socialism and After*. Oxford: James Currey, pp. 117–32.

Tesfaye Tafesse. 1995. *Villagization in Northern Shewa, Ethiopia: Impact Assessment*. Munster: Lit Verlag.

World Bank. 2014. 'Ethiopia: Promoting Basic Services Phase III Project (P128891), *Investigation Report of the Inspection Panel*. Retrieved 12 May 2015 from http://ewebapps.world bank.org/apps/ip/PanelCases/82-Inspection%20Panel%20Investigation%20Report%20 -%20Ethiopia%20PBS%20-%20Phase%20III%20Project.pdf.

Zinabu Endalfer. 2014. 'Villagization in Contemporary Ethiopia: The Experience of Gambella Region, Anywaa Zone, from Human Rights Perspective', M.A. thesis. Addis Ababa University, Centre for Human Rights.

Part IV
Underdeveloping South Omo

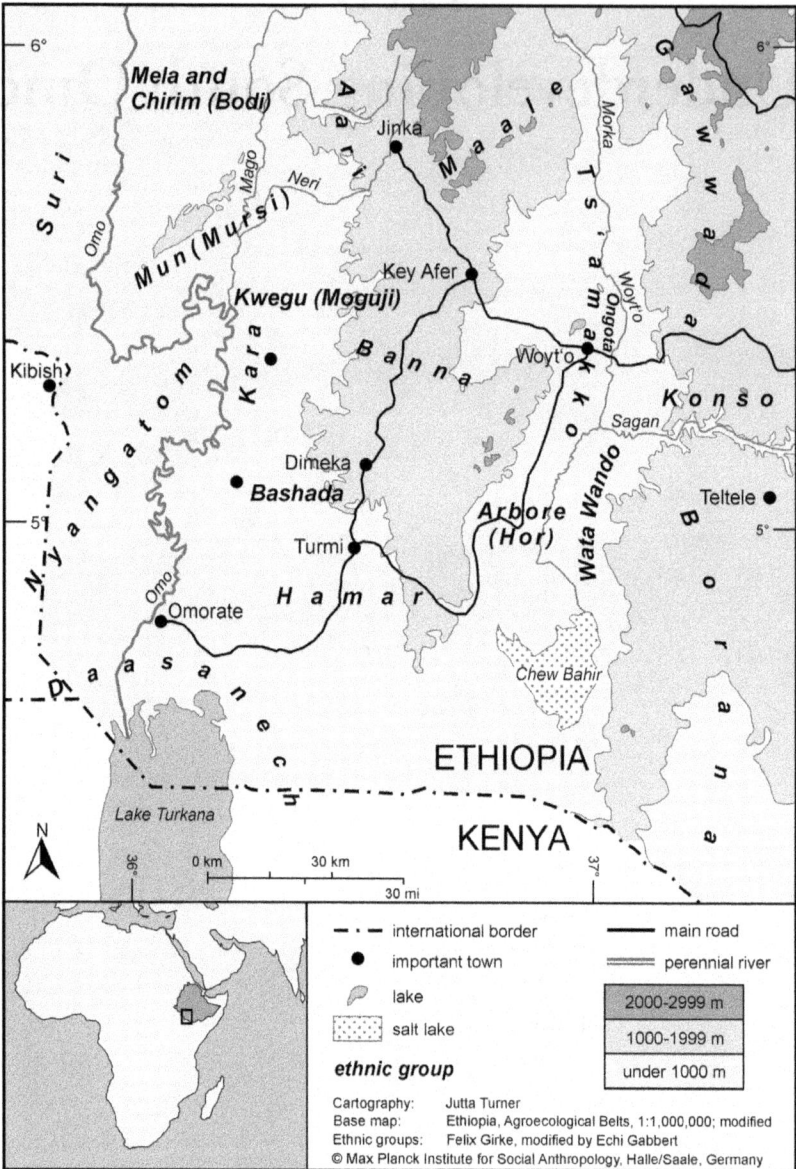

Map PIV.1. Peoples of South Omo.

Chapter 10

'Breaking Every Rule in the Book'

The Story of River Basin Development in Ethiopia's Omo Valley

David Turton

I originally wrote the paper on which this chapter is based for a panel on 'Land Policies and their Consequences for Vulnerable Populations in East Africa', organized by Professor Elliot Fratkin at the annual meeting of the American Anthropological Association in 2012. The Gibe III hydroelectric dam in the middle basin of the Omo River[1] had then been under construction for six years, and the associated Kuraz Sugar Development Project of the Ethiopian Sugar Corporation had just been announced. This project, more than 200 kilometres downstream from the dam, called for the forced resettlement ('villagization') of thousands of agro-pastoralists, without consultation or compensation, and their transformation into 'outgrowers' for the Sugar Corporation. It was already glaringly apparent that both the sugar project and the dam itself had been planned without taking into account the considerable worldwide literature that had accumulated over the previous half century on how to avoid the impoverishment of people displaced by dams and other infrastructural development projects.

The purpose of the paper was to add my voice to those of others – NGOs, academics and human rights activists – who were warning that unless changes were made in the way these projects were being planned and implemented they would have disastrous consequences for the people and environment of the Lower Omo and Lake Turkana basin. For it was still possible at that time to hope that the planners and policymakers would listen to our concerns and take some basic steps to avoid at least the worst effects of the impending disaster. All we were asking for was that there should be genuine consultation with the affected people and properly funded schemes for compensation, benefit sharing and livelihood reconstruction.[2] Today, seven years on and with no sign of our concerns and suggestions being taken seriously, let alone acted upon, we can no longer speak of an 'impending' disaster. As Lucie Buffavand reports of the Mela (Bodi), who were the first group of agro-pastoralists in the Lower Omo to bear the full brunt of the Kuraz Sugar Project, 'The Mela are arguing . . . that the neglect of their knowledge and the rejection of their meaningful participation in the development project can only have disastrous consequences, *which are already unfolding*' (2016: 489, emphasis added). The best we can do now (and who knows whether this may yet have beneficial consequences for the people of the Lower Omo) is document these 'disastrous consequences', detail the failures of planning that have brought them about and understand better the political conditions that made them not only possible but inevitable.

The last two of these aims form the subject matter of the present chapter, which is divided into four parts. First, I outline the history of the Gibe III project and discuss some of the more glaring shortcomings of its preparatory documentation. I then describe the Kuraz Sugar Development Project and the extent of its likely impact on people and the environment. In the third part of the chapter, I summarize the lessons learned from past cases of development-forced displacement about how to minimize its adverse effects on the displaced. Finally, I ask how it came about that river basin development in the Omo Valley has become such a textbook example of 'how *not* to do it'. I find the answer in a certain way of 'seeing' the people of the southern Ethiopian lowlands, which has been deeply entrenched in the state-building activities of successive Ethiopian governments since the nineteenth century.

The Dam

The River Omo rises in the well-watered western highlands of Ethiopia at about the same latitude as Addis Ababa. It flows for nearly 1,000 kilometres and drops 1,600 metres from its source to its end point in Lake Turkana, the world's largest desert lake, which lies almost wholly within Kenya but takes nearly 90 per cent of its water from the Omo. These climatic and topographic features give the Omo a hydropower potential second only to that of the Blue Nile, which accounts for half the hydropower potential of the entire country (Kloos and Worku 2010: 77). The Gibe III Dam,[3] the tallest in Africa, began generating electricity in October 2015 and was officially inaugurated in December 2016, ten years after construction had begun. With an 'installed capacity' of 1,870 megawatts (meaning its turbines will produce electricity at this level continuously), it is expected to increase Ethiopia's electricity generating capacity far beyond the present domestic demand.[4] Unlike many large dams, Gibe III will not require significant resettlement of local people from its reservoir area, which, although stretching back 150 kilometres from the dam wall, is relatively sparsely populated. But the characteristics that gave the Omo its impressive hydropower potential have also made its lower basin a highly attractive location for human settlement, not the least of its attractions being the annual Omo flood, which Gibe III, being designed (like any hydropower dam) to regulate the river flow, is bound to eliminate.

Around 90,000 people,[5] speaking six different languages (from north to south, Bodi (Mela and Chirim), Mursi (Mun), Kwegu/Muguji, Nyangatom, Kara and Dassanech) make up the present-day population of the Lower Omo, between 300 and 500 kilometres downstream from the dam. Virtually all combine agriculture with cattle herding, and all depend heavily on 'flood-retreat' or 'recession' agriculture. Planting – mainly of sorghum but also of maize, cow peas, mung beans and tobacco – takes place in September and October as the flood recedes, with the harvest coming at the height of the dry season in December and January. Harvests are bigger in the southern part of the lower basin than further north because the area flooded is more extensive. But rainfall is more reliable in the north, making it possible for the Bodi, Kwegu and Mursi to practise both flood-retreat and rain-fed cultivation. The principal constraint on flood cultivation is the size of the area inundated, which in turn depends on the amount of highland rainfall; the principal constraint on rain-fed cultivation is the availability of adequate and timely local rainfall; and the principal constraint on pastoralism is the availability of adequate dry season grazing and watering points. For the Bodi and Mursi, each of these subsistence activities would be insufficient on its own, or even in combination with one of the other two, but the three together make possible a viable agro-pastoral economy. Further downstream, where rainfall is not sufficient for reliable rain-fed cultivation, the flood submerges not only the delta but also large areas of grassland away from the immediate banks of the river. This enables the Dassanech to produce all (and more) of the grain they need from flood cultivation alone, while the flooded 'flats' provide excellent dry season grazing between November and March (Carr 1977; Almagor 1978).

So how did the dam builders propose to compensate the downstream population[6] for the loss of the flood? To begin with, this question was ignored by the simple (though almost laughable) device of limiting the environmental impact assessment[7] (CESI 2006: 38, Fig. 3.1) to the so-called 'project area' – essentially the middle basin of the Omo – thereby excluding any mention of the impact on the environment and people of the Lower Omo and Lake Turkana basin. In April 2008, after mounting international criticism and, no doubt, with the loan conditions of the multilateral development banks in mind, a revised impact assessment was produced (CESI S.p.A and Mid-Day International 2008), now called *Environmental and Social Impact Assessment* (henceforth, ESIA). This included selected findings and recommendations drawn from another study (Agriconsulting S.p.A. and Mid-Day International 2008) called *Environmental Impact Assessment: Additional Study on Downstream Impact* (henceforth *Additional Study*). These documents were belatedly approved by the Ethiopian Government's Environmental Protection Agency in July 2009 as the construction process entered its fourth year.

The revised impact assessments proposed a 'downstream mitigation plan', the centrepiece of which would be an artificial or 'controlled' flood, to be released from the dam reservoir over a ten-day period in late August or early September. This, it was claimed, would sufficiently replicate the natural flood to compensate the downstream population for 'all adverse effects' of the dam (CESI S.p.A and Mid-Day International 2009: 231), while at the same time 'guaranteeing [the] regularity and yields' of flood-retreat cultivation and avoiding the 'severe damage to downstream communities' caused by 'large unregulated floods' (Agriconsulting S.p.A. and Mid-Day International 2009: 3). It would be difficult to imagine a more striking example than this of the well-known tendency of impact assessments commissioned by developers to ignore or play down the negative effects of a project and to exaggerate or, as in this case, fabricate its positive effects.

In the first place, the idea that residents of the Lower Omo are regularly subjected to 'devastating' floods is a fiction. The only flood ever mentioned in support of such a claim occurred in 2006, and this was described in a government appeal to donors as the worst Omo flood for 100 years (SNNPRS 2006: 5). Even so, the official human death toll of over 350 proved puzzlingly difficult to verify, even with the help of colleagues who were working in the area at the time. The Japanese anthropologist Toru Sagawa, for example, who was in the worst affected area, was told that although a few men had drowned while trying to lead stranded cattle to safety at night, these amounted to no more than ten or twelve (personal communication, March 2009). In any case, there can be no doubt that the people of the Lower Omo, like those living in other floodplains such as that of the Awash in Ethiopia or the Nile in Sudan, have a profound knowledge of the flood regime, which they see as life-giving rather than life-threatening.[8]

Second, the three pages (165–167) describing the proposal for a controlled flood in the 2008 version of the *Additional Study* are plainly inadequate. Managed flood releases from dams are a highly complex and relatively untried method for maintaining flood basin ecosystems, requiring, amongst other things, 'close collaboration with the users of flood plain resources' (Acreman 2000: 29 and passim). But the authors of the *Additional Study* appear to have calculated the size and duration of the controlled flood purely from mathematical models of the river flow. The three pages devoted to this topic in the 2008 version of the study are reprinted in the 2009 version and followed by a new section, 'Assessment of Controlled Flooding' (Agriconsulting S.p.A and Mid-Day International 2009: 168–74), in which observations made during the 2008 flood season are used to confirm the adequacy of the calculations. These observations consisted of the collection of daily flow and water level data at the dam site, and a one-day helicopter flight by a 'team of river geomorphologists and an expert in Omo valley agriculture' (op. cit.: 169). It is clear that the proposal for a controlled flood contained in these pages is neither derived from a detailed analysis of the agricultural and pastoral practices of the downstream population, nor informed by their profound practical knowledge of the flood regime.[9]

Third, and equally striking, is the failure of the *Additional Study* to include a calculation of the cost of a controlled flood in lost electricity production.[10] This calculation was made, however, by the French consultancy firm SOGREAH in an independent review of the project commissioned by the European Investment Bank (EIB). It concluded that the annual cost of the controlled flood would be between 7.8 and 10.8 million US dollars (2010: 87) and that this was enough to make it 'probable' that, in choosing between the competing claims of electricity production and the maintenance of downstream livelihoods, 'priority will not be given to recession agriculture' (ibid.: 85). The overall verdict of the SOGREAH consultants on the proposal for a controlled flood was that information on the relationship between river flow and environmental and socio-economic conditions in the lower basin, particularly the delta, 'is . . . still dramatically missing' (ibid.: 120). The authors of the *Additional Study* had 'planned a solution without fully qualifying the problem' (ibid.: 122), and further studies were necessary to fill the gaps.

Soon after the completion of the SOGREAH review (May 2010), BMT Cordah Ltd, submitted a report to the EIB in which terms of reference were set out for studies to address three 'major weaknesses' in the Gibe III documentation: inadequate baseline data on the Omo River; no cumulative assessment of the impacts of the Omo-Gibe hydropower cascade (including the planned Gibe IV and V) on the lower basin and no consideration of the possible negative impacts of Gibe III on Lake Turkana (BMT Cordah 2010: 7). Amongst the studies recommended was 'a carefully designed and targeted community development programme' (op. cit.: 10). Following the decision of the Industrial and Commercial Bank of China, in July 2010, to make a loan of 450,000 USD to the project, the EIB decided against making a loan itself[11] and did not commission any of the recommended further studies.

Even before the SOGREAH review was submitted, however, a press release had been issued by Salini Construttori that effectively tore up the downstream mitigation plan. The purpose of the press release was to rebut criticisms of the Gibe III project coming from Survival International, but it made, in passing, a highly revealing reference to the controlled flood: 'This will enable the local people to have a *transitory period of a suitable duration* when it is deemed opportune to switch from flood-retreat agriculture to more modern forms of agriculture' (Salini Construttori, 30 March 2010, emphasis added). One could almost hear the cat being let out of the bag. It was now clear that the dam builder, and presumably also the Ethiopian Electric Power Corporation (EEPCO), had a very different understanding of the role of the controlled flood from that of the authors of the *Additional Study*. For the latter, it was clearly intended to be the central component of the 'downstream mitigation plan'. For the former, it would operate only for a limited period, after which flood-retreat cultivation would stop altogether, dry season grazing areas would no longer be sustained by the annual flood and the local population would take up 'more modern' forms of agriculture, presumably as 'outgrowers' for the Sugar Corporation. No official confirmation of this was forthcoming from EEPCO or the Gibe III project office,[12] and it was to be another ten months before the then Prime Minister, the late Meles Zenawi, let the cat fully out of the bag in a carefully staged act of political theatre.

The Plantations

On 25 January 2011, Meles went to Jinka, the capital of South Omo Zone, to make a speech that was to be the centrepiece of the 13th Annual Pastoralists' Day celebrations, held that year in Jinka. The burden of his speech was that work would soon begin on a huge commercial irrigation scheme in the Lower Omo that would lift local pastoralists out of 'poverty and backwardness' and give them a 'modern life'.

> The Gibe III dam is developing rapidly and when it is finished the flood, which has been a huge problem for years in this region, will end forever. It will then be possible to create a big irrigation system in this wide and fertile area of South Omo. Following the good results we have achieved in the Afar region, the government is planning, and working hard to establish, a 150,000 hectare sugarcane development in this area starting this year. When this development work is done, we believe that it will transform the entire basis of the area. This will benefit the people of this area and hundreds of thousands of other Ethiopians by creating employment . . . I promise you that, even though this area is known as backward in terms of civilisation, it will become an example of rapid development. (Meles Zenawi 2011: 2)

It might be thought deliberately provocative to choose an event intended to celebrate pastoralism to announce that thousands of local pastoralists were about to be forced off their land to make way for a government irrigation scheme. But in fact, this was entirely consistent with the long-standing view of successive Ethiopian governments of what constitutes 'pastoral development'; namely, 'phased voluntary sedentarization along the banks of the major rivers' (FDRE 2002: 5). But although described as 'voluntary', this process cannot be resisted by legal means, given the historically weak level of protection that is provided for communal land ownership in Ethiopian land tenure legislation.[13] The Prime Minister mentioned in his speech that local pastoralists would be given irrigable land for their own use. He failed to mention that in return for this 'gift' they would lose all their best agricultural and grazing land, including access to the Omo River itself. They would thereby be forced – because they would have no reasonable alternative – to give up their former herding activities and move into a limited number of government-planned resettlement villages, situated close to the plantations.

A few days after the Prime Minister's speech, it was reported in the Addis press that a total of 245,000 hectares had been allocated to the Ethiopian Sugar Corporation in the Lower Omo, although only 150,000 hectares of this were considered suitable for sugar cane production. Six cane-crushing mills would be required to deal with the expected level of production, and up to 100,000 jobs would be created (Addis Fortune 2011). No maps of the proposed plantations, feasibility studies or impact assessments were made available for public discussion before implementation of the project began. But in March 2012, Survival International published on its website a map of the sugar project,[14] taken from a leaked report prepared by members of the Ethiopian Wildlife Conservation Authority (Cherie, Derbe and Girma 2011). The authors of the report were concerned about what the project would mean for wildlife conservation, but anyone familiar with the human ecology of the area would have known that the implications for the human population of what was described in the report would be devastating.

The map showed that the plantations would stretch for over 100 kilometres, from north to south, along both banks of the Omo. They would be irrigated by two main canals, running from north to south on each side of the Omo and taking water from the river at the northern end of the project area. Starting in the north, Block 1 would occupy land currently used for flood-retreat and rain-fed cultivation by Bodi, Kwegu and Mursi and a large area west of the river that currently lies within the Omo National Park. Block 2 would take more land from the Omo National Park, and Block 3 would occupy land currently used by Nyangatom, Kara and Muguji for both cultivation and grazing. The map also showed that a further 74,000 hectares in the more arid southern part of the lower basin, occupied principally by Dassanech, had been leased to private investors for irrigated farms. It was mentioned in the report, though not indicated on the map, that an additional 30,000 hectares, to be taken from the south-western part of the Mago National Park, would be added to the sugar plantations in due course. It is worth noting that although the value of both National Parks as protected areas would be greatly reduced by these developments this was not so much because they would be reduced in size but because much of the buffer area that existed around and between them, and through which game animals were free to move, would be taken over by sugar plantations.[15]

According to these projections, the total irrigated area in the Lower Omo would eventually amount to at least 250,000 hectares, making this by far the largest irrigation complex in Ethiopia and at least doubling the total irrigated area in the country. The social and environmental impact of potential irrigation development on anything like this scale is nowhere considered in the Gibe III impact assessments. This is extraordinary given, first, that the irrigation potential of the Omo-Gibe basin has long been recognized, with estimates of the total irrigable area ranging from 73,000 hectares to 445,000 hectares (Avery 2010: 1–5). Second, it was noted in the impact assessments that irrigated agriculture would be an attractive proposition for private investors, once river flow had been regulated. The ESIA itself estimated the area suitable for large-scale irrigation in the lower basin to be 142,000 hectare (CESI 2006: 172). And yet, despite all this, in the few sentences devoted to large-scale commercial plantations in the *Additional Study*, it is assumed, 'for the sake of argument', that these will cover no more than 5,000 hectares and that they will 'almost certainly' be confined to the delta plain. Cotton is considered to be the most likely crop and sugar the least likely because of its high infra-structural costs (Agriconsulting S.p.A. and Mid-day International 2009: 83–84). It came as no surprise, then, that during my meeting at the Ministry of Water and Energy in December 2010 the Minister insisted that no large-scale commercial irrigation schemes were planned for the Lower Omo. This was less than two months before the Prime Minister announced plans to turn the Lower Omo into the largest irrigation complex in Ethiopia.

Even after implementation of the sugar project had begun, the government continued to insist that irrigation development in the Lower Omo should not be taken into account in the discussion of the downstream impacts of Gibe III (Turton 2012). Given that the Lake receives 90 per cent of its inflow from the Omo and that large-scale irrigation in the Lower Omo would be impossible without the regulated river flow created by Gibe III, this was an absurd proposition. Its public relations advantages for the Ethiopian government, however, are plain to see.[16] First, it enabled the downstream impact of the dam to be discussed without reference to its potentially devastating impacts on the ecology and level of Lake Turkana. In studies commissioned by the African Development Bank and the University of Oxford and drawing on projections of total irrigable area made by both the ESIA and the Omo-Gibe Master Plan, the civil engineer Sean Avery estimated that potential irrigation abstraction could cause the lake level to drop by as much as 20 metres (its current average depth being roughly 30 metres) and that the regulation of the Omo flow by the dam will have a devastating impact on the productivity of Lake Turkana's fisheries (Avery 2010, 2012 and 2013). Second, by ignoring the connection between Gibe III and large-scale irrigation development, it was possible to maintain the fiction of a controlled flood as an effective downstream mitigation measure. In fact, the scale of the irrigation development now being implemented rules out an effective controlled flood of any kind, whether temporary or not. This is because a flood that reached a level sufficient to benefit the downstream ecology and livelihoods would also inundate irrigation infrastructure along the banks of the Omo. In effect, the proposal for a controlled flood acted as a subterfuge that helped, at least for a time, to disguise the government's true development intentions in the Lower Omo from local residents, donors and regional neighbours alike.

A Few Things We Know about Development-Forced Displacement

What, then, will the 'rapid development' and 'modern life' promised by the Prime Minister to his Jinka audience mean in practice? In the civilizational discourse of government officials and planners, the hope seemed to be that 'backward' pastoralists, who are forcibly dispossessed of their land, livelihoods and cultural identities by the sugar plantations, would nevertheless benefit automatically from generalized economic and infrastructural 'development' and 'modern' forms of agriculture. Unfortunately, the considerable research literature that now exists on past cases of 'development-forced displacement and resettlement' tells a very different story.

One thing we know from this literature is that most displaced people today are not victims of wars or natural disasters but of development – large infrastructural projects such as hydroelectric dams, irrigation schemes, urban clearances and roads. It has been estimated that around 15 million people a year are displaced by such projects (Cernea 2008: 20), to which must be added the millions more who lose access to vital economic resources (because, for example, they live downstream from large hydroelectric dams) without themselves being physically displaced. We also know that those affected not only tend to come from economically disadvantaged and politically marginalized sections of a population – often ethnic minorities[17] – but they also tend to be made worse off as a result. It follows that projects that have been deliberately designed and implemented by governments to improve the well-being of their own citizens must be counted amongst the principal causes of world poverty. This does not, of course, mean that such projects should not be carried out. It does mean that they should be carried out in a way that ensures that they become genuine 'development opportunities' for those who have had to get out of the way to make them possible. How to achieve this objective is the main question dealt with in the literature on development-forced displacement.

Michael Cernea, formerly Senior Policy Adviser at the World Bank and the principal architect of its 'Involuntary Resettlement Guidelines', has done more than anyone to answer this question. Based on what he calls a 'vast body of empirical data', Cernea identified eight different 'impoverishment risks', some or all of which will attach, in varying degrees, to any project involving forced displacement (1997: 1569). Those most relevant to the Omo case are loss of common property resources, especially land; economic and social marginalization; increased morbidity and mortality; and loss of 'social capital' – the social support mechanisms people had formerly relied on during periods of hardship. Cernea's overall point is that 'general and vague predictions' (1997: 1571) and well-meaning aspirations will not protect displaced populations from the risks of impoverishment. Rather, planners should identify the risks *in advance* and put in place specific mechanisms and strategies to deal with them. In so doing there must be open and transparent communication and genuine consultation between planners and people, such that the knowledge and interests of those affected are fully reflected in decisions made about their future lives and livelihoods. And, finally, there must be adequately funded and detailed schemes for compensation, long-term investment and benefit sharing (Cernea and Mathur 2008). I hope it is clear from what I have written above that 'general and vague' is an accurate description of the way planners, government officials and politicians have talked about the likely impacts of Gibe III and the plantations on the people of the Lower Omo.

For an instructive comparative example, we need look no further than irrigation development in the Awash Valley of Ethiopia's Afar Regional State, to which the Prime Minister referred approvingly in his Jinka address. Like the Omo, the Awash is a major river of the Ethiopian Rift, rising in the central highlands and flowing north-eastward for around 1,000 kilometres across semi-arid and arid lowlands. The Wonji Shoa and Metehara sugar estates were established in the upper Awash Valley in the 1950s and 1960s, and the Awash National Park was set up in 1969, just a little after the Omo National Park. Despite the Prime Minister's reference in his Jinka speech to 'the good results we have achieved in the Afar Region', studies of the impact of plantation development on the two main pastoral groups of the area, the Karrayu Oromo and Afar, show that the population as a whole became poorer and more vulnerable to food insecurity as a result (Kloos 1982; Ayalew and Getachew 2009; Kloos et al. 2010). The forced displacement of herders from thousands of hectares of their most valuable grazing lands and the loss of access to watering points along the Awash River put increased pressure on remaining resources. This led to land degradation, violent conflict between neighbouring groups and increased vulnerability to drought, while employment opportunities on sugar estates were monopolized by migrant workers from the highlands. The same studies make it clear that the impoverishment of local people by irrigation development in the Awash Valley could have been avoided if two simple and indeed obvious conditions had been met. First, detailed feasibility studies and socio-economic impact assessments should have been completed and made publicly available, *before* the plans were finalized. Second, local people (not just administrators) should have been genuinely involved in the consultation and planning process, and their needs and interests should have been fully and systematically addressed, *from the start*.

The same well-documented mistakes that were made in the Awash Valley by previous governments were subsequently made in the Omo Valley: no public discussion of feasibility studies and impact assessments, no genuine consultation with local people, no compensation and livelihood reconstruction plans and no political will to allow the affected population a genuine role in decision-making. On the contrary, the planning process was entirely top-down, and implementation was surrounded by a wall of secrecy. The attitude of the government appears to have been that its plans must be pushed through with the utmost speed and with no concession to local objections. So far from genuinely consulting the affected population, strenuous efforts were made, with the help of police and army units, to intimidate them into compliance with government wishes and to prevent them from talking about the project to outsiders, especially foreigners. Indeed, implementation of the project appears to have been conceived as a quasi-military operation, with the army acting as an occupying force amongst a recalcitrant civilian population.[18] The predictable result has been growing local anger and resentment against what is seen as an aggressive government 'land grab' of the kind that has defined the relationship between the Ethiopian state and the peoples of its lowland periphery since the nineteenth century.

It is difficult to see how river basin development in the Omo Valley is going to have less dire consequences for local people and the environment than it has had in the Awash Valley. Indeed, there are good reasons to predict the opposite. These include the sheer scale of the developments, in progress and planned; the size of the affected human population, both in Ethiopia and Kenya; the potential transboundary impacts on the world's largest desert lake; and the particularly blatant disregard shown by planners and policymakers for the lessons learned from past cases about how to protect from impoverishment those displaced by development projects. One cannot help asking, 'How did it come to this?' How could the Ethiopian government have allowed its most ambitious hydropower and irrigation project yet, situated in one of the most iconic landscapes in Africa,[19] to become such a textbook example of how *not* to do river basin development?

How Did It Come to This?

It is, of course, far from unheard of for well-intentioned schemes to improve the human condition to have tragic consequences for those whom they were intended to help. But, as James C. Scott has argued, this is far more likely to occur in states with a 'prostrate civil society' where leaders are 'driven by an authoritarian disregard for the values, desires and objections of their subjects' and are willing and able to use coercive power to achieve their objectives (1998: 4–7). States fitting this description, of which Ethiopia under the Ethiopian Peoples' Revolutionary Democratic Front (EPRDF) has certainly been one, constitute, according to Scott, 'a mortal threat to human well being' (loc. cit.). There are two other, more specific, factors we need to take into account in order to understand how the current threat to human well-being in the Lower Omo has come about.

First, there was the decision of the EPRDF leadership, following its near defeat in the 2005 election, to 'rip off the façade of democratisation' that it had carefully put in place during its first decade in power (Markakis 2011: 255). It now saw its overriding aim of long term political survival as being dependent on (a) closing down all possible avenues of political opposition and dissent (Aalen and Tronvoll 2009; Hagmann and Abbink 2011), and (b) basing its claim to legitimacy on the rapid achievement of highly ambitious economic growth targets. The adoption of this Chinese model of 'developmental authoritarianism' helps to explain the willingness of policymakers and planners to bypass international norms (and even national laws) designed to protect people and the environment, particularly in the hydropower and commercial agriculture sectors. The official explanation was that speed is of the essence in the fight against poverty and in the drive to make Ethiopia a middle-income country by 2025. The government was therefore determined not to be held back in this fight by what the then Chief Executive of the Ethiopian Electric Power Corporation, Meheret Debebe, in a BBC documentary on Gibe III, called 'luxurious preconditions'.[20]

The linking of political survival with authoritarian rule on the one hand and rapid economic growth on the other meant that constructive criticism of the way the Gibe III project and large-scale irrigation development were planned and implemented was routinely brushed aside by government representatives as coming from the 'enemies' of Ethiopia, who want to hold back its development. In his Jinka speech, for example, the Prime Minister referred to those who criticized government policy on environmental and human rights grounds as 'the promoters of backwardness and poverty'. This in turn made it virtually impossible for a constructive dialogue to take place between the government and its critics, whether domestic or foreign. In the absence of legal mechanisms for mobilizing and expressing local opposition to government policies, it also risked provoking violent forms of resistance along ethnic lines. A ready legitimizing rationale for such resistance was provided by the principles of 'ethnic federalism', which were enshrined in the Ethiopian constitution[21] in 1995 (Turton 2006).

The second and most important additional factor we need to take into account in answering the question 'How did it come to this?' is the state-building project that has shaped government policy towards Ethiopia's lowland periphery and its predominantly pastoral population since the end of the nineteenth century. Ethiopia, like the United Kingdom, and unlike most other African states, is a product of 'dominant group nation-building' (Kymlicka 2006) through which the small highland kingdom of Abyssinia established its control over its highland and lowland peripheries during the nineteenth century (Markakis 2011). Today's rulers are perhaps as much the victims of this legacy as were their predecessors in the Imperial and Derg regimes. As Ayalew and Getachew point out in their discussion of the marginalization of pastoralists in the Awash Valley, a 'major determinant' of this process has been 'the general tendency in the mindset of government policy-makers to associate agriculture with development and pastoralism with primitivism' (2009: 79). This 'general tendency' was plainly evident in

Meles' Jinka speech, in which he persistently linked pastoralism with 'backward-ness', thereby also linking forced resettlement and 'villagization' in the lowland periphery with the 'civilizing' mission of the Ethiopian state.

The extension of state control from Ethiopia's highland core to its lowland periphery mirrors in remarkable detail Scott's description of state expansion into the huge upland border area of mainland Southeast Asia (2009). For the highland peasant farmers of the Ethiopian state, we need to substitute the lowland wet rice cultivators of the Han Chinese state; and for the pastoralists and agro-pastoralists of the Ethiopian lowlands, we need to substitute the shifting cultivators and for-agers whom Scott describes as occupying 'zones of refuge' in the hills of the Southeast Asian mainland. From the point of view of both states, the problem was how to appropriate these peripheral areas, with their diverse, fluid and mo-bile populations, and 'illegible' subsistence economies, into the 'fiscally legible economy of wage labour and sedentary agriculture' (op. cit.: 10). In the border areas of mainland Southeast Asia, this was achieved by, amongst other things, the resettlement of land-hungry people from the central areas to the periphery,[22] where they could replicate the settlement patterns and agriculture of the centre, and by the establishment of development projects that would 'project govern-ment administration' into the periphery (op. cit.: 20).

As this process gained pace, and communications between centre and pe-riphery improved, it became clear that these previously 'neglected and seemingly useless territories' were in fact of great potential value to 'the economies of mature capitalism' (op. cit.: 11). Meanwhile, the 'civilizational discourse' common to both the Chinese Han and the Ethiopian state was deployed to insist that those who occupied these territories would automatically benefit by being drawn in to the 'modern life' of wage labour and sedentary agriculture. This perhaps helps to explain why those planning hydropower and irrigation development in the Omo Valley did not think to produce detailed and credible plans for compensation, benefit sharing and livelihood reconstruction. For they might have thought that even if the people of the Lower Omo were now destined to lead a life of food aid dependence and occasional employment on sugar plantations 'at starvation wages'[23] they would still have been rescued by the state from the 'backwardness' of their former lives.

In a letter to the Russian Czar in 1872, the Abyssinian Emperor Yohannes IV wrote, '[T]he borderlands of Ethiopia are inhabited by savage people but now, by the grace of God, I do what is possible to civilise and subject them' (quoted by Reid 2007: 29). If Meles' Jinka speech is anything to go by, these words, *mutatis mutandis*, could well be seen as summing up the thinking of current Ethiopian policymakers on the future of lowland Ethiopians: pastoralists must take up set-tled plough agriculture in order to become true citizens of Ethiopia. Or, in the words of Muhammad Yusuf, Chair of the Pastoralist Affairs Standing Committee of the House of Peoples' Representatives, 'civilisation did not come from pastoralists but from agriculture. They must work on the land to be good citizens' (Levitt 2012, quoted in Fratkin 2014: 110). This 'mindset', as Ayalew and Getachew call it (loc. cit.), must go a long way towards explaining the failure of today's politicians to 'see', let alone respect and learn from, the knowledge, skills and wisdom of those whom they aspire to lift out of 'poverty and backwardness'. While we have no reason to doubt the sincerity of this aspiration, it is difficult not to conclude that the disaster now being played out in the Lower Omo is the result of a fundamentally authoritarian, repressive and racist state-building project in Ethiopia, going back at least to the time of Yohannes IV.

David Turton is a social anthropologist who was formerly Director of the Refugee Studies Centre at the University of Oxford. Before moving to Oxford, he taught in the Department of Social Anthropology at the University of Manchester. He has carried out long-term field research amongst the agro-pastoral Mursi of the Lower Omo Valley, south-western Ethiopia, focusing on the impact of long term ecological change on migration, settlement and political identity.

Notes

1. The Omo is known as Gibe in its upper and middle basins.
2. I myself had already (December 2010) had meetings in Addis Ababa, organized for me by the Ethiopian Ambassador in London, with the Minister of Water and Energy and his staff, the Chief Executive Officer of the Ethiopian Electric Power Corporation and the Gibe III project manager. All were hospitable and generous with their time, but it was clear that they saw the meetings (some of which were video recorded for a purpose that was not explained to me) as public relations exercises rather than as opportunities to hear the concerns and suggestions of someone who had been working as an anthropologist in the Lower Omo for the previous forty years.
3. The first dam to be completed along the Omo-Gibe began operating in 2004 and is known as Gilgil ('Lesser') Gibe 1. In 2010, a power plant known as Gibe II and drawing its water through a 26 kilometres tunnel from the Gilgil Gibe I reservoir was opened further downstream. Two more dams, which are still at the planning stage, Gibe IV and V, will complete the Omo-Gibe hydropower cascade.
4. The plan is to export up to 50 per cent of the electricity to neighbouring countries, including Djibouti and Kenya.
5. This figure is based on the Ethiopian Government's 2007 census (Federal Democratic Republic of Ethiopia 2008: Table 5, 98–99), which almost certainly underestimates population numbers in the Lower Omo.
6. In this chapter, the phrase 'downstream population' refers primarily to people living along the lower course of the Omo before it enters Lake Turkana. It must not be forgotten, however, that the dam will have considerable impacts, direct and indirect, on Lake Turkana and that these will adversely affect the lives of around 300,000 people who live around the Lake. The elimination of the annual flood will drastically reduce the productivity of the lake's fisheries, and the lake level could drop by as much as twenty metres because of the abstraction of irrigation water from the Omo. For an instructive summary of the likely extent of these impacts, see Avery (2013).

7. This was commissioned by the contractor Salini Construttori and completed in 2006, the year in which construction began. Salini had also been the principal contractor for the Gilgil Gibe I Dam and Gibe II power plant.

8. See Acreman (2000: 14–18) for a useful summary of the natural resource systems of floodplains and of the crucial role of the 'recession zone' in floodplain productivity.

9. For more details on the shortcomings of the Gibe III impact assessments, see two independent reviews commissioned by the European Investment Bank, SOGREAH (2010) and BMT Cordah (2010).

10. This cost arises because the rate at which water must pass through the dam to create a flood exceeds that at which it can be allowed to pass through the turbines.

11. Both the World Bank and the African Development Bank also declined to lend directly to the Gibe III project.

12. It was, however, verbally confirmed to me during my meeting with the Minister of Water and Energy and members of his staff in December 2010.

13. 'In practical terms, the pastoral lands have not been covered by specific national legislation granting security of tenure to the people who live from pastoralism' (Helland 2006: 2).

14. http://assets.survivalinternational.org/documents/744/ewca-location-map-of-the-proj ect-area.pdf (accessed 19 August 2018).

15. See Homewood (2004: 129): '. . . it is not the size of [a] protected area, but the extent of the wider savanna ecosystem within which the protected area sits, that determines . . . [its] . . . species richness.'

16. It is more surprising that the United Nations Environment Programme also ignored the huge potential impact of large-scale irrigation on the level of Lake Turkana in its report entitled 'Ethiopia's Gibe III Dam: Its Potential Impact on Lake Turkana Water Levels' (UNEP 2012).

17. Fifty per cent of those displaced by the Namada Dam, in Gujarat Province of north-western India, for example, belonged to 'tribal' populations, which account for only 8 per cent of the Indian population as a whole. Commenting on this, the novelist Arundhati Roy, who has campaigned on behalf of those displaced by the Namada Dam, writes: 'The ethnic otherness of their victims takes some pressure off the Nation Builders. It's like having an expense account. Someone else pays the bills. People from another country. Another world' (1999: 18–19).

18. See Lucie Buffavand's account, in her contribution to this book, of the introduction of supposedly 'voluntary' villagization amongst the Mela (Bodi), where plantation development and resettlement are most advanced.

19. In 1980, the Lower Omo Valley was declared a UNESCO World Heritage Site in recognition of its 'fundamental importance in the study of human evolution', which has made it 'renowned the world over' (http://whc.unesco.org/en/list/17). Amongst the important fossil discoveries made in the Lower Omo were two Homo sapiens skulls known as Omo I and Omo II. These have been dated to about 195,000 years ago, making them 'the earliest well-dated anatomically modern humans yet described' (McDougall, Brown and Fleagle 2005) and making the Lower Omo Valley the oldest landscape in the world known to have been inhabited by modern humans.

20. 'Power Rules', shown on the BBC News Channel in 2009 in the 'Our World' series, presented by Peter Greste and produced by Natalie Morton.

21. See 'Constitution of the Federal Democratic Republic of Ethiopia, Proclamation 1/1995', which begins 'We, the Nations, Nationalities and Peoples of Ethiopia . . .' and goes on (Article 39.5) to define 'Nation, Nationality or People' as 'a group of people who have or

share a large measure of a common culture . . . mutual intelligibility of language . . . and who inhabit an identifiable, predominantly contiguous territory.'

22. This strategy was also employed in the Lower Omo with the resettlement of thousands of Konso farmers from the southern highlands to the territory of the Bodi (Mela), beginning in 2004. See Ayke Asfaw (2005) and Buffavand (this volume).

23. See John Markakis commenting on the likely consequences for Afar pastoralists of the Tendaho Dam and Sugar Project in the Awash Valley: '[T]he fate of the Afar people is sealed. Their future lies in seasonal work at starvation wages in the sugarcane fields' (2011: 300).

References

Aalen, L., and K. Tronvoll. 2009. 'The End of Democracy? Curtailing Political and Civil Rights in Ethiopia', *Review of African Political Economy* 36(120): 193–207.

Acreman, M. 2000. 'Managed Flood Releases from Reservoirs: Issues and Guidance', *submission to the World Commission on Dams Report to DFID and the World Commission on Dams*. Wallingford: Centre for Ecology and Hydrology.

Addis Fortune. 2011. 'Waterworks Enterprise Begins Surveying for New Sugar Dev't', 30 January.

Agriconsulting S.p.A. and Mid-Day International Consulting Engineers. 2008. 'Gibe III Hydroelectric Project, Environmental Impact Assessment: Additional Study on Downstream Impact'.

———. 2009. 'Gibe III Hydroelectric Project, Environmental Impact Assessment: Additional Study on Downstream Impact'.

Almagor, U. 1978. *Pastoral Partners: Affinity and Bond Partnerships among the Dassanetch of South-West Ethiopia*. Manchester: Manchester University Press.

Avery, S. 2010. 'Hydrological Impacts of Ethiopia's Omo Basin on Kenya's Lake Turkana Water Levels and Fisheries', *Final Report, prepared for the African Development Bank, Tunis*. Nairobi. Retrieved 24 May 2018 from http://www.mursi.org/pdf/Avery%20final%20report.pdf.

———. 2012. *Lake Turkana and the Lower Omo: Hydrological Impacts of Major Dam and Irrigation Developments*. University of Oxford, African Studies Centre. Retrieved 24 May 2018 from http://www.africanstudies.ox.ac.uk/sites/sias/files/documents/Volume%20I%20Report.pdf.

———. 2013. *What Future for Lake Turkana? The Impact of Hydropower and Irrigation Development on the World's Largest Desert Lake*. University of Oxford, African Studies Centre. Retrieved 1 March 2019 from https://www.africanstudies.ox.ac.uk/sites/default/files/africanstudies/documents/media/whatfuturelaketurkana-_update_0.pdf.

Ayalew Gebre, and Getachew Kassa. 2009. 'The Effects of Development Projects on the Karrayu and Afar in the Mid-Awash Valley', in A. Pankhurst and F. Piguet (eds), *Moving People in Ethiopia: Development, Displacement and the State*. Oxford: James Currey, pp. 66–80.

Ayke Asfaw. 2005. 'Challenges and Opportunities of "Salamago Resettlement": The Resettlement of Konso Farmers in the Ethnic Land of the Bodi Agro-Pastoralists, South-West Ethiopia', Paper submitted to the Forum for Social Studies, Addis Ababa.

BMT Cordah Ltd. 2010. 'Gibe III: Terms of Reference', *Report to the European Investment Bank*, June.

Buffavand, L. 2016. '"The Land Does Not Like Them": Contesting Dispossession in Cosmological Terms in Mela, South-West Ethiopia', *Journal of Eastern African Studies* 10(4): 489.

Carr, C. 1977. *Pastoralism in Crisis: The Dasanetch and Their Ethiopian Lands*. Chicago: University of Chicago Press.

Cernea, M. 1997. 'The Risk and Reconstruction Model for Resettling Displaced Populations', *World Development* 25(10): 1569–87.

———. 2008. 'Reforming the Foundations of Involuntary Resettlement: Introduction', in M. Cernea and H.M. Mathur (eds), *Can Compensation Prevent Impoverishment? Reforming Resettlement Through Investment and Benefit-Sharing*. Oxford: Oxford University Press.

Cernea, M., and H.M. Mathur (eds). 2008. *Can Compensation Prevent Impoverishment? Reforming Resettlement through Investment and Benefit-Sharing*. Oxford: Oxford University Press.

CESI (Centro Elletrotecnico Sperimentale Italiana). 2006. 'Gibe III Hydroelectric Project: Environmental Impact Assessment'. Milan.

CESI S.p.A and Mid-Day International Consulting Engineers. 2008. 'Gibe III Hydroelectric Project: Environmental and Social Impact Assessment'. Milan.

———. 2009. 'Gibe III Hydroelectric Project: Environmental and Social Impact Assessment'. Milan.

Cherie Enawgaw, Derbe Deksios and Girma Timer. 2011. *Existing Challenges: Plantation Development versus Wildlife Conservation in the Omo-Tama-Mago Complex*. Addis Ababa: Ethiopian Wildlife Conservation Authority.

Federal Democratic Republic of Ethiopia (FDRE). 2002. *Statement on Pastoral Development Policy*. Addis Ababa: Ministry of Federal Affairs.

———. 2008. *Summary and Statistical Report of the 2007 Population and Housing Census: Population Size by Age and Sex*. Addis Ababa: Population Census Commission.

Fratkin, E. 2014. 'Ethiopia's Pastoralist Policies: Development, Displacement and Resettlement', *Nomadic Peoples* 18(1): 94–114.

Hagmann, T., and J. Abbink. 2011. 'Twenty Years of Revolutionary Democratic Ethiopia, 1991–2011', *Journal of Eastern African Studies* 5(4): 579–95.

Helland, J. 2006. 'Land Tenure in the Pastoral Areas of Ethiopia', *International Research Workshop on Property Rights, Collective Action and Poverty Reduction in the Pastoral Areas of Afar and Somali, National Regional State, 30–31 October*. Addis Ababa: International Livestock Research Institute.

Homewood, K.M. 2004. 'Policy, Environment and Development in African Rangelands', *Environmental Science & Policy* 7: 125–43.

Kloos, H. 1982. 'Development, Drought, and Famine in the Awash Valley of Ethiopia', *African Studies Review* 25(4): 21–48.

Kloos, H., and Worku Legesse. 2010. *Water Resources Management in Ethiopia: Implications for the Nile Basin*. Amherst, NY: Cambria Press.

Kloos, H., Worku Legesse, S. McFeeters and D. Turton. 2010. 'Problems for Pastoralists in the Lowlands: River Basin Development in the Awash and Omo Valleys', in H. Kloos and Worku Legesse (eds), *Water Resources Management in Ethiopia: Implications for the Nile Basin*. Amherst, NY: Cambria Press, pp. 253–83.

Kymlicka, W. 2006. 'Emerging Western Models of Multination Federalism: Are They Relevant To Africa?', in D. Turton (ed.), *Ethnic Federalism: The Ethiopian Experience in Comparative Perspective*. Oxford: James Currey, pp. 32–64.

Levitt, T. 2012. 'Crisis or Rebirth? The Future of Ethiopia's Pastoralist Tribes', *The Ecologist*, 3 May. Retrieved 17 June 2018 from https://theecologist.org/2012/may/03/crisis-or-rebirth-future-ethiopias-pastoralist-tribes.

Markakis, J. 2011. *Ethiopia: The Last Two Frontiers*. Woodbridge: James Currey.

McDougall, I., F.H. Brown and J.G. Fleagle. 2005. 'Stratigraphic Placement and Age of Modern Humans from Kibish, Ethiopia', *Nature* 433: 733–36.

Meles Zenawi. 2011. 'Speech During the 13th Annual Pastoralist Day Celebrations, Jinka, South Omo', 25 January. Retrieved 17 June 2018 from http://www.mursi.org/pdf/Meles %20Jinka%20speech.pdf.

Reid, R. 2007. *War in Pre-Colonial Africa*. Oxford: James Currey.

Roy, A. 1999. *The Cost of Living*. New York: The Modern Library.

Salini Construttori S.p.A. 2010. 'Gibe 3: The Survival Figures Are Obviously Incorrect', Press Release, 30 March.

Scott, J.C. 1998. *Seeing Like a State: How Certain Schemes to Improve the Human Condition Have Failed*. New Haven: Yale University Press.

———. 2009. *The Art of Not Being Governed*. New Haven: Yale University Press.

SNNPRS (Southern Nations, Nationalities and Peoples Regional State). 2006. 'South Omo Floods, 2006', *Flash Appeal*, August.

SOGREAH. 2010. 'Independent Review and Studies Regarding the Environmental and Social Impact Assessments for the Gibe 3 Hydroelectric Project', *Final Report*. Echirolles, France.

Turton, D. 2006. 'Introduction', in D. Turton (ed.), *Ethnic Federalism: The Ethiopian Experience in Comparative Perspective*. Oxford: James Currey, pp. 1–31.

———. 2012. 'Ethiopia Responds to UNESCO's World Heritage Committee on Lake Turkana', *Mursi Online*. Retrieved 20 May 2018 from http://www.mursi.org/news-items/ethiopia-responds-to-unescos-world-heritage-committee-on-lake-turkana.

UNEP (United Nations Environment Programme). 2012. *Ethiopia's Gibe III Dam: Its Potential Impact on Lake Turkana Water Levels*. Division of Early Warning and Assessment (DEWA), United Nations Environment Programme.

Chapter 11

State-Building in the Ethiopian South-Western Lowlands

Experiencing the Brunt of State Power in Mela

Lucie Buffavand

In August 2017, after the main rainy season, when the Mela should have been busy storing maize cobs in their granaries and planning large gatherings for dances, hunger had settled in.[1] 'We remain seated on our stools', an elder said, meaning that the adults were skipping meals to let their children eat the little they had.

Earlier that year, on the banks of the Omo River to the west, there were none of the patches of ripening sorghum usually to be found at the height of the dry season. The banks remained dry year-round now that the Gibe III dam's reservoir, filled in 2015, regulated the movements of the river. A system of irrigation, meanwhile, was watering thousands of hectares of sugar cane that stretched along the eastern bank of the Omo. The Ethiopian Sugar Corporation had reserved a strip of irrigated land at the edge of its plantation for the local population, who were pressured into growing maize and forced to disrupt their pastoralist way of life by settling nearby. But the lack of control the Mela had over the opening of the irrigation gates, and the arbitrary size of the plots assigned to them, meant that, for many, the yields did not match their needs. These frustrating results had driven the Mela to rely even more on their own sickles. They had opened large fields along the Gura River, not far from the plantation, for rain-fed cultivation. But that year, a drought and an invasion of crop pests – fall army worms – had reduced their efforts to nothing. The only consolation was that their herds of cattle had not been decimated by epidemic.

Coping strategies were limited. The most destitute families, who could not afford to sell the few cattle they had, attempted to trap warthogs and sell their meat – the consumption of warthog meat being taboo in Mela – to migrant workers in the plantation at ridiculously low prices: less than 100 Ethiopian birr (ETB; then about 4 US dollars) per animal. Some Mela men had taken up work in the plantation as watchmen. The often superfluous nature of their tasks – men being hired to watch over every possible piece of machinery, construction, and so on – made it clear to all that the salaries they received were a way to buy their consent to the taking of their land. Women had once been recruited to weed the sugar cane fields, where they were watched 'like cattle' by plantation personnel, but when after a full month of work they received a pay far lower than that of the migrant workers, they left the fields, lacking any means to make their case for a more equitable wage.[2]

The hunger that settled in among them brought back memories of the drought in the early 1970s.[3] At that time, the Mela had fallen back on another resource: the land of intermediate altitude on the slopes of the Dime highlands, in the east. 'Now, if we had planted over there, the maize would have grown', a Mela man surmised. To the question of why they did not go there to cultivate this year, an elder retorted: 'We would shit ourselves (*geser jo*)!' The first man explained: 'The government would chase us, most probably when the plants would have already reached our waist.' The most commonly shared feeling was that of being stranded on the plain where their resources were being depleted – to move eastward was no longer an option.

Why would the government forbid the Mela to cultivate in areas to which they had headed seasonally for more than a century? How did the Mela come to anticipate that government repression would prevent them from accessing resources even in critical times? These questions address the wider phenomena of state-building and the making of a state's subjects. Among the 'set of practices and processes and their effects' that is 'the state' (Trouillot 2001: 131), the arrangement of populations, and especially their sedentarization, so as to make them 'legible' to state agents, has been identified as a key corollary of state-building (Scott 1998). But people can be made to comply with this form of control only if mechanisms of state domination have been implemented. In other words, the disciplinary methods of power, such as villagization, that work internally at a detailed level and are meant to produce isolated individuals receptive to state demands follow or are accompanied by state power as an exterior constraint – that is, as authoritative commands backed by force (Mitchell 1991: 92–93). This chapter examines the various means by which the Ethiopian state has attempted to secure the compliance of people whose land it takes, by placing the Mela's current situation in the broader frame of an actualization of state power in the south-western Ethiopian lowlands. The form that such land dispossession takes will be related herein to the specific history of state presence in the region.

Although the Ethiopian state had been considering the construction of hydroelectric dams and accompanying irrigation schemes in the Omo River basin since the 1990s (Kamski 2016: 572), their actual implementation in the 2010s is part of a series of ambitious projects of infrastructure building launched by the government. In response to the mounting opposition to the regime, which was expressed during the 2005 national elections, the ruling coalition, despite its Marxist-Leninist heritage, shifted its economic strategy towards a market-oriented one, with a focus on trade and the integration of Ethiopia into the world economy (Lefort 2015). The development of the sugar industry in the Lower Omo Valley is envisioned as a major component of the national economy: the initial size of the plantation was intended to comprise nearly half the total hectarage of sugar plantations in Ethiopia (Tewolde and Fana 2014: 119), with the government aiming to place the country among the top ten sugar exporters in the world (Asnake and Fana 2014: 257).[4]

The seemingly impressive economic growth that followed the party's economic turn secured its legitimacy claims to stay in power (Hagmann and Abbink 2011: 586). Concomitantly, the political strategy was to extend the reach of the party to the lowest level so as to realize the late prime minister's aspiration for a 'coalition with the people' (Vaughan 2011). Hence the paradox of the party's position: while officially proclaiming the advent of an economy driven by market forces, the party consolidates its firm control over all domains of Ethiopians' lives (Lefort 2015). The resulting model of this peculiar combination of a market economy with centralized political control has been called 'vanguard capitalism' (Weis 2015). Observers of the Ethiopian highlands have analysed the results of this Ethiopian version of the 'developmental state': the encompassing reach of the state through bureaucratic methods (Planel 2014); the control of the rural economy, which operates through a narrative of farmer dependency (Little 2014); the disempowerment of the peasantry (Lefort 2012); and the use of coercion and the rise of authoritarianism in general (Hagmann and Abbink 2011), which produce the sense of a 'diffuse threat' and a 'formidable self-censorship' (Bach 2016: 14).

In the highlands, the current strengthening of state power represents a continuation of a history of peasant-state relations characterized by the strict verticality and arbitrariness of state power (Poluha 2002). In the southern highlands, state power was already experienced through land appropriation for settlers, investors or state farms (Tadesse 2009). Owing to this historical background, the actual application of force in rural Ethiopia by state agents is often unnecessary, as the constant use of threats has been sufficient to ensure the people's compliance with government policies, such as the broad use of fertilizers (Planel 2014: 430ff). Although the methods are coercive, the state has not needed to resort to inflicting physical harm. In the lowlands, however, where land had not previously been confiscated and state presence had been weak (Markakis 2011), the implementation of development projects has been accompanied by the state's demonstration of force. The deployment of the military and its utilization of violence aim to subdue a population whose land has been taken for commercial agriculture. The state seeks to actualize in the lowlands its 'claim to power', which for a long time had been left 'unresolved' (Abbink 2002; Girke 2015), by exercising a power that lowlanders previously had only experienced in quite circumscribed realms.

This chapter considers the encounters between state agents and the Mela, in the context of this new land appropriation by the state. Mela land has been allocated to settlers from the southern highlands, the Konso, since 2004 and to state-run plantations since 2012. These two phenomena – the resettlement of land-hungry people and the development of commercial agriculture – have applied unprecedented and increasing pressure to agro-pastoralists. Further-more, each reinforces the other: the heavy military presence that accompanies the development schemes is also used for the freeing up of land for southern highlanders whom the government plans to resettle. I outline the two types of interventions through which state agents seek to enforce state power: actions of military personnel and meetings with government workers (which sometimes overlap). Comparisons to other areas in the Ethiopian lowlands (see, for instance, Wagstaff 2015) where land has been taken by force from populations that had enjoyed relative political autonomy reveal a pattern of land appropriation marked by threats, violence, the banning of local populations' livelihood strategies and the indiscriminate labelling of their men as outlaws. The study of the Mela's movements in and out of specific parts of their territory shows how, in this con-text of repression, the Mela are forced into renouncing some of their resources that are still available, even in the face of chronic hunger.

Power Relations at the Margins of the State

The present demonstration of state power in South Omo can be viewed in rela-tion to the historic relationships in Ethiopia between centre and periphery. After the initial conquest in the late nineteenth century, which was marked by cattle and slave raids, the south-western lowlands were only administered remotely by the government. The lack of interest cut both ways: Turton (2005: 270) notes that the Mursi (Mun)[5] had adopted 'a strategy of avoidance – amounting almost to denial – in their dealings with agents of the state'; this general attitude not-withstanding, there was an intermediary role with the state that some individuals were to play. The denial of state rule was still evident in early 2011 during the meeting in which people were first informed of the government plans, when a Mursi man pronounced: '*Mangesti* (government/state), when you say that the land is yours, I do not even know what you are talking about. This is the land of my father, the land of my ancestors'.[6]

The indifference towards the state's pretensions that the Mursi, Mela and others display in their encounters with state agents is supported in no small part by their armed power. Possession of arms is a result of state expansion itself: the Mela first acquired guns from northern traders who had settled in the surrounding highlands. This in turn furthered the disengagement of the state from these areas, as Haberland (1959: 400; my translation) witnessed in the early 1950s during his short visit to the Chirim: 'Until now, [the state] has always preferred to avoid coercive measures against a people numbering more than 500 armed men and living in a hostile territory.' At the beginning of the twenty-first century, the state was still in 'unresolved competition' with lowlanders regarding the latter's failure to acknowledge its political power (Abbink 2002: 158). Girke (2015: 183, 186) explores the resulting negotiations of claims to power in Kara: well aware that 'they can get away with a lot' as rules are not systematically enforced, the Kara 'act as if they did think [that they could assert themselves militarily vis-à-vis state authorities]'. The lowlanders' resistance to full submission to state power, as well as their economic self-sufficiency and even wealth, irritate state officials, who accuse them of 'arrogance' (Wagstaff 2015: 22).

There are at least two domains in which complete avoidance of the state is recognized as counterproductive: taxes and interethnic conflicts. Mela men comply with the yearly payment of taxes,[7] long perceived as a tribute that keeps state interference at bay. The mediating or punitive role of the state in interethnic conflicts was at times instrumentalized: following a Mela raid on Mursi in late 1971, during which the Mela stole a lot of Mursi cattle, the Mursi appealed to state authorities, who then ordered the Mela to return the stolen cattle; less than a year later, the first police post in Mela land was established. In order to stop Mela raids on neighbouring cultivators, the police often resorted to the imprisonment of the Mela *komorutiya*, their most important ritual figures – the local authorities viewed this as a cost-effective form of punishment, and Mela men were never sent to jail *en masse*. More devastating uses of force were exceptions rather than the rule. The most significant event in this regard was a military operation carried out against the Nyomony in 1999 – with whom many Mela were also living.[8] It was intended to punish these agro-pastoralists for a series of large-scale raids that they had launched against the Malo people, an Omotic-speaking group of highland cultivators living in the Gamo Gofa zone. The military assembled the Nyomony men and shot them; about two hundred died.[9]

A Demonstration of Force

The reliance on the military for the establishment of commercial farms on communal land is a pattern found across the different Ethiopian regimes.[10] However, characteristics of the present regime tie development projects such as the sugar cane plantation in the Omo even more closely with a warlike discourse and the use of the military. It is above all a question of governing style. The threat of campaigns and a warlike vocabulary pervade development policies in Ethiopia (Little 2014: 125–26). Words such as 'fight', 'enemies' and 'struggle' are ubiquitous in the party's programmes and developmental discourse (Bach 2011: 654;

Fana 2014: 69). This martial discourse is a legacy from the TPLF's seventeen-year armed struggle against the Derg.[11]

In addition, the continuity of a warlike mindset is matched by a continuity of personnel. The staff of the state-owned Metals and Engineering Corporation (MetEC), in charge of building the first sugar cane processing plant in the southern region, are military (Asnake and Fana 2014: 257), including many former Tigrean fighters from the liberation struggle. Abay Tsehaye, director general of the Ethiopian Sugar Corporation (ESC) from 2010 to 2013, had ministerial rank and was also a veteran of the TPLF and a former national security adviser.[12] The presence of military or party leaders on the board of these newly created state companies, who are charged with a major part of the infrastructural work that is supposed to produce the desired economic transformation, contributes to 'the forging of a closer economic nexus between state, party, and . . . military' (Weis 2015: 298). After a period of gradual separation of these institutions in the 1990s, the coalition is orchestrating a return to the 'vanguard' mode of governance of the TPLF during its guerrilla years (ibid.: 316).

Finally, the party-state has contended that development is a matter of survival, and thus demands extraordinary means. The developmental discourse, which in the early 2000s was communicated primarily to party members and civil servants, became hegemonic after the contested 2005 elections (ibid.: 252f). Development was then framed as the only solution for the Ethiopian nation itself; it was 'securitized' – that is, presented as an issue that trumped all others and superseded political debate (Fana 2014). The rulers sought to emulate the developmental model of South Korea and Taiwan, but the presence of an outside threat (North Korea and China respectively) was missing in Ethiopia (ibid.: 67). They thus crafted an internal threat: poverty became the peril that threatened the very survival of the Ethiopian nation, and '[r]esistance against such extraordinary measures [would] be treated similarly to wartime dissidence' (ibid.: 71) – hence the speed with which the plans were executed in the Omo and the heavy military presence (Turton, this volume).

In May 2011, troops led by the head of the Southern Region's Special Police Force came to Hana town in Mela land as part of a coordinated large-scale security operation, with police forces arriving in Suri, on the other side of the Omo, at the same time (Wagstaff 2015: 30). The operation consisted first in the registration of all arms and munitions possessed by the Mela: a registration number was painted on their rifle stocks. The security forces then proceeded to arrest the 'bandits' (*shifta*) – that is, Mela men who had allegedly committed homicides or thefts in the past years against their agriculturalist neighbours, based on testimonies hastily collected in meetings during which the local government officials pressed Mela elders to provide names. These measures were intended to end, in the most brutal fashion, the past decades of weak administration in the region, during which homicides may have gone unpunished. The troops also rounded up many young Mela men who had not been accused of committing any crime. The troops who carried out these arrests sported a purposely exaggerated display of military might – helmets, shields, batons and modern rifles.

This 2011 operation represented an initial demonstration of force, which mostly targeted young men.[13] Overall, the authorities detained more than 120 men in a camp, where the prisoners were regularly beaten. They were hastily sentenced to many years of imprisonment and sent to jails in Jinka and Sawla. Wagstaff (2015: 24) also reports of Suri complaints regarding 'the biased court judges (all non-Suri . . .) in the *woreda* and zone courts, proclaiming disproportionate verdicts against the Suri based on flimsy evidence'. As some Mela said at the time, the prison in Jinka had become the compound of the new generation (*dirr*) because of the unprecedentedly high number of young men who were detained there.

The Mela have not opposed the land alienation and mass detentions head-on. Rather, they have framed their contestation of the legitimacy of state power in cosmological terms, in discourses that do not surface in encounters with state agents (Buffavand 2016). Although open resistance has been generally deemed too costly, the Mela reacted violently when their people were repeatedly hit and killed by vehicles of the ESC driving at high speed on the new roads. Before the start of the project, there were no known precedents of people being run over by vehicles. The Mela treated these incidents as homicides perpetrated by *habesha* (highlanders), and in some cases, the relatives or age-mates of the victims sought revenge by killing drivers, townspeople or military men. In October 2012, after a pregnant woman and a herding boy had already been killed on the road, a truck, driving at high speed during the night, hit and killed a young Mela man; an all-out confrontation between Mela fighters and the military ensued. About fifty Mela men were then put in prison.[14]

The sequence of events that starts with homicides on the road and then leads to retaliation and eventually to imprisonment has continued to occur regularly. The most significant was the killing of a young Mela man in December 2017, after which some Mela men shot at passing cars on the road, killing a dozen *habesha*. Mela men and also some women were sent to jail in Jinka, and the local government confiscated thirty-five guns from the Mela. More generally with respect to weapons, since the registration of arms in 2011, no disarmament campaign has been attempted and the painted numbers on the guns have faded away. Nonetheless, it is probable that the aforementioned confiscation has made the Mela's position an even more vulnerable one vis-à-vis the state authorities and also vis-à-vis the neighbouring groups who are still armed.

Violence against the Mela also occurred in the form of arbitrary beatings by soldiers near market or plantation towns where the military are permanently based. These beatings were on the rise during the state of emergency from October 2016 to August 2017.[15] In one instance, the dead body of a Mela man was found next to the police checkpoint on the road to the plantation; no one was prosecuted for this crime. The Mela have become increasingly infuriated by the government's double standard, as they are invariably targeted as the sole perpetrators of crimes. This is evident in conflicts between the Mela and highland or resettled cultivators, for which the authorities punish the Mela people but not members of the other warring group. In a response to a conflict between Mela-Chirim people and Konso settlers that broke out in February 2014, and during which killings happened on both sides,[16] the military surrounded the Konso settlements and shot the Mela and Chirim who approached, killing and wounding unarmed women and children.[17] A more recent case provides yet another example of a justice system that is consistently biased against Mela people. In August 2017, a young Mela woman, last seen leaving a village during the evening, was found dead the next morning in the sugar cane fields, her body butchered by a machete. The Mela know that the only people present in the fields at night are the migrant workers operating the irrigation system; however, only the Mela watchmen who had worked the day shift were taken into custody, and no migrant worker was ever interrogated.

The violent actions of the military and the strong bias of the judicial system and police forces have certainly created a pervading feeling of fear and insecurity among the Mela. The military tanks stationed in the vicinity of the sugar cane plantation ominously suggest to the Mela that their greatest dread – that the government will eventually decide to finish them off – is not totally implausible.[18]

Gunpoint and the Maze of Words

Government meetings, at which state officials gather representatives of the communities to inform them regarding development policies or to make peace between groups in conflict, have proven to be 'the most important performative sites' of the relation between the state and the lowlanders (Girke 2015: 177). Inhabitants of such peripheral areas as Mela or Kara land could once use such meetings, in a masterful use of irony, to challenge state claims to power (ibid.). But the militarization of development has transformed the style and tenor of the meetings (ibid.: 189).

In January 2011, authorities held a meeting in Hana town, where representatives of local communities (Chirim, Mela, Mursi and Kwegu) were to be informed about the development plans project.[19] Roads had already been cut through the bush, and airplanes had regularly surveyed the land at low altitude. Whereas previously the implementation of major schemes (such as the resettlement of Konso people in Mela land) had been preceded by a round of meetings to obtain the attendants' acquiescence, this time the government had gone ahead with transformative plans before informing people about them – a change some Mela representatives noted with concern during the meeting. In this first meeting, people still dared to express their opposition to the government's project, but in subsequent meetings soldiers surrounded the attendants, and those who persisted in speaking their minds were put in jail for a few days. The government's meetings, whose frequency increased, were convened to achieve the objectives they had so far often fallen short of: to obtain people's obedience, to deny their agency and to suppress any challenge to state power.

The Mela indeed feel that their consent has been obtained at gunpoint. One regular attendee to such meetings explained it as follows: 'the government is putting its gun on our ear like this [mimicking someone pointing a gun]: "Why don't you agree? Why don't you agree?" Don't we beg them to stop? So we agreed. "All right, go and cultivate"'.[20] In the government meetings, when not faced with actual death threats, the Mela are confronted with a maze of words. To illustrate this, a Mela man showed me the string game *kuyekuye* (cat's cradle): with the string stretched between his hands, in a few manipulations he created a complicated web of criss-crossing paths. 'This is the government's discourse: it goes there and comes back here – one gets lost.'[21] Officials hide the true motives of the government; they say one thing and then often do another.

Officials find themselves striving to impose their dominance by force or through deceit to an audience of dubious allegiance. This climate of suspicion has been pervasive in the highlands, especially since the Derg regime. Poluha (2002: 129) delineates the process that occurred under the Derg and now the current regime and how this has shaped peasant-state relations: there is an official 'we' against 'them', the latter including ex-officials or supporters of the former government. More than twenty-five years after the fall of the military junta, the Mela are regularly asked by officials which of the two governments – the Derg or the EPRDF – is the better one (see also Girke 2015: 179). Failing to express unflinching loyalty towards the powerholders automatically classifies one as an opponent (Poluha 2002: 130). It is not surprising, then, that the meetings are held more as a gauge of the audience's allegiance to the regime than as an opportunity to discuss problems that the communities may encounter.

The exchanges during a government meeting as reported to the author by a Mela attendant offer a clear example of the wall of suspicion with which the Mela are regularly confronted. By mid-2014, following the long conflict with the Konso settlers, only a few Mela people had remained in the new villages that the government had established close to the plantation and laid out according to a grid (Stevenson and Buffavand 2018: 120). This was not their first or only attempt at evading the state scheme of villagization (ibid.: 124). Worried this time that the Konso could steal or harm their cattle, Mela heads of household felt safer to stay permanently in the cattle camps that they had kept further east; or, as some explained, it also provided a good excuse to stay out of the resettlement villages. Local government officials seemed indeed to have been too busy dealing with the conflict to be able to pressure people to stay in the villages. But when the confrontations ceased, officials resumed their harassment with renewed vigour. During the first government meeting since the conflict had broken out, a Mela attendant, who had managed to slip away before the end, joined another Mela man, a Kwegu man and me. In our conversation, he reported what had been said in the meeting:

First Mela man [*imitating a government official*]: 'Only a very few people are in the resettlement villages. The Chirim, and the people from Hana, and the people from Magolony, now, today, the fact that you refuse to go to the resettlement villages, we brought you all here and here you are. Now, today, tell us this message, and we will listen! Who is preventing you from going into the resettlement villages? This is it. Only this idea, only one. "What is preventing us from going in the resettlement is . . .", is it another government which advises you that? And tells you not to move in the resettlement villages? Tell us this one idea. "Government, you do things badly for us, and we don't want this!" These two ideas, don't say three or four ideas, I want only two ideas.' I went to pee and I came and hid. After that, the Mela must have been eating shit; they must have been in real trouble. [Imitating the government official]: 'I want only these two ideas!'

Kwegu man: If you had said: 'We left, with the Chirim and the Mela of Hana. Where can we seed? You are planting sugar cane'.

First Mela man: Kolayholi[22] said: 'You the government, there is no problem, you are good to us! Now, you divided the [maize] fields into very little plots. There are some people who want a big plot. Maybe the people don't move in the resettlement villages because of this. Now with the sugar cane, you just go on seeding it; before for the maize fields you showed us the plots for each of us, you said: "Your boundary is here, your boundary is there". Now for the sugar cane you don't show us anything, maybe the people are afraid and say that you are stealing the land and they run away'. [Imitating a government official]: 'All right, Kolayholi, sit down and be quiet. So this is your message? Stop with it! Leave it. Tell us only these two ideas I told you about, I want only these two ideas. The one who wants to say this idea he waits and you tell us only about these two ideas and when this is finished, now you tell us what you want to say'.

Second Mela man, to me [imitating a government official]: 'Stop it! Name us the people who advise you!' They're imagining only you, the Westerners (*ferenji*) [as our advisers]![23]

This informal report of a government meeting exemplifies the politics of suspicion at work: the official tried to obtain a confession of the Mela's disloyalty towards the Ethiopian government, even though he had seemingly allowed the voicing of an alternate explanation (the 'second idea') for the evasion of the villagization scheme – a criticism of the government.

Kolayholi had been rather cautious in introducing the problems the Mela encountered in the irrigated plots. The ESC had originally given to each household a 0.75 hectare plot on which to cultivate maize. Some people had started to cultivate only because they were pressured into it and later abandoned their fields to the weeds. Others were discouraged by the constant work required by the irrigation and weeding; irrigated agriculture is more labour intensive than the shifting cultivation that they customarily practice, and thus creates problems allocating labour between the fields and the cattle camps. In the end, a good portion of the maize fields were overgrown with weeds. The ESC apparently perceived this as a waste of land and, claiming that the Mela were 'unable' to productively utilize plots of such size, decided to reduce the maize fields to a 0.25 hectare plot per household, promising the people that it would be extended to 0.75 when they could cultivate sugar cane as outgrowers. But Kolayholi's explanation as to why the Mela abandoned the government's scheme was not something that the authorities wanted to hear; he was silenced, and the official sought to reduce the matter to one of disloyalty, thus implying that the Mela were unable to reach their own informed decisions without outside influence.

The position of the Mela or Chirim working in the administration as translators for government meetings or as members of the justice and security office is a very precarious one: under intense suspicion, they must demonstrate on which side of the dividing line they stand. Besides the use of force and intimidation, the recruitment of personnel from the dominated group as temporary watchmen or in more long-term positions within the administration is an important component in the securement of compliance. Beyond the setting of the meetings, these administrators are often sent to bend the resistance of the population in times of high tension, when highland officials do not want to confront the armed lowlanders directly.

Civil servants in Ethiopia are regularly evaluated through sessions of criticism and self-criticism (in Amharic: *gimgema*), which are essentially directed by party officials (Labzaé 2015). Given the tight control of the administration by the party-state and the pressure from above to fulfil certain goals, the vast majority of state workers resort to intimidation tactics towards those whom they administer (ibid.: 103). The Mela and Chirim workers are no exception, and because they are a 'subordinate elite' (Markakis 2011: 11), dominated within the administrative structure as they are in the overt ethnic hierarchy, they sometimes resort to using the harshest methods of intimidation against their own people. Conversely, the majority within the community distrusts their own members appointed to administrative positions. Gabbert (2012: 230) reports the speech of an Arbore elder, in which he draws the line between the community and its elected representatives, who can only be loyal to one side: by accessing such government positions, they exclude themselves from the community. It has been observed that in Tigray state policies can be adapted and negotiated at ground level by state workers, which challenges the usual state/peasant dichotomy (Villanucci and Fantini 2016). In South Omo, however, this grey zone where negotiation can occur rarely exists, and so the dichotomy remains strong.

Shrinking Resources

The application of force and the use of a threatening discourse by state agents have effects on Mela livelihood strategies that go beyond the already significant limitations imposed by the damming of the river and the establishment of plantations. This is partly because the securitization of the sugar industry has ramifications for other government schemes. As mentioned in the introduction, land appropriation by the state in the south-western lowlands takes two forms: the resettlement of highland farmers from regions that suffer land shortages and the development of commercial agriculture. In the present case, the strong military presence in investment areas has hastened the freeing up of land for settlers within the region.[24] This is particularly evident in the easternmost part of Mela territory, the Oso Valley, hemmed in by the Dime mountains to the west and the Basketo and Aari highlands to the north and east.[25]

Konso were resettled in Mela's and Chirim's dry season grazing land in the early 2000s; yet more Konso were resettled in the Oso Valley starting in 2010, along with people from Sidama and Wolayta and spontaneous settlers from the Amhara region.[26] Benefiting from higher rainfall than in the Omo Valley, the Oso Valley offers fertile lands for cultivation and lush grazing grounds. Oral traditions and ancient gravestones testify to the past presence of the Mela. But they were forced to flee after a devastating raid in the early nineteenth century, probably by the army of the then powerful Kafa kingdom; at the turn of the twentieth century, the troops of Menelik II coming from the east chased them out of the valley again. Abandoned by the Mela and their cattle, the bush grew dense and the tse-tse flies thrived, preventing the Mela from grazing their cattle there when the raiding threat ceased, because of the prevalence of trypanosomiasis.

The Mela did not resume cattle herding in the Oso Valley until around 2000.[27] But ten years later, they found themselves surrounded by the new settlers; furthermore, the Basketo Woreda had demarcated land for a private investor, and a private hunting reserve had been established in the southern part of the valley. In 2011, after clashes between the Mela and Amhara settlers, and between the Mela and Aari highlanders, the government ordered the Mela of Oso to leave the valley: accused of being the sole instigators of conflicts, they were told that they ought to leave the land for 'hungry people'. The security operation that preceded the clearing of land for the sugar cane plantation in the Omo Valley was by then in full swing. Troops were sent to the Oso. Young men were put in prison, and the Mela complied and left the valley.

During the following years, however, many came back. With the end of flood-retreat cultivation and the difficulty in accessing dry season grazing land along the Omo because of the dam and the plantations, the Oso Valley had become an even more critical resource for the Mela as a whole. In early 2017, even more violent methods were used to push Mela people out of the northern Oso. Men were arbitrarily beaten up by the police forces, whose numbers had risen with the state of emergency and the imminent visit of the Ethiopian and Sudanese heads of states, and a Mela member of the local administration ordered the police to burn Mela's houses and granaries.[28] Although the pervasive presence of the military is meant to protect the state's development venture, it is also used in support of the resettlement of people from other regions at the expense of agro-pastoralists, whose customary use of the land is not acknowledged.

First fleeing conquering armies of the empire at the end of the nineteenth century, the Mela of the Oso were now being forced to leave their land by the military and police forces of the 'developmental state'. Such events – massacres, forced evictions, indiscriminate incarceration, and so on – inform the Mela's relations to the state and their decisions as to where to move – and if to move at all.[29] The violent eviction from the Oso conveys the same message as the injunction to settle in government-designed villages along the sugar cane plantations: the Mela are supposed to remain confined in a narrow territory that cannot provide adequately for their subsistence. This order was hammered home once more in a government meeting by the officials' insidious and threatening discourse, which was reported by a Mela attendant as follows:

[Government officials]: How many fields do you have?

[Mela attendant]: One field I cultivate in such place.

[Government officials]: One?

[Mela attendant]: Another one [I cultivate somewhere else].

We didn't know [what they had in mind]. We enumerated all the fields that we had ever cultivated . . . and reached many.

[Government official]: How is it that you cultivate so many fields?

They brought up a new discourse.

[Mela attendant]: 'When there's hunger, over there it's the highlands, I go and cultivate in the highlands, then I come down, I cultivate here [in the plain], and then I go and cultivate on the [Omo] river banks.

[Government official]: 'You are a boaster. This land is left idle, some people remain [in other regions], when they'll come, I will put these people there. In those fields. And you will hold only one [field]'.[30]

Afraid that cultivation outside of the area to which they were now assigned would be sanctioned as it had been in the Oso Valley, the Mela were then reticent to use the full range of their resources: they did not dare to cultivate the lands of intermediate altitude that have not been given to resettled communities of farmers, and which had saved them from hunger more than four decades ago (see this chapter's introduction).

Conclusion

The sudden actualization of state power in the Lower Omo is apparent in the military violence that is regularly inflicted on the Mela, and by an intimidating discourse in government meetings that rests on this background of violence, on the use of deceit and on the persistent suspicious attitude exhibited by state agents.

As a result of a history of strong state presence in the highlands, Ethiopian peasants have learned that 'in order to survive it is best to delegate both initiative and responsibility to government officials' (Poluha 2002: 134). The thorough application of authoritarian methods has created fear and insecurity among the Mela, and although they do not yet systematically rely on government officials, they have had to relinquish some of their strategies. They pay the price of this defeat with hunger (see also Wagstaff 2015: 22).

Even though the agro-pastoralists of the Lower Omo were only distantly administered by the government before the start of the development scheme, they already felt constrained by the state incorporation, in that they had realized that 'the activities of the nation-state . . . [had] blocked their potential movement into new areas' (Turton 2005: 271). It is now not only potential movements that are curtailed; migration between resource sites is also curtailed, and the sites themselves are being depleted. The Mela have not remained passive in the face of the state domination – many have evaded the state scheme of villagization and continued to clear land for rain-fed cultivation despite the government's injunctions to farm only in the irrigated plots, but this evasion is spatially constrained to the lower altitudes of the Omo plain. The Mela for the most part have renounced their former areas of cultivation in higher altitudes. Hemmed in by the sugar cane plantations on one side and the resettlement of highlanders on the other, they are forced to abandon a livelihood strategy that relies on varied activities and ecological settings. Their subsequent insertion into the economy of the plantation is compromised by the competing presence of the migrant workers.

Land dispossession in the Lower Omo has therefore accelerated the state-building process and its requisite to make populations legible (see chapters by

Asebe and Fana in this volume). Through the sorts of population engineering that Ethiopian governments have consistently favoured – the resettlement of highlanders to more fertile regions and the villagization programmes – the Mela find themselves forced ever closer to the state's model subject of the sedentary farmer who cultivates his sole plot of land. In the highlands, government authorities have recently come to realize that the use of force cannot be counted on to indefinitely contain people's grievances. The historical trajectory in which lowlanders such as the Mela find themselves might be at odds with this shift towards a less coercive mode of governing at the national level, the implications of which have yet to be evaluated. And as long as the government remains an essentially repressive and predatory force in the lowlands, the Mela's lives are bound to become increasingly difficult.

Lucie Buffavand is an affiliated researcher to the Institut des Mondes Africains (France). She has carried out fieldwork in Mela, south-west Ethiopia, since 2007. She was awarded a postdoctoral research grant by the Fyssen foundation for the year 2018, in affiliation with the Laboratoire d'Anthropologie Sociale in Paris. Her research focuses on the relation between social identities and place-making practices, and on local responses to large-scale development schemes.

Notes

1. The Mela are a group of Me'en speakers living on the eastern side of the Omo River. Together with the Chirim, another Me'en group and the northern neighbours of the Mela, they are known as 'Bodi' to Ethiopian authorities and foreigners (see Map PIV.1 Peoples of South Omo, this volume).
2. Mela women said they had received on average 200–300 ETB for a month, whereas migrant workers are officially paid 40 ETB per day.
3. Crop failures had then been worsened by the war with the Mursi, which impeded the normal course of subsistence activities. Also, food aid deliveries were virtually absent.
4. In April 2017, the Ethiopian prime minister Haile Mariam accompanied the Sudanese president Omar al-Bashir on a visit to the second sugar-processing factory being built in South Omo, as part of the Sudanese head of state's three-day stay in Ethiopia. This visit testifies to the importance of the project with respect to highlighting Ethiopia's leading role in the economic integration of the wider region ('Al-Bashir Visits Omo Kuraz II Sugar Factory', *Walta info*, 6 April 2017, retrieved 5 February 2018 from https://www.waltainfo.com/news/national/detail?cid=28790).
5. Mursi is the name used by most outsiders for the Mun (see LaTosky, this volume).
6. Mursi man, January 2011, Hana.
7. In Mela, taxes had been collectively paid in cattle until towards the end of the empire; married men then had to pay in cash, but arrangements were made with the local administration that relieved men who had very few or no cattle from having to pay. Nowadays, there is increasing pressure on every married man to pay – they may be asked at the local clinic to show the receipt of their tax payment before receiving any treatment – and the yearly amount is 500 ETB. Payment in cattle, however, persists: one or two head are demanded from each district (*kebele*) on top of the individual payments in cash.

8. The Nyomony are a group of a few thousand Me'en-speaking people living on the western side of the Omo.

9. See also Abbink (2006: 398) on the haphazard use of force during government interference in interethnic conflicts in the Maji area.

10. See, for instance, Tadesse (2009: 148) on the strengthening of the army and the police in Gamo under Haile Selassie, when the state gave communal land to its various clients.

11. The Tigrayan People's Liberation Front (TPLF) is the core party of the Ethiopian People's Revolutionary Democratic Front (EPRDF), the ruling coalition.

12. Bewket Abebe, 'State-Owned Sugar Corporation Welcomes New Director General', *Addis Fortune*, 13 October 2013, retrieved 20 November 2014 from http://addisfortune.net/articles/state-owned-sugar-corporation-welcomes-new-director-general/.

13. A few Mela women were victims of rape by military personnel during this period.

14. After the first vehicular-inflicted deaths, the ESC dismissed the more reckless drivers and laid down a road for pedestrians alongside the track of the main car road. It did not prevent other deadly incidents from taking place. This can be compared with the much stricter rules observed by the BGP and Tullow Oil companies during an oil exploration in Arbore, which included a monitored speed limit of 40 km/hour for all drivers; there were no casualties during the operation (Gabbert 2014: 20).

15. A nationwide state of emergency was declared following a wave of protests in the Oromia and Amhara regions in 2016. It gave more power to the security forces, whose presence was strengthened near investment areas such as the ESC plantations.

16. Following the government-led resettlement of Konso people in 2004 in what were dry season pastures for the Mela and Chirim, there have been regular conflicts between the two groups. The authorities have turned a blind eye to the arrival of new Konso settlers over the years and to the steady encroachment of Konso fields on Mela and Chirim pastures and cultivation areas.

17. A new search for 'bandits' followed in December 2014; it targeted Mela men who had allegedly made use of their fighting sticks. Another contingent of Mela men was imprisoned, and one young man who tried to escape from the police was shot dead.

18. The killing of 200 men in Nyomony, another Me'en speaking group, is a precedent (see above). This fear of genocide is shared by the Anywaa people in Gambella, who were dispossessed of their land in favour of private investors: 'The aim of the government is to reserve enough land and give it to investors. [Villagization] is also a technique that is made to gather this tribe at one place and kill them all without missing one . . . The aim of the government is gather us and kill us in one place' (leaked interview transcripts of the World Bank Inspection Panel, February 2014, retrieved 4 March 2015 from https://www.documentcloud.org/documents/1678822-gambella-inspection-panel-transcripts.html, pp. 5 and 7).

19. This was the only government meeting I was able to attend. Halfway through the meeting, an official demanded that I leave.

20. Mela elder, November 2011.

21. Mela man, October 2015.

22. Pseudonym.

23. Conversation with two Mela men and a Kwegu man, June 2014.

24. These two state-led phenomena had been even more tightly connected in other parts of Ethiopia. In Gamo, the resettlement of Amhara people was used to secure the development of cotton plantations: the settlers were given land and enrolled in the imperial army with the hope that they would crush any Gamo resistance to the taking of their land for plantations (Tadesse 2009: 148).

25. Oso is the Me'en name of the river, whose upper course the authorities call Usuno and the lower course Sala.
26. It appears that the administration of the Basketo Special Woreda had gone ahead with the resettlements, although the South Omo zone was claiming the land where people were resettled as part of their district. The case was brought to the regional level, which decided in favour of the Basketo Woreda, mostly because smallholder farmers are deemed more deserving of land than pastoralists.
27. They could cope with the trypanosomiasis thanks to the availability of cattle medicines in nearby towns.
28. See also Wagstaff (2015: 30) on arsonists who burned down Suri houses to force them to move into the resettlement sites.
29. These traumatic events also leave traces in a people's very identity. Gabbert (2012: 46ff) shows how the Arbore's memories of the oppression and exile endured during and after the imperial conquest live on as a 'history of scars' in oral traditions and in the landscape and have shaped their collective identity.
30. Mela man, August 2017.

References

Abbink, J. 2002. 'Paradoxes of Power and Culture in an Old Periphery: Surma, 1974–98', in W. James, D.L. Donham, E. Kurimoto and A. Triulzi (eds), *Remapping Ethiopia: Socialism and After*. Oxford: James Currey, pp. 155–72.

———. 2006. 'Ethnicity and Conflict Generation in Ethiopia: Some Problems and Prospects of Ethno-Regional Federalism', *Journal of Contemporary African Studies* 24(3): 389–413.

Asnake Kefale, and Fana Gebresenbet. 2014. 'The Expansion of the Sugar Industry in the Southern Pastoral Lowlands', in Rahmato Dessalegn, Meheret Ayenew, Asnake Kefale and B. Habermann (eds), *Reflections on Development in Ethiopia: New Trends, Sustainability and Challenges*. Addis Ababa: FSS and FES, pp. 247–68.

Bach, J.-N. 2011. '*Abyotawi* Democracy: Neither Revolutionary nor Democratic, a Critical Review of EPRDF's Conception of Revolutionary Democracy in Post-1991 Ethiopia', *Journal of Eastern African Studies* 5(4): 641–63.

———. 2016. 'L'Éthiopie après Meles Zenawi: L'autoritarisme ethnique à bout de souffle?', *Politique Africaine* 142: 5–29.

Buffavand, L. 2016. '"The Land Does Not Like Them": Contesting Dispossession in Cosmological Terms in Mela, South-West Ethiopia', *Journal of Eastern African Studies* 10(3): 476–93.

Fana Gebresenbet. 2014. 'Securitization of Development in Ethiopia: The Discourse and Politics of Developmentalism', *Review of African Political Economy* 41(S1): 64–74.

Gabbert, E.C. 2012. 'Deciding Peace: Knowledge about War and Peace among the Arbore of Southern Ethiopia', Ph.D. thesis. Halle: Martin Luther University Halle-Wittenberg, Institute for Social Anthropology.

———. 2014. 'The Global Neighbourhood Concept: A Chance for Cooperative Development or *Festina Lente*', in Mulugeta Gebrehiwot Berhe (ed.), *A Delicate Balance: Land Use, Minority Rights and Social Stability in the Horn of Africa*. Addis Ababa: Institute for Peace and Security Studies, Addis Ababa University, pp. 14–37.

Girke, F. 2015. 'The Uncertainty of Power and the Certainty of Irony: Encountering the State in Kara, Southern Ethiopia', in R. Hariman and R. Cintron (eds), *Culture, Catastrophe, and Rhetoric: The Texture of Political Action*. Oxford, New York: Berghahn, pp. 168–93.

Haberland, E. 1959. *Altvölker Süd-Äthiopiens*. Stuttgart: Kohlhammer.

Hagmann, T., and J. Abbink. 2011. 'Twenty Years of Revolutionary Democratic Ethiopia, 1991 to 2011', *Journal of Eastern African Studies* 5(4): 579–95.

Kamski, B. 2016. 'The Kuraz Sugar Development Project (KSDP) in Ethiopia: Between "Sweet Visions" and Mounting Challenges', *Journal of Eastern African Studies* 10(3): 568–80.

Labzaé, M. 2015. 'Les travailleurs du gouvernement: Encadrement partisan et formes du travail administratif dans l'administration éthiopienne', *Genèses* 98: 89–109.

Lefort, R. 2012. 'Free Market Economy, "Development State" and Party-State Hegemony in Ethiopia: The Case of the "Model Farmers"', *Journal of Modern African Studies* 50(4): 681–706.

———. 2015. 'The Ethiopian Economy: The Developmental State vs. the Free Market', in G. Prunier and É. Ficquet (eds), *Understanding Contemporary Ethiopia: Monarchy, Revolution and the Legacy of Meles Zenawi*. London: Hurst, pp. 357–94.

Little, P.D. 2014. '"The Government Is Always Telling Us What to Think": Narratives of Food Aid Dependence in Rural Ethiopia', in P.D. Little, *Economic and Political Reform in Africa: Anthropological Perspectives*. Bloomington and Indianapolis: Indiana University Press, pp. 116–40.

Markakis, J. 2011. *Ethiopia: The Last Two Frontiers*. Rochester and Woodbridge: James Currey.

Mitchell, T. 1991. 'The Limits of the State: Beyond Statist Approaches and Their Critics', *American Political Science Review* 85(1): 77–96.

Planel, S. 2014. 'A View of a Bureaucratic Developmental State: Local Governance and Agricultural Extension in Rural Ethiopia', *Journal of Eastern African Studies* 8(3): 420–37.

Poluha, E. 2002. 'Learning Political Behaviour: Peasant-State Relations in Ethiopia', in E. Poluha and M. Rosendahl (eds), *Contesting 'Good' Governance: Cross-Cultural Perspectives on Representation, Accountability and Public Space*. London: Routledge, pp. 101–36.

Scott, J. 1998. *Seeing Like a State: How Certain Schemes to Improve the Human Condition Have Failed*. New Haven, CT: Yale University Press.

Stevenson, E.G.J., and L. Buffavand. 2018. '"Do Our Bodies Know Their Ways?" Villagization, Food Insecurity, and Ill-Being in Ethiopia's Lower Omo Valley', *African Studies Review* 61(1): 109–33.

Tadesse Wolde Gossa. 2009. '"We Have Been Sold": Competing with the State and Dealing with Others', in G. Schlee and E.E. Watson (eds), *Changing Identifications and Alliances in North-East Africa, Vol. 1: Ethiopia and Kenya*. Oxford and New York: Berghahn, pp. 135–53.

Tewolde Woldemariam, and Fana Gebresenbet. 2014. 'Socio-Political and Conflict Implications of Sugar Development in Salamago *Wereda*, Ethiopia', in Mulugeta Gebrehiwot Berhe (ed.), *A Delicate Balance: Land Use, Minority Rights and Social Stability in the Horn of Africa*. Addis Ababa: Institute for Peace and Security Studies, Addis Ababa University, pp. 117–43.

Trouillot, M.R. 2001. 'The Anthropology of the State in the Age of Globalization', *Current Anthropology* 42(1): 125–38.

Turton, D. 2005. 'The Meaning of Place in a World of Movement: Lessons from Long-Term Field Research in Southern Ethiopia', *Journal of Refugee Studies* 18(3): 258–80.

Vaughan, S. 2011. 'Revolutionary Democratic State-Building: Party, State and People in the EPRDF's Ethiopia', *Journal of Eastern African Studies* 5(4): 619–40.

Villanucci, A., and E. Fantini. 2016. 'Santé publique, participation communautaire et mobilisation politique en Éthiopie: La Women's Development Army', *Politique Africaine* 142: 77–99.

Wagstaff, Q.A. 2015. *Development, Cultural Hegemonism and Conflict Generation in Southwest Ethiopia: Agro-Pastoralists in Trouble*. Note 13. 'Observatoire des Enjeux Politiques et Sécuritaires dans la Corne de l'Afrique'. Les Afriques dans le Monde (LAM) / Sciences Po – Bordeaux. Retrieved 3 October 2017 from www.lam.sciencespobordeaux.fr/sites/lam/files/note13_observatoire.pdf.

Weis, T. 2015. 'Vanguard Capitalism: Party, State, and Market in the EPRDF's Ethiopia', Ph.D. thesis. Oxford: Exeter College, University of Oxford.

Chapter 12

Customary Land Use and Local Consent Practices in Mun (Mursi)

A New Call for Meaningful FPIC Standards in Southern Ethiopia

Shauna LaTosky

> FPIC cannot exist where a people does not have the option to meaningfully withhold consent.
> —G.G. MacDonald and G. Zezulka, 'Understanding Successful Approaches to FPIC in Canada'

Introduction

When the United Nations Declaration on the Rights of Indigenous Peoples (UNDRIP) made specific mention of free, prior and informed consent (FPIC) in 2007 as a prerequisite for any activity that affects the traditional lands and resources of indigenous peoples, the purpose was to prioritize and affirm the rights of indigenous peoples to self-determination (Article 32). In more recent years, FPIC processes have come to include 'any and all marginalised and vulnerable people who could be affected by proposed development activities and land deals' (Franco 2014: 14; see also FAO 2016: 3–4). Implementation has been difficult due not only to constraints on how the diverse legal challenges surrounding FPIC standards are recognized and enforced but on how the actual meaning of the words Free, Prior, Informed, Consent are interpreted (Dunlap 2018: 106), in particular, 'consent', which is often loosely interpreted as 'participation' or 'consultation' (Franco 2014).[1]

In the literature on development in southern Ethiopia today, consultation is a familiar topic. This is because of evidence that consultative procedures run contrary to international human rights standards of 'free, prior and informed consent' (FPIC).² Corporate-state investors, like sugar cane development and villagization schemes in South Omo Zone, struggle to honour appropriate FPIC guidelines with agro-pastoralist communities. While state media reports declare that the government uses sound consultative procedures and that the agro-pastoralist peoples have 'consented' to the largest state-run sugar project in Ethiopia, empirical studies show that consent processes continue to be 'narrowly defined as participation' (Yidneckachew 2015: 295), and that public forums are a unidirectional campaign of convincing communities – with information and promises cascading down from above (Tewolde and Fana, forthcoming).

The Mun³ are one of several marginalized communities impacted by the massive Kuraz Sugar Development Project (KSDP) that began in 2011, as well as the near-complete South Omo Villagization Plan, which includes the Salamago Woreda. Both projects are supervised by the state-owned Ethiopian Sugar Corporation (ESC)⁴ and impact the lives of the Mun, Bodi and Kwegu in unprecedented ways: the construction of the Gibe III dam, which controls the seasonal flooding of the Omo and lends itself to irrigation schemes for the sugar plantations, has already disrupted traditional riverbank flood-retreat agricultural practices (Turton, this volume); the construction of Kuraz I, II and III,⁵ in the Salamago Woreda, which have involved the clearing of vast tracts of land for sugar estates, roads and infrastructure (including towns for migrant labourers) encroach on the traditional grazing lands and cultural use areas of the Mun and their neighbours. A third major development is the government planning of five villages (two in southern Munland and three in northern Munland), which the Mun are expected to relocate to in order to adopt a more sedentary way of life through irrigation-based farming. One of the most pressing concerns for the Mun is the future protection of their heritage and resources as a result of these large-scale developments, in particular their cultivation sites along the Omo River, traditional grazing lands, and important sacred sites.⁶ Mun express these concerns as a lack of sufficient support, time and information, especially on the social and environmental impact assessments provided by the government and other parties involved (see also Turton, this volume). There is concern that promises made by the ESC to communities (i.e. access to jobs, clinics, schools, water wells and irrigation technology to improve crop yields⁷) were empty rhetoric.

This chapter adds to the growing body of literature on FPIC and consultation procedures being followed in the Salamago Woreda in the South Omo Zone of Ethiopia. This chapter is a call for developing more humanizing ways of advancing FPIC (e.g. procedural guidelines, local consent protocols and strategic land use planning) in order to develop more transparent and context-specific guidelines and also to demand their application retrospectively to projects in advanced stages of development (Anaya, Evans and Kemp 2017: 2). While consent in retrospect does not constitute FPIC, it is possible, however, for the ESC to retrospectively address prior impacts on customary land and resource rights (ibid.:

29) as experienced, for example, by the Mela and Chirim (referred to as Bodi by outsiders), who have been the first to relocate (Buffavand, this volume). This is not only critical for restoring the dignity[8] of the Mun (see Atuahene 2016 on the importance of 'dignity restoration') but also for determining their conditions for entering into FPIC negotiations prior to their anticipated relocation. Since the Mun have not yet moved to any government-planned villages, most Mun base their ideas of 'prior consent' on the experiences of the Mela and Chirim and see them as conditional to remedying those problems associated with the transition to irrigation farming (see Anaya, Evans and Kemp 2017: 29), which has so far been a dehumanizing experience (Stevenson and Buffavand 2018; Buffavand, this volume). In the quest for equitable solutions to the prospect of development in southern Ethiopia, one of the challenges inherent in the current model of rapid, large-scale development is the lack of any meaningful understanding of the concerns and knowledge of customary land use practices and local consent practices of Mun and other agro-pastoralists.

In this chapter, I draw on the work of scholars such as Owen and Kemp, who insist that in order for FPIC to be meaningful and transparent, 'the users of the framework must be capable of identifying, analysing and incorporating local socio-historical knowledge and anthropological data into decision-making frameworks' (2014: 96). However, questions arise such as: whose responsibility is it to decide on the kind of social knowledge to include? Is it realistic to expect that industry leaders become conversant in such topics? (ibid.). In considering these questions, I look at current FPIC research, including empirical studies on the KSDP, its consultation procedures and the initial impacts of and local responses to the project.[9] I argue that comprehensive baseline studies that include local knowledge are the responsibility of ESC industry leaders and are still urgently required.[10] Research shows that if all stakeholders, especially industry leaders, are socially responsible when it comes to developing a deep knowledge base of existing land use practices, networks of social exchange and local decision-making processes, development agreements will be more equitable and conflicts in the area will be far fewer (Owen and Kemp 2014; see Gabbert 2018).[11] While my focus is mainly on local consent procedures associated with customary land use in Mun, I also consider legal and policy protections within the context of FPIC as recommended in the literature and by the Mun community.

I begin, however, by providing some background context with respect to the Mun, the ESC and growing criticism about consent procedures related to sugar cane development and villagization programmes in southern Ethiopia. I then consider how such criticism compares to local Mun experiences, framing them within the context of international human rights discourse, which emphasizes that 'FPIC processes must be free from manipulation or coercion; allow adequate time for traditional decision-making processes; facilitate the sharing of objective, accurate, and easily understandable information; and ensure community agreement' (UN

2011). Finally, I present ethnographic evidence of local consent processes associated with customary land use in Mun, with the intention of motivating those interested in improving FPIC standards in the Salamago Woreda and beyond.

The Mun, the Ethiopian Sugar Corporation and Its Critics

The Mun are an agro-pastoral people of southern Ethiopia with a population of 6,916 according to most recent official figures (CSA 2007). The name they use for themselves is 'Mun' (sing. 'Muni') or 'Taama' (in ritual/historical contexts), and they speak *tuga Munin* (the 'Mun' language), a Surmic, Nilo-Saharan language that is closely related to but also distinct from that of the Suri to the west and north-west. They live along and between Mago and Omo National Parks and identify themselves in terms of the families, clans, geographical places and territorial sections (called *bhuranyoga*) of which they are a part. The Mun herd mainly cattle but also goats and sheep. They cultivate sorghum and maize, beans and squash, and collect over fifty varieties of edible leaves and other wild plants, as well as medicinal plants, for both people and livestock (LaTosky and Olibui, forthcoming). They engage in transhumant agro-pastoralism, which involves flood-retreat and rain-fed cultivation of sorghum and maize and the seasonal migration of livestock between lowland and highland areas. In 2011, the future of Munland (*baa Munin*) became more uncertain than ever, as the state-owned ESC entered Mun with the intention of turning 200,000 hectares of land along the Omo River into sugar cane plantations.[12] Other areas within Mun (e.g. Makki) have been earmarked for private and state-owned investments, but information is limited. The majority of Mun have little knowledge of how (and by whom) their customary lands will be used and accessed in the future, and even fewer details of when they will relocate to five government-planned villages.[13] While the principles of customary land ownership are straightforward to the Mun, the realities are much more complex. The most obvious point of complexity is that the Ethiopian state does not formally recognize the land tenure and resource rights of agropastoralists.[14] To date, the government has not sought to demarcate traditional lands or provide legislative or administrative protections of customary land use and occupancy rights as mandated by most international human rights courts.

Within the South Omo Zone, Bench Maji Zone and Keffa Zone of SNNPRS, the KSDP has cleared vast tracts of land for sugar cane plantations and has built processing factories, all of which are at different phases of construction and financial uncertainty.[15] Owned and operated by the state-run ESC, the KSDP has sugar estates in the Salamago Woreda, which affects mainly the Mun (Mursi) and Mela and Chirim (Bodi) agro-pastoralists and the Kwegu, who have some cattle but mainly fish and cultivate along the banks of the Omo River. The ESC has never had to declare that it is operating on the collective lands of the Mun, Mela, Chirim and Kwegu because according to the Ethiopian Constitution land is owned by the state.

While the ESC claims that it has demonstrated an awareness of 'social responsibility' towards agro-pastoralists like the Mun, Mela and Chirim,[16] many critics disagree that the ESC and KSDP have embraced the core principles of corporate social responsibility, which includes transparent FPIC procedures (Tewolde and Fana forthcoming).[17] In the absence of proper consultation, Yidneckachew (2015: 294) contextualizes the current state of development in Salamago Woreda as follows:

> OKSDP [Omo Kuraz Sugar Development Project], which acquired vast land, has abrogated the traditional communal land title and administration,[18] access to the river, grazing land and the forest of Bodi, Mursi, Bacha [Kwegu] and Dimme[19] ethnic groups in the Salamago district of South Omo. This commercial farming is a potential threat that restricts access to biodiversity, wild food and environmental interaction and eliminates valuable resources such as climate-resilient crops and medicinal plants. Besides, it evicts them from their land, territories and resources; and marginalizes them from their spiritual, cultural, social and economic relationship with their traditional lands. Further, the project has the intent to transform the socio-economic and cultural reality of pastoralists. These situations call for proper consultation of the pastoralist communities.

Claims of improper consultation procedures have been made for other parts of Ethiopia as well. The Oakland Institute's report from November 2014 on consultative procedures in Suri (Chai and Tirmaga), the majority of whom live in the Bench Maji Zone (on the western side of the Omo River), was one of the first to critique the government for its lack of transparency when consulting local communities about villagization plans (see especially Wagstaff (2015: 15) on the absence of any rights-based approach to development in Suri).[20]

> Research and interviews in the area suggest that the '*sefara*' [resettlement] process has been marked by an absence of meaningful consultations with communities to be displaced, contradicting the Ethiopian government and international donors' claim of voluntary settlement. When the government does approach the community for consultations, the meetings function primarily as announcements of relocation. (Oakland Institute 2014: 14)

A recent study by Stevenson and Buffavand (2018: 115) makes similar claims for the Salamago Woreda:

> It was not until planning was well underway that the government arranged public meetings to announce the villagization plan, and little

effort was made to accommodate local ideas about the layout of the sites or the kinds of livelihood that would be possible there.

Despite these and other empirically grounded critiques that 'proper consultation is still needed' and that 'meetings function primarily as announcements of relocation' and 'a test of allegiance than a discussion of the problems communities may encounter' (Buffavand, this volume),[21] the ESC defends its procedures and claims of obtaining 'full consent' even though a clear FPIC agenda has yet to be implemented or made available.[22]

> The EPRDF government, while launching Omo-Kuraz Sugar Development Project and also other projects some six years back, gave priority to all forms of benefit of natives of the project areas. Accordingly, prior to the inception of the project, the government had held successive discussions with the locals of the area as well as the concerned people and had started running the project [after] getting [what they claimed was] their *full consent*. (ESC 2017; emphasis added)

The question of what 'full consent' means – or should mean – in the context of development in Ethiopia, and more specifically South Omo, is precisely what critics have come to challenge. While it is nothing new or novel in proposing that obtaining FPIC should have been – and should continue to be – a priority for investors, including state-run corporations like the ESC, what is still overlooked by the ESC is the retrospective application of clear guidelines on 'free, prior, informed consent', how it can (or should) be validated and how local knowledge and notions of 'consent' factor into such consent processes. Otherwise, the definition of FPIC could impose a non-consensual understanding of consent and FPIC on Indigenous and minority groups (Young 2020: 6).

In the next part of the chapter, I explore what FPIC is and how it is interpreted in Ethiopia and practised in southern Ethiopia today (see also Tewolde and Fana, forthcoming), and I outline what it means for agro-pastoralists such as the Mun of South Omo to give informed consent. Finally, I highlight some of the recommendations made in the literature as well as those made by the Mun, who have come to recognize that their rights to FPIC are being violated. Here I suggest a proactive position that the ESC and its partners should take in order to engage seriously in meaningful and transparent consultation processes (Laplante and Spears 2014).

FPIC, UNDRIP and the Multiple Meanings of Informed Consent

FPIC is used to describe a fundamental human right of indigenous peoples to give consent to or withhold consent from developments that may impact their lands or resources (MacDonald and Zezulka 2015: 8). However, there is no universally accepted definition of FPIC, no agreement on what an FPIC process must entail and no clarity about what constitutes 'consent' (Owen and Kemp 2014). The process of FPIC centres on voluntary participation and the ability of individuals and groups to comprehend a full range of relevant, adequate and complete information about development procedures and their benefits and risks. Although most international guidelines suggest that consent processes should be determined locally, not all states, Ethiopia among them,[23] feel obliged to honour the final version of Article 32 of the UN Declaration on the Rights of Indigenous Peoples (UNDRIP), which establishes that:

> [States] shall consult and cooperate in good faith with the indigenous peoples concerned through their own representative institutions in order to obtain their free and informed consent prior to the approval of any project affecting their lands or territories and other resources.[24]

Although it is probably unrealistic to develop a universal definition of consent given the diversity of legal systems and cultures in which these laws operate, a range of initiatives and useful guidelines and definitions are advocated through international policy.[25] Mauro Barelli's article 'Free, Prior and Informed Consent in the Aftermath of the UN Declaration on the Rights of Indigenous Peoples' provides a useful starting point for defining free, prior and informed consent:

> Free – no coercion, intimidation or manipulation.

> Prior – consent must be sought in advance of any authorization or commencement of activities; agents should guarantee enough time for the indigenous consultation/consensus processes to take place.

> Informed – people must receive satisfactory information in relation to key areas, including the nature, size, pace, reversibility and scope of the proposed project, the reasons for launching it, its duration, and a preliminary assessment of its economic, social, cultural and environmental impact. Crucially this information should be accurate and in a form that is accessible, meaning that the language used should be fully understood by the peoples affected.

> Consent – a process of which consultation and participation represent central pillars. Consultation should be undertaken in good faith, while full and equitable participation of indigenous peoples should be guaranteed. Indigenous peoples should also have equal access to financial, human and material resources in order to engage constructively in this

discussion. Moreover, indigenous peoples should be able to participate through their own freely chosen representatives and according to their customs. (Barelli 2012: 2)

While many companies and government organizations in Ethiopia include the rhetoric of stakeholder engagement – inclusiveness, transparency, participatory, consensus building, flexibility, effective communication[26] – details of consultative procedures are usually lacking. Consultation seems to be used synonymously with consent, and the Ethiopian state, which sees itself as acting in the best interests of agro-pastoralists, does not formally recognize the land use and occupancy rights of agro-pastoralists.

Fulfilling the duty to consult and receiving 'full consent' are used interchangeably (ESC 2017) without defining the conditions for fulfilling either. Yidneckachew (2015: 281) explains, 'the FDRE Constitution clearly specifies the right of nations, nationalities and peoples to participate in national development and, in particular, to be consulted with respect to policies and projects affecting them', 'to be consulted' is not the same as 'to give consent'.[27] Legal scholars Laplante and Spears (2014: 87) make a distinction between consultation and consent:

FPIC differs importantly from consultation in the way decision-making authority is exercised and legitimated. Whereas consultation processes require only that extractive industry companies hear the views of those potentially affected by a project and take them into account when engaging in decision-making processes, consent processes require that host communities actually participate in decision-making processes.

While the provisions and laws of the Ethiopian Constitution, according to Adem (2009: 36), include 'assurance against displacement' and 'the right to FPIC', these rights become meaningless if there is no option to 'meaningfully withhold consent' (MacDonald and Zezulka 2015), a point to which I return later. For now, I only reiterate Adem's point to show that 'the right to FPIC' is as arbitrary as the right to occupy and use land.

The Constitution prescribes the right to private ownership of property of every Ethiopian citizen (Article 40). This is, however, an individual right that does not apply to groups like indigenous peoples. Moreover, the right to land and natural resources therein are exclusively vested in the state and the peoples of Ethiopia: 'Ethiopian pastoralists have the right to freely obtain land for grazing and cultivation and are guaranteed against displacement.' The assurance against displacement seems absolute; hence, the right to FPIC features with this package.

When addressing the arbitrary nature in which the government expropriates land, Data Dea (2017: 243n13) reminds us that any assurance against the forced relocation of agro-pastoralists is far from absolute:

While it is clearly stated in article 40(3) of the constitution that 'the right to own land is exclusively vested in the state and peoples of Ethiopia,' in practice, . . . the state routinely violates land rights of the people. For example, in its proclamation 456/2005, the EPRDF government discarded the constitutional disguise on who actually owns land. Article 5(3) of this proclamation is worded 'Government being the owner of rural land'.

A similar picture emerges when assessing the arbitrary actions of the government with regard to large-scale sugar cane development and villagization in southern Ethiopia.

How Did the Mun Give Their 'Full Consent'?

Mun accounts, as I will show below, are consistent with what researchers have found in Mela and Chirim and other parts of Ethiopia where agro-pastoralists are affected by large-scale development and villagization plans.[28] The main predicaments that the Mun are facing in their area are the result of coercion and a lack of access to both information and decision-making. The interviews conducted with Mun informants mainly between 2011 and 2014, shortly after the government had announced its plans and began to build the KSDP in South Omo, are outlined below.[29] While these summaries could be interpreted as biased, since all informants experienced coercion on some level, further interviews since 2014 have shown that these cases are not isolated and have become more the norm than the exception.[30]

Coercion was evident in the use of overt threats – harassment, intimidation, disarmament, imprisonment by the South Omo Police, Salamago Woreda and South Omo zonal officials – and, in several recent cases, the use of lethal force, especially by military personnel, but also in more insidious ways, like restricted access to information, decision-making, persuasion through payments, the lack of grievance mechanisms and various other 'encroachments on dignity' (McSherry and Freckelton 2013).[31] The majority of informants reported that 'instead of asking our permission, they [the government] came, set up a military base in the Mun village of Meganto, and announced their plans'. As one Muni informant explained to me in 2011 and, again, in 2013:

They began to talk to us after the military and bulldozers had already arrived. Three military tanks arrived after these initial talks in Meganto [photos of the tanks are shown]. The Mun said that they would only move once they had seen if the Bodi produce enough corn on their one-hectare plots. Even if local officials think we have agreed, for the Mun, to give consent means something more than simply saying, 'Yes, we agree'. What they [the government officials] don't understand is that an agreement is always conditional; it is based on future observations and obligations. If we don't like what we see in the future, say in one or two years from now, we will not consent to anything. They [government officials] do not understand that 'yes' means 'yes, we will see'. (Personal communication with a Muni man, name withheld, 12 May 2013)

My findings show that the majority of Mun did not have enough information to make an informed decision as to why they should 'voluntarily' move in the future to the one-hectare plots (that people were told would be available by 2017) in government-planned villages, some of which had still not been officially decided on.[32] None of the informants felt that they had any power to veto the decision without incurring negative consequences. Many men and women said that they were afraid to attend government meetings or express their grievances.[33] Of the 32 Mun men and 18 Mun women selected for this chapter, not one of them reported being asked by government officials about the chosen location of the new villages. Both of the two literate informants complained that no information sheets, maps or documents were provided beforehand to show where the government was planning to settle the Mun. All of the people whom I interviewed from Baruba said that they felt pressured to settle and that they did not know if they would be able to return to their homes once they moved to the new government villages, especially if promises were not kept and their quality of life did not improve. One unanswered question was whether some people would be allowed to opt out of villagization and continue their agro-pastoralist life.[34] Many informants suspected that their homes would be destroyed and their land taken by the government once they were relocated to one of the five villages: Makki (near the Mago River), Romos (approximately 9 km from the Mara River), Muturro (near the Omo River crossing to Omo National Park), Madhok (near Moizo) and Tawanya (south of Moizo).

While over 60 Mun men and 30 Mun women were formally and informally interviewed between 2011 and 2014, the informants included here were selected because (a) they had been directly involved in consultative processes, (b) they were respected in their communities and (c) they represented clans from the five territorial sections that overlap with the planned resettlement sites. When asked about the purpose of 'villagization', over 95 per cent said that the government had promised to bring them schools and health clinics (see Fana, this volume). While many informants were open to the idea of sending their children to school, all agreed that a mobile school and clinic in their area was better than moving to the lowlands. Most expressed discontent about the open lowland areas selected, which the people of Baruba declared as 'mosquito infested' and inhospitable. Most participants reported never being told about the development procedures (the location of government-planned villages, building roads, cutting off grazing areas or having limited, if any, access to seasonal cultivation sites along the Omo River).[35] The benefits and risks were not explained in an understandable way. Direct benefits beyond education and healthcare included grinding mills, irrigation systems and water pumps, but social risks involved in resettlement (e.g. alcoholism, HIV, rupture in the social order) were never clearly discussed, with the exception of informants from Makki, who were said to be hard negotiators with more experience talking to the government. All participants claimed that the Mun from Romos and Muturro who had 'agreed' to the resettlement had been paid a per diem for attending meetings and discussions and/or were being paid government salaries. It remains unclear how individual consent was validated by the ESC, although payments seems to be one means for obtaining consent (see Buffavand, this volume). As one Muni informant explained: 'The one they call "*balabat*" (leader in Amharic) in Romos gets 2,000 Ethiopian birr per month [roughly 62 Euro] to keep the peace. He just goes along with their plans and tries to convince others to do the same.' The same informant, whose name remains anonymous, continued:

> They are paying some of us 1,000 Ethiopian birr to be watchmen, though I do not live in Romos. I have gone there [to Romos] three times now [a four-hour round trip on foot] to get my salary, but they keep telling me to come back again. That's their way to keep me working. They make me run like a dog back and forth for my salary . . . I tell them that I agree, but nobody from Mara wants to go there. You know the place. We will burn up [in the sun] – this is no place for our children or cattle.[36]

By 2014, around a dozen Mun were employed as watchmen, drivers and translators, and several dozen young men were recruited into the South Police force for the first time in history. Even if it were true that there have been '6,695 jobs created for locals in 2015' (ESC 2015), which includes not only the Mun but also the Mela and Chirim (Bodi), Kwegu, Dime, Konso and Ari, so far it has not been the Mun who have benefitted from jobs promised by the ESC.[37] Young Mun men who finished school and then started to work at the sugar factories have 'forgot [*sic*] about their people, [and started] drinking, chew(ing) [*sic*] the *khat* and [became] violent'.[38]

The informants also highlighted the use of intimidation and discrimination by migrant workers, military and government officials.[39] Such discriminatory attitudes also include ambitious campaigns to eradicate so-called 'harmful cultural practices', which are often blamed as being a deterrent for development in agro-pastoralists communities (LaTosky 2015: 170).[40]

> Romos is bad! The workers call us 'baboons', insult us and cheat us at the clinic. I wear clothes so they respect me. . . . But even then Mun are

not allowed to shower in the [common] shower house built for [migrant] workers, which now has a big fence around it to keep the Mun out.[41]

The majority of men feared that refusing to move to the government-planned villages in the future would have political repercussions. Women also feared that their husbands would be put in prison if they did not move with their children to Romos or Muturro in the future. Everyone knew of *at least* one Muni man who had been imprisoned or arrested for unknown reasons since 2011(see also Buffavand on figures in Mela, this volume).

From this preliminary evaluation of the first consultative procedures in Mun, it becomes increasingly evident that the ESC has not incorporated the Mun peoples' fundamental right to free, prior and informed consent with respect to their ongoing relationship with their traditional lands. That is, socially appropriate and meaningful consultation with the Mun has not taken place, and receiving their 'full consent' is still urgently required if the Mun are to be left with some dignity, a say in protecting affected areas and the opportunity to retrospectively renegotiate benefits and compensation based on prior impacts in Mela and Chirim. Makki is an exceptional case, since elders and younger men who attended the meetings have had more frequent and open conversations with the zonal authorities from Jinka and managers of the ESC than in other areas of Mun. First of all, the Mun of Makki have already voluntarily 'settled' along the Mago River after migrating there in the early 1980s in search of a cooler environment,[42] and therefore do not have to relocate as do the majority of Mun. Second, Mun living in Makki were the first to receive and accept basic healthcare and education services provided by missionaries over two decades ago, and thus have more experience negotiating with the government about basic needs and benefits. Their past experiences working with the government and missionaries have thus made it easier for the Mun of Makki to negotiate their terms, at least on a conditional basis, although the development plans in their area are on a much smaller scale than those along the Omo River. In short, the Mun in Makki can remain in an area that they have already chosen and where they had already negotiated a number of basic services (e.g. a clinic and the first mother-tongue Mun school – grades 1–3) with missionaries and government.

As one elder explained:

In Makki, the elders agreed to the government's [villagization] plans, but only if we get the things we asked for – a grinding mill, ambulance service, a school [from grades 5–8]. Also, the training of Mun teachers and healthcare workers should continue. Now the clinic is run by the government. The missionaries always had all the medicines, but now this has changed. They used to walk from Meganto to Makki to get medicine because the government clinic never had anything. Now, already the medicines are lacking here too. We hope this is not a bad sign for the future.

. . .

In the beginning, the chief administrator, Moloka, went to Makki; he spent three days talking to elders. It was good. . . . Now, they say they will start to build irrigation canals. The village is not in the place that we would have chosen, but now we will wait and see if they keep their promises. In Makki we want another school, but we don't know if irrigation will be good or not. Paul [an Australian missionary] showed us this, but we went back to our ways [of growing sorghum]. We will wait and see. (Interview with a Muni elder, name withheld, 8 July 2014).

So that meaningful consent processes could take place, rather than just strategic bargaining, as was the case in Makki, I spoke with those involved in the Makki meetings and other public consultations in order to draft a list of recommendations of how FPIC should – and should not – be approached in Mun, particularly within the context of current changing land use practices.[43] The main suggestion for improving participation in FPIC was to understand local consent processes and land use planning, which I highlight below.

Obtaining Consent in Mun

Consent is a complex issue associated with the communication of information, comprehension, autonomy and choice. In Mun, to say 'I agree' '*Anye kigomoinyo*' (pl. '*Agge kigomnoinyo*') means the same as 'I consent' and is almost always conditional.[44] In other words, to agree or to give consent is a fluid concept and can be negotiated and renegotiated depending on the circumstances. To agree/consent to something is often an indirect expression to avoid hurting or insulting others, or to save face (for example, to avoid being thought of as a stingy person, called a *gongai*, by refusing someone's request). I learned early on in my fieldwork that refusal to agree is almost never expressed with a curt 'no' (LaTosky 2013). Instead, one usually says, 'Yes, I'll give it to you later on' (*Eeh miso na hali kariye*) or 'Wait and we'll give it to you in the future' (*Ga meso na hali hali kariye*). That is, one usually agrees, at least partially, to a direct request because it is considered unacceptable, even rude, to blatantly refuse the request of another. This is why many agreements carry with them the explicit understanding that they need not be fulfilled immediately. There is also the implicit understanding that they are reversible, not definitive, if the person does not honour his end of the agreement.[45] An agreement (or debt) can persist across generations (Turton 1973) and is a kind of tacit understanding, which means that others understand what they have in mind and what they are agreeing to without necessarily being told. Given the high illiteracy rates in Mun, many still view informed written consent with great suspicion, as it reminds them of past misunderstandings with the government.[46] One recent example of such a misunderstanding occurred in 2004, when the Ethiopian government entered into a public–private partnership with African Parks Foundation (APF) and signed a 25-year agreement that would allow APF to manage Omo National Park (ONP) without first consulting the Mun and other local communities who use and occupy areas within and around the park (see www.mursi.org).

Cultivating and Grazing Within and Between *Bhuranyoga*

When it comes to obtaining consent about land and resources, the Mun divide land into three main categories: cultivated land (*baa gunyang*),[47] grazing land (*missa iwoyn*) and sacred lands (*badhinya*) or ritual places (*baa barrara*). The Mun people also live in and identify with five territorial sections called *bhuranyoga*. These are Baruba (or Mara), Mugjo, Biyogolokarre, Gongolobibi and Ariholi (Turton 1979). People move freely across and between *bhuranyoga* with their cattle and can cultivate in any area, although along the banks of major river courses such as the Omo River, Mago River and Elma River, verbal consent must be obtained to use cultivation sites and water resources that belong to certain families and clan members. People must inform others before moving to new cultivation sites. The same does not apply to grazing land, which is considered open access for every Mun, just as hot springs (*ra*) and salt licks (*garsan*) can be openly accessed by all Mun (Tefera et al. 2016). If one is a guest in another *bhuranyoga* or neighbouring ethnic community, he will inform those in the area, drawing also on social exchange networks, such as bondfriends.[48]

Decisions about when and where to herd and cultivate are made only by men, including the young men and boys who herd the cattle (ibid.). Serious matters, like the clearing of new cultivation sites, are discussed between families and clans and ultimately decided upon by the ritual leader (called a *komoru*) and his advisors.[49] If a certain area is to be banned from grazing, only the *komoru* can decide on this, together with elders. If the *komoru* makes such a decision, nobody will move to that area or interfere with his decision. To impose restrictions on traditional grazing areas is a violation of Mun customary law, especially if no consent is sought from the local priest and his advisors. To deny open access rangelands is considered a great offence and the cause of many conflicts (ibid.).

Sacred Land (*Baa barrara*)

When the Mun refer to sacred places, this includes powerful ritual sites, called *badhinya* (sing. *badhi*) in Mun, which include ancestral and protected landscapes (e.g. sacred groves) accessed only by ritual leaders. Other sacred sites used for public ritual purposes are called *dhebinya* (clay pits for traditional rituals) and *ngawunya* (sing. *ngawu*), which are places for important community rituals (e.g. cattle blessing rituals called *bio lama*). Information disclosure is a big issue when it comes to sacred lands, since the Mun themselves are not allowed access to all of them (some of which, like the *badhinya*, serve as secret ritual sites for Mun ritual leaders and ancestral burial grounds).[50] To not seek consent when it comes to entering land considered sacred (*baa barrara*) is to disrespect the *komoru*, ancestral spirits, customs and religion, as well as the future well-being of the people. These areas are protected by the community. A person who trespasses on a *badhi*, cuts a tree or fetches firewood from such a site, will bring misfortune, according to Mun beliefs. The most common consequence is that a person or his cattle will be killed by a snake or attacked by a hyena or lion.

To summarize, in all three categories of land there is a necessity of disclosure to individuals, clans, families and, in cases of restricted access, the *komoru*. The first example of consent in Mun shows how people must seek permission to cultivate on someone else's land. If people want to move into or share a new area, they will come together and kill a favourite ox. As one Muni man explained:

> For the Mun, killing the favourite ox is like signing a document; it means a big decision has been made that cannot be reversed. So far, the Ethiopian Sugar Corporation has not respected Mun customary traditions, nor has there been any discussion of compensating the Mun for the loss of cultivation sites along the Omo River.

In the second example, anyone can be permitted to use traditional grazing lands. The only time that official consent is needed is when cattle are moved to a new area, or when grasslands are burned or certain rangelands banned, in which case consent must be obtained from the *komoru*. Younger men, even herding boys, can advise. Thus, to be told that grazing is not permitted in a certain area is a violation of Mun customary law, especially if the *komoru* has not been consulted and alternative grazing areas have not been negotiated.

A final example in which consent is needed is in relation to decisions about the hundreds of sacred sites in Munland. To disrespect access rights – for example, by refraining from seeking permission to enter a certain sacred place – will bring, according to Mun, serious harm to others. One Muni informant explained that 'to destroy a *badhi* is the same as destroying a church or a mosque'. The ESC is not aware of their existence and is clearing sacred sites of the Mun people. Informed consent is, according to the Mun, straightforward if local consent processes regarding land use decisions – especially those related to seasonal grazing zones, cultivation sites and important sacred sites – are understood and respected.

Conclusion

In southern Ethiopia, obtaining free, prior and informed consent from the Mun community still requires a 'radical recalibration' (Owen and Kemp 2014) of how to engage openly in critical discussions about land use planning without fear of reprisals. This will only be possible if investors like the ESC and the government relinquish their defensive positions and firmly believe that FPIC standards must be enforced, enduring and meaningful (Laplante and Spears 2014: 69). For Mun, a meaningful agreement is based on certain conditions and a tacit understanding of how and when the agreement should be honoured. Mun consent can be reversible, as it relies on others to disclose information, especially when it comes to land use practices. The destruction of sacred sites is, for the Mun, proof that their customary rights and cultural values are disrespected. In the legal discourse, the Mun would be referred to as victims of 'dignity takings', which occur when property is destroyed or confiscated by the state from owners or occupiers who are not paid just compensation and who are treated in dehumanizing and infantilizing ways (Atuahene 2016).

Understanding the Mun social and political order includes, above all, respecting how decisions are made, how they assert their own categories of 'territory', or *bhuranyoga*, and their preferences for using and maintaining culturally significant places and resources now and in the future. Another priority is that future resettlement to government-planned villages, if at all, should be decided on by the Mun and carried out according to their social organization and political institutions and in ways that respect their territorial organization (see Turton 1973). There was a general consensus that people should be resettled but not be put together (especially ritual leaders) with people from different *bhuranyoga*. A refusal by the ESC to respect the nature of Mun relationships and their obligations to particular territorial sections and the ritual leaders and inhabitants of those places were, based on the majority of informants, to be grounds to refuse consent to move to government-planned villages.

Many concerned scholars have already provided recommendations about mitigating negative impacts of large-scale development on agro-pastoralists in Ethiopia. One promising suggestion comes from legal scholar Adem (2009: 45), who urges a careful reconsideration of the UNDRIP, and domestic laws around the world, in order to recognize that Ethiopia's Indigenous peoples, which includes agro-pastoralists like the Mun, obtain the dignified and collective right to access and occupy their land and to transparent FPIC procedures:

> [T]he Ethiopian government should ratify ILO 169 and adopt a new law dealing with the rights of indigenous peoples explicitly recognising their collective right to land and FPIC. It should require identification of existing indigenous peoples based on international and African standards

and establish independent monitoring institutions. The Constitution should be amended to guarantee the right to FPIC regarding indigenous peoples.

Besides giving priority to the legal recognition of land rights and the right to FPIC (FAO 2016), others are pushing for more political representation and participation of agro-pastoralist peoples in Salamago Woreda in formal decision-making bodies (Tewolde and Fana 2014). Many researchers are also encouraging donors, investors and government to consider the value of long-term anthropological studies for understanding social knowledge, which includes, but is by no means limited to, local consent processes (Abbink et al. 2014). Turton's work on the Mun, which spans over 40 years, is invaluable proof of this. My sharing of Mun experiences and highlighting their local consent processes within the context of customary land use is to advance the idea that any discussion about FPIC should be characterized by mutual respect and understanding of the practical knowledge and expertise of agro-pastoralists in sustainably shaping land use. Only through meaningful FPIC procedures, applied retrospectively, can the dignity of the Mun and other indigenous peoples of the Salamago Woreda be restored.

For many years, the Mun have been asking anthropologists, missionaries, wildlife conservationists, political scientists, government and industry leaders and members of civil society organizations to help them develop their own 'basic services' and, more recently, a strategic land use plan that would allow for agro-pastoralism, wildlife conservation and sugar cane plantations to coexist (see Little et al. 2010). I would like, therefore, to ask fellow colleagues, industry leaders from ESC, the Mun community, government ministries and civil society to come together to draft an integrated land use plan that includes the right to meaningful consultation. Giving the Mun a meaningful role in decision-making 'might result, for example, in the introduction of mobile schools and in policies (like mobile veterinary services) designed to encourage and facilitate the combination of settled agriculture with mobile herding'.[51] Moreover, giving priority to an FPIC agenda, retrospectively, that includes local knowledge of consent and customary land use planning will not only improve the ESC's reputation, both locally and globally, but such knowledge will help to mitigate conflicts and possibly avoid potential public litigation in the future.

Shauna LaTosky is a research affiliate at the Max Planck Institute for Social Anthropology (Halle/Saale), where she served as Director of the South Omo Research Center and completed her postdoctoral studies in 2015. She has written on Mun women, health, education and traditional land use practices. Her current research consists of an extensive ethnobotanical study of Mun edible and medicinal plants for which an ethnographic film in the *Guardians of Productive Landscapes* series is underway.

Notes

I am grateful to the Max Planck Institute for Social Anthropology for its financial and intellectual support. I would also like to thank David Turton for his encouragement, and all Mun informants for sharing what it means to give (and withdraw) consent and struggle for environmental and social justice.

1. FPIC procedures are sometimes used as a bureaucratic tool to legitimize state and corporate control over controversial development and land grabs as a result of 'interpretive manipulations' (Dunlap 2018).
2. FPIC principles are backed by the United Nations Declaration on the Rights of Indigenous Peoples (UNDRIP), the Convention on Biological Diversity, and the International Labour Organization Convention 169.
3. Mun (sing. Muni) is their self-designation, and Mursi is the name used by outsiders.
4. The ESC has been responsible for all aspects of the KSDP project (Kamski 2016b: 570), which is supposed to include 'basic social services, infrastructures, employment opportunities and social development schemes as negotiated benefits so as to penetrate the society and to transform the pastoralist communities into a more settled way of life' (Yidneckachew 2015: 289).
5. See Kamski (2016a: 2) for a map of the project.
6. Flood-retreat cultivation has not been possible for several consecutive years because of the disruption of the flow of the Omo River.
7. Yields from experimental irrigated plots near Kuraz III disappoint, in part because of their lack of control over water.
8. Dignity is meant in the sense of 'empowering people to assume full control over their own lives and, as a corollary, preventing others from intruding into those lives, unless free, prior, informed consent has been granted' (Somsen 2017: 356). Mun dignity could be restored, for example, with ecological protection and restoration and financial compensation.
9. See Stevenson and Buffavand (2018).
10. Kamski (2016b: 567) points to the pressure on the ESC to complete the KSDP to meet Growth and Transformation Plan I targets as the main reason why 'the corporation has skipped important preparatory works'. This ought to include the assessment and disclosure of potential operational hazards and local vulnerabilities, and baseline studies on the agricultural and pastoral practices of peoples like the Mun and 'their profound practical knowledge of the flood regime' (Turton, this volume).
11. For effective approaches to FPIC, see MacDonald and Zezulka (2015) and Young (2020).
12. Originally, 245,000 hectares were allocated by the government to the ESC in SNNPRS and later reduced to 175,000 hectares (Kamski 2016b: 569). As of 2016, 10,600 hectares of land had been cultivated and an additional 13,000 hectares cleared in Salamago Woreda for sugar cane (ibid.: 574).
13. Tewolde and Fana (2014: 123 fn14) quote an official saying that the original plan was '[t]o put all Mursi in one village, [but] based on demand from the Mursi community, a second village will be prepared near the Maki River'. This is inconsistent with the first 'Villagization Plan in Salamago Woreda', in which three villages were planned in Hailewoha (known as Meganto in Mun) (SNNPRS 2012). By 2018, five villages were being prepared.
14. See Turton, this volume.
15. See Kamski (2016a and 2016b) and Turton (this volume). See also Kamski (2019) on the growing concerns over ESC's indebtedness and planned privatization of sugar estates.

16. Remarkably, the ESC's website observes that 'social responsibility' refers to helping 'willing natives' to settle in villages to prevent them from 'wandering around in search of grazing land and water' (ESC 2017).

17. Criticism also points to gaps and contradictions in the ESC's understanding of the social and environmental impacts. While some claim that 'controlled flooding' will be a permanent measure taken to compensate people for any adverse impacts from the upstream dam, others claim that controlled flooding will only be temporary (Turton, this volume).

18. 'Communal land rights' would have been more accurate than 'title' here, since one cannot refer to 'title' without an administrative process of defining ownership and generating title certificates (email communication from John Galaty, 12 July 2018).

19. The Dime are highland agriculturalists who do not rely on flood-retreat agriculture along the Omo River.

20. The first report, by Human Rights Watch (2012: 5), made recommendations that development strategies 'should strive to find a balance between respecting the traditional way of life of indigenous communities and the duty to respect their free, prior, and informed consent, while allowing the government of Ethiopia to meet its own development goals for the area'.

21. According to Buffavand (this volume), 'Mela feel that their consent has been obtained at gunpoint.'

22. Similar allegations have been made for the Suri (see Wagstaff 2015: 24), the Afar (Rettberg 2010) and in the Gambella region, where government villagization programmes are said to 'lack free, prior and informed consent of the indigenous minority groups in the area' (SMNE [Solidarity Movement for a New Ethiopia], quoted in Meckelburg 2014: 158).

23. Ethiopia was not a signatory of this declaration.

24. UNDRIP (2007). A number of states that have included FPIC in their legislation (e.g. the Philippines and Peru) are also heavily criticized for repeatedly failing to enforce it (Fox and Sutton 2012: 12).

25. See especially Greenspan (2014), UN-REDD Programme (2013) and FAO (2014) on practical guidelines, which have had their own share of complications, especially in terms of undermining indigenous autonomy (see Laltaika and Askew, this volume).

26. See, for example, Ethiopian Wildlife Conservation Authority (2013).

27. For an analysis of how consultation is framed in both English and Amharic versions of the Constitution, see Tewolde and Fana (forthcoming).

28. See especially Stevenson and Buffavand (2018); Rettberg (2010); Turton, this volume.

29. Many of these interviews were incidental to other research. As one of the only researchers present when the bulldozers and military vehicles arrived in Jinka in 2011 to initiate the first stages of a so-called 'public consultation' with local communities, it was impossible to ignore the concerns and anxieties of people. Many agro-pastoralists came to the South Omo Research Centre (where I worked as its director) from northern Mun and Mela to share their concerns without fear of reprisals.

30. Reports of intimidation, harassment, imprisonment and use of lethal force by the police and military were shared in April 2018, between May and December 2019 and, again, in July 2020. Targeted were educated boys and men accused of being 'friends of the whites' and/or 'anti-development agents' (see Yidneckachew 2015: 287). On 30 August, 2018, Ethiopian soldiers surrounded the village of Bhele and attacked its residents, killing one Muni man and critically wounding another. Between October and December 2019, forced disarmament campaigns resulted in unprecedented violence carried out by the Ethiopian military against the Mun, Mela and Chirim (see Concerned Scholars Ethiopia

(CSE), 2019). In July 2020, military attacked unarmed Mun men, beat an elder, shot a young man in the leg and killed Lugolonybanna Ngosoni and Olichagi Dorwa. In August 2020, busloads of soldiers arrived in the Salamago Woreda as part of the government's continued efforts to militarize development operations.

31. See Fana (2014) to further understand the 'Securitization of Development in Ethiopia'.

32. Mun have not yet relocated to any of the villages. The fifth village in Tawanya, southern Munland, was declared in April 2018.

33. During fieldwork in 2014, many Mun men expressed a fear of being detained and therefore avoided meetings whenever possible. The refusal to attend was also perceived as a form of resistance (see Stevenson and Buffavand 2018: 124).

34. Evidence that pastoralism will be allowed is based on scant findings (e.g. that 'cattle corridors will remain') (Tewolde and Fana 2014: 123).

35. Tawanya was chosen by the government before *komoru* Bioitongiya (a ritual leader) was asked to relocate Mun there.

36. Interview with a Muni informant from Mara, name withheld, 14 July 2014.

37. Thirty-four Mun men and several Mun girls and women were employed by ESC in the sugar factories, which the Mun refer to as 'China'. Email communication with a Muni informant, name withheld, 16 May 2018.

38. Ibid.

39. Tewolde and Fana (2014: 135) confirm that the 'incoming [migrant] population predominantly holds the perception that it has the "higher culture" which contributes to implicitly or explicitly, knowingly or inadvertently, discriminating against local people'.

40. For example, AMREF Canada paid women to sew back their lips, since pottery lip-plates are deemed by the government as a 'harmful cultural practice'. As I argue elsewhere, the actual perceived harm is that the Mun women with lip-plates harm Ethiopia's reputation as a modern African state (LaTosky 2015).

41. Interview with Muni informant from Mara, name withheld, 14 July 2014.

42. See Turton (1985, 1988) for details about this migration.

43. See Tefera et al. (2016).

44. Email communication with a Muni informant, name withheld, 16 May 2018.

45. This is unlike the European understanding of 'consent', which is based on a '[a] definitive agreement . . . made at a specific moment in time', and closer to how 'consent' is defined in the Congo basin context, as '[a]n ongoing relationship of exchange between parties which undergoes revision and renegotiation' (Lewis et al. quoted in Gabbert 2014).

46. See also Human Rights Watch (2012: 38).

47. Other important areas include foraging sites called *baa kinnawng* (sing. *baa kinoiyi*).

48. Agreeing on access helps to avoid potential conflict (see Tadie and Fischer 2017: 453, 457 for parallels in Hamar and Bashada).

49. Every *bhuranyoga* has its own *komoru* (Turton 1979).

50. Ritual places *are* associated with particular locations and cannot be simply transferred as some officials have claimed (Tewolde and Fana 2014: 131).

51. Email communication with David Turton, 7 September 2018.

References

Abbink, J. et al. 2014. 'Lands of the Future: Transforming Pastoral Lands and Livelihoods in Eastern Africa', *Max Planck Institute for Social Anthropology Working Paper* No. 154. http://www.eth.mpg.de/cms/de/publications/working_papers/.

Adem Kassie Abebe. 2009. 'The Power of Indigenous Peoples to Veto Development Activities: The Right to Free, Prior and Informed Consent (FPIC) with Specific Reference to Ethiopia', Thesis for LLM. Moka. Mauritius: University of Mauritius.

Anaya, J., J. Evans and D. Kemp. 2017. 'Free, Prior and Informed Consent (FPIC) within a Human Rights Framework: Lessons from a Suriname Case Study', RESOLVE FPIC Solutions Dialogue: Washington DC. Retrieved 12 April 2018 from https://www.csrm.uq.edu.au/publications/free-prior-and-informed-consent-fpic-within-a-human-rights-framework-lessons-from-a-suriname-case-study.

Atuahene, B. 2016. 'Dignity Takings and Dignity Restoration: Creating a New Theoretical Framework for Understanding Involuntary Property Loss and the Remedies Required', *Law and Social Inquiry* 41(4): 796–823.

Barelli, M. 2012. 'Free, Prior and Informed Consent in the Aftermath of the UN Declaration on the Rights of Indigenous Peoples: Developments and Challenges Ahead', *International Journal of Human Rights* 16(1): 1–24.

CSA (Central Statistical Agency). 2007. 'Population and Housing Census'. Addis Ababa: Central Statistical Agency. Retrieved 24 May 2018 from http://catalog.ihsn.org/index.php/catalog/3583.

CSE (Concerned Scholars Ethiopia). 2019. 'Memo on Violence in South Omo Areas, SNNPRS, Ethiopia (October 2019): A Call for Preventive Action and Rule of law'. Omo-Turkana Research Network. Michigan State University. Retrieved 20 March 2020 from https://www.canr.msu.edu/news/concerned-scholars-for-ethiopia-issue-urgent-call-for-action-to-end-violence-in-south-omo-zone.

Data Dea Barata. 2017. 'Goldmine and Minefield: A Native Anthropologist's Review of Eike Haberland's Culture-Historical Research on Wolaita Ethiopia', in S. Dinslage and S. Thubauville (eds), *Seeking Out Wise Old Men: Six Decades of Ethiopian Studies at the Frobenius Institute Revisited*. Berlin: Reimer, pp. 237–49.

Degu Tadie, and A. Fischer. 2017. 'Natural Resource Governance in Lower Omo, Ethiopia: Negotiation Processes Instead of Property Rights and Rules?', *International Journal of the Commons* 11(1): 445–63.

Dunlap, A. 2018. '"A Bureaucratic Trap": Free, Prior and Informed Consent (FPIC) and Wind Energy Development in Juchitán, Mexico', *Capitalism Nature Socialism*. DOI: 10.1080/10455752.2017.1334219.

ESC (Ethiopian Sugar Corporation). 2015. 'Project Created Job Opportunities to 6,695 Citizens', *Sweet* (Ethiopian Sugar Corporation Newsletter), Vol. 3, June 2013. Retrieved 28 May 2018 from https://www.slideshare.net/meresaf/newsletter-env3.

———. 2017. 'The Triumphant Journey of Omo-Kuraz Sugar Development Project'. Retrieved 17 April 2018 from http://ethiopiansugar.com/index.php/en/news/articles/274-the-triumphant-journey-of-omo-kuraz-sugar-development-project.

Ethiopian Wildlife Conservation Authority. 2013. 'Proceedings of Consultative Meetings on Reconciling Conservation and Development in the Lower Omo Valley'. Mizan-Teferi. Addis Ababa: EWCA. Retrieved 27 May 2018 from https://phe-ethiopia.org/pdf/Mizan_proceding_Final_draft.pdf.

Fana Gebresenbet. 2014. 'Securitization of Development in Ethiopia: The Discourse and Politics of Developmentalism', *Review of African Political Economy* 41(S1): 64–74.

FAO (Food and Agriculture Organization of the United Nations). 2014. 'Respecting Free, Prior and Informed Consent: Practical Guidance for Governments, Companies, NGOs, Indigenous Peoples and Local Communities in Relation to Land Acquisition'. Retrieved 27 May 2018 from http://www.fao.org/3/a-i3496e.pdf%20%20.

————. 2016. 'An Indigenous Peoples' Right and a Good Practice for Local Communities', *Manual for Project Practitioners.* Retrieved 27 May 2018 from http://www.fao.org/3/a-i6190e.pdf.

Fox, S., and T. Sutton. 2012. 'Ground Rules: Cultivating Investments through Free, Prior, and Informed Consent', Retrieved 1 June 2018 from http://veracityworldwide.com/wp-content/uploads/2015/05/Ground-Rules-----Cultivating-Investments-Through-Free-Prior-and-Informed-Consent.pdf.

Franco, J. 2014. 'Reclaiming Free Prior and Informed Consent (FPIC) in the Context of Global Land Grabs'. *Transnational Institute (TNI) for Hand off the Land Alliance.* Retrieved 9 September 2019 from https://www.tni.org/files/download/reclaiming_fpic_0.pdf.

Gabbert, E.C. 2014. 'The Global Neighbourhood Concept: A Chance for Cooperative Development or Festina Lente', in Mulugeta Gebrehiwot Berhe (ed.), *A Delicate Balance: Land Use, Minority Rights and Social Stability in the Horn of Africa.* Addis Ababa: Institute for Peace and Security Studies, pp. 14–37.

————. 2018. 'Future in Culture: Globalizing Environments in the Lowlands of Southern Ethiopia', in J. Abbink (ed.), *The Environmental Crunch in Africa: Growth Narratives vs. Local Realities.* New York: Palgrave, pp. 287–317.

Greenspan, E. 2014. 'Free, Prior, and Informed Consent in Africa: An Emerging Standard for Extractive Industry Projects', *Oxfam America Research Backgrounder Series.* Retrieved 27 May 2018 from www.oxfamamerica.org/publications/fpic-in-africa.

Human Rights Watch. 2012. 'What Will Happen if Hunger Comes?' Abuses against the Indigenous Peoples of Ethiopia's Lower Omo Valley'. Retrieved 18 May 2018 from https://www.hrw.org/sites/default/files/reports/ethiopia0612webwcover.pdf.

Kamski, B. 2016a. *The Kuraz Sugar Development Project.* OTuRN Briefing Note Nr. 1. Lansing, MI: Omo-Turkana Research Network.

————. 2016b. 'The Kuraz Sugar Development Project (KSDP) in Ethiopia: Between "Sweet Visions" and Mounting Challenges', *Journal of Eastern African Studies* 10(3): 568–80.

————. 2019. 'Omo Investors Won't Scrub Away Kuraz's Sugary Stain', *Ethiopia Insight.* Retrieved 10 September 2019 from https://www.ethiopia-insight.com/2019/08/01/omo-investors-wont-scrub-away-kurazs-sugary-stain/.

Laplante, L.J., and S.A. Spears. 2014. 'Out of the Conflict Zone: The Case for Community Consent Processes in the Extractive Sector', *Yale Human Rights and Development Journal* 11(1): 69–116.

LaTosky, S. 2013. *Predicaments of Mursi (Mun) Women in Ethiopia's Changing World.* Köln: Rüdiger Köppe.

————. 2015. 'Lip-Plates, "Harm" Debates, and the Cultural Rights of Mun (Mun) Women', in C. Longman and T. Bradley (eds), *Interrogating Harmful Cultural Practices: Gender, Culture and Coercion.* London: Ashgate, pp. 169–91.

LaTosky, S., and Olisarali Olibui. Forthcoming. 'Cultivating the Agro-pastoralist Diet in Southern Ethiopia Now and in the Future: The Role of Wild Edible Plants for Food Security and Well-Being in Mun (Mursi)'. Proceedings of the 20th International Ethiopian Studies Conference, Mekelle University, October 1–5, 2018.

Little, P.D. et al. 2010. 'Policy Options for Pastoral Development in Ethiopia and Reaction from the Regions', *Report Number 4.* Pastoral Economic Growth and Development Policy Assessment, Ethiopia.

MacDonald, G.G., and G. Zezulka. 2015. 'Understanding Successful Approaches to FPIC in Canada. Part I. Recent Developments and Effective Roles for Government, Industry, and Indigenous Communities', *Boreal Leadership Council.* Retrieved 24 May 2018 from

http://borealcouncil.ca/wpcontent/uploads/2015/09/BLC_FPIC_Successes_Report_
Sept_2015_E.pdf.

McSherry, B., and I. Freckelton (eds). 2013. *Coercive Care: Rights, Law and Policy*. Milton Park: Routledge.

Meckelburg, A. 2014. 'Large Scale Land Investment in Gambella, Western Ethiopia – The Politics and Policies of Land', in Mulugeta Gebrehiwot Berhe (ed.), *A Delicate Balance: Land Use, Minority Rights and Social Stability in the Horn of Africa*. Addis Ababa: Institute for Peace and Security Studies, pp. 144–65.

Oakland Institute. 2014. *Engineering Ethnic Conflict: The Toll of Ethiopia's Plantation Development on the Suri People*. Oakland, CA: Oakland Institute, pp. 1–23.

Owen, J.R., and D. Kemp. 2014. '"Free Prior and Informed Consent", Social Complexity and the Mining Industry: Establishing a Knowledge Base', *Resources Policy* 41: 91–100.

Rettberg, S. 2010. 'The Impact of Sugar Cane Plantations on Pastoral Livelihoods within the Afar Region of Ethiopia', in Altare Caroline (ed.), *Sugar Cane and Indigenous People*. Montpellier SupAgro: Ethical Sugar, pp. 6–11. Retrieved 25 May 2018 from https:// ethicalsugar.files.wordpress.com/2014/02/sugarcane-and-indigenous-people-final-report .pdf.

SNNPRS (Southern Nations, Nationalities and Peoples Regional State). 2012. 'Government, Pastoral Affairs Bureau, S. Omo Zone, Salamago Woreda and Kaffa Zone, Decha Woreda. Villagization Plan of 2005 (E.C)', submitted to Kuraz Sugar Development Project (August 2012), Hawassa.

Somsen, H. 2017. 'The End of European Environmental Law: An Environmental Programme for the Anthropocene', in L.J. Kotzé (ed.), *Environmental Law and Governance for the Anthropocene*. Oxford and Portland: Hart, pp. 353–72.

Stevenson, E.G.J., and L. Buffavand. 2018. '"Do Our Bodies Know Their Ways?" Villagization, Food Insecurity, and Ill-Being in Ethiopia's Lower Omo Valley', *African Studies Review* 61(1): 109–33.

Tadie, D., and A. Fischer. 2017. 'Natural Resource Governance in Lower Omo, Ethiopia: Negotiation Processes Instead of Property Rights and Rules?', *International Journal of the Commons* 11(1): 445–63.

Tefera, S. et al. 2016. 'Pastoralists Do Plan! Community-Led Land Use Planning in the Pastoral Areas of Ethiopia', *Rangelands* 6. Rome, Italy: International Land Coalition.

Tewolde Woldemariam, and Fana Gebresenbet. 2014. 'Socio-Political and Conflict Implications of Sugar Development in Salamago Wereda, Ethiopia', in Mulugeta Gebrehiwot Berhe (ed.), *A Delicate Balance: Land Use, Minority Rights and Social Stability in the Horn of Africa*. Addis Ababa: Institute for Peace and Security Studies, pp. 117–43.

———. Forthcoming. 'The Developmental State in South Omo: Sugar Industrialization, Politics of Development and Conflict', in Dereje Feyissa and K. Tronvoll (eds),

Turton, D. 1973. 'The Social Organization of the Mun: A Pastoral Tribe of the Lower Omo Valley, South West Ethiopia', Ph.D. thesis. London: University of London. Retrieved 5 June 2018 from http://www.Mun.org/pdf/social-organisation-of-the-Mun.pdf.

———. 1979. 'A Journey Made Them: Territorial Segmentation and Ethnic Identity among the Mun', in H. Ladislav (ed.), *Segmentary Lineage Systems Reconsidered*. Belfast: Queen's University Press, pp. 119–43.

———. 1985. 'Mursi Response to Drought: Some Lessons for Relief and Rehabilitation', *African Affairs* 84(336): 331–46.

———. 1988. 'Looking for a Cool Place: The Mursi, 1890s–1990s', in D. Anderson and D. Johnson (eds), *The Ecology of Survival: Case Studies from Northeast African History*. London: Lester Crook, pp. 261–82.

UN. 2011. 'Expert Mechanism Advice No. 2: Indigenous Peoples and the Right to Participate in Decision-Making'. Retrieved 18 April 2018 from http://www.ohchr.org/Documents/Issues/IPeoples/EMRIP/Advice2_Oct2011.pdf.

UNDRIP (United Nations Declaration on the Rights of Indigenous Peoples). 2007. Adopted 2 October. A/RES/61/295. http://social.un.org/index/Indigenous, Peoples/Declarationon theRightsofIndigenousPeoples.aspx.

UN-REDD Programme (United Nations Programme on Reducing Deforestation and Forest Degradation). 2013. 'Guidelines on Free, Prior and Informed Consent', *UN-REDD Programme*. Retrieved 27 May 2018 from http://www.unredd.net/.index.php?option=com docman&task=doc_download&gid=8717&Itemid=53.

Wagstaff, A.Q. 2015. 'Development, Cultural Hegemonism and Conflict Generation in Southwest Ethiopia: Agro-Pastoralists in Trouble', *Observatoir des Enjeux Politiques et Securitaires dans la Corne de L'Afrique*, Note 13.

Yidneckachew Ayele. 2015. 'Policies and Practices of Consultation with Pastoralist Communities in Ethiopia: The Case of Omo-Kuraz Sugar Development Project', in Yohannes Aberra and Mahmmud Abdulahi (eds), *The Intricate Road to Development: Government Development Strategies in the Pastoral Areas of the Horn of Africa*. Addis Ababa: Institute of Peace and Security Studies, pp. 274–96.

Young, S. 2020. *Indigenous Peoples, Consent and Rights: Troubling Subjects*. Oxon and New York: Routledge.

Chapter 13

Ethiopia's 'Blue Oil'?

Hydropower, Irrigation and Development in the Omo-Turkana Basin

Edward G.J. Stevenson and Benedikt Kamski

Introduction

In debates about the politics of large dams in the twenty-first century, Ethiopia has secured itself a prominent place. Since the year 2000, multiple mega-dam projects have been launched, and the ideas that 'water is Ethiopia's oil' and that 'hydropower can end poverty' are frequently invoked by government representatives and water resources experts in Addis Ababa. These discourses, however, fly in the face of a large literature showing that mega-dams have massive, unaccounted costs (e.g. Richter et al. 2010; Ansar et al. 2014). Negative outcomes include loss of prime riverside farmland, collapse of fisheries, extirpation of endemic wildlife and impoverishment and displacement of peoples reliant on the ecosystems that are transformed by dams (see Scudder 2005; Kirchherr and Charles 2016).

How is it, then, that large dams and poverty reduction remain so tightly connected in so many people's minds? One answer is a utilitarian one. Classically, utilitarians argue that the suffering of a minority is justified if it is instrumental to providing the greatest good for the greatest number of people. On these grounds, people who believe that dams generate wealth for the nation might not be concerned that they also impoverish certain groups – for instance, populations downstream – so long as the net benefits outweigh the costs. Although this utilitarian calculus is not always stated explicitly, it is common in the Environmental and Social Impact Assessments (ESIAs) that are supposed to guide planners in the identification of worthy projects (see McCully 2001: 54ff.).

Official impact assessments, however, play a relatively small part in the drama of large dams. Prior to ESIAs, and informing their commissioning, are narratives about dams and development. In this chapter, we review some of these narratives and their pragmatic implications. Metaphors such as 'blue oil', we demonstrate, illuminate some aspects of the issues but render other aspects invisible.[1]

The empirical material on which the chapter is based relates to hydro-agricultural development (i.e. hydropower and large-scale irrigation) in the Omo-Turkana basin, a region encompassing parts of southern Ethiopia and northern Kenya.[2] In this context, the most troublesome and least visible facts (those which planners have been most resistant to acknowledging) concern the physical hydrology of the Omo-Turkana basin and the hydrosocial systems – the connections between hydrological rhythms and indigenous livelihood systems – that large dams and plantations serve to interrupt. After a brief review of the politics of land and water in Ethiopia, we appraise the strengths and weaknesses of the 'blue oil' narrative in relation to the Gilgel-Gibe III dam (referred to as Gibe III in the remainder of this chapter) on the Omo River and the irrigated sugar cane estates that have been established downstream of the dam. This appraisal involves accounting for the fiscal costs of the dam and plantation schemes and the revenues they are expected to generate. It also requires consideration of the livelihood systems of people downstream and the implications of these interventions for them.

In the latter part of the chapter, we consider alternative narratives that critics have deployed in relation to the hydro-agricultural projects in the Omo-Turkana basin: framings that portray them as variously an ecological disaster, an abuse of human rights and an instance of development-forced displacement. These alternative narratives represent the Gibe III dam and associated plantation schemes as part of an elaborate, costly and violent process of incorporating a peripheral region and population. Which set of narratives one endorses depends largely on whether one focuses on how the projects use water to produce commodities, or how, in doing so, they deprive certain people of food, water and homes.

The Politics of Land and Water in Ethiopia

In agrarian societies, including Ethiopia, land tenure and the exercise of power are closely intertwined. Over the course of the twentieth century, successive regimes were accompanied by changing modes of land ownership (Dessalegn 1999; Tafesse 2006). The framers of the constitution of the Federal Democratic Republic of Ethiopia wrote that 'ownership of land is vested in the state and the people' (FDRE 1995: Art. 40.3), but they also recognized the rights of 'nations, nationalities, and peoples' in the plural, establishing a political contract with the diverse groups that make up the Ethiopian polity. While the Ethiopian People's Revolutionary Democratic Front (EPRDF) has not changed the constitution since it assumed power in the early 1990s, a decisive shift in agricultural policy took place in the early 2000s, when, alongside the previous policy of supporting smallholders, the government began to promote large-scale commercial farming as a means of modernizing the agricultural sector (see Dessalegn 2011, 2014; Dorosh and Rashid 2012). This initiative gained momentum in the wake of the so-called global 'land rush' that occurred after 2008 as investors sought to capitalize on the potential for commodity production in the global South (Hall 2011).

One of the most important assets that Ethiopia offered in the global marketplace for land and agriculture was its freshwater endowment, because of abundant rainfall in the temperate highland regions (Yacob and Imeru 2005; Matthews et al. 2013; Mehta et al. 2012).[3] Occasionally referred to as one of the 'water towers' of East Africa (UNEP 2010), the country possesses twelve primary river basins that form four major drainage systems, namely the Nile basin, Rift Valley, Shebelli-Juba and North-East Coast. A key feature of most river basins is extreme fluctuation in river flow caused by the seasonality of rainfall in the highlands.[4] The outward inclination of the highlands also creates steep river profiles – in the case of the Omo River, dropping from more than 2,500 metres in altitude to just a few hundred meters in the lowlands (Avery 2012). Estimates of national hydropower capacity range from 30,000 to 45,000 megawatts, ranking Ethiopia second on the continent after the Democratic Republic of Congo (UNEP 2010; Block and Goddard 2012).

This claim – that Ethiopia's rivers are convertible to a certain number of megawatts of electricity – is central to the 'blue oil' narrative. It is the hydrological equivalent of seeing land as simply a resource to be exploited, as opposed to a place or a home with its own history and significance (Turton 2011; Girke 2013). Large dams, as they are usually planned and built, are incompatible with the livelihood systems of the downstream river valleys, which in the Horn of Africa tend to be semi-arid regions where river flooding provides water and nutrients that are vital for farming and herding (Kloos et al. 2010). This feature of the mega-dam model – the destruction that it visits on pre-existing systems of land use and farming in the lowlands – means that it is inevitably controversial as a development option. To the extent that they ignore this controversy, government narratives that represent the building of mega-dams as a national priority are based on a narrow interpretation of national identity that privileges highlanders over lowlanders and permanently settled agricultural populations over nomadic pastoralists or agro-pastoralists (see Schlee 2013). These dynamics are clearly illustrated in the case of the Gibe III dam in the Omo-Turkana basin.

The Gibe III Dam and the End of the Annual Flooding of the Omo

We use the term Omo-Turkana basin to refer to the Lake Turkana drainage basin (Butzer 1971; Avery 2010), a closed transboundary river basin comprising the lake (located almost entirely in Kenya) and its major tributary, the Omo River (located in Ethiopia).[5] The Gibe dam cascade on the Omo River comprises Gibe III

(1,870 MW), together with Gibe IV (aka Koysha, 1,470 MW), currently under construction, and Gibe V (660 MW), currently in the planning stage.[6] The Gibe III dam, the centrepiece of this cascade, was officially inaugurated in December 2016, ten years after the Italian engineering group Salini Impregilo had been awarded the contract by the Ethiopian Electric Power Corporation. Although the cost of the dam is hard to verify, the Ethiopian government reportedly allocated at least $572 million, and the Industrial and Commercial Bank of China provided $459 million (Verhoeven 2011).[7] The official cost of the major dam-building projects currently undertaken by Salini in Ethiopia (including the Grand Ethiopian Renaissance Dam, Gibe III and Koysha) is more than €7.35 billion.[8]

In order to appraise the strengths and weaknesses of the 'blue oil' metaphor in the case of the Omo, we need to consider, in addition to the price tags attached to the dams, the ways Gibe III and associated projects have affected the lives of people in the region. We do so first by reviewing the immediate effects of the projects in terms of employment and infrastructure development, and second by examining the implications of the changes in hydrology brought about by the dam.

At its high point, the Gibe III project employed eight thousand people. While the dam itself is located in the middle Omo, new infrastructure was also installed downstream. The construction of bridges across the Omo established a permanent linkage between the eastern and western banks of the river in its lower catchment, and the expansion of roads and mobile phone networks provided unprecedented communication links between the Lower Omo basin and the towns and cities of southern Ethiopia. With electric power generated by Gibe III transmitted across Ethiopia's borders, the project also established new transboundary links. Revenues from electricity export to Kenya were projected to reach $400 million by 2020; Sudan and Djibouti were also slated to receive electricity via transmission lines financed by the African Development Bank (African Development Fund 2012).

Hydrologically, the Gibe III dam created a novel division of the river basin: upstream of the reservoir, where the Omo and its major tributaries – the Gibe and Gojeb rivers – largely maintained their natural hydrological cycle, and downstream, where the power plants and water level of the reservoir determined the flow volume of the Omo River. The implications of this change in natural regime for the livelihoods of people downstream are far-reaching. By holding back waters in the reservoir, and releasing them continually to power turbines, the dam interrupts the prior pattern of annual flooding to which the natural and social systems of the Lower Omo and Lake Turkana are adapted.

Considering the livelihood systems of one of the indigenous groups of the Lower Omo helps to clarify the importance of the flood for the livelihoods of the region's peoples in general. The traditional livelihoods of the Mursi (Mun) rest on three pillars: (1) farming on land inundated by the annual rise of the river, sometimes referred to as 'flood recession agriculture' (a practice that provides highly predictable yields, including for the primary staple grains, sorghum and maize), (2) rain-fed farming on land that receives enough rain to grow crops (an unpredictable venture, sometimes providing valuable supplementary grain), and (3) cattle herding (a crucial source of dairy products, meat and blood) (Turton 1989; Carr 2012). As Turton (this volume) notes, 'each of these subsistence activities would be insufficient on its own, or even in combination with one of the other two, but the three together make possible a viable agro-pastoral economy.' Other groups of the region, who have less access to land suitable for rain-fed agriculture, depend even more on the flood – for example, the Kwegu, who rely on flood-retreat farming, fishing and small stock (as opposed to cattle), and the Dassanech, who are unable to practise rain-fed farming because of lower rainfall in the vicinity of the Omo delta.

The relationship between the annual flood and the food systems of the Lower Omo may be usefully considered as part of a hydrosocial system – that is, a set of cultural and economic practices adapted to a particular ecological niche in which hydrology is a crucial component (see Bakker 2012; Linton and Budds 2013). In a remarkable misreading of this system, planners and engineers working on Gibe III had initially cast the annual flooding of the Omo as posing a hazard to downstream communities, and proposed that by eliminating it, the dam would improve conditions (see Turton, this volume). In the face of criticism, Salini subsequently acknowledged the negative implications of the end of the annual flooding and claimed the regulation of the river by the dam could be combined with 'artificial floods' released from the reservoir that would preserve the possibility of flood recession agriculture (Salini 2016). But evidence for the success of such floods, or rather of the flood recession farming they supported, has not been provided by Salini, and testimonies from independent sources suggest that they have fallen far short of what would be required for people to continue to practise flood recession agriculture. Releases of water from the Gibe III reservoir in September 2016 (at a time when the river would ordinarily have been at its height) were not sufficient to inundate the river banks (L. Buffavand, pers. comm.); and in 2017, the rise of the river was again negligible (W. Hurd, pers. comm.). Indeed, engineers familiar with the scheme acknowledged that the headworks of the irrigation system installed downstream (to serve new plantations, discussed further below) would reportedly not withstand releases of water anywhere near the volume of the prior flooding. All of this casts doubt on the viability of artificial floods as a mitigation measure.

To summarize, although the construction of the Gibe III dam and associated infrastructure offered tangible benefits to project employees and to road users in the region, and although the dam has succeeded in supplying electricity to urban centres, it has also jeopardized the food security of people downstream. At issue in terms of the socio-economic outcomes of the dam is not only the electricity generated, or the volume or tempo of the pre- and post-dam floods, but also the environmental and cultural adaptations to the river system that the various peoples of the Lower Omo developed over historical time. Rather than taking these hydrosocial systems seriously, the rhetoric of Salini regarding artificial floods reads like a smokescreen, providing distraction and allowing the frame of 'large dam as positive development' to remain in place. As we go on to show, similar misreadings and simplifications underlie the project of expanding plantation agriculture in the Omo.

'We Can Change This Grassland to Sugar'

In January 2011, the global price for refined sugar had reached a twenty-year high, selling for US $ 0.30 per pound (USDA 2016). It was against this backdrop that the Ethiopian government placed a bet on the expansion of the sugar industry in its first Growth and Transformation Plan (GTP-I, 2010/11–2014/15). According to planners, increased national sugar-processing capacities would ease the challenge of rising domestic demand for processed sugar and allow the export of surpluses to boost foreign currency earnings. Moreover, the cultivation and processing industry would provide employment opportunities to both unskilled labourers and the increasing numbers of university graduates.[9]

The Kuraz Sugar Development Project (KSDP) was the flagship site for sugar production under GTP I. With a projected area of 175,000 hectares, it would dwarf any other plantation in East Africa (Avery 2012). The rhetoric that surrounded the KSDP, like that concerning Gibe III, was hyperbolic. 'We can change this grassland to sugar, which will become money, just as we can change the people and the whole country,' said an ESC official in 2014.[10] Alongside the KSDP, a number of domestic and foreign investors took advantage of favourable investment conditions created by the Ethiopian government by reportedly leasing more than 90,000 hectares of land in Salamago, Nyangatom, Dassanech and Hamar Woreda (districts) in South Omo Zone, with leasehold areas ranging from less than 500 hectares to as many as 10,000 hectares.[11] Large-scale agriculture in the semi-arid climate of the Lower Omo is possible only with artificial irrigation, and the public and private investments alike depended on a system of canals channelling water through the newly established estates. Extracting enough water from the Omo River to irrigate 200,000–300,000 hectares would have serious implications for Kenya.

Transboundary Implications

Before the construction of the Gibe III dam, the annual flood of the Omo – the main source of fresh water for Lake Turkana – provided a pulse of water and nutrients on which the reproductive cycles of the lake's fish depended (Hopson 1982). Because of high evaporation rates, the lake is brackish, but the fresh water of the Omo, which provides more than 90 per cent of the lake's inflow, makes it habitable for a wide variety of aquatic life (Kolding 1995). According to fish biologists, the end of the flood alone would reduce the fish population of the lake by two-thirds (Gownaris et al. 2016). These fish constitute a valuable food source for pastoralists in regions bordering the lake and produce fish traded as far afield as the Democratic Republic of Congo.

Despite the mobilization of civil society organizations in Turkana (e.g. Friends of Lake Turkana; see Leakey 2009) and a few dissenting voices in the Kenyan parliament (see Hansard 2008, 2010), the Gibe III and Kuraz schemes have been neither openly challenged nor obstructed by the government of Kenya. Only in 2018, more than two years after the completion of Gibe III, was a joint commission proposed to study the environmental and social implications of the dam and irrigation projects for Kenyans.[12] The silence of the Kenyan government on the Omo-Turkana issues contrasts strikingly with the state of affairs regarding the Blue Nile – site of the other major dam project underway, the 6,000 MW Grand Ethiopian Renaissance Dam (GERD) – which has been the subject of numerous treaties and covenants involving the downstream states, Sudan and Egypt.[13] This is all the more remarkable given that, unlike GERD, the Gibe dams are accompanied by massive irrigation schemes that will abstract large quantities of water from the basin at the expense of downstream users.

Counternarratives

Although the Kenyan government has been slow to act, a diverse range of other international actors is active in the region, including engineers and contractors (notably Salini), financiers (multilateral development banks and the Chinese state), foreign investors (e.g. those investing in cotton production), Western governmental aid organizations, and environmental and human rights activists. We have touched already on the role of Salini and the financiers; here we focus on international activists, as it is they who have most efficiently propagated counternarratives emphasizing the interests of local peoples and ecosystems. These counternarratives centre on the concepts of ecological disaster, human rights abuses and development-forced displacement. Although not necessarily conflicting with one another, each highlights different aspects of the situation. We consider each of these counternarratives in turn.

The ecological disaster narrative is emblematized by the analogy between Lake Turkana and the Aral Sea in Central Asia. Once the world's fifth largest body of fresh water, the Aral Sea largely dried up in the 1980s, when Soviet planners, with a focus on maximizing cotton production, neglected the implications of the massive abstractions of water that the irrigated plantations required. In relation to the Omo, this framing came to prominence in reports by the hydrologist Sean Avery (2010, 2012, 2013) and by the US-based NGO International

Rivers (2013).[14] If the Ethiopian government's projections for the Kuraz plantation scheme were realized, Avery (2013: 47) calculated, they would require the abstraction of up to 50 per cent of the Omo flow, which would cause a drop of approximately 20 metres in the level of Lake Turkana. The Aral Sea narrative was taken up by international media outlets such as The Guardian and influenced UNESCO's (2018) decision to include the Lake Turkana National Parks in Kenya on its list of World Heritage Sites in danger.[15]

The second framing emphasized by advocacy groups in relation to the Omo focuses on human rights abuses. In 2011, the US-based NGO Human Rights Watch reported that 'local government and security forces had carried out arbitrary arrests and detentions, used physical violence, and seized or destroyed the property of indigenous communities' in the Lower Omo (HRW 2012: 2). Mass arrests by the military forces of Ethiopia's southern region were also reported by the Oakland Institute (2013: 6). The strength of the human rights abuse narrative is that it produces litigable claims, which might provide leverage for the protection of community interests. The weakness of the approach is that it generally requires proof of specific criminal acts, by identifiable individuals or institutions, and a court that is willing to hear the case. In the Omo, these components have been difficult to assemble. Attempts to hold the Ethiopian government accountable for the abuses suffered by local peoples – for example, by the UK-based NGO Survival International, using the African Union as an arbiter – have so far failed to yield a judgment.[16]

The literature on Development-Forced Displacement and Resettlement (DFDR) offers another lens through which to view events. The DFDR narrative takes the phenomena reviewed above – including the end of annual flooding and the annexation of large territories for plantations – not so much as paradoxes to be explained but as common features of actually existing development, which routinely lead to impoverishment for some people while at the same time generating wealth for others. As Turton (2015) has argued, the failures of development in the Omo, rather than being exceptional, reprise a catalogue of errors that have been made elsewhere since at least the twentieth century (see Cernea 2000; Mitchell 2002; Oliver-Smith 2015). Indeed, their recurrence suggests that they might be better understood not as errors but as deliberate sacrifices.

Although the narratives of ecological disaster, human rights abuse and DFDR have been summarily dismissed by the Ethiopian government, the chorus of criticism from international activists and scholars has not gone unnoticed by Ethiopia's aid partners in Europe and North America. One sign of this was the initiative of the Donor Assistance Group (DAG) – a consortium including the World Bank, USAID and the European Union – to carry out a series of missions to the Lower Omo, meeting with local government officials and residents, ostensibly to uncover the facts of the matter.[17] Rather than clarifying the situation, however, the mission reports themselves led to further controversy. In 2012, a translator employed by one of the DAG missions independently published the transcripts from conversations that had taken place between DAG staff and members of a Mursi community during a visit to the Lower Omo. Allegations of beatings and rapes carried out by government soldiers had been omitted from the official report, suggesting that the DAG preferred to ignore these claims rather than to risk offending the Ethiopian government (Oakland Institute 2013). The hazards associated with the Gibe III dam and Kuraz had forced the aid community into a precarious 'balancing act' – criticizing enough to placate domestic constituencies but not so much as to jeopardize their relationship with the Ethiopian government (Turton 2014).

Denouement

As the first decade of hydro-agricultural development in the Omo draws to a close, the weakness of the 'blue oil' narrative is becoming ever more apparent. At the KSDP, delays in building the factories required for turning sugar cane into marketable products meant that, after at least four seasons of cultivation, the massive investments in sugar cane estates had failed to yield the anticipated economic results. From its high point in 2011, the global price for refined sugar fell by half to US $ 0.15 per pound in January 2018 (McConnell 2018: 29). To the astonishment of local people (both those employed by the sugar estates and those displaced to make way for the plantations), large parts of the first years' potential harvests of ripe sugar cane were either burned or left to rot in the fields (Kamski 2016b: 575).[18] Further, incomplete planning and capital shortages forced the ESC to downscale the projected cultivation area from 175,000 hectares to 100,000 hectares (Kamski 2016b: 574). Meanwhile, none of the private investors had successfully developed their entire leasehold areas. Investors claimed that, despite the low lease rates and generous fiscal incentives granted by the Ethiopian state, the high initial investment required for reclaiming land for large-scale irrigation had slowed progress.[19]

At the same time, the government of Ethiopia and its aid partners found themselves under fire from critics regarding the treatment of indigenous people in the context of the expanding plantations. The component of development planning in the Omo that has generated the most international controversy was the one designed most consciously with local populations in mind, namely the programme of 'villagization' (moving indigenous people into large, government-designed villages) (FDRE 2012).[20] Because the programme was implemented without meaningful consultation of locals regarding where they might resettle, or what kinds of livelihoods they might practise there, it bred resentment (Tewolde and Fana 2014; Yidneckachew 2015). And because, unlike the dam and plantation projects, villagization involved face-to-face engagement between officials and the people, it provided an opportunity for local resistance in a way that other interventions that affected them did not (Stevenson and Buffavand 2018). For advocacy groups, meanwhile, the fact that the villagization also implied eviction,[21] and was accompanied by the use of food aid as a bargaining chip, made it potentially litigable in a way that river basin engineering on its own was not.[22]

Conclusion: Changing the Frames?

Whether the campaigns of advocacy groups, or grassroots resistance by locals, will succeed in changing the way development is pursued in the Omo-Turkana basin remains to be seen. What we have tried to do in this chapter is not to pick a winning horse but to clarify the narratives that are commonly invoked to make sense of the situation, and to articulate the pragmatic possibilities and interpretive risks that each narrative implies.

As we have seen, the metaphor of 'blue oil' implies that fresh water, like petroleum, constitutes a resource that might be tapped to raise the living standards of all Ethiopians. And to some extent, the policy of hydro-agricultural development pursued by the EPRDF in the Omo-Turkana basin does correspond to a petrochemical model: treating the river's water as a resource to be parcelled out and sold to foreign corporations or governments, investors or commodity traders. Water, however, is different from petroleum and other precious minerals, in that while it is necessary for the production of other commodities it is only exceptionally treated as a commodity in its own right (Bakker 2011). Crucially, it is convertible into other commodities such as crops or electricity only after extensive operations that are politically charged. As we have argued here, the ways in which water is tied up in hydrosocial systems makes its exploitation highly contentious.

The most prominent alternative framing employed in reference to the current historical conjuncture in the Omo-Turkana basin, namely the Aral Sea disaster, also carries interpretive risks. By focusing attention on likely future impacts on the water level of Lake Turkana, the Aral Sea analogy distracts attention from the real damages that the Gibe III dam has already done to people who depended on the Omo's annual flood for their livelihoods. The analogy with the Aral Sea also foregrounds transboundary and geopolitical dimensions of the situation – the indemnity that Ethiopia owes to Kenya – which, while important in their own right, distract from the costs incurred by the people of the Lower Omo.

If the dominant narratives are misleading, what better alternatives are available? For answers to this question, we might do well to listen to the people whose lives are threatened by these projects. In an important contribution to the debate, Buffavand (2016) relates how the Mela (known by outsiders as Bodi) have enlisted cosmological knowledge to the cause of preserving their homeland, including beliefs in the sacredness of the land and the power of Divinity to punish those who treat the land wrongly. Analogous models from other parts of Ethiopia include the Borana Oromo notion of *fidnaa*, or flourishing in place (a literal analogue of the Amharic *limat*), which in its original sense connotes fertility and natural growth (Dahl and Gemetchu 1992).[23] The great value of these concepts is that they orient us to the importance of the ecological and social systems that development operates upon and which are commonly discounted by planners. The risk of these narratives is that they fall on deaf ears: to unsympathetic audiences, the ways of thinking and perceiving that they represent may be construed simply as baffling or quaint.

The narrative of Development-Forced Displacement and Resettlement, although it does not necessarily correspond to indigenous views, avoids the most obvious blind spots of the other narratives reviewed in this chapter. In the Omo-Turkana case, a DFDR lens foregrounds the impacts on people and ecosystems on both sides of the international border and invites comparison with the many other cases in the historical record in which development projects have brought about unjustified suffering for already marginalized people (Oliver-Smith 2015). This narrative is (or ought to be) intelligible to planners and bureaucrats and renders visible important aspects of development planning – including the tendency of many development projects to leave the 'beneficiaries' worse off – that are too often ignored. Coupled with an appreciation of the importance of hydrosocial systems, it draws attention to outcomes that, with foresight, might be prevented and, with hindsight, demand to be redressed.

Edward G.J. Stevenson is an Assistant Professor of Anthropology at Durham University. He holds a PhD in Anthropology and a Master's in Public Health from Emory University. With Jennifer Hodbod, he coordinates the Omo-Turkana Research Network (OTuRN).

Benedikt Kamski is Senior Researcher at the Arnold-Bergstraesser-Institute (ABI) and political analyst working across the Horn of Africa. He holds a PhD in Political Science from the University of Freiburg and is also a founding member of the Omo-Turkana Research Network (OTuRN).

Notes

We acknowledge with gratitude the openness of people in Ethiopia – notably including employees of the government and the Ethiopian Sugar Corporation – in sharing their knowledge with us. For feedback that helped to improve this chapter, we owe thanks to Gordon Bennett, Lydia Khennache and Kay Gilliland Stevenson. We have also benefitted from many conversations over the years with David Turton. The opinions we express in this chapter are, however, ours alone, and it is we who bear responsibility for any errors the chapter may contain.

1. This observation derives from Lakoff and Johnson's (1980) book, *Metaphors We Live By*.

2. We use the phrase 'hydro-agricultural development' to refer to the development of irrigated commercial farming schemes as well as hydropower dams, both being contingent upon the same resource – that is, fresh water flowing through major rivers.

3. Agricultural water use generally refers to water resources abstracted from groundwater and surface water for irrigation uses (blue water) but excludes green water resources such as precipitation onto farmland and soil moisture as part of crop water consumption (see Falkenmark and Rockström 2006).

4. Mean annual rainfall on a countrywide basis is around 848 mm, with a peak precipitation amount of 2,000 mm in the south-western lowlands and fewer than 100 mm in the western Afar Triangle (FAO Aquastat 2005).

5. The term Omo River basin (or Omo-Gibe River basin), by contrast, refers to the catchment of the Omo River from its source in the Shewa highlands to its terminus in Lake Turkana. Lake Turkana was formerly referred to as Lake Rudolf.

6. Gibe I and II are on the Gibe River, located further upstream and effectively a tributary of the Omo. Gibe IV and Gibe V would constitute two additional reservoirs and power stations envisaged in the lower catchment of the Omo River (Gibe III HEP 2015). For more information on the Gibe dam cascade, see Carr (2017).

7. Several international banks (including the World Bank Group, European Investment Bank and African Development Bank) declined to fund the project (Carr 2017: chaps. 2, 10).

8. This accounts for approximately 11 per cent of the total cost of all projects planned under the Growth and Transformation Plan (a five-year plan for national development) between 2010/11 and 2014/15. Salini changed its name to Webuild in 2020.

9. In 2015, the urban unemployment rate in Ethiopia was 17 per cent, of whom college graduates constituted 14 per cent of the unemployed (World Bank 2016: 2, 29). The Ethiopian Sugar Corporation (ESC) estimates that four workers would be employed per hectare in the cultivation and processing industry; indirect employment – for example, in the service sectors – might raise this figure substantially (Kamski 2016a).

10. Personal interview with ESC Project Management conducted by BK on the KSDP project site, July 2014.

11. These numbers were provided to BK by the South Omo Zone Investment Directorate (March 2017). Systematic inventories of land leased to investors and the status of these schemes are not available at present. On the processes and conditions of large-scale land deals, see Keeley et al. (2014) and Dessalegn (2011).

12. At the time of writing, the Ethiopian Sugar Corporation was seeking a consultant to carry out the study on behalf of the commission (ESC official, pers. comm. to EGJS, Addis Ababa, 2018/2/19).

13. On treaties and covenants that have sought to regulate use of the Nile by riparian states, see, for example, Cascão (2009) and Khennache et al. (2017).

14. The analogy between Lake Turkana and the Aral Sea is reviewed further by Stevenson (2018).

15. For media reports, see, for example, Vidal (2014).

16. Survival International submitted its petitions to the African Commission on Human and Peoples' Rights, an African Union body tasked with upholding the African Charter of 1986. The ACHPR passed judgment in 2009 against the government of Kenya for the eviction of the Endorois people from a game reserve in the Rift Valley in the 1970s (ACHPR 2009). Although the judgment is yet to be enforced, the Endorois case constitutes a legal precedent that might be leveraged on behalf of residents of the Omo-Turkana

basin. On the AUC's involvement in the Lower Omo, see United Nations Human Rights Council Periodic Review for Ethiopia April/May 2014 (UN-HRC 2014; see AUC-2013: Item 27).

17. DAG supported the Ethiopian government to the tune of $4 billion in 2016. See http:// dagethiopia.org/new/, accessed on 15 February 2018.

18. As the quality of sugar cane deteriorates rapidly after cutting, transporting cane to other parts of the country for processing was unfeasible. While the Kuraz II factory, one of four processing plants under construction, started trial production in March 2017, the installed capacity remained too low to process the sugar cane thus far produced.

19. Interviews with investors conducted by BK in South Omo in June 2014 and March 2017.

20. Formally, villagization was implemented by the regional and zonal governments, whereas the construction of settlements and related infrastructure on the KSDP project site was the financial and administrative responsibility of the ESC (Kamski 2016a).

21. The annexation of valuable riverside land for sugar estates deprived some communities among the Bodi and Kwegu (neighbours of the Mursi) of the opportunity to cultivate during the last floods, in 2014, while the clearing of 'bush' land earmarked for sugar also meant the loss of wild plants and game animals on which people relied as fallback options in previous droughts (Buffavand 2016; see also the chapters by LaTosky and Buffavand in this volume). (Bodi is the name used by most outsiders for the Mela and Chirim people, a territorial group of the Me'en who live on the eastern side of the Omo River [see Buffa-vand, this volume]. Mursi is the name used by most outsiders for the Mun [see LaTosky, this volume].)

22. Litigation regarding villagization in Ethiopia's western province of Gambella provides a precedent here. In 2014, the High Court in London heard the case of an Ethiopian citizen known as Mr O., who alleged that British aid money was used for programmes that forced him from his home. This led the Department for International Development (DFID) to cancel its support of the Protection of Basic Services (PBS) fund, which law-yers argued was underwriting villagization (Rawlence 2016).

23. The reappropriation of *limat* under the Derg and EPRDF, to refer to industrial as opposed to natural growth, constitutes a semantic shift that is parallel to the redefinition of the English word 'development' in the twentieth century (Sachs 2010). See also Lakoff (2005) on 'freedom'.

References

African Commission on Human and Peoples' Rights (ACHPR). 2009. 'Centre for Minority Rights Development (Kenya) and Minority Rights Group (on behalf of Endorois Welfare Council) / Kenya. Communication 267/03'. Retrieved 15 February 2018 from http:// www.achpr.org/communications/decision/276.03/.

African Development Fund. 2012. *Ethiopia-Kenya Electricty Highway: Project Appraisal Report*. Retrieved 3 August 2020 from https://www.afdb.org/fileadmin/uploads/afdb/ Documents/Project-and-Operations/Ethiopia-Kenya_-_Ethiopia-Kenya_Electricity_ Highway_-Project_Appraisal_Report_.pdf.

Ansar, A. et al. 2014. 'Should We Build More Large Dams? The Actual Costs of Hydropower Megaproject Development', *Energy Policy* 69: 43–56.

AUC. 2013. '35th Activity Report of the African Commission on Human and People's Rights'. Retrieved 15 February 2018 from http://www.achpr.org/files/activity-reports/35/achpr 54eos14_actrep35_2014_eng.pdf.

Avery, S. 2010. 'Hydrological Impacts of Ethiopia's Omo Basin on Kenya's Lake Turkana Water Levels and Fisheries', *Final Report*. Tunis: African Development Bank.

———. 2012. *Lake Turkana and the Lower Omo: Hydrological Impacts of Major Dam and Irrigation Developments*, vol. 1 Report. Oxford: African Studies Centre.

———. 2013. *What Future for Lake Turkana?* Oxford: African Studies Centre.

Bakker, K. 2011. 'Commons versus Commodities: Political Ecologies of Water Privatization', in R. Peet, P. Robbins and M. Watts (eds), *Global Political Ecology*. London: Routledge, pp. 347–70.

———. 2012. 'Water: Political, Biopolitical, Material', *Social Studies of Science* 42(4): 616–23.

Block, P., and L. Goddard. 2012. 'Statistical and Dynamical Climate Predictions to Guide Water Resources in Ethiopia', *Journal of Water Resources Planning and Management* 138(3): 287–98.

Buffavand, L. 2016. '"The Land Does Not Like Them": Contesting Dispossession in Cosmological Terms in Mela, South-West Ethiopia', *Journal of Eastern African Studies* 10(3): 476–93.

Butzer, K.W. 1971. *Recent History of an Ethiopian Delta*. Chicago: University of Chicago Press.

Carr, C. 2012. 'Humanitarian Catastrophe and Regional Armed Conflict Brewing in the Transborder Region of Kenya, Ethiopia and South Sudan: The Proposed GIBE III Dam in Ethiopia'. Africa Resource Working Group (ARWG). Retrieved 15 February 2018 from https://www.academia.edu/8385749/Carr_ARWG_Gibe_III_Dam_Report.

———. 2017. *River Basin Development and Human Rights in Eastern Africa: A Policy Crossroads*. Cham: Springer Open. DOI 10.1007/978-3-319-50469-8.

Cascão, A.E. 2009. 'Changing Power Relations in the Nile River Basin: Unilateralism vs. Cooperation?', *Water Alternatives* 2(2): 245–68.

Cernea, M.M. 2000. 'Risks, Safeguards, and Reconstruction: A Model for Population Displacement and Resettlement', in M.M. Cernea and C. McDowell (eds), *Risks and Reconstruction: Experiences of Resettlers and Refugees*. Washington, DC: World Bank.

Dahl, G., and Gemetchu Megerssa. 1992. 'The Spiral of the Ram's Horn – Boran Concepts of Development', in G. Dahl and A. Rabo (eds), *Kam-ap or Take-Off: Local Notions of Development*, vol. 29, Stockholm Studies in Social Anthropology. Stockholm: Stockholm University Press.

Dessalegn Rahmato. 1999. 'Revisiting the Land Issue: Options for Change', *Economic Focus* 2(4): 9–11.

———. 2011. *Land to Investors: Large-Scale Land Transfers in Ethiopia*. Addis Ababa: Forum for Social Studies.

———. 2014. 'Large-Scale Land Investments Revisited', in R. Dessalegn, A. Meheret, K. Asnake and B. Habermann (eds), *Reflections on Development in Ethiopia: New Trends, Sustainability and Challenges*. Addis Ababa: Forum for Social Studies, pp. 219–45.

Dorosh, P., and S. Rashid (eds). 2012. *Food and Agriculture in Ethiopia: Progress and Policy Changes*. Philadelphia: University of Pennsylvania Press.

Falkenmark, M., and J. Rockström. 2006. 'The New Blue and Green Water Paradigm: Breaking New Ground for Water Resources Planning and Management', *Journal of Water Resources Planning and Management* 132(3): 129–32.

FAO Aquastat. 2005. 'Aquastat Survey Ethiopia'. Retrieved 2 August 2020 from http://www.fao.org/nr/water/aquastat/countries_regions/eth/ETH-CP_eng.pdf.

FDRE. 1995. *Constitution of the Federal Republic of Ethiopia*. Addis Ababa: Federal Democratic Republic of Ethiopia.

———. 2012. *South Omo Villagization Plan*. Addis Ababa: Federal Democratic Republic of Ethiopia.

Gibe III HEP. 2015. 'Gibe III Hydroelectric Project'. Available at http://www.gibe3.com.et/.

Girke, F. 2013. 'Homeland, Boundary, Resource: The Collision of Place-Making Projects on the Lower Omo River, Ethiopia', *Max Planck Institute for Social Anthropology Working Paper* No. 148. Retrieved 2 August 2020 from http://www.eth.mpg.de/pubs/wps/pdf/mpi-eth-working-paper-0148.

Gownaris, N.J. et al. 2016. 'Fisheries and Water Level Fluctuations in the World's Largest Desert Lake', *Ecohydrology*. DOI: https://doi.org/10.1002/eco.1769.

Hall, R. 2011. 'Land Grabbing in Africa and the New Politics of Food', *Policy Brief* No. 041. Brighton: Future Agricultures Consortium.

Hansard. 2008. 'Question 428: Extensive Damming of River Omo pp. 4063–4065', *Kenya National Assembly Official Record*, 11 December 2008. Retrieved 2 August 2020 from https://books.google.com/books?id=EA4voQLzkmkC&pgis=1.

———. 2010. 'Point of Order: Effects of Construction of Gibe III Dam', *Kenya National Assembly Official Record*, 21 October 2010. Retrieved 2 August 2020 from https://books.google.com/books?id=vydMozkeMUMC&pgis=1.

HRW. 2012. *What Will Happen if Hunger Comes? Abuses against the Indigenous Peoples of Ethiopia's Lower Omo Valley*. Amsterdam: Human Rights Watch.

Hopson, A.J. (ed.). 1982. *Lake Turkana: A Report on the Findings of the Lake Turkana Project (1972–75)*, vols. 1–6. London: ODA.

International Rivers. 2013. *The Downstream Impacts of Ethiopia's Gibe III Dam: East Africa's "Aral Sea" in the Making?* Berkeley, CA: International Rivers.

Kamski, B. 2016a. 'The Kuraz Sugar Development Project', *OTuRN Briefing Note* No. 1. Lansing, MI: Omo-Turkana Research Network.

———. 2016b. 'The Kuraz Sugar Development Project (KSDP) in Ethiopia: Between "Sweet Vision" and Mounting Challenges', *Journal of Eastern African Studies* 10(3): 568–80.

Keeley, J. et al. 2014. *Large-Scale Land Deals in Ethiopia: Scale, Trends, Features and Outcomes to Date*. London: IIED.

Khennache, L., J. Adamowski and N. Kosoy. 2017. 'The Eastern Nile River Waterscape: The Role of Power in Policy-Making and Shaping National Narratives', *International Negotiation* 22: 123–61.

Kirchherr, J., and K. Charles. 2016. 'The Social Impacts of Dams: A New Framework for Scholarly Analysis', *Environmental Impact Assessment Review* 60: 99–114.

Kloos, H. et al. 2010. 'Problems for Pastoralists in the Lowlands: River Basin Development in the Awash and Omo Valleys', in H. Kloos and L. Worku (eds), *Water Resources Management in Ethiopia: Implications for the Nile Basin*. Amherst, NY: Cambria Press, pp. 321–51.

Kolding, J. 1995. 'Changes in Species Composition and Abundance of Fish Populations in Lake Turkana, Kenya', in T.J. Pitcher and P.J.B. Hart (eds), *The Impact of Species Changes in African Lakes*. Dordrecht: Springer, pp. 335–63.

Lakoff, G. 2005. *Whose Freedom?* New York: Farrar, Strauss, and Giroux.

Lakoff, G., and M. Johnson. 1980. *Metaphors We Live By*. Chicago: University of Chicago Press.

Leakey, R. 2009. 'The Gibe III Dam Must Be Stopped'. Retrieved 15 February 2018 from http://richardleakey.wildlifedirect.org/2009/03/26/the-gibe-iii-dam-must-be-stopped/.

Linton, J., and J. Budds. 2013. 'The Hydro-Social Cycle: Defining and Mobilizing a Relational-Dialectical Approach to Water', *Geoforum* 57: 170–80.

Matthews, N., A. Nicol and W. Michago Seide. 2013. 'Constructing a New Water Future? A Reanalysis of Ethiopia's Current Hydropower Development', in J.A. Allan (ed.), *Handbook of Land and Water Grabs in Africa*. New York: Routledge, pp. 311–23.

McConnell, M.J. 2018. 'Sugar and Sweeteners Outlook'. SSS-M-358, U.S. Department of Agriculture, Economic Research Service, June 18.

McCully, P. 2001. *Silenced Rivers: The Ecology and Politics of Large Dams*, 2nd edn. London: Zed Books.

Mehta, L., G.J. Veldwisch and J. Franco. 2012. 'Introduction to the Special Issue: Water Grabbing? Focus on the (Re)appropriation of Finite Water Resources', *Water Alternatives* 5(2): 193–207.

Mitchell, T. 2002. *Rule of Experts: Egypt, Techno-Politics, Modernity*. Berkeley, CA: University of California Press.

Oakland Institute. 2013. *Ignoring Abuse in Ethiopia: DFID and USAID in the Lower Omo Valley*. Oakland, CA: Oakland Institute.

Oliver-Smith, A. 2015. *Defying Displacement: Grassroots Resistance and the Critique of Development*. Austin: University of Texas Press.

Rawlence, B. 2016. 'The Refugee Who Took on the British Government', *The Guardian online*. Retrieved 2 August 2020 from https://www.theguardian.com/world/2016/jan/12/ethiopian-refugee-who-took-on-the-british-government.

Richter, B.D. et al. 2010. 'Lost in Development's Shadow: The Downstream Human Consequences of Dams', *Water Alternatives* 3(2): 14–42.

Sachs, W. (ed.). 2010. *The Development Dictionary: A Guide to Knowledge as Power*, 2nd edn. Chicago: University of Chicago Press.

Salini. 2016. 'Gibe III Hydroelectric Project: Salini Impregilo in Ethiopia'. Retrieved 15 February 2018 from https://www.salini-impregilo.com/minisiti/etiopia/en/projects/gibe-iii-hydroelectric.html.

Schlee, G. 2013. 'Why States Will Destroy Pastoralism and How They Can Learn That in Their Own Interest They Should Not', *Nomadic Peoples* 17(2): 6–19.

Scudder, T. 2005. *The Future of Large Dams: Dealing with Social, Environmental, Institutional and Political Costs*. London: Earthscan.

Stevenson, E.G.J. 2018. 'Plantation Development in the Turkana Basin: The Making of a New Desert?', *Land* 6(7): 1–11.

Stevenson, E.G.J., and L. Buffavand. 2018. '"Do Our Bodies Know Their Ways?" Villagization, Food Insecurity and Ill-Being Ethiopia's Lower Omo Valley', *African Studies Review* 61(1): 109–33.

Tafesse Olika. 2006. 'Ethiopia: Politics of Land Tenure Policies under Three Regimes: A Carrot-And-Stick Ruling Strategy', in Alexander Attilo, Kassahun Berhanu and Yonas Ketsela (eds), *Ethiopia: Politics, Policy-Making and Rural Development*. Addis Ababa: Addis Ababa University Press, pp. 1–26.

Tewolde Woldemariam, and Fana Gebresenbet. 2014. 'Socio-Political and Conflict Implications of Sugar Development in Salamago Wereda, Ethiopia', in Mulugeta Gebrehiwot Berhe (ed.), *A Delicate Balance: Land Use, Minority Rights and Social Stability in the Horn of Africa*. Addis Ababa: Institute for Peace and Security Studies, pp. 117–43.

Turton, D. 1989. 'Warfare, Vulnerability and Survival: A Case from Southwestern Ethiopia', *Cambridge Anthropology* 13(2): 67–85.

———. 2011. 'Wilderness, Wasteland, or Home? Three Ways of Imagining the Lower Omo Valley', *Journal of Eastern African Studies* 5(1): 158–76.

———. 2014. 'Donor Balancing Act on Human Rights in the Lower Omo Valley', *Mursi Online*. Retrieved 2 August 2020 from http://www.mursi.org/news-items/donor-balancing-act-on-human-rights-in-the-lower-omo-valley.

———. 2015. 'Hydropower and Irrigation Development in the Omo Valley: Development for Whom?' Paper presented at the International Conference on Ethiopian Studies, Warsaw, Poland.

UNEP. 2010. *Africa Water Atlas*. Nairobi: United Nations Environment Programme.

UNESCO. 2018. *Lake Turkana National Parks (Kenya) Inscribed on List of World Heritage in Danger*. Retrieved 2 August 2020 from http://whc.unesco.org/en/news/1842.

UN-HRC. 2014. *Working Group on the Universal Periodic Review*. United Nations Human Rights Council, A/HRC/WG.6/19/ETH/3. Retrieved 2 August 2020 from https://www.ecoi.net/en/file/local/1125450/1930_1398866271_g1410567.pdf.

USDA. 2016. *World and U.S. Sugar and Corn Sweetener Prices: Economic Research Services*. United States Department of Agriculture. Retrieved 15 February 2018 from http://www.ers.usda.gov/data-products/sugar-and-sweeteners-yearbooktables.

Verhoeven, H. 2011. 'Black Gold for Blue Gold? Sudan's Oil, Ethiopia's Water and Regional Integration', *Chatham House Briefing Paper*, AFP BP 2011/03. Retrieved 2 August 2020 from https://www.chathamhouse.org/sites/files/chathamhouse/19482_0611bp_verhoeven.pdf.

Vidal, J. 2014. 'Ethiopian Dam's Ecological and Human Fallout Could Echo Aral Sea Disaster', *The Guardian*, 5 March. Retrieved 2 August 2020 from http://www.theguardian.com/global-development/2014/mar/05/ethiopian-dam-gibe-iii-aral-sea-disaster.

World Bank. 2016. *Why So Idle? Wages and Employment in a Crowded Labor Market, 5th Ethiopia Economic Update*. Retrieved 2 August 2020 from http://documents.worldbank.org/curated/en/463121480932724605/pdf/110730-REPLACEMENT-WP-thEthiopiaEconomicUpdatevweb-PUBLIC.pdf.

Yacob Arsano, and Imeru Tamrat. 2005. 'Ethiopia and the Eastern Nile Basin', *Aquatic Sciences* 67(1): 15–27.

Yidneckachew Ayele. 2015. 'Policies and Practices of Consultation with Pastoralist Communities in Ethiopia: The Case of Omo-Kuraz Sugar Development Project', in Yohannes Aberra and Mahmmud Abulahi (eds), *The Intricate Road to Development: Government Development Strategies in the Pastoral Areas of the Horn of Africa*. Addis Ababa: Institute of Peace and Security Studies, pp. 282–304.

Conclusion

Pastoralists for Future

Echi Christina Gabbert, Fana Gebresenbet and Jonah Wedekind

As we finalize this volume, worldwide attention has turned to the future of land. The magnitude of land deals in the Global South in the past decade – from Indonesia, across Africa to the Amazon – has visibly increased the imbalance between the interests of large corporations, consuming classes and states, on one hand, and of pastoralists, agro-pastoralists, smallholders, and landless workers, on the other hand. The negative effects of agro-industrial monocultures on ecosystems and climate underline the urgency for effective future-oriented land policies (IPCC 2019). Pastoralists and agro-pastoralists[1] living on and from arid lands will most likely be among the most affected by the climate crisis. Yet, precisely the landscapes they inhabit can be productively guarded and restored with their indigenous knowledge and land use practices. How we live on, with and from land plays an undeniable role on a planetary scale in the present, and will continue to do so in the future. We want to conclude with relating the findings in this volume to the challenges this observation contains.

Limits on Ideals about Land

Once it was thought that 'the whole planet will end up modernizing toward some convergent omega point called the Globe' (Latour 2018: 218). We know now that this is not possible. Latour compares the situation of the 'moderns' to a flight on a plane that keeps circling in the air because its destined landing ground has disappeared. It becomes increasingly clear that modernity cannot escape the spectre of 'finitude', not only of resources themselves but also of limited ideas that resources represent mere commodities. Soil quality, water availability and climate variability are increasingly becoming unpredictable (IPCC 2019: Chapter 2), and global lands and food policies do not reflect the challenges that continued careless use of resources poses. On the contrary, since the unprecedented spikes in food and fuel prices of 2007/08, the global land rush has resulted in highly speculative, conflictive and destructive scenarios acted out at the last frontiers of the world, such as in pastoralist territories in Eastern Africa. Securing and speculating with land, labour, food and fuel have become symptoms of the looming end of 'cheap nature' (Moore 2014: 289). Instead of co-managing precious 'resources' with indigenous experts and with extra care to find ways to live within planetary limits, many governments in the Global South invite investors to access and use indigenous and pastoralist lands in often unproductive and speculative ways. This has resulted in dysfunctional socio-ecological, economic and political outcomes. In the current climate crisis, uncertainty has become the new *status quo*. No one can be sure where and when it will be possible to produce food in the future (IPCC 2019: Chapter 5), or, to return to the circling airplane, which climate policies will prove consequential in securing landing grounds in the future.

In this context, Ethiopia's climate policy agenda seems visionary. Despite Ethiopia being one of the least carbon emitting countries, it (cl)aims to take seriously its global responsibility to reduce the economy's carbon emissions. Ethiopia's Climate Resilient Green Economy strategy acknowledges that '[b]eyond the economic impact, the conventional development path would lead to a lower quality of life and health problems' (FDRE 2011: 17). Therefore, Ethiopian land use planning policies pledge to lower Green House Gas (GHG) emissions in various sectors, including agriculture and energy. However, as some of our contributions have shown, in practice the implementation of the Green Economy strategy has seen the enforcement of modernist projects (e.g. large-scale hydroelectric dams and biofuel plantations) with devastating socio-ecological effects. Nevertheless, reducing GHG emissions, without producing more social-ecological ills on the ground, resonates with voices from all fields and disciplines in the sciences that call for planetary cooperation in pursuing food and climate justice (see Ripple et al. 2017; Hagedorn et al. 2019). This relates to an argument that we wish to make here: what or who is considered 'modern' needs to be redefined. But why?

Questioning Modernism, Invoking Pastoralism

If so-called 'developing' countries were to consider urgent global paradigm shifts more seriously than the generations and governments of 'moderns' who are largely responsible for having engendered the ecological and climate crisis, this in itself would be remarkable. To realize this paradigm shift, small-scale farmers and (agro-)pastoralists, as the guardians of time-tested practices to produce food, play key roles. Unfortunately, when looking at the implementation of land policies in (agro-)pastoralist territories, our findings are less promising.

With examples from Ethiopia, Kenya and Tanzania, we aim to fill knowledge gaps about the socio-ecological outcomes of neoliberal and state-led development projects (see Johnsen et al. 2019). We have shown how pastoralists have been repeatedly excluded from policymaking, and we have mapped the very fields to which they can contribute: future-oriented land use, sociocultural diversification, indigenous-led conservation and ecological biodiversity, bottom-up state-building, conflict resolution, as well as inclusive citizenship, democracy and development. All these are possible starting points for cooperation and transformation. We describe and refute the misleading tropes about and of pastoralists as 'backward' or 'romanticized people' and object to the declaration of their land as 'unused' and 'empty'. We describe how coercion, forced displacement and violent intimidation have been combined with the implementation of investment schemes that have failed ecologically, socially and economically, making people's livelihoods ever more precarious. We have underlined the fact that different groups of pastoralists live under different conditions, with different needs, possibilities and aspirations, and we acknowledge that they react to development schemes in variable ways, including through adaptation, change and diversification of livelihoods, adopting various forms of resistance and subversion, but also resigning to disillusionment and doom. What most (agro-)pastoralists share, however, is, firstly, limitations of the political space, citizenship rights and land use rights through which to make their own, free choices in the present and for the future, and, secondly, lack of recognition of the legitimacy of their knowledge as relevant to land use planning, with practices that encompass sustainable biodiversity conservation strategies and will be of increasing importance in the future.

The profound failure of projects of large-scale land investments, described in this volume, resonates with the results of more extended case studies; for example, of the Beni Shangul and Gambella Regions of Ethiopia by Atkeyelsh Persson (2019), the very region that released unexpectedly large quantities of CO_2 into the biosphere in 2015/16 (Palmer et al. 2019). Evidence suggests that government-enforced conversion of shifting cultivation to mono-cropping was responsible for releasing sub-soil organic carbon and nitrogen reserves (Berhanu and Kim 2019). Such effects of large-scale land use conversions contribute to the climate crisis. Indeed, if pastoralism is abolished, this also eradicates pastoralist's 'adaptive capacity to respond imaginatively to climatic uncertainties' (Mehta, Adam and Srivastava 2019: 1531). Pastoralists are experienced in living with strong fluctuations between times of scarcity and times of abundance. Mobility, as a time-tested way of life, secures access to erratic resources with the least cost to the environment. Thus, pastoralist knowledge provides an important foundation to develop solutions for living in otherwise uncultivable lands in the future.

We acknowledge efforts arising out of the need to ensure rights to food and human welfare by governments. The present climate crisis calls for awareness of all possible ways of organizing state relations with societies and ecologies on a planetary scale in the future. Desirable relations would affirm the 'autonomous dignity of all' (Wainwright and Mann 2018). Although we criticize the notion of 'modernism' as *mot d'ordre* for top-down development schemes, we do not foster ideas about 'bad moderns' and 'illuminated traditionalists'. On the contrary, our volume includes a variety of visions for the future of land and its people that can complement each other. Yet, state policies for pastoral territories in East Africa, which this volume has described and analysed, continue to ignore inclusive solutions that challenge 'modernist' preconceptions of progress that by definition exclude most rural peoples. The establishment of monocultures instead of polycultures, sedentarization of pastoralists, violent dispossession in the name of development and the commodification of land under a rigorous developmental paradigm neither constitute innovative, equitable, peaceful and future-friendly policies nor – following Latour's *dictum* – have such approaches ever been 'modern'.

On 23 January 2019 at the 17th Pastoralist Day in Jinka, Ethiopia's Deputy Prime Minister, Demeke Mekonnen, assured his audience of the respect held by the Ethiopian government for pastoralists' knowledge and culture as the basis for land use and, moreover, for national reconciliation. But in September and October 2019, Ethiopian military killed and tortured members of the Mela and Chirim (Bodi) and Mun (Mursi) in southern Ethiopia in a humiliating disarmament campaign. To date, there have been no statements or reports from the government on these human rights violations (see CSE 2019). This horrific violence against agro-pastoral men, women and children in the vicinity of new sugar plantations shows that the destruction of pastoralist livelihoods continues despite a promising trend of democratization and commitments to a more measured use of force by security forces at the national level since PM Abiy assumed power in April 2018. The ties between pastoralists and states – not to mention between mobile and sedentary modes of life – have been stressed and even ruptured for centuries, and more so over the last decade, as the land rush widened this rift in the name of development and modernism.

In this context the recent demands for the creation of new federal states in SNNPR, already achieved in Sidama and ongoing in other zones including Wolaita and South Omo and the continued push of the current administration to intensify large-scale agro-industrial monoculture by eradicating local knowledge based integrated practices, highlight the danger of the top-down policies on land we have discussed in this volume. If the recognition of historical and recent injustices against pastoralist communities are not met with accountability and transparency, peaceful futuremaking lacks its basis. Necessary truth and reconciliation processes cannot be bypassed without risking disintegration and destabilization of affected citizens, regions and even entire countries.

Who holds the tools to bridge the rifts between states and pastoralists, or sedentary and mobile modes of living? '[T]he current trajectory of food systems in Europe is unsustainable and must be changed' states a collective of experts from all fields (De Schutter 2019: 6).[2] 'However, current policies have proven slow to adapt to these new challenges, and are locked into the paradigms of the past' (IPES 2019: 26). Indeed, nations considered as 'modern' or the 'most developed' are also the leading CO_2 emitters (e.g. US, China and the EU member states) and have so far not been fast, flexible or determined enough to react adequately to the climate crisis. Yet this would be necessary in order to counter the crisis of climate change and ecological destruction that bears dire consequences for life on earth. The key is doing so in a socially and economically just way.

In this context, the prediction of the philosopher Achille Mbembe that 'it might be that the future of the planet is being played out on the (African) continent' (Mbembe and Nuttall 2017) gains additional significance. He stresses the need for planetary action and responsibility in order to open the door to a future for all (Mbembe 2017). Planetary responsibility requires philosophical, aesthetic and political imagination in times of climate crisis. To be open to seeing the world like a pastoralist is part of this. Most food in Africa is produced by small-holders and (agro-)pastoralists, African countries have the lowest CO_2 emissions worldwide and the continent contains large sub-soil carbon stores. Some might say that these are merely indications of 'backwardness' and 'underdevelopment'. Yet when regarded as reflecting the history of smallholders' taking good care of the land, biodiversity and climate instead, the soundness of their land use practices and those of (agro-)pastoralists can be acknowledged, supported, refined and combined with other future-oriented land use practices. While being aware of the cynicism that accompanies expectations that Africa should bear the responsibility for rescuing what was destroyed in other parts of the world – often through market-mechanisms such as REDD+ carbon trading schemes – it is conceivable that if the major polluters finally have to pay sufficient taxes for carbon emissions this could contribute to a global transformation. If African governments then would not copy and impose exploitative schemes in their own countries – for example, by bypassing indigenous populations in land use planning and carbon trade – cooperative planning could open up possibilities for supporting holistic solutions for food production. Climate-friendly land use practices would not be eradicated but rewarded for producing food without destroying the environment.[3] Among these are common practices of agro-pastoralists such as low-till hoeing with little soil disturbance, maintaining land cover zones and retaining flood-retreat cultivation, as well as pursuing extensive forms of land use with seasonal grazing mobility and shifting cultivation to sustain biodiversity. Moreover, balanced assessments of the value of livestock products for human nutrition (especially for infants), health, ecology and economy can be combined with detailed studies about the reduction of the carbon footprint of livestock production and about livestock systems that are effective at carbon sequestration (see Varijak-shapanicker et al. 2019).[4]

Agro-Pastoral Modes of Living

Our volume can only shed light on a few realities. The search for places to land on and for transformative alternatives for creating an 'ecologically wise and so-cially just world' contains many more realities (Kothari et al. 2019: xxi). Yet, this unsettling moment in history provides sufficient reasons to replace Eurocentric modes of knowledge production that have been adopted and pushed by states in the Horn of Africa and elsewhere against 'their' pastoralist citizens, small-scale farmers and indigenous groups. Now is a point in time when we should posi-tively activate the decolonization of knowledge and epistemologies. It is time to accept the multiplicity of worlds, in which humans and non-humans co-exist in an entangled and co-constituted manner. Accordingly, there should be no single mandatory approach, certainly not one that demands high expenditures of energy for limited output, but rather openness to a diversity of approaches that together can reach an ethical–political orientation towards a desirable qual-ity of life defined by people in emancipatory ways. Among these, pastoralist worldviews and cosmologies inspire alternative meanings of inhabiting and pro-tecting places that connect the living with the ancestors and the practical with the divine in order to live on and with land, now and in the future. With our studies, we aim to lay a realistic ground on which to start working on more peaceful, and future-oriented, policies and practices that fully incorporate the perspectives and rights of pastoralists and smallholders in order to bridge the rifts that now exist. Positive and informed futuremaking is critical in order to embrace divergent views that envisage a common existence. The contributors of this book, while sitting at their desks or while moving through pastures in the drylands, hope that readers from all backgrounds will feel invited to facili-tate dialogue across the rifts that define pastoral history, to correct the injustices and to address grievances and blind spots that define both the past and the present, and together, with greater respect and responsibility, envision land in a common future on a common planet, where – at last – all can find a common ground.

Echi Christina Gabbert is an anthropologist and a lecturer at the Institute for Social and Cultural Anthropology at Göttingen University, Germany. Her re-search foci are agro-pastoralism, music and oral history, political ecology and peace and conflict studies. Her long-term fieldwork in Ethiopia resulted in the award-winning PhD thesis 'Deciding Peace'. She extended the 'Cultural Neigh-bourhood Approach' to 'Global Neighbourhood' scenarios, where global invest-ment schemes meet smallholder's livelihoods, and is coordinating the *Lands of* *the Future* Initiative, an interdisciplinary project about pastoral livelihoods in the twenty-first century.

Fana Gebresenbet is Assistant Professor at the Institute for Peace and Security Studies of Addis Ababa University. He wrote his PhD on 'The Political Economy of Land Investments: Dispossession, Resistance and Territory-Making in Gambella, Western Ethiopia'. He has been researching state-building and development in Ethiopia's lowlands for more than a decade.

Jonah Wedekind is a political ecologist working on large-scale biofuel investment projects in Ethiopia at Humboldt-Universität zu Berlin, Germany. His research interests include agrarian and environmental transformations, property relations and anthropologies of the state. He was a Marie Curie Early Stage Career fellow within the EU research project ENTITLE – The European Network for Political Ecology (2013–2016) and is a co-editor of undisciplinedenvironments.org and ethiopia-insight.com. Formative years spent in Ethiopia as a third-generation expatriate of linguists and human rights workers resulted in his deep-rooted interest in Ethiopian Studies.

Notes

1. Many groups that are called pastoralists are also practising agriculture and are therefore easily misrepresented in land use decisions; therefore, we also use the term agro-pastoralists, which often means horticulture-cum-animal husbandry.
2. The collective included 'more than 400 farmers, food entrepreneurs, civil society activists, scientists, and policymakers consulted throughout a three-year process of research and reflection' (IPES 2019: 11).
3. This approach has been supported by the *Guardians of Productive Landscape* Project: 'In other words, the actual guardians of productive landscapes would not have to beg for aid anymore but would earn a seasonal income for their help in the combat against climate collapse' (Schlee et al. 2017: 19).
4. It remains to be seen whether Ethiopia's newly drafted *Pastoralist Development Strategy and Policy* (MoP 2019), currently under review at the Prime Minister's Office, shall learn from past mistakes and respectfully build on indigenous knowledge and land use practices and work collectively towards figuring out questions of land rights and land jurisdiction in the future.

References

Atkeyelsh G.M. Persson. 2019. *Foreign Direct Investment in Large-Scale Agriculture in Africa: Economic, Social and Environmental Sustainability in Ethiopia*. Abingdon and New York: Routledge.

Berhanu Terefe, and D-G. Kim. 2019. 'Shifting Cultivation Maintains but its Conversion to Mono-cropping Decreases Soil Carbon and Nitrogen Stocks Compared to Natural Forest in Western Ethiopia'. *Plant and Soil*. DOI: 10.1007/s11104-019-03942-0.

CSE (Concerned Scholars Ethiopia). 2019. 'Memo on Violence in South Omo areas, SNN-PRS, Ethiopia (October 2019): A Call for Preventive Action and Rule of Law'. Retrieved 4 November 2019 from https://www.canr.msu.edu/oturn/Memo_(4.0)_on_violence_in _South____Omo_areas_SNNPRS_Ethiopia_(26_October_2019).pdf.

De Schutter, O. 2019. 'Preface' in IPES (International Panel of Experts on Sustainable Food Systems), 'Towards a Common Food Policy for the European Union: The Policy Reform and Realignment that is Required to Build Sustainable Food Systems in Europe', pp. 6–7. Retrieved 10 October 2019 from http://www.ipes-food.org/_img/upload/files/CFP_Full Report.pdf.

FDRE (Federal Democratic Republic of Ethiopia). 2011. *Ethiopia's Climate-Resilient Green Economy Green Economy Strategy*. Addis Ababa, Ethiopia.

Hagedorn, G. et al. 2019. 'The Concerns of the Young Protesters are Justified: A Statement by Scientists for Future Concerning the Protests for More Climate protection', *GAIA – Ecological Perspectives for Science and Society* 28(2) 79–87.

IPCC (Intergovernmental Panel on Climate Change). 2019. 'Climate Change and Land'. IPCC Special Report on climate change, desertification, land degradation, sustainable land management, food security, and greenhouse gas fluxes in terrestrial ecosystems. Summary of Policymakers. Retrieved 10 October 2019 from https://www.ipcc.ch/site/assets/uploads/2019/08/Fullreport-1.pdf.

IPES (International Panel of Experts on Sustainable Food Systems). 2019. 'Towards a Common Food Policy for the European Union: The Policy Reform and Realignment that is Required to Build Sustainable Food Systems in Europe'. Retrieved 10 October 2019 from http://www.ipes-food.org/_img/upload/files/CFP_FullReport.pdf.

Johnsen, K.I. et al. 2019. *A Case of Benign Neglect: Knowledge Gaps about Sustainability in Pastoralism and Rangelands*. United Nations Environment Programme and GRID-Arendal, Nairobi and Arendal. Retrieved 20 October 2019 from http://www.grida.no/publications/428.

Kothari, A. et al. (eds). 2019. *Pluriverse: A Post Development Dictionary*. Shahpur Jat, New Delhi: Tulika Books.

Latour, B. 2018. 'On a Possible Triangulation of Some Present Political Positions', *Critical Inquiry* 44(2): 213–26.

Mbembe, A. 2017. 'Time on the Move'. Lecture. April 8, 2017 at the Institute for Cultural Inquiry, Berlin. Retrieved 10 October 2019 from https://www.ici-berlin.org/events/achille-mbembe/.

Mbembe, A., and S. Nuttall. 2017. 'Discussion with Achille Mbembe and Sarah Nuttall' (Part I). April 8 2017 at the Institute for Cultural Inquiry, Berlin. Retrieved 10 October 2019 from https://www.ici-berlin.org/events/achille-mbembe/.

Mehta, L., H.N. Adam and S. Srivastava. 2019. 'Unpacking Uncertainty and Climate Change from "Above" and "Below"', *Regional Environmental Change* 19: 1529–32

Moore, J.W. 2014. 'The End of Cheap Nature, or: How I learned to Stop Worrying about "the" Environment and Love the Crisis of Capitalism', in C. Suter and C. Chase-Dunn (eds), *Structures of the World Political Economy and the Future of Global Conflict and Cooperation*. Berlin: LIT Verlag, pp. 285–314.

MoP (Ministry of Peace). 2019. *Pastoral Development Policy and Strategy Framework. Draft Unpublished document*. Addis Ababa (March 2019).

Palmer, P.I., et al. 2019. 'Net Carbon Emissions from African Biosphere Dominate Pan-tropical Atmospheric CO_2 Signal', *Nature Communications* 10: 3344. DOI: 10.1038/s41467-019-11097-w.

Ripple, W.J., et al. 2017. 'World Scientists' Warning to Humanity: A Second Notice', *BioScience* 67(12): 1026–28.

Schlee, G., et al. 2017. 'Guardians of Productive Landscapes', *Max Planck Institute for Social Anthropology, Report 2014–2016*. Department 'Integration and Conflict', pp. 17–19.

Varijakshapanicker, P., et al. 2019. 'Sustainable Livestock Systems to Improve Human Health, Nutrition, and Economic Status', *Animal Frontiers* 9(4): 39–50.

Wainwright, K., and G. Mann. 2018. *Climate Leviathan: A Political Theory of Our Planetary Future*. London and New York: Verso.

Glossary

Abbreviations: Af. for Afar (Qafar af); Am. for Amharic; Ar. for oho Arbore/Hor; Or. for Afan Oromo; Me'en (Bodi); Mun. for tuga Munin (Mursi)

Aba Gandaa (Or.)	village elder
Afkeek-Maada (Af.)	tribal section
Afran Qallo (Or.)	Oromo clan/subgroup
agle (Af.)	Afar custom, taking care of animals on a usufruct basis
amba (Am.)	flat-topped mountains and hills
amoyta askar (Af.)	Sultan's militia
arbto ader (Am.)	livestock producer
ardaa (Or.)	neighbourhood
baa (Mun.)	land, place
baa barrara (Mun.)	ritual places
badhi (sing.) (Mun.) badhinya (pl.)	sacred lands
balabat (Am.)	leader
bhuranyoga (Mun.)	territorial section in Munland

biʕida (Af.)	oryx
bosona (Or.)	jungle
caasaa gandaa (Or.)	village structure
Derg (Am.)	committee; the military government that ruled Ethiopia between 1974 and 1991
dhebinya (Mun.)	clay pits for traditional rituals
dhugaa lafaa (Or.)	the truth of the land
dirr (Me'en)	compound of a generation-set, usually in a cattle camp
ferenji	Westeners
foora (Or.)	seasonal grazing
Gadaa (Or.)	political and sociocultural age- and generation-grading system of democratic governance of the Oromo
garee misooma (Or.)	development groups
gimgema (Am.)	cadre critique/evaluation
giber (Am.)	tax
gongai (Mun.)	stingy person
gosa (Or.)	clans
gott (Or.)	quasi-governmental sub-kebele structures
gulo (Am.)	castor
guza (Or.)	reciprocal form of sharecropping
habesha (Am.)	Amharic speaker, Ethiopian descending from the highlands
herega (Or.)	water point
Jaarsolii Biyyaa (Or.)	elders' council
Jaarsummaa (Or.)	reconciliation process
kaloo (Or.)	enclosed pasture reserved for calves, milk cows and weak animals
kalo saga (Af.)	cow paid as tax for the use of dry season grazing
kebele (Am.)	lowest administrative unit in Ethiopia
khat	stimulant cash crop

kilil (Am.)	federal states
komoru (Mun.)	important ritual figure in Munland
komorut (sing.)/ komorutiya (pl.) (Me'en)	important ritual figures in Mela
Liyu police (Am.)	special paramilitary police contingent
malak(sing.)/ malokti (pl.) (Af.)	tax collector
mengist (mangɛsti)	state/government
meret werariwoch (Am.)	land invaders/land grabbers
ngawunya (Mun.)	places for important community rituals
nungu (Ar.)	slowly, with care
Odaa (Or.)	sacred sycamore tree, symbolizing peace and stability
Qaalluu (Or.)	a religious institution that is believed to enable a connection between the people and their supernatural authority, central to conflict resolution in the Oromo society
qeerroo (Or.)	bachelor or unmarried man
qobbo (Or.)	castor
reera (Or.)	large customary grazing unit with generally defined users
seelii (Or.)	party organizational cells
seera yabbii (Or.)	customary enclosures set aside for calves and lactating or sick cattle
sefara (Am.)	resettlement programme of the 1980s in Ethiopia
shifta (Am.)	bandits
Taama (Mun.)	self-designation for Mun in ritual contexts
tuga Munin (Mun.)	Mun language
woreda (Am.)	district, second lowest administrative level in Ethiopia
Zamača (Am.)	campaign – students sent out to teach the rural population about the new reforms following the 1974 revolution
zelan (Am.)	derogatory term for nomads and pastoralists
ɛidi saaka (Af.)	end of Ramadan

Index

www.ingramcontent.com/pod-product-compliance
Lightning Source LLC
Chambersburg PA
CBHW070610030426
42337CB00020B/3734